GUNS OF THE WILD WEST

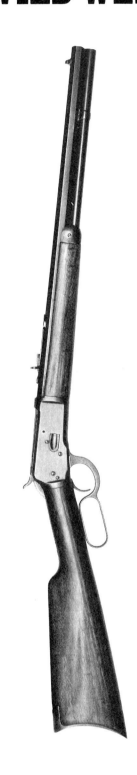

In series with *Guns of the Wild West*
Guns of the Elite
Guns of the Empire
Guns of the Reich

GEORGE MARKHAM

GUNS OF THE WILD WEST

Firearms of the American Frontier, 1849–1917

The handguns, longarms and shotguns of the Gold Rush, the American Civil War,
the Wild West and the
Armed Forces.

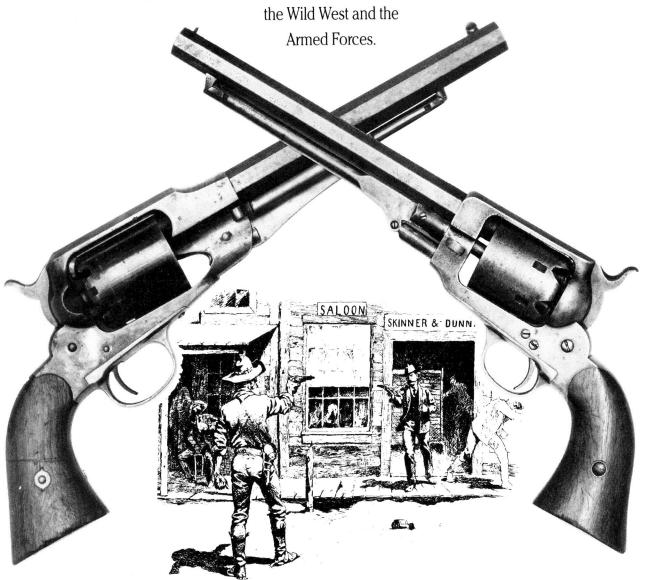

ARMS & ARMOUR PRESS

PREFACE AND ACKNOWLEDGEMENTS

First published 1991. Reprinted 1993
First published in paperback in 1993 by
Arms & Armour Press
A CASSELL IMPRINT
Villiers House
41/47 Strand
London WC2N 5JE

Distributed in the USA by
Sterling Publishing Co., Inc.,
387 Park Avenue South, New York, NY 10016.

Distributed in Australia by
Capricorn Link (Australia) Pty. Ltd,
P.O. Box 665, Lane Cove,
New South Wales 2066,
Australia.

**British Library Cataloguing in
Publication Data**

Markham, George
    Guns of the wild West: firearms of the
    American frontier, 1849–1917
    I. Title
    623.440978

ISBN 1-85409-105-0 (hardback)
ISBN 1-85409-197-2 (paperback)

1: half-title. The Winchester rifle epitomised the Wild
West. This is a ·44–40 Model 1892 rifle, no. 726431,
with a 20-inch octagonal barrel. Courtesy of Wallis &
Wallis.

2, 3: title page. Two typical Civil War period cap-lock
revolvers—a ·44 New Model Army Remington (left)
and a ·36 Whitney Navy (right)—flank 'A Fight in the
Street' by Frederic Remington, published in *Century
Magazine* in 1889, which portrays the average Wild
West gunfight far better than any Hollywood
shoot-out. Guns courtesy of Wallis & Wallis.

Edited and designed by John Walter.
Produced by Elex Research Services using
Typefit® from The Typesetting Bureau Ltd.
Camerawork by Service Twenty-Four Ltd.
Quality printing by The Bath Press,
Lower Bristol Road, Bath, BA2 3BL,
Great Britain.

What constitutes a 'Gun of the Wild West'
can be defined in differing, but equally
satisfactory ways. Excellent books and well
researched articles have been written on the
subject, but each author has had to decide
what should be included; I have tried to
provide a balanced coverage of the handguns,
longarms and shotguns introduced after the
first pocket-pattern Colt revolver appeared in
1849—creating a whole new market for
personal-defence guns, just as the California
Gold Rush was hastening the opening of the
Western Seaboard.

Fortunately, a great many detailed studies of
individual guns have been produced; the affairs
of Colt, particularly, have attained the status of
a religion among collectors. It is impossible to
do more here than summarise the history of the
best known guns, readers seeking additional
information being directed to the bibliography.

Most highly recommended are Joseph Rosa's
excellent *The Gunfighter. Man or Myth?* (1969)
and *Guns of the American West, 1776–1900*
(Arms & Armour Press, 1985). These books are
appreciably more anecdotal than my approach
and provide an entertaining read.

Firearms of the American West, 1803–1865
and *Firearms of the West, 1866–1894* were
published by the University of New Mexico
Press in 1984 and 1985 respectively. The work
of Louis Garavaglia and Charles Worman, these
large, handsome and expensive volumes can
afford the space—over 800 pages—to deal with
their subject in meticulous detail, though the
subjection of technical history to anecdotal
documentation is slightly disappointing.

Guns of the Wild West pays special attention
to the weapons of the Civil War, and to the
development of the US Army's smallarms.
These are all too often ignored in studies of
Wild West firearms, even though they served
the army in campaigns against the Indians
or along the troubled border with Mexico
before many—condemned as obsolescent—
found their way into civilian hands.

Excepting guns such as the pioneering Smith
& Wesson Model No. 1 cartridge revolvers, ·22
rimfires have been omitted. Though small
calibre rimfire rifles taught many a Western
youngster to shoot, particularly as the Wild
West era drew to a close, they had little real
impact. An adequate classification of the many
rimfire longarms would significantly reduce
coverage of more battle-worthy guns. Problems
are always encountered in the cataloguing of

firearms, and *Guns of the Wild West* has faced
its share. Conflicting pattern-dates are by no
means uncommon, and there is a tendency
among collectors to classify guns made in
the nineteenth century much too precisely.
Modern enthusiasts are prone to overlook that,
though the US gunmaking industry was better
mechanised than any other prior to the First
World War, only the products of the leading
makers were truly mass-produced.

As accurate dating is often difficult, phrases
such as 'about' or 'it is believed ' have been
used more than I would have liked. Should
better information be forthcoming, I shall be
pleased to acknowledge it in any subsequent
editions. Material should be sent by way of my
publishers.

Unless stated otherwise, all patent numbers
quoted in the text refer to those granted in the
USA. Applications were often submitted some
time before patents were granted, and three
years or more could easily elapse; production,
therefore, could precede or ante-date grants of
patents—a vital (but all too often overlooked)
factor determining order of precedence. The
controversy that still surrounds the use of
'Deringer' and 'derringer' has been resolved by
restricting the former to guns made by Henry
Deringer of Philadelphia, and the latter to a
generic term.

Many people have contributed to this book,
and I hope that by a corporate 'thank you' I
shall not offend any of them unwittingly. I
am particularly pleased to acknowledge the
assistance of Ian Hogg, John Batchelor, Philip
Haythornthwaite, Roy Butler and Wallis & Wallis,
without whom the pictorial coverage would be
much poorer. The Photographic Libraries of the
Royal Armouries, HM Tower of London, the US
National Archives, the patent offices in Britain
and the USA, Dr Francis Lord, Milwaukee Public
Museum, the John M. Browning Museum,
Fabrique Nationale Herstal SA, Colt's Inc.,
Joseph J. Schroeder, and the Amon Carter
Museum in Fort Worth, Texas, have all
contributed. Their help is greatly appreciated.

Quotations have been kept to a minimum, but
I am pleased to acknowledge material extracted
from Joseph Rosa's *Guns of the American West*.

After all is said and done, of course, the faults
are mine alone; hopefully, they too have been
kept to a minimum.

George Markham
Ashby de la Zouch

SUMMARY OF CONTENTS

SELECT BIBLIOGRAPHY

¶ BADY, Donald B.: *Colt Automatic Pistols, 1896–1955.* Borden Publishing Company, Alhambra, California; revised edition, 1973.

¶ BARNES, Frank C.: *Cartridges of the World* ('The Book for Every Shooter, Collector and Handloader'). DBI Books, Inc., Northbrook, Illinois; fifth edition, 1985.

¶ BATTY, Peter, and PARISH, Peter: *The Divided Union* ('The Story of the American Civil War, 1861–65'). The Rainbird Publishing Group, London; 1987.

¶ BOWMAN, Hank Wieand: *Antique Guns.* Fawcett Publications, Greenwich, Connecticut; 1963.
Antique Guns from the Stagecoach Collection. Fawcett Publications, Greenwich, Connecticut; 1964.
Famous Guns from the Smithsonian Collection. Fawcett Publications, Greenwich, Connecticut; 1966.
Famous Guns from the Winchester Collection. Fawcett Publications, Greenwich, Connecticut; 1958.

¶ BROWNING, John, and GENTRY, Curt; *John M. Browning, American Gunmaker.* Doubleday & Company, New York; 1964.

¶ BUTLER, David F.: *Winchester '73 & '76* ('The First Repeating Centerfire Rifles'). Winchester Press, New York; 1970.
United States Firearms; The First Century, 1776–1875. Winchester Press, New York; 1971.

¶ CAMPBELL, Clark S.: *The '03 Springfields.* Ray Riling Arms Books Company, Philadelphia, Pennsylvania; 1971.

¶ COCHRAN, Keith: *Colt Peacemaker Encyclopedia.* Published privately, Rapid City, South Dakota; 1986. A supplement was produced in 1989.

¶ DU MONT, John S.: *Custer Battle Guns.* Phoenix Publishing, Canaan, New Hampshire; 1988.

¶ EDWARDS, William B.: *Civil War Guns.* The Stackpole Company, Harrisburg, Pennsylvania; 1962.

¶ FULLER, Claud E.: *The Breech-Loader in the Service, 1816–1917* ('A History of All Standard and Experimental U.S. Breech-Loading and Magazine Shoulder Arms'). N. Flayderman & Company, New Milford, Connecticut; 1965.

¶ GARAVAGLIA, Louis, and WORMAN, Charles: *Firearms of the American West, 1803–1865.* University of New Mexico Press, Albuquerque, New Mexico; 1984.
Firearms of the American West, 1866–1894. University of New Mexico Press, Albuquerque, New Mexico; 1985.

¶ GARDNER, Colonel Robert E.: *Small Arms Makers* ('A directory of fabricators of firearms, edged weapons, crossbows and polearms'). Crown Publishers, Inc., New York; 1958.

¶ GLUCKMAN, Colonel Arcadi: *Identifying U.S. Muskets, Rifles and Carbines.* The Stackpole Company, Harrisburg, Pennsylvania; 1965.

¶ HATCH, Alden: *Remington Arms in American History.* Remington Arms Company, Inc., Ilion, New York; revised edition, 1972.

¶ HATCHER, Major General Julian S.: *Hatcher's Notebook* ('A Standard Reference Book…'). The Stackpole Company, Harrisburg, Pennsylvania; third edition, 1962.

¶ HAVEN, Charles T., and BELDEN, Frank A.: *A History of the Colt Revolver.* William Morrow & Company, New York; 1940.

¶ HICKS, Major James E., USA: *U.S. Military Firearms, 1776–1956.* James E. Hicks & Son, La Vineta, California; 1962.

¶ HOGG, Ian V., and WEEKS, John S.: *Pistols of the World* ('A comprehensive…encyclopedia of the world's pistols and revolvers from 1870 until the present day'). Arms & Armour Press, London; 1978.

¶ JINKS, Roy G.: *History of Smith & Wesson.* Beinfeld Publishing Company, North Hollywood, California; 1977.

¶ KIRKLAND, K.D.: *America's Premier Gunmakers.* Bison Books, London; 1990.

¶ KOPEC, John A., GRAHAM, Ron, and MOORE, Kenneth C.: *A Study of the Colt Single Action Army Revolver.* Published by the authors, La Puente, California; 1976.

¶ LAKE, Stuart N.: *Wyatt Earp, Frontier Marshal.* Boston, Massachusetts; 1931.

¶ LEWIS, Colonel Berkeley R.: *Small Arms and Ammunition in the United States Service, 1776–1865.* Smithsonian Institution, Washington DC; 1968.

¶ LORD, Dr Francis A.: *Civil War Collector's Encyclopedia.* Volume 1, The Stackpole Company, Harrisburg, Pennsylvania, 1963; volume 2 ('Military Matériel, Both American and Foreign, Used by the Union and Confederacy'), Lord Americana & Research, West Columbia, South Carolina, 1975.

¶ McAULAY, John D.: *Civil War Breech Loading Rifles* ('A survey of the innovative infantry arms of the American Civil War'). Andrew Mowbray, Inc., Lincoln, Rhode Island; 1987.
Carbines of the Civil War, 1861–1865. Andrew Mowbray, Inc., Lincoln, Rhode Island; 1985.

¶ MACDONALD, John: *Great Battles of the American Civil War.* Michael Joseph, London; 1988.

¶ MILLER, W.T. (Editor): *Photographic History of the Civil War.* New York; twelve volumes, 1911.

¶ NEAL, Robert J., and JINKS, Roy G.: *Smith & Wesson 1857–1945.* A.S. Barnes & Company, Inc., South Brunswick, New Jersey, 1966.

¶ PARSONS, John E.: *Henry Deringer's Pocket Pistols.* William Morrow; New York, 1952.
Smith & Wesson Revolvers: The Pioneer Single Action Models. William Morrow, New York; 1957.
The First Winchester. Winchester Press, New York; 1969.
The Peacemaker and its Rivals. William Morrow, New York; 1950.

¶ ROOSEVELT, Theodore; *Hunting Trips of a Ranchman.* G.P. Putnam's Sons, New York; 1885.

¶ ROSA, Joseph G.: *The Gunfighter: Man or Myth?* University of Oklahoma Press, Norman, Oklahoma; 1969.
They Called Him Wild Bill: The Life and Adventures of James Butler Hickok. University of Oklahoma Press, Norman, Oklahoma; 1974.
Colonel Colt, London. Arms & Armour Press, London; 1976.
Guns of the American West (1776–1900). Arms & Armour Press, London; 1985.

¶ SCHUMAKER, P.L.: *Colt's Variations of the Old Model Pocket Pistol, 1849–72.* Fadco Publishing Company, Beverly Hills, California; 1957.

¶ SELL, De Witt E.: *Handguns Americana.* Borden Publishing Company, Alhambra, California; 1972.

¶ SELLERS, Frank M., and SMITH, Samuel E.: *American Percussion Revolvers.* Museum Restoration Service, Ottawa, Ontario, Canada; 1971.

¶ SERVEN, James E.: *Colt Firearms from 1836.* The Foundation Press, La Habra, California; seventh printing, 1972.

¶ STEFFEN, Randy: *The Horse Soldier, 1776–1943.* University of Oklahoma Press, Norman, Oklahoma; four volumes, 1977.

¶ STERN, Daniel K.: *10 Shots Quick* ('The Fascinating Story of the Savage Pocket Automatics'). Globe Printing Company, San Jose, California; 1967.

¶ SUTHERLAND, Robert Q., and WILSON, R. Larry: *The Book of Colt Firearms.* R.Q. Sutherland, Kansas City, Missouri; 1971.

¶ SWAYZE, Nathan L.: *'51 Colt Navies.* Published privately, Yazoo City, Missouri; 1967.

¶ WATROUS, George R.: *The History of Winchester Firearms, 1866–1966.* Winchester-Western Press, New Haven, Connecticut; third edition, 1966.

¶ WILLIAMSON, Harold F.: *Winchester—The Gun that Won the West.* A.S. Barnes Company, Cranbury, New Jersey; 1964.

¶ WILSON, R.L.: *The Colt Heritage* ('The Official History of Colt Firearms from 1836 to the Present'). Simon & Schuster, New York; undated [1979].

¶ WINANT, Lewis; *Firearms Curiosa.* Ray Riling Arms Books Company, Philadelphia, Pennsylvania; 1961.

INTRODUCTION

When Rodrigo de Triana, a seaman aboard the caravel *Pinta*, sighted the island that was to be named San Salvador in the evening of Friday 11 October 1492, the New World had been inhabited for thousands of years. The earliest explorers called the native tribes 'Indians', believing that they had indeed found the elusive passage westward to the Indies. The name stuck.

Gradually, the expansion-minded states in the Old World—Spain, England, France, the Netherlands, France—each laid claim to territory in the New. Spaniards reached Florida in 1513, moving into New Mexico by 1540; Frenchmen began tracing the Mississippi valley northward in 1673, and the Russians, crossing eastward across the Bering Strait, had penetrated deep into Alaska by 1741.

Ultimately, however, colonialization depended greatest on Englishmen. Their first settlement in North America was founded in what was to become the province of Virginia—Jamestown, proclaimed in 1607, was named after King James I. In 1620, after a perilous voyage across the Atlantic in the ship *Mayflower*, the Pilgrim Fathers founded the township of New Plymouth. Within a few yeas, Puritans had arrived by the hundred to escape persecution; townships along Massachusetts Bay grew so rapidly that, by the end of the seventeenth century, the Puritans had established settlements all over what would become 'New England'.

One huge area of wilderness had been granted by Charles I to a Catholic, George Calvert (later Lord Baltimore). Calvert called his new possession 'Maryland' after the Virgin Mary, the first settlement being established in 1634.

4, right. The fascinating 'County Map', a decorative hand-coloured map by Samuel Augustus Mitchell of Philadelphia and 'Entered according to Act of Congress in the year 1863...' Even at the time of the Civil War, the Dark and Bloody Ground was still sparsely settled. Courtesy of Robert Jeeves.

5, right. This photograph, taken in the unspoiled foothills of the Rocky Mountains, shows why the progress of settlement westward across North America was so slow. The combination of dense forestation, lakes, fast-flowing rivers and near-vertical mountain peaks provided a near-impenetrable barrier. Author's collection.

6, right. This hand-tinted postcard—'A Quaint Old Street'—was published by Richard M. Cook of Marblehead, Massachusetts, from a photograph taken about 1910. It is typical of the area in which the US firearms industry grew. Author's collection.

Nearby, another tract was seized from the Swedish in 1664 and chartered to Quaker William Penn in 1681; he named his impressively wooded possession Pennsylvania.

Albemarle Colony was the subject of a charter granted by Charles I in 1629; settled from Virginia in the 1650s, it was subsequently granted to group of English aristocrats in 1663. The first permanent settlement was established at Charles Town in 1670. Renamed 'Carolina Colony' in 1691, the area was divided in 1712. The present Delaware, New Jersey and New York were taken by the British from the Dutch in 1664. By 1732, when Georgia was formed by James Oglethorpe as a refuge for convicts, debtors, gamblers and the poor, there were thirteen states.

A treaty was agreed with France in 1748, bringing many years of sporadic large scale fighting to an end, but bickering continued for many years. As late as 1755, the British suffered a humiliating reverse at the hands of the French and their Indian allies. Casualties were horrendous, the British losing about eight hundred men from a force mustering less than 1,500, compared with about ten dead Frenchmen. Lessons were clear. The French made best use of cover, while the British advanced across open ground. The mistake was to be repeated many times in the next fifty years.

In 1759, however, the British Army crushed the French on the Plains of Abraham in Quebec, ending the threat to Canada virtually with a single volley. Within a few years, however, the size of the standing army had been greatly reduced and the financial burden of maintaining garrisons adroitly switched from the British taxpayer to the North American colonists.

After the French had been ousted, efforts were made to draw the fledgling united states closer to the Crown. Revenues were raised in the form of taxes; attempts were made to enforce the whim of a government several thousand miles away, across a broad ocean. The British authorities controlled the pattern of settlement with little regard to the views of the colonists. As many of the latter had left Britain to escape just such restrictions, an undercurrent of resentment grew perceptibly after 1763.

Incidents such as the Boston Tea Party in December 1773, when a band of colonists disguised as Red Indians dumped a large consignment of tea in Boston harbour, swelled into full-blown hostility. The British reacted by sending troops to enforce decrees emanating from London. The colonists reacted so strongly that fighting broke out in 1775.

British troops were dispatched to Concord, Massachusetts, in the middle of April 1775 to seize arms and ammunition being collected for patriotic use. On 19 April, in the small town of Lexington on the way to Concord, the first shots were fired when eight hundred Britons commanded by Major John Pitcairn of the Royal Marines confronted about a hundred American Minutemen. When the smoke had cleared, eight Americans lay dead.

A subsequent skirmish at Concord caused losses on both sides, and then came the bloody battle of Bunker's Hill; unspoken war had begun. On 4 July 1776, the Second Continental Congress ratified the independence from Britain of the United States of America, which had been declared two days previously. Local skirmishes had escalated into a major war.

7, right. Part of "Asher & Adams' New York and Part of Ontario", a lithographed map 'Entered in according to Act of Congress in the year 1871...' This shows the eastern margins of New York state, parts of northern Pennsylvania, plus most of Massachusetts and Connecticut—the cradle of the USA's gunmaking industry.

Courtesy of Robert Jeeves.

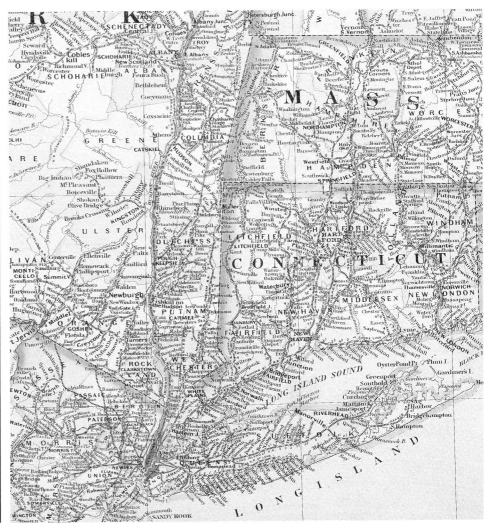

CREATION OF A FIREARMS INDUSTRY

At the beginning of the War of Independence, the colonists had nothing but a series of local militias, with no central leadership and no clear strategy. However, the first steps towards forming a 'Continental Army' had been taken during the Second Continental Congress on 14 June 1775. It was placed under the control of a five man civilian commission, and intended to supplement local militias during the war most people could see looming. Experience gained during the War of Independence was vital to the development of the US armed forces. Though the Continental Army stood down on 2 November 1783, it was reactivated whenever the embryo USA was threatened. It had been placed under direct control of the President under the constitution adopted in 1788.

The lack of facilities to train the Minutemen was matched by a dearth of weapons. The first regulation pattern weapons made in what became the United States were five hundred British-style muskets made in the mid-eighteenth century by Hugh Orr of Bridgewater, Massachusetts, for the Province of Massachusetts Bay. When war began, all the colonists could muster were a few muskets that had survived the Indian Wars—British Brown Bess and French Charleville patterns being amongst the most numerous.

These were far from sufficient to arm the large numbers of men mustering to serve the Continental Army, and so any serviceable rifle, musket and fowling piece was pressed into service. In November 1775, Congress requested the individual states to 'manufacture good fire locks with bayonets; each fire lock to be made with a good bridle lock, three quarters of an inch bore—barrel to be three feet and eight inches in length, the bayonet to be eighteen inches in the blade, with a steel ramrod...' On 23 February 1776, Congress authorized the Committees of Safety, formed to ensure supplies of arms and equipment, to contract for muskets and bayonets to serve the United States.

Activities in Maryland typified the period. The establishment of a military gun making industry in the province dated from August 1775, when the Maryland

8, right. American militiamen in action during the War of Independence, showing them in line in the foreground—aping contemporary European techniques—and in skirmish order (background). The US troops were much more effectual when fighting their own irregular battles. Courtesy of Philip Haythornthwaite.

Convention—predecessor of the state legislature—reported that twelve suitable shops existed in the area: four in Frederick Town, three in Baltimore, two in Hager's Town and one each in George Town and Jerusalem. Each smith was thought to be capable of producing twenty serviceable muskets monthly. Rifles could also be made, in addition to swords and tomahawks.

Production began immediately, the muskets being '3½ feet in the barrel, ¾-inch bore, with good double bridle locks, black walnut or maple stocks, and plain strong brass mountings; bayonets with steel blades, 17 inches long; steel ramrods,

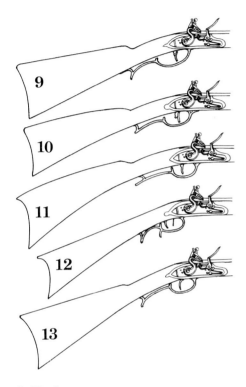

9–13, above.
The principal butt shapes that characterised the Long Rifle schools:
9, Lancaster County, Pennsylvania;
10, Reading County, Pennsylvania;
11, Bethlehem County, Pennsylvania;
12, Bedford County, Pennsylvania;
13, Maryland.
Note the differing comb designs and the shaping of the butt-belly.

double screws; priming wires and brushes fitted thereto; with a pair of brass moulds for every 80 muskets to cast 12 bullets on one side, and on the other to cast shot of such size as the musket will chamber three…'

Participants in the scheme included Isaac Behr of Baltimore, William Wheatcroft of Annapolis, Henry Hollingsworth of Elkton and Elisha Winters of Frederick Town, though most of the guns bore nothing but MARYLAND. Most barrels were made by Hollingsworth or Isaac Harris.

The Committee of Safety Muskets often included locks cannibalized from old unserviceable British or French muskets, or new locks imported from Europe. In detail, however, they vary greatly; some have plain British-style stocks, others follow French patterns, while a few even display profiles based on indigenous North American long rifles.

The Long or Kentucky Rifle, indelibly associated with the War of Independence, evolved from the Jaeger rifle of southern Germany, northern Austria and Bohemia.

During the eighteenth century, in the period between the War of the Spanish Succession (1701–14) and the Seven Years War (1756–63), many people fled from the horrors of religious persecution to settle in the New World. Puritans came from England, Huguenots from France; there were Lutherans from central Europe, still dominated by Catholicism. People fled to escape hunger, or from compulsory military service.

The immigrants included many German-speaking gunmakers. Entering through the port of Philadelphia, most men settled in the interior of Pennsylvania. The area surrounding the settlement of Lancaster was typical of many European gun making centres. Rich in iron ore and coal, Pennsylvania ("Penn's Wood") had plentiful forests to provide good-quality charcoal, and a myriad streams to power water-wheels.

The first guns made in North America followed the traditions of their Old World antecedents—short, heavy and firing large-calibre balls. Such guns were common in Europe, not only for sporting purposes but also as the weapons of the élite riflemen in the armies of Prussia and Austria-Hungary.

However, the needs of the settlers who moved inland from Philadelphia differed from those who remained along the Atlantic seaboard. Remote from maritime or riverine trade, the uplanders needed a weapon that could take large game: animals such as deer provided not only food but also clothes, in the form of buckskin. They could not be taken effectually with the smooth-bore fowling pieces popular along the coastal margins. Fowling pieces had neither the range nor the accuracy to down the game found in the interior.

In 1769, backwoodsmen led by Daniel Boone ventured through the Cumberland Gap to explore the wilderness beyond. Now comprising much of the states of Kentucky and Tennessee, this they called 'Kentucky' from an old Indian word meaning 'dark and bloody (or brooding) ground'. The term was soon associated with the Long Rifles, even though they may have been made in Maryland, North Carolina, Pennsylvania or Virginia.

The establishment of the Wilderness Trail, as the route into Kentucky was known, encouraged many settlers to seek their fortune in the flat and fertile land west of the Appalachian mountains. Virtually all carried guns made in up-state Pennsylvania, where the first Long Rifles had been made by Martin Meylin in the early eighteenth century.

As the decades had passed, the guns had been lengthened—improving accuracy—but also lightened to a point where they had an elegance unmatched by any amorphous Jägerbüchse. The gradual refinement of the Long Rifle was accompanied by a steady reduction in calibre, the average dimension by the time of the War of Independence being about ·45–·50 compared with ·60–·65 twenty years earlier. The reduction in calibre had been due partly to elongation of the barrel, which improved accuracy, but also to a desire to conserve materials: a ·45-diameter ball contained only a little more than a third of the lead in a ·65 example (·048in compared with ·143in³). Barrels measured 40–44in, though some pre-1760 examples could be 48–50in. They were generally octagonal, rifled with seven or eight grooves. A slow constant-pitch twist was standard, though a few straight groove barrels were made alongside smooth-bore versions which could handle ball or shot with equal facility.

Changes in barrel length and calibre, and the refinement of the stock, were accompanied by other changes. For example, lock plates were reduced from the old flat-plate musket styles until they were delicately arched. This allowed the breech and butt-wrist to be very slender. Butt plates, originally flat, were curved to fit the shoulder; sliding wooden patch-box covers in the butt-sides, common to most European designs, were replaced by hinged brass lids retained by spring latches. The clumsy European trigger guards, often heavy brass castings or carved from wood, were replaced by plain ovals and a simple curved finger-spur.

Changes in the style of the patch boxes, particularly, are often valuable aids to dating guns that were rarely signed. Most Long Rifles made prior to the War of Independence had plain-lid boxes without side bars, though stock carving was already being practised in moderation. Shortly after the war, perhaps about 1790–5, Lancaster gunsmiths such as Jacob Dickert adopted a stylised flower at the head of the patch box. This remained in vogue until at least 1815, and may be encountered on guns made by Albright, Fondersmith, Graeff, Haeffer, Henry, Resor and others in the Lancaster area.

The practice of decorating patch boxes spread widely after 1800. Henry Albright and Melchior Fordney used horses' heads; others used birds or scroll work. Hinges were beautified, while pierced work was applied to side bars. Carving was applied to the right side of the butt around the patch box, and to form a raised cheek piece on the left. The cheek-piece flat often contained a decorative inlay such as a stylised starburst. Guns made by the Voglers of Salem, North Carolina, often featured eagle motifs not only on the cheek piece but also at the head of the patch box. Other devices include 'x' (a talisman to ward off evil), a crescent moon, a shield or a heart.

Most early guns were made in Lancaster County, Pennsylvania, in meagre workshops. Though this limited output, it did not prevent the appearance of some elegant, highly serviceable and often most attractively decorated guns. The apogee of the Long Rifle is generally agreed to be 1780–1820, though production continued well into the cap-lock era in isolated parts of the Appalachians.

The initial gunmaking centres in Lancaster County were supplemented by newer ones in York County, to westward, and then by others in the more northerly Lebanon and Dauphin counties. Some gunsmiths followed the northward course of the state rivers before reaching the Susquehanna and, ultimately, the state of New York. Another group moved progressively southward into North Carolina by way of Maryland and Virginia.

The seeds of the later gunmaking industry in New England, most notably in the states of Massachusetts and neighbouring Connecticut, were sewn largely by smiths trained in Pennsylvania. Local needs, however, ensured that muskets and fowling pieces predominated; only in the uplands of New York and the most northerly states did the rifle retain its importance.

THE WAR OF INDEPENDENCE, 1776–83

The first major skirmish occurred when, on the instructions of General Thomas Gage, a British detachment was sent from Boston to Concord to seize equipment destined for the colonists. After fighting at Lexington and Concord on 19 April 1775, the rebel forces besieged Boston. The siege lasted until General William Howe evacuated to town in March 1776.

The British sent a large fleet under the command of Admiral Lord Howe, brother of the Boston general, with instructions either to request the rebels to surrender—with the promise of pardon—or to force them into submission. On 4 July 1776, however, the United States of America delared independence.

General Howe landed men on Long Island, forcing the American commander, George Washington, to retreat into Manhattan. General Lord Cornwallis, having taken Washington's garrison at Fort Lee, drove the rebels across New Jersey to the western bank of the Delaware river; however, on Christmas night, Washington crossed the Delaware under cover of darkness and caught the British unaware at Trenton. The action was short and sharp, and the Britons lost a thousand men. Though Trenton was soon retaken, Washington escaped to regroup his forces and inflicted a severe defeat on Cornwallis at Princeton.

1777 opened with the advance of a British expedition from Canada into the northern United States. Commanded by General Sir John Burgoyne, with a detached column under Colonel St Leger, the British made steady progress until being checked first at Oriskany and then at Albany. Finally, on 17 October 1777, Burgoyne was forced to surrender to the American general Horace Gates after the battle of Saratoga.

14, below. This dramatized rendering of the Battle of Lexington, 19 April 1775, was published in the USA early this century. It bears the legend 'Buckman Tavern to the left, meeting house in the center, and Old Belfry to the right, which, in the Revolutionary period, stood on the battlefield'.

Author's collection.

Buckman Tavern to the left, meeting house in the center, and Old Belfry to the right, which, in the Revolutionary period, stood upon the battlefield

Fighting continued to be unpredictable, with neither side able to land the conclusive blow. Cornwallis defeated Washington at the Battle of Brandywine Creek in September 1777, then took Philadelphia on 25 September. During the winter of 1777/8, when campaigns were reduced to a minimum by the harsh conditions, Washington quartered his army at Valley Forge. Here, with the able assistance of a Prussian officer, Wilhelm von Steuben, the Continental Army became ever more effectual. On 28 June 1788, Washington's men overcame British forces at the battle of Monmouth, penning the Britons remaining in the northern USA around New York.

The southern theatre gained in importance as British fortunes declined in the north. The French navy laid siege to Savannah and Yorktown, preventing the British replenishing military stores, and though Cornwallis destroyed General Gates's army at Camden (16 August 1780), he suffered severe setbacks at the battles of King's Mountain and Cowpens (7 October 1780 and 17 January 1781).

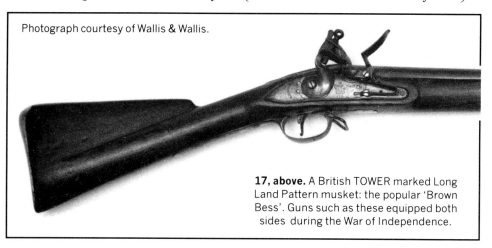

Photograph courtesy of Wallis & Wallis.

17, above. A British TOWER marked Long Land Pattern musket: the popular 'Brown Bess'. Guns such as these equipped both sides during the War of Independence.

A defeat of American forces at Guilford Court House in the middle of March 1781 allowed Cornwallis to advance into Virginia to establish a base at Yorktown. There, cut off by Franco-American land forces and the French Navy, he was starved into submission. The seven-thousand strong British army surrendered on 19 October 1781.

Though the war on land had ended, maritime campaigns continued. The British merchant marine suffered considerably at the hands of American privateers, most notably John Paul Jones; with the Spanish and Dutch fleets controlling much of the waters around the British Isles, the Royal Navy was never able to come to terms with the depredations of the embryo US Navy. Finally, in November 1783, the Treaty of Paris sealed the borders of the USA from the Atlantic seaboard westward to the Mississippi river.

The defeat of the vaunted British Army came as a shock to many European observers. By a happy combination of better generalship, guerilla tactics, better equipment, guile, luck, and the participation of the French, the Colonial Army had defeated forces mustering far greater numbers of men under arms. It has been estimated that the rebels rarely managed to field more than twenty thousand men at one time, while the British numbered 42,000 backed by about thirty thousand irregulars raised in Hesse and other German states.

By 1793, only Spanish Florida among Old World possessions in southern north America retained its independence, though it was some years before the political organisation of the new country stabilised. The original articles of confederation soon proved insufficient, so a new constitution was drafted in 1786–7. This led to the inauguration of the first president, George Washington, in 1789.

15, top. The death of American General Richard Montgomery during the attack on Quebec, 31 December 1775/1 January 1776. From a nineteenth-century engraving. Courtesy of Philip J. Haythornthwaite.

16, above. 'Declaration of Independence, U.S. Capitol'. A lithographed postcard published by B.S. Reynolds Co., Washington DC, after a painting by John Trumbull. John Hancock, President of Congress, is seated at the table facing the Committee of Five—Thomas Jefferson, John Adams, Benjamin Franklin, Roger Sherman and Robert Livingston. Author's collection.

18, top. This engraving, based on
*A Plan of Discipline Composed for the Use of
the Militia of the County of Norfolk*, dating
from the early nineteenth century, shows the
use of 'Light Fusils by Officers, as commonly
adopted in North America [during the War of
Independence]. Courtesy of Philip J.
Haythornthwaite.

19, right. Washington's crossing of the
Delaware, Christmas Eve 1776. From a
painting by Emanuel Lütze, once in the
Kunsthalle, Bremen. Author's collection.

20, right. The surrender of General Sir John
Burgoyne at Saratoga, 17 October 1777. A
lithographed postcard published by B.S.
Reynolds Co., Washington DC, after a painting
by John Trumbull. Author's collection.

LONG RIFLES IN WAR

There is a popular misconception that every man in the Continental Army carried a Long Rifle during the War of Independence. This is far from the truth; the American regulars were armed largely with French and British muskets, the latter impressed into service after capture. The first US-made musket was subsequently patterned on a French prototype.

Only a few irregulars carried Long Rifles, though the value of these guns was sufficiently well-known for many backwoodsmen to be used as sharpshooters and skirmishers. Eight rifle companies were raised in Pennsylvania during the early days of the War of Independence, befitting the state in which the Long Rifle had been born; two more came from Maryland, and others from Virginia.

Yet the success of the guns, in British eyes at least, was wholly disproportionate to their numbers; in October 1777, for example, a ball fired by rifleman Timothy Murphy had killed British General Simon Fraser, one of Burgoyne's most able commanders, and there had been many similar incidents.

Among the most important actions in which Long Rifles contributed greatly to victory was the Battle of King's Mountain, fought in North Carolina on 7 October 1780. American forces under Colonel Sevier defeated a mixed British and Loyalist forces led by Major Patrick Ferguson. The British, in a poor position on top of a hill, were unable to stem the advance of the riflemen up the wooded hillside. A desperate charge down the hill proved a failure, costing Ferguson his life, and the Americans carried the day; Loyalist casualties amounted to 224, plus six hundred

taken prisoner, while the colonials lost 28 killed and about ninety wounded. It was ironic that a rifle ball should have killed Ferguson, inventor of the breech-loading flintlock rifle that bore his name and a long-time advocate of riflemen.

The Long Rifle also proved its worth at the Battle of New Orleans, fought on 8 January 1815—after the Treaty of Ghent had concluded the war of 1812 between Britain and the United States. The British forces, recklessly confident of victory, had advanced against such a well fortified and defended position that they were cut to ribands. Great bravery was no substitute for tactical skill, and the casualty figures favoured the defending American forces by more than sixty to one.

21, right. An engraving of the breech of the flintlock Hall rifle, Model 1819. The chamber and lock unit were removed to reload; in an emergency, they made a passable pocket pistol.

From W.W. Greener, *The Gun and its Development* (1910).

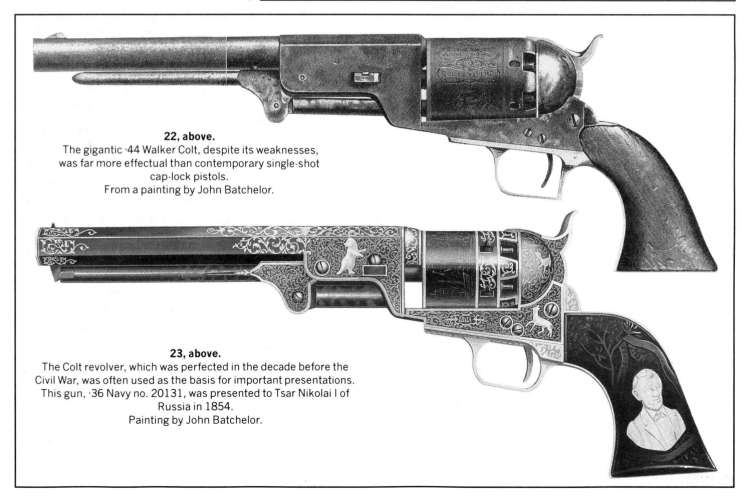

22, above.
The gigantic ·44 Walker Colt, despite its weaknesses, was far more effectual than contemporary single-shot cap-lock pistols.
From a painting by John Batchelor.

23, above.
The Colt revolver, which was perfected in the decade before the Civil War, was often used as the basis for important presentations. This gun, ·36 Navy no. 20131, was presented to Tsar Nikolai I of Russia in 1854.
Painting by John Batchelor.

24, right. 'Old Fort Wilkins, 1844. Copper Harbor, Mich.' A photo-postcard, dating from the 1940s, showing a reconstruction of a typical stockade fort of the mid nineteenth century. Author's collection.

THE EARLY NINETEENTH CENTURY

The USA soon pursued expansionist aims of its own, the Louisiana Purchase of 1803 all but doubling its size. By this time, the thirteen original states had been joined by four more—Vermont had been admitted to the Union in 1791, Kentucky in 1792, Tennessee in 1796 and Ohio in 1803. Soon, adventurers such as Lewis & Clark were despatched to report on the land to the west of the Mississippi.

The War of 1812 arose from US suspicions about the behaviour of the British during the Napoleonic Wars. Though the British and French had violated American shipping during the period, Napoleon had wisely vowed not to interfere with Anglo-American trade.

In 1807, the British, confident of maritime supremacy, had enacted an Order in Council perpetuating the blockade of French ports and adding the demand that neutral shipping would be allowed through the blockade only after stopping at a British port and paying customs duties! The Royal Navy was also stopping ships to remove 'deserters', even though they may have claimed US citizenship.

Additionally irked by the supply of British arms to the Shawnee indians and by wrangles over the border with British Canada, the USA went to war on 18 June 1812. Plans to invade Canada miscarried. Though the US Navy was successful in the earliest naval engagements off the Atlantic seaboard and on the Great Lakes, the British seized the initiative at the battle of Bladensburg and then set light to Washington, DC. After several months of inconclusive skirmishing, both sides acknowledged the Treaty of Ghent on 14 December 1814. Ironically, the greatest US victory, the Battle of New Orleans, was gained after peace had been signed.

Few of the USA's goals had been achieved during the war, though popular opinion soon formed the view that it had been a great victory. The greatest long term gains were considerable reduction of the Union's dependence on Europe and diminution of Indian power. Shawnee chief Tecumseh had been killed in battle on the Canadian border, while the defeat of the Creek Indians in the south hastened the entry of Spanish Florida into the Union in 1819.

Like other nations, the USA began to industrialize during the first quarter of the nineteenth century, spurred partly by a desire to compete with the Old World, whose goods were filling New World requirements, but also to create a base from which the thrust westward could be supported.

25, above. The Greene carbine was typical of the breech-loaders touted in the mid-nineteenth century. This is one of the British trial guns, made by the Massachusetts Arms Company in 1856. It bears the cypher of Queen Victoria and the mark '1–G.–17 R.D.M.R.'. Note the Maynard Tape Primer, and the leaf-pattern back sight graduated to 600yd; the barrel pivots sideways to the right to load. Courtesy of Wallis & Wallis.

WAR WITH MEXICO

The Texas of the 1830s was a semi-autonomous, near desolate province of Mexico in which thirty thousand American immigrants had been allowed to settle. In 1836 General Antonio López de Santa Anna, then the Mexican president, ratified a new constitution limiting provincial rights. Texas promptly seceded, declaring itself an independent republic.

Santa Anna mustered a sizable army, marching northward with little resistance until he reached the Alamo, a little-known fort in the little-known Texan town of San Antonio. The siege began on 23 February 1836 and lasted a mere thirteen days, whereupon 183 of the estimated garrison of two hundred were massacred in revenge for at least a thousand casualties inflicted on a Mexican army mustering perhaps three thousand men. The dead included William Travis, Jim Bowie and Davey Crockett, but Santa Anna was delayed sufficiently for the Texan army to prepare to face him. Thus the Alamo—'cottonwood' in Spanish—has become a particular embodiment of heroic resistance and selfless sacrifice for a noble cause.

Santa Anna was soon captured, then released when the Mexican government promised not to interfere in Texan affairs. At this time, the independence of Texas was still not recognized in Mexico, though influential thought in the United States—the so-called 'Manifest Doctrine'—was beginning to see the province as fit to be added to the Union.

The USA annexed Texas in 1845, causing Mexico to sever relations. Santa Anna was overthrown; and when President Polk suggested stabilising the US-Mexican border on the Rio Grande, his overtures were rebuffed. The US Army was ordered into disputed territory. Forces clashed in April 1846, outraging public opinion: American blood had been spilled on what was widely believed to be American soil. Action was required.

The campaigns were brief and unspectacular. US Army troops soon captured New Mexico and large tracts of California, while General Zachary Taylor achieved rapid success south of the Texas border.

Santa Anna was restored to the presidency in 1846 and immediately took the offensive, but was checked at the the bloody but otherwise inconclusive battle of Buena Vista in February 1847. A change in strategy saw a US thrust on Mexico City, General Winfield Scott defeating Santa Anna at the battle of Cerro Gordo in April 1847 and taking the Mexican capital on 14 September.

The Mexicans then sued for peace and the Treaty of Guadeloupe Hidalgo ended the war on 2 February 1848. In return for fifteen million dollars in gold, Mexico ceded to the USA land bounded by the Rio Grande and Gila river, along the Colorado to the Pacific coast. Land south of the Gila was transferred by an adjustment made in 1853.

The wars with Mexico were the first in which Colt revolvers attained any military prominence: the Paterson Colts in the hands of the Texans, and then the huge Walker Colts with the US Army after 1847. Their story is told in greater detail in the section devoted to cap-lock revolvers.

SEEDS OF CIVIL WAR

The drive to open up the West brought clashes between the forces of slavery and Abolitionists opposing them. The problem was highlighted in the ever-growing contrast between the northern states, where industrialization was at its most vibrant, and a largely agrarian south dependent on tobacco and cotton.

Several states had already declared their rights to repeal federal laws, Virginia doing so as early as 1798, but the periodic compromises rarely lasted; South Carolina had attempted to repeal or 'Nullify' a federal law in 1832, provoking a crisis so severe that President Andrew Jackson threatened to send in the federal army unless the state complied.

The co-called Compromise of 1850 arose when California asked to be admitted to the Union. The basis of representation was that each state, regardless of size or population, should elect two men to the Senate. The admission of California, whose constitution expressly prohibited slavery, would have given the abolitionists a majority. However, as the slavery question had not been resolved in territories ceded to the USA by Mexico in 1848, Senator Henry Clay proposed the admission of California as a free state, counterbalanced by the organization of New Mexico and Utah with slavery to be resolved by 'Popular Sovereignty'.

Clay's proposals were backed strongly enough to be implemented immediately, but succeeded only in postponing the slavery question for a few years. In 1854, Kansas Territory demanded a settlement by Popular Sovereignty. This caused the bitterest violence in the years preceding the Civil War. In addition, the effects of Clay's harsh Fugitive Slave Law were enough to turn many a liberal conscience into a rabid abolitionist.

Finally, the election of Republican Abraham Lincoln to the presidency in 1860 caused South Carolina to secede from the Union. Ten more states followed South Carolina's lead in 1861. Lincoln refused to recognize the right of the states to secede if they wished to do so, and, after a tense stand-off, the USA was plunged into the Civil War.

THE AMERICAN CIVIL WAR, 1861–5

The Civil War was contested between the federal government and eleven northern states on one side, and the eleven secessionists on the other. Though now largely seen as a conflict of slavers and abolitionists, the war was as much about trade and constitution.

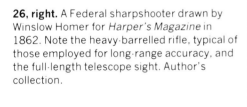

26, right. A Federal sharpshooter drawn by Winslow Homer for *Harper's Magazine* in 1862. Note the heavy-barrelled rifle, typical of those employed for long-range accuracy, and the full-length telescope sight. Author's collection.

27, right. The Confederate Steam Gun was only one of the outlandish weapons proposed for use in the war. Made by Ross Winans of Baltimore to the designs of Charles Dickinson, it had a single barrel fed from a hopper and was allegedly capable of throwing 200 balls a minute to a maximum range of two miles. Captured by the Federal army in May 1861, it was never used in anger.

From a contemporary engraving in *Harper's Magazine*, 1861.

The southern, Confederate or Rebel forces were raised from the states of South Carolina, Mississippi, Florida, Alabama, Georgia, Louisiana, Texas, Virginia, Arkansas, Tennessee and North Carolina. Under the Presidency of Jefferson Davis, the Confederate States of America relied on patriotic fervour and the international value of cotton, the South's staple crop, to promote their cause. The northern, Federal or Union side, under the guidance of Abraham Lincoln, contained more than twice as many men and the lion's share of manufacturing facilities.

The first shots of the war were fired on 12 April 1861 by Confederate guns aimed at Fort Sumter, the strong Federal battery guarding the secessionist port of Charleston, South Carolina. Sumter surrendered after a bombardment, without a casualty, but the die had been cast. By 21 July, thirty thousand Union troops massing for an attack on the rebel capital—Richmond, Virginia—were halted at the first battle of Manassas (known to the Union as 'Bull Run') and driven back on Washington by Confederate forces commanded by generals Jackson and Beauregard.

The unexpected defeat, and the spectacle of their forces fleeing in disorder through the streets of the nation's capital, galvanized the Union into raising the half-million strong Army of the Potomac under the command of General George McClellan.

The first major campaigns began in the Spring of 1862, when General Ulysses Grant captured Confederate forts Henry and Donelson in western Tennessee. This was followed by the capture of New Madrid, Missouri, and the bloody but inconclusive battle of Shiloh (Tennessee) on 6–7 April 1862. By June, the Union forces had occupied Memphis, Tennessee, while Commodore David Farragut and the Union navy had gained control of New Orleans.

McClellan, meanwhile, had landed a 100,000-man force near Fort Monroe, Virginia, in another attempt to take Richmond. Erring too much to caution, McClellan's Army of the Potomac was turned back by Confederate generals Lee, Jackson and Johnson at the bloody Seven Days Battles contested from 26 June to 2 July 1862.

At the second battle of Manassas, 29–30 August 1862, Lee drove a Union army under General John Pope out of Virginia and then invaded Maryland. This seemed to pose a great threat to the border states, especially in those such as Delaware, where there were strong pro-slavery feelings. However, fortified by advance knowledge of the Confederate battle plan, McClellan stopped Lee at the battle of Antietam on 17 September.

The setback proved temporary, as Lee, after regrouping, defeated Union forces under General Ambrose Burnside at the battle of Fredericksburg (13 December). Whatever his merits as a firearms designer, Burnside was soon seen to be an ineffectual commander and superseded by General Joseph "Fightin' Joe" Hooker. Hooker decided on an immediate offensive, but was comprehensively defeated by Lee at Chancellorsville, Virginia, at the beginning of May 1863.

Lee then re-invaded the Union, dodging through Maryland and onward into Pennsylvania. However, a series of skirmishes developed into the climatic battle of Gettysburg (1–3 July 1863). Under a new commander, General George Meade, the Union forces turned a defensive position into one of strength: decisively checked, Lee and his men fell back into Virginia.

Concurrently, Ulysses Grant captured Vicksburg in the West and, after the last few Mississippi outposts had fallen, the main trade route to the Gulf of Mexico fell under Union control. In the East, however, General Rosecrans was defeated by Confederates at Chickamauga, Georgia, and Grant was recalled to replace him.

Grant and his principal lieutenant, William Sherman, drove the Confederate General Braxton Bragg out of Chattanooga in late November 1863; Sherman took Knoxville, whereafter the remaining rebels were cleared from Tennessee. Grant's success persuaded Lincoln to give him supreme command of the Federal armies in the Spring of 1864. Taking personal charge of the Army of the Potomac, Grant elected to grind the Confederacy down, confident that superiority in manpower and armaments would be the telling factor. His efforts began badly in May, losing large numbers of men in the Virginian battles of The Wilderness, Spotsylvania and Cold Harbor, but soon penned Lee's forces by Petersburg.

While Grant was doggedly reducing Lee's positions, Sherman captured Atlanta and then began his famous 'March through Georgia', reaching the Atlantic coast at Savannah on 10 December 1864. In his wake was a swathe of destruction, the result of a deliberate scorched-earth policy.

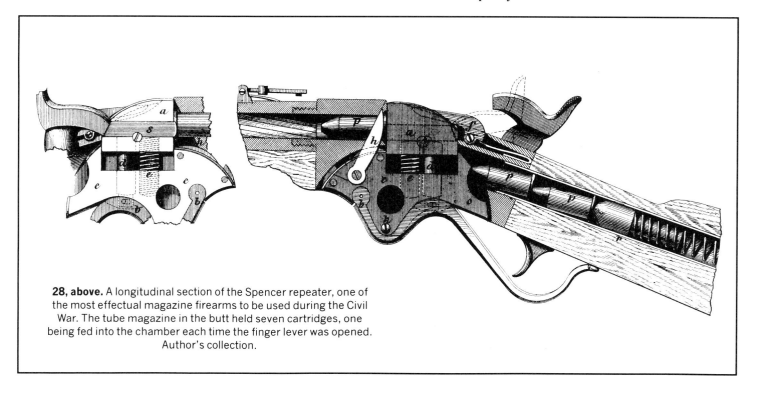

28, above. A longitudinal section of the Spencer repeater, one of the most effectual magazine firearms to be used during the Civil War. The tube magazine in the butt held seven cartridges, one being fed into the chamber each time the finger lever was opened. Author's collection.

By the Spring of 1865, the Confederate forces were in a terrible way; near to starvation, with neither ammunition or equipment, they could do little but wait. General Grant began his final advance with a minor battle at Five Forks, on 1 April, then took Richmond two days later. On 9 April, Lee surrendered at Appomattox Court House, and the capitulation of General Johnson in North Carolina on 26 April effectively ended the war.

AFTERMATH OF WAR

The Union had gained an upper hand largely owing to the concentration of industrial might in the north, but also partially to the reliance placed by the South on imported weapons. Though Confederate forces had begun with encouraging victories, and though the skill of Lee came close to gaining strategic victories more than once, the result was rarely in doubt after 1863. However, the war had been costly not only in fiscal terms but also, more importantly, in human suffering. The death toll in a war in which brother had raged against brother was appalling, and a divisive scar festered for many years.

29, below. The headquarters of General Raphael Meade at Gettysburg, from a lithographed postcard printed in Germany for The Hugh C. Leighton Company, Portland, Maine. The caption notes that "From this homely little cottage, General Meade directed the battle of the second and third days until fire from the Confederate batteries, preliminary to Pickett's charge, became so severe that twenty seven horses of his headquarter's guard lay dead about the door. Then he mounted and rode to the position…in time to witness the retreat of the survivors of Pickett's men." Author's collection.

30, above. Zouaves—Federal troops dressed in French colonial-style uniforms—practice their musket-and-bayonet defence against cavalry. From a contemporary engraving. Courtesy of Philip J. Haythornthwaite.

31, above right. This engraving of the Battle of Resaca, 13–15 May 1864, shows the advance of the Federal troops against a strong Confederate hill-top position. Note the conventional tactics: ranks of infantrymen (foreground) advancing in rigid order behind a screen of skirmishers. Slavish adherence to traditional principles contributed greatly to the horrendous casualty rate in the Civil War. Courtesy of Philip J. Haythornthwaite.

Lincoln had intended to be lenient with the Rebels, but his assassination in Ford's Theatre, Washington, in 1865, allowed a Congress dominated by radical northern Republicans to embark on its own programme of pacifying the south. This did not end until Federal troops withdrew from south of the Mason-Dixon Line in 1877.

After the end of the Civil War, the USA consolidated an industrial base from which it had risen to become a world-ranked power by the turn of the century. Immigrants flocked to the USA by the million, fleeing religious, state or racial persecution in their native lands. Others, such as the Scots and Irish, chose to escape the Enclosures of the Highlands after the Jacobite Rebellion of 1745 or the great famines of the 1840s. It has been estimated that five million people entered the USA between 1820 and the beginning of the Civil War in 1861, almost ninety per cent from Britain, Ireland or Germany.

From the earliest times, immigrants had contributed much to the North American gunmaking. The Kentucky Rifle, for example, was refined from the Jaeger rifle of central Europe by generations of émigré German Büchsenmacher.

THE INDIANS

One of the less savoury aspects of American expansionism was the gradual disenfranchisement of the American Indians. The native Americans were goaded, pursued and herded away from tribal lands—which the settlers wanted—into reservations on poor ground. Thousands died during the enforced transfers; thousands more perished in bleak winters, denied access to traditional hunting grounds where the buffalo were being slaughtered to extinction.

Though the Indians fought long and hard for their lands and then their rights, tribal squabbling prevented them presenting a cohesive force against the US Army. Some believed that Custer sealed his fate by ignoring the treaty, signed in 1868, that forbade entry to the Black Hills. Soon, settlers backed by the US Army were making such steady inroads into the area that cattle grazed in the grasslands that fringed the southern margins of the Black Hills.

In December 1875, the Indian Agent at Standing Rock received orders to tell Sitting Bull and the Hunkpapa Sioux—later destined to be villains in the Custer

32, right. A ·50–70 Gatling on a US Navy landing carriage, 1875. Essentially similar guns were used during the Civil War, the earliest relying on percussion caps. From a contemporary engraving, courtesy of Ian Hogg.

33, below. The maker's plate of an early Colt-made Gatling Gun. Note the repesentations of the rampant Colt and two Root side-hammer revolvers above the last line. By courtesy of Ian Hogg.

drama—to move inside the borders of the minuscule reservation prepared for them. The deadline for compliance was set as 31 January 1876, or the Indians would be considered as hostile.

The tribe was encamped for the winter on the Powder River, more than two hundred miles away from Standing Rock across plains that were deep in snow. Sitting Bull replied that the tribe could not move across Dakota until the summer of 1876, but the advice was ignored; troops were ordered in.

The Battle of the Little Big Horn, fought on 25 June 1876, was one-sided. When the smoke had cleared, Companies C, E, F, I and L of the 7th Cavalry had died to a man. Springfield single-shot carbines and Colt Single Action Army revolvers had been no match for the ferocity of the huge band of Indians numbering roughly three thousand.

The desire for revenge, fanned by public pressure, led to further restrictions. Sitting Bull, by now seen as the principal enemy, met generals Nelson Miles and Alfred Terry but could obtain few concessions. Eventually, in the summer of 1881,

34, right. The Indian as a subjugated showman. This British postcard by Gale & Polden Ltd, Aldershot, dated July 1909, shows the "Sole Survivors of the Black Hawk Massacre Episode. Now taking part in the Red Man's Spectacle, Earls Court". Author's collection.

35, right. The driving of the Last Spike effectively joined the railways driven from the West and East coasts of the USA. This famous picture shows the meeting at Promontory Point, Utah, 7 May 1869. On the left is the Central Pacific Rail Road locomotive No. 60 *Jupiter*; on the right is Union Pacific's No. 119. From a lantern slide. Author's collection.

a small band of the remaining Hunkpapa Sioux surrendered at Fort Buford. After a period of imprisonment, the chief was allowed to rejoin his people at Standing Rock in 1883. However, the US government was soon demanding that half the reservation be surrendered. The attitude of the white settlers towards the Indians was pithily expressed by Senator John Logan, who berated Sitting Bull: 'you have no following, no power, no control, and no right to control. You are on an indian reservation merely at the sufferance of the government'.

Eventually, partially by excluding Sitting Bull from negotiations, the government obtained the consent of the Hunkpapa Sioux to cede the land. A poor winter was compounded by government callousness over food allocations; the young, the old and the sickly died in droves. The hopeless situation brought a hopeless solution, in the form of a religion known as the Ghost Dance. Originating among the Paiutes in the late 1860s, this promised resurrection of the dead, return of the buffalo—they had long since been exterminated in the Dakotas—and new grass to bury the white men. Once more would the Indians be masters of their lands.

The re-appearance of the Ghost Dance after a solar eclipse early in 1889 coincided with the agonies being faced by the Hunkpapa Sioux. Unfortunately, the intensity with which the Indians embraced the Ghost Dance terrified the settlers into petitioning the government for protection. The Standing Rock agent, McLaughlin, pronounced it a 'pernicious system of religion'. Even though the Dance was based on non-violent principles, the army was ordered to detain Sitting Bull. Mistakenly, the old chief was seen by Washington as the power behind the Ghost Dance.

As 15 December 1890 dawned, with the connivance of the army, the Indian Bureau and agent McLaughlin, more than forty 'friendly' Indians dressed as Agency policemen were sent to detain Sitting Bull. What happened remains unclear, but the aged man was shot through the head by one of the policemen and the ensuing skirmish between rival factions claimed the lives of several men.

Attempts to negotiate led only to a confrontation between the remaining Indians—numbering perhaps three hundred men, women and children—and 470 men of the US Army, backed by Hotchkiss revolver cannon. The Battle of Wounded Knee apparently began when hotheads among the Sioux fired on the soldiers as the Indians were being disarmed. It resulted in the needless deaths of about 200 Indians and 25 soldiers, at a time when the US Government had officially declared the idea of the Western frontier to be moribund.

The Indian nations had made no real contribution towards the history of the firearm in North America. Though many tribes used guns, occasionally to good effect, the weapons were taken in battle or from settlers; others were simply obtained through the trading posts, most notably after the passing of the Indian Intercourse Act in 1834.

Particularly popular were flint- and cap-lock trading muskets, often bearing the marks of Henry Leman, and (in later days) the brass-mounted 1866-model Winchester. These guns can be identified by decorative tacks driven into their woodwork, or by crude wrapped-rawhide repairs to the butt wrists.

OPENING OF THE WEST

Among the important events that forged a nation out of the United States was the discovery of gold near Sutter's Mill, an obscure township in California, on 24 January 1848. News travelled slowly at first, which was fortunate: little more than

36–9, right. The pepperbox was the forerunner of the modern revolver, distinguished by a cluster of full length barrels. In addition to guns imported from Britain, France and Belgium, substantial quantities were made in the USA by Robbins & Lawrence, Ethan Allen and Stocking & Co. The guns shown here are a ring-trigger Belgian 'Mariette' (36), a typical British-made bar-hammer gun (37), an Allen & Thurber (38) and a ·28 six-shot Stocking (39) with an extended cocking spur. The self-cocking Allen guns were quite popular in the West at the time of the California Gold Rush, though soon displaced by the small cap-lock revolvers.

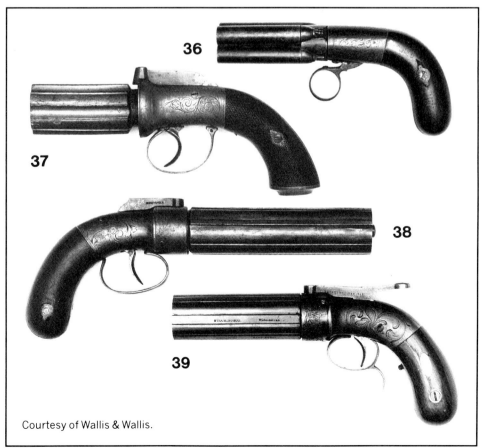

Courtesy of Wallis & Wallis.

Photographs
courtesy of
Wallis & Wallis.

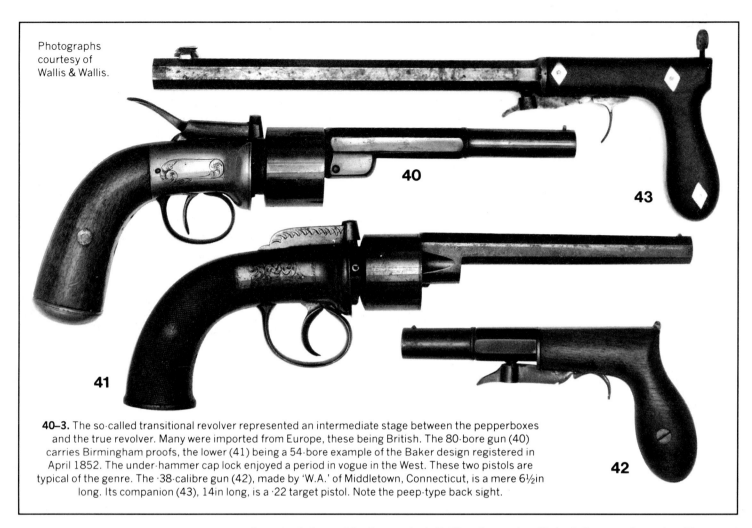

40-3. The so-called transitional revolver represented an intermediate stage between the pepperboxes and the true revolver. Many were imported from Europe, these being British. The 80-bore gun (40) carries Birmingham proofs, the lower (41) being a 54-bore example of the Baker design registered in April 1852. The under-hammer cap lock enjoyed a period in vogue in the West. These two pistols are typical of the genre. The ·38-calibre gun (42), made by 'W.A.' of Middletown, Connecticut, is a mere 6½in long. Its companion (43), 14in long, is a ·22 target pistol. Note the peep-type back sight.

a week later, Mexico ceded California to the United States when the Treaty of Guadeloupe Hidalgo finally ended hostilities between the two countries.

Eventually, news of the lucky strike filtered back to the eastern USA. Chaos ensued as thousands of men, often accompanied by their families, set out on the dangerous journey across the uncharted Great Plains towards the foothills of the Rocky Mountains. Few of the western states had been organised by 1848, and a trek westward to California was quite as dangerous as it was arduous. Potential prospectors died of thirst on the plains and deserts, or froze on uncharted mountains. Others fell victims to marauding Indians. Some simply disappeared without trace, though completion of the transcontinental railways—which met at Promontory Point, Utah, in 1869 for the driving of the 'Last Spike'—eventually eased the hardships of westward migration.

Many men began their journeys from towns such as Cincinnati, where Benjamin Kittredge & Company (one among many) plied them with arms and ammunition. Others trecked from St Louis, in Missouri, then out westward along the Oregon Trail and the Platte river until they reached Fort Laramie. The route led westward through what is now Wyoming to Forkham, at the head of the Snake river, and the commencement of the California Trail.

Prospectors who had survived to Forkham turned south-westward to Sacramento, San Franciso and the Pacific Ocean. Gradually, the staging posts on their route expanded into townships, then became cities.

For many, California, the land of opportunity, was where their troubles began. By 1850, what had once been small Spanish colonial towns had often become hotbeds of saloons, brothels and tricksters. The population of California tripled in a year, and was ten times its 1848 levels by 1851. There were fortunes to be made—and then lost at the gaming tables. Crime soared; life was cheapened to almost nothing. In September 1851, the *Illustrated London News* reported that:

"The crime of homicide continues to prevail all over the country to an extent which [elsewhere]. would be taken as proof that civil society was completely disorganised. Our 'Homicide Calendar' for June, lately published in the *San Francisco Chronicle*, the 'total of Killed' for the first six months of the present year is set down at 219 persons; and in the same period, 'Hung by the sheriff, 2; hung by the mob, 24'. But whether the two judicial and twenty-four lynch executions are included…I am not able to determine. "The number of 'killed' in the month of June was twenty—a fact which it is sincerely to be hoped may be taken as evidence that the homicidal epidemic is abating."

Into this market poured the output of gunmakers nearly three thousand miles distant on the eastern seaboard of the United States. Colt revolvers, Deringer pistols, and Hawken rifles were merely three of the weapons to achieve a sudden (and largely unexpected) notoriety. The success of the machine-made Colts,

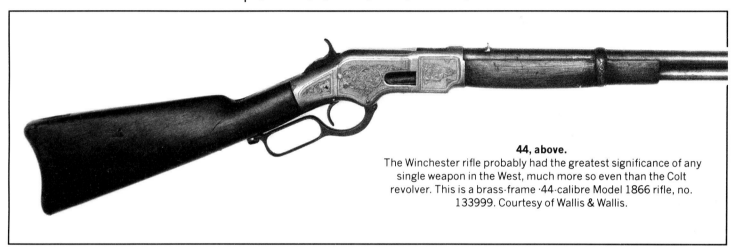

44, above.
The Winchester rifle probably had the greatest significance of any single weapon in the West, much more so even than the Colt revolver. This is a brass-frame ·44-calibre Model 1866 rifle, no. 133999. Courtesy of Wallis & Wallis.

particularly, helped to lay the foundations of an arms industry which would fuel a bloody Civil War little over a decade later.

THE WEAPONS OF THE WEST

The popular conception that every lawman and outlaw carried a Colt Peacemaker and a Winchester rifle, fuelled by western fiction and countless Hollywood films, still dies very hard.

Strenuous efforts have been made in recent years to prove that the Western handguns ranged from tiny derringers and ·22-calibre Suicide Specials to the largest revolvers. The most popular handguns prior to the mid 1870s were cap lock Colts and Remingtons, large quantities of which had either been touted commercially or sold out of military service at the end of the Civil War. James Butler 'Wild Bill' Hickok was presented with a matched pair of scroll-engraved ·36 Colt M1851 Navy revolvers in 1869, their carved ivory grips displaying an eagle motif; outlaw Sam Bass was carrying a well-worn ·44 1860-pattern Colt Army revolver when he was fatally wounded during a bank-raid in Round Rock, Texas, in the summer of 1878.

The advent of the metal-cased cartridge changed matters appreciably, though the Single Action Army Colt never gained ascendancy in the years prior to 1917. The staggering output of Iver Johnson, for example, shows that sales of low-cost guns could not have been confined to the Eastern states.

Lawmakers and lawbreakers alike never agreed on the perfect weapon. Many favoured shotguns, which were particularly deadly at short range and more likely to correct minor deficiencies in aim than a revolver; others used knives or axes in preference to firearms, and a few men even extolled the virtues of the bow. Many of the most notorious Westerners changed weapons whenever the opportunity arose: balance and handling qualities have always been subjective. Identifying their guns, therefore, may be difficult. The late Hank Wieand Bowman, in *Antique Guns from the Stagecoach Collection*, quoted the collection's founder, Osborne Klavestad, as saying:

"Zerelda Samuels, the crafty old mother of the James bandits, talked my uncle into buying Jesse's 'very own six shooter'… My uncle was greatly elated over his prize until he learned that the female mountebank kept a whole bushel basket of guns on hand to sell to gullible tourists. Legend has it that Borax Smith's Twenty Mule Team would have bent an axle if…loaded with all the Jesse James guns Zerelda Samuels tearfully parted with."

A display board of guns owned by Jesse James and 'authenticated by his son' included a M1873 Winchester lever-action rifle, two Colt Single Action Army revolvers, a Schofield Smith & Wesson and a round-butt Merwin & Hulbert. The large-calibre Merwin & Hulbert pattern was very popular in its short-barrel guise, one ·44 single-action gun being taken from Bass Outlaw in El Paso in 1892 and a ·44 double-action example from Pearl Hart in 1899.

When he was shot by Robert Ford in 1882, Jesse James owned a ·45 first pattern Smith & Wesson Schofield revolver, no. 366. Ironically, the murder weapon was a New Model No.3 Smith & Wesson.

Alexander Franklin 'Frank' James, Jesse's elder brother, carried two ·44–40 M1875 Remington revolvers (one being no. 15116). When he surrendered in 1882, Frank James stated that he preferred the Remingtons because they were 'the hardest and surest shooting pistol made', and because they chambered the same cartridges as his Winchester rifle. In addition to a Colt Single Action Army revolver and a ·36 M1851 Colt Navy cap lock, no. 109168, Thomas Coleman 'Cole' Younger

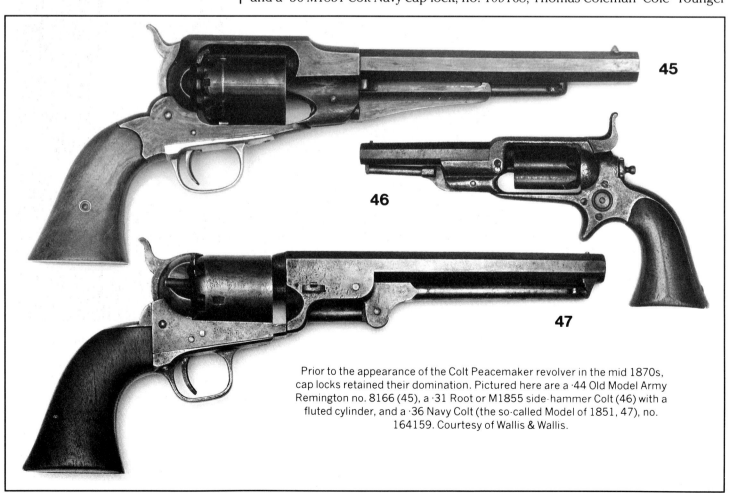

Prior to the appearance of the Colt Peacemaker revolver in the mid 1870s, cap locks retained their domination. Pictured here are a ·44 Old Model Army Remington no. 8166 (45), a ·31 Root or M1855 side-hammer Colt (46) with a fluted cylinder, and a ·36 Navy Colt (the so-called Model of 1851, 47), no. 164159. Courtesy of Wallis & Wallis.

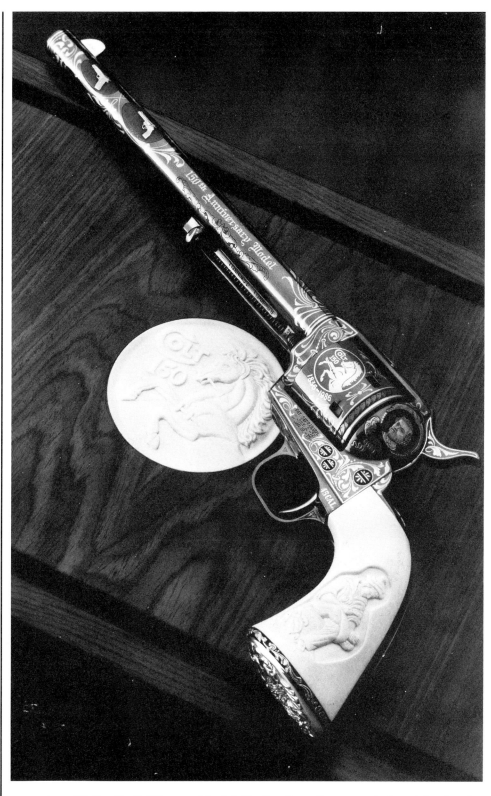

48, right. The Colt New Model Army Revolver, Peacemaker or M1873 is undoubtedly the best known of all cartridge revolvers. This picture shows the ultra-ornate Colt 150th Anniversary Exhibition Gun, created in 1986 in a bid to rival the best of the guns made in the nineteenth century—a far cry from the weapons of the plains!

owned a ·32 Smith & Wesson Model No.2, allegedly presented to him by the infamous guerilla William Quantrill some time prior to the latter's death in 1865. Charlie Pitts of the James-Younger gang was carrying a ·44 third or New Model Smith & Wesson Russian revolver, no. 40369, when he was killed in 1876 during a raid on Northfield, Minnesota.

Dallas Stoudenmire, one-time City Marshal of El Paso, owned a ·44 Smith & Wesson American revolver, no. 7056, and a ·44 Richards-Mason conversion of a Colt M1860 cap-lock army revolver. Wyatt Earp is said to have carried a Smith & Wesson Model No.3 during the gunfight at the O.K. Corral in 1881, though he

49, right. The James Boys: Jesse (left) and Frank (right), flanking their mother Zerelda. From a photograph taken about 1880 and published in postcard form at a later date. Author's collection.

50, right. By 1900, the first automatic pistols were being perfected. Among them were several designed by John Browning and made by Fabrique Nationale d'Armes de Guerre in Belgium. This is an example of the ·38 Colt Model 1900, no. 1653, from the US Army test series. Note the 'U.S.' mark on the trigger guard. Courtesy of Joseph J. Schroeder.

acquired Colt Single Action Army revolver no. 69562 shortly afterwards; Virgil Earp owned a nickelled ·44 Smith & Wesson New Model No.3, no. 14289.

John Wesley Hardin had a variety of revolvers, including ivory-grip Smith & Wesson ·44 first pattern (or 'Old Old Model') Russian revolver no. 25274 and ·44 Double Action no. 352. Shortly before being killed by a bullet from ·45 Colt Single Action Army revolver no. 141805, fired by El Paso lawman John Selman in 1895, Hardin surrendered engraved ·41 double-action Colt no. 73728. Two additional Colt revolvers were found on his body, but doubt remains whether one was an ivory-grip ·45 Single Action Army (no. 126680) and the other a ·41 double action. One eye-witness reported that both were double-action guns.

There is substantially less doubt that Sherriff Pat Garrett used Colt Single Action Army revolver no. 55093 to kill Billy the Kid in 1881. The gun was shipped from Hartford to Benjamin Kittredge & Company of Cincinnati in April 1880. Among the many guns presented to Garrett by the grateful citizens of Missouri were a ·41 Colt double action (no. 138671), a cased ·38 folding-hammer Merwin & Hulbert, no. 16648, and ·32 Hopkins & Allen Model XL no. 3164.

William H. Bonney, Jr, better known as Billy the Kid, favoured Colts. Though he carried a new ·41 double-action gun in 1878, a ·44 Single Action Army revolver was surrendered to Garrett's possee near Stinking Springs, New Mexico, at the end of 1880. Many lesser guns reached the West. The compact Webley

'British Bulldog'—and a legion of European-made copies—was a popular import, favoured for its large bore, while small-calibre 'Suicide Specials' were preferred for the ease with which they could be concealed. Owing to their ability to fire several shots without reloading, cheap revolvers steadily eclipsed derringers in the last decades of the nineteenth century.

Lieutenant-Colonel George Armstrong Custer carried a pair of Webley Bulldog revolvers during his Last Stand on the Little Big Horn, and a ·38-calibre version was taken from the body of outlaw Robert 'Bob' Dalton after an abortive raid on Coffeyville, Kansas, in October 1892. An unidentifable ·22 Suicide Special was taken from John McCall in 1876 after he had murdered Wild Bill Hickok in Deadwood, South Dakota. The popular image of the Western duel is wildly inaccurate, as most men tipped the odds in their favour whenever possible. A shot in the back prevented the victim returning fire, and a stealthy attack out of the shadows guaranteed more success than a confrontation in the midday sun. The

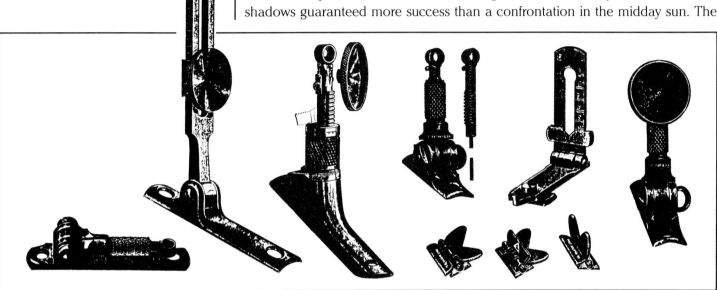

51, above. Some of the many Colt and Lyman sights offered with the original Lightning magazine rifles in the 1890s. Author's collection.

following extract from Joseph Rosa's fascinating *Guns of the American West* (1985) gives an idea of the performance of the average gunslinger:

"A…less publicised event took place on 9 March 1877, at Cheyenne, Wyoming, when gamblers Charlie Harrison and James Levy shot it out after a dispute at a gaming table. The pair had been drinking heavily all evening, and the more they consumed the more belligerent they became, until finally Levy pulled a gun on Harrison… They stepped into the street and Harrison hurried into the Senate Saloon to pick up a revolver. He emerged to find Levy waiting for him outside Frenchy's Saloon. Charlie promptly opened fire, but missed, and Levy shot back. Six shots were exchanged before Harrison fell, struck in the chest. Raising himself, he fired once more but missed, and then fell back. Levy ran across the street, stood over him, and deliberately fired another bullet into him before…hurrying away."

Reality was not always what celluloid wished it to have been.

GLOBAL RECOGNITION

US interest in central and south America was a constant source of friction with Old World powers. The brutality with which the Spanish put down a rebellion in Cuba in 1895 provoked a particularly jingoistic campaign in the leading US national newspapers.

The destruction of USS *Maine* on a visit to Havana harbour on 15 February 1898 was ascribed in many war-mongering quarters to sabotage, overlooking the reasonable explanation that it was due simply to negligence and sweating cordite: the wreck was raised some years after the war, revealing a hole in the plating in the region of the forward magazine.

One relic of the event was a series of 6mm Lee Straight-Pull M1895 navy rifles and a few Trapdoor Springfields, sold by Francis Bannerman & Sons in 1909.

Concerned by the *Maine* incident, the Spanish government announced that the Cubans would be granted limited autonomy. However, the US Congress demanded that Cuba be granted total independence, which meant the removal of Spanish troops; believing that the Spanish were unlikely to concur readily, Congress also granted President McKinley the right to use force to free Cuba from Spanish domination.

Spain declared war on the USA on 24 April 1898. In Europe, it was anticipated that the Spanish, though known to be in decline militarily, would not surrender easily. But the campaigns were ridiculously one-sided. A US Navy squadron commanded by Commodore George Dewey destroyed virtually the entire Spanish Pacific squadron during the Battle of Manila Bay (1 May 1898), at the cost of seven wounded, while the Spanish Caribbean squadron, threatened by large numbers of regular and volunteer troops landed on the Cuban coast, was annihilated during the battle of Santiago on 3 July. The surrender of the city of Santiago to General William Shafter on 17 July brought fighting to an end.

It had been remarkable principally for the naval action in the Pacific, which raised many an eyebrow in Europe, and for the participation of Theodore Roosevelt and the 1st Volunteer Cavalry. Nicknamed the Rough Riders, this unit attained notoriety for its participation in the battle of San Juan Hill.

The Treaty of Paris, signed on 10 December 1898, ended Spanish colonial rule in Latin America and the Pacific. Spain renounced all claims to Cuba, ceded Guam and Puerto Rico to the USA, and transferred sovereignty to the Philippine Islands for twenty million dollars in gold. It elevated the United States of America to the status of a world power, with a far-flung colonial empire, and reduced the once-vaunted Spanish domination of Latin America to virtually nil.

It was the first time a New World power had defeated an Old World nation since the American War of Independence had ended British interest in the United States. Even though Spanish power had been waning for years, the American victory in the war—and the ease with which it had been achieved—was genuinely unexpected in Europe. Clearly, the USA was no longer to be taken lightly.

By 1917, and the entry of the United States of America into the First World War, civilisation was pushing back the borders of the Wild West—particularly from the east, as the Sierra Nevada mountains of eastern California and the deserts of Arizona and Nevada presented obstacles in the west.

52, right. Men of the US Army on the border with Mexico man a ·30-calibre 1909-model Benet-Mercié machine rifle—the so-called 'Daylight Gun', named after a rumour that its Hotchkiss-pattern feed strips could not be loaded in the dark. From a postcard copyrighted by the International News Service ('Machine Guns in Action', Mexican War Series No. 1) *c*.1916. Author's collection.

THE HANDGUNS

The first Colts were cap lock rifles, made in Hartford in 1832 and then in Baltimore. They were successful enough to encourage Colt to apply for what became English Patent 6,909, granted on 22 October 1835, and comparable US 136 of 25 January 1836. Each claimed ease of loading, and rapidity of fire by connecting the hammer and cylinder-rotating pawl.

Emboldened by the limited success of his early rifles, and fuelled by his own vision, Colt then founded the Patent Arms Manufacturing Company in Paterson, New Jersey, in 1835. His products included revolver-rifles and the first Paterson Revolvers, readily identifiable by triggers that sprang down out of the frame when the hammer was thumbed back for the first shot.

About 180 No.5 Holster Pistols were acquired by the government of the independent State of Texas in 1839–41, for the state navy. Withdrawn when the navy was disbanded, they passed to the Texas Rangers. Ironically, an encounter between the Texan and Mexican navies in 1843 provided the inspiration for the maritime battle scene rolled into the cylinder peripheries of many later Colts.

Colt's own enthusiasm was not matched by success in a traditionally cautious market, and so the Patent Arms Manufacturing Company was forced into liquidation in 1842. When war with Mexico began in 1846, an army commanded by General Zachary Taylor was sent southward to the border between Mexico

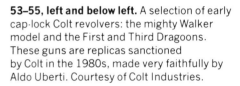

53–55, left and below left. A selection of early cap-lock Colt revolvers: the mighty Walker model and the First and Third Dragoons. These guns are replicas sanctioned by Colt in the 1980s, made very faithfully by Aldo Uberti. Courtesy of Colt Industries.

and Texas. Taylor's men included Samuel H. Walker, who had become acquainted with Paterson Colts during the Seminole Wars.

When it became clear that the problems with Mexico were serious, Walker was ordered northward to recruit volunteers and obtain firearms. He immediately sought out Colt, to whom the 1836 US master patent had reverted, and the two men successfully refined the Paterson Colt into a battle-worthy weapon.

A thousand-gun government contract was obtained in January 1847, the guns being made in the Whitneyville, Connecticut, factory of Eli Whitney. The cumbersome 1847-vintage six shot Walker Colts were more than 15in long and weighed in excess of 4½lb, but their efficacy soon brought another order. On the strength of this contract, Colt founded his own manufactory in the small Connecticut town of Hartford in 1848.

CAP-LOCK COLTS, 1848-60

The ·44 Model 1848 or Colt Dragoon Revolver (1848–50) initially embodied old Whitney parts, but improvements were soon made. It had a square-back trigger guard and ovoid cylinder-stop slots. The Second Model (1850–1) had squared cylinder-stop slots, pins between the nipples, a roller on the hammer and a leaf-type main spring, while the Third Model (1851–61) had a round-back trigger guard, an improved back sight and could accept a shoulder stock. In addition, there was

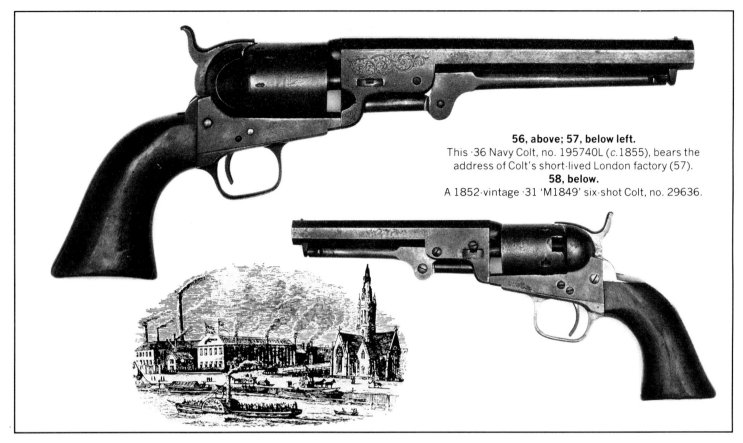

56, above; 57, below left.
This ·36 Navy Colt, no. 195740L (*c.*1855), bears the address of Colt's short-lived London factory (57).
58, below.
A 1852-vintage ·31 'M1849' six-shot Colt, no. 29636.

a transitional pattern incorporating Walker-Colt parts. This was produced for the US Army in 1848, to replace defective Walker Colts; 239 of the latter are known to have failed in service, mostly owing to ruptured cylinders.

The Dragoon revolvers were Colt's first major success; about twenty thousand were made in 1849–55, 9,380 of which were purchased by the US Army.

The success of the Colt Dragoon revolver inspired the introduction in 1848 of the first ·31 five-shot Colt pocket-model revolver. The earliest pattern, known colloquially as the 'Baby Dragoon', had a distinctive square-back trigger guard, rounded cylinder-stop slots and (except on the last guns) lacked a rammer beneath the barrel. The revolvers were normally reloaded by substituting cylinders, though the cylinder axis pin was specifically designed to double as a rammer.

The barrels measured 3–6in. A motif of Texas Rangers chasing Indians was rolled into the surface of the cylinder, replaced by a stagecoach robbery scene on transitional guns made in 1850. About fifteen thousand Baby Dragoons were made in 1848–50.

They were superseded in 1850 by the very similar ·31 Pocket Revolver, now misleadingly (but conveniently) labelled 'Model 1849', which proved such a tremendous success commercially that production had exceeded 300,000 when the new-pattern pocket models

appeared in the early 1860s. The last 1850-type Pocket Revolver did not leave Hartford warehouses until 1873.

Such variety will be encountered among these guns that a complete collection would exceed two hundred individual guns. The ·31 revolvers were made with five or six-shot cylinders, the former being regarded as standard. Barrels measured 3–6in; squared cylinder-stop slots were normal, together with the stagecoach

59, below. Men of the Federal Navy at gun drill. Note that, in addition to their cutlasses, they are armed with ·36 Colt Navy revolvers. One butt is clearly visible on the gunlayer's hip. Courtesy of US National Archives, Washington DC.

60, right. An exploded-view drawing of the ·36 Navy Colt, or Model of 1851. Note that the weapon was essentially simple—especially the lock components. Author's archives.

robbery cylinder scene. Most guns were blued, with some colour case-hardening, while grip straps were often silvered. However, a wide range of engraving was offered alongside ivory grips and virtually any barrel-length purchasers suggested. In addition to the 314,000 guns made in Hartford, about eleven thousand guns were made in the London factory in their own special number-series.

The success of the small-calibre cap lock Colts was helped by an extension of the 1836 master patent to 1857, as a result of a successful lack of profit claim filed in the US courts.

The most sought versions of the ·31 'M1849' Colt revolver include early guns with a small trigger guard; the so-called 'Wells Fargo', which lacked a rammer; and a special three-inch barrel gun with a greatly abbreviated rammer.

The improved ·36 Navy Colt, otherwise known as the Old Model Belt Pistol (or Model of 1851), was a contemporary of the ·31 Pocket Model. Made in great numbers—215,348 in Hartford (1850–73) plus forty thousand in London—it was 13in overall, had a 7½-inch barrel and weighed 2½lb. Its 'navy' connotation arose from the small calibre and the naval scene rolled into the cylinder periphery in honour of the so-called Battle of Campeche, when the Texans defeated

the Mexicans in an otherwise insignificant skirmish on 16 May 1843. Few guns ever saw the sea, most being used during the land campaigns of the American Civil War.

The Navy revolvers were sold in a myriad styles, from the plainest military issue (the first thousand-gun consignment was accepted by the US Army in 1855) to gems of the gunmaker's art.

The principal variations are mostly easily recognizable. The earliest guns had square back trigger guards, and the barrel wedge lay above the retaining screw; this was replaced by a similar gun with the wedge below the screw. The third pattern had a small round-back guard, and the otherwise identical fourty type had a large round-back guard. A few shoulder stocks were made after 1859, but were distinctly unpopular.

Among the best-known recipients of presentation-grade Navy Model Colt were two Russian tsars, Nikolai I and Aleksandr II, Napoleon III of France, and Mormon leader Brigham Young. Another went to Queen Victoria's consort, Prince Albert, to mark the Great Exhibition of 1851. It was accompanied by a matching Dragoon Colt and a Baby Dragoon to amuse the Prince of Wales.

Out West, the Navy Colt was favoured for its balance. Though its popularity waned after the elegant and harder-hitting ·44 Army revolver appeared in 1860, the Navy pattern was still widespread into the 1870s. James Butler 'Wild Bill' Hickok owned a pair of ·36 Colts, with which Robert Kane saw him offering:

"...to do a little shooting for us...outside the city limits... His last feat was the most remarkable of all: a quart can was thrown by Mr Hickok himself, which dropped about 10 or 12 yards distant. Quickly whipping out his weapons, he fired alternately with right and left. Advancing a step with each shot, his bullets striking the earth just under the can, he kept it in continuous motion until his pistols were empty."

Colt was particularly keen to establish a foothold in the British military market, opening a factory in Pimlico (London) in 1854 after exhibiting successfully at the Great Exhibition. Among the fascinated visitors was Charles Dickens, who recorded:

"Under the roof of this low, brick-built, barrack-looking building, we are told that we may see what cannot be seen under one roof elsewhere in all England, the complete manufacture of a pistol, from dirty pieces of timber and rough bars of steel, till it is fit for the gunsmith's case."

Unfortunately for Colt, Britain already had an effectual revolver designed by Robert Adams. His guns had some superior features: their calibre was greater—38, 54, 80 and 120 Bore— and the solid frame was stronger than Colt's open top. In addition, Adams' double-action trigger eliminated thumb cocking.

Government trials proved to be inconclusive, allowing each inventor to claim victory even though the Board of Ordnance preferred the Colt. The British acquired nearly 24,000 Navy Colts during the Crimean War, and many similar weapons were bought privately.

Experience soon revealed the superior man stopping qualities of 38 Bore (·500) and 54 Bore (·442) Adams revolvers. The addition of Rigby's and Kerr's patent rammers to the basic Adams design, and the advent of improved lock-work patented by Lieutenant Frederick Beaumont of the Royal Engineers, eventually persuaded the Board of Ordnance to replace the Colts.

The Model 1855, or Root Pattern, pocket revolver supplemented the ·31 Pocket Model. Developed by Elisha Root, superintendent of the Hartford factory, the new cap locks were derived from the contemporary side-hammer muskets. They had solid frames and sheath triggers, but the most obvious feature was the cranked side hammer that allowed the axis pin to enter the cylinder through the back of the frame. A new rack-and-pinion or 'creeping' rammer was used; Root's patent described it as a method of 'combining the plunger of a many-chambered rotating-breech pistol...with a lever with a cogged sector engaging the cogs of a straight rack'. Though the new Colt revolvers were very sturdy, and undeniably very

NAVY COLT

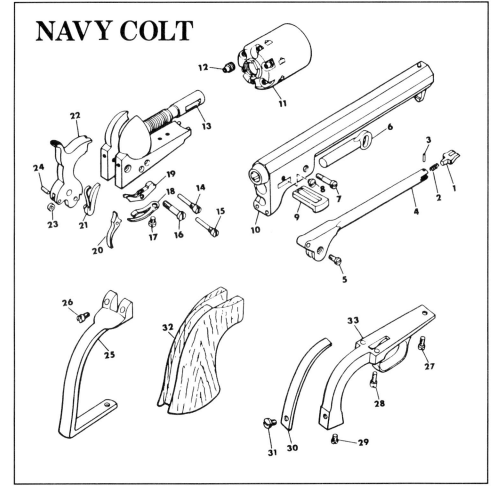

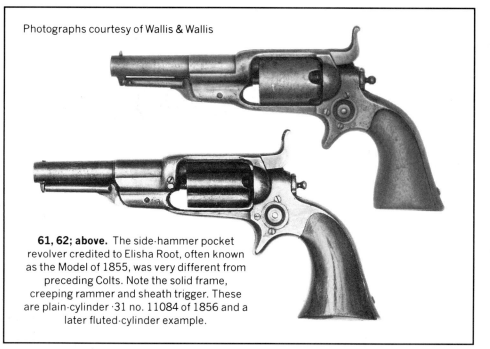

Photographs courtesy of Wallis & Wallis

61, 62; above. The side-hammer pocket revolver credited to Elisha Root, often known as the Model of 1855, was very different from preceding Colts. Note the solid frame, creeping rammer and sheath trigger. These are plain-cylinder ·31 no. 11084 of 1856 and a later fluted-cylinder example.

well made, the expiry of Colt's master patent in 1857 exposed them to the keen competition afforded by cheaper and cruder guns. Only about forty thousand were made in 1855–70. There were two major variations—five-shot ·28 and ·31—with barrels of 3½ or 4½in. Barrels were cylindrical, excepting for a few octagonal 3½-inch examples made in the late 1850s. Apart from small quantities made with fully fluted cylinders, side hammer Colts display either a log cabin and Indian motif or (more rarely) the standard rolled stagecoach-robbery pattern.

THE TRUE DERINGER, 1848–70

The legions of small-calibre revolvers produced after the introduction of the first pepperboxes and Colts did nothing to reduce the popularity of easily concealable single-barrel pistols, which continued in vogue into the late nineteenth century.

The archetypal design was the cap-lock made in Philadelphia by the gunsmith Henry Deringer, whose reputation had been made by the manufacture of US Model 1817 flintlock rifles in the 1820s. Deringer began making cap-lock pistols in the 1830s, ranging from a large duelling pistol to a tiny gun that could easily be hidden in a hand.

There has been much debate about the origin of 'derringer' as a generic term. It is popularly supposed to have arisen from the assassination of Abraham Lincoln by John Wilkes Booth, in Ford's Theater, Washington, on 14 April 1865; however, Joseph Rosa, in his fascinating *Guns of the Wild West* (1985), has drawn attention

to the killing of General William Richardson by Charles Cora in lawless San Francisco in November 1855. Even the local newspapers described the murder weapon as a 'derringer' and the term has since become applied to any readily concealable pistol.

Guns of this type were very popular on both sides of the law. William F. 'Buffalo Bill' Cody purchased a pair of genuine Deringers in 1865, while a double-barrel Remington was used by embittered Leon Czolgosc to fatally wound President William McKinley in September 1901.

The classic Deringer was a ·41-calibre back action cap-lock with a rifled seven-groove

barrel of about 1·9in and an overall length of merely 4½in. True Deringers were invariably marked DERINGER PHILADEL. on the lock; they had distinctive side plates and pineapple pattern escutcheons retaining the transverse barrel key. The barrels were finished in a false damascus twist achieved by streaking, locks were case-hardened, and most of the metal work was blued—excepting trigger guards and the escutcheons, which were sometimes silver plated.

Deringer pistols were produced in appreciable numbers in the 1840s, but achieved no real notoriety until the later part of the California Gold Rush. Thereafter, many other gunmakers attempted to cash in on the pistols' success among the gaming tables and bordellos of the West Coast. Among the copyists were Slotter & Company and A.J.Plate of San Francisco, together with J. Deringer of Philadelphia—a tailor who allowed his name to be used by gunsmiths seeking spurious legitimacy.

Henry Deringer died in 1867, though his executors immediately took action against infringers of his name. His work had inspired legion of copyists, content merely to copy his miniature cap-lock. Others were more ambitious. Jesse Butterfield of Philadelphia produced a near-facsimile of the Deringer design, though his ·38-calibre cap locks were usually fitted with a patented priming tube mounted vertically ahead of the hammer. This fed a pellet over the nipple each time the hammer was cocked.

Apart from copies of the Deringer, cap-lock pistols of this general pattern are scarce. However, the smallest Lindsay Young America single-barrel cap-lock pocket pistol could be

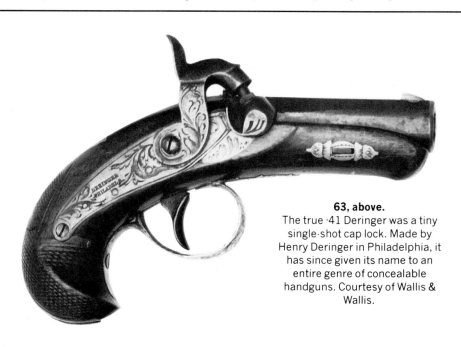

63, above.
The true ·41 Deringer was a tiny single-shot cap lock. Made by Henry Deringer in Philadelphia, it has since given its name to an entire genre of concealable handguns. Courtesy of Wallis & Wallis.

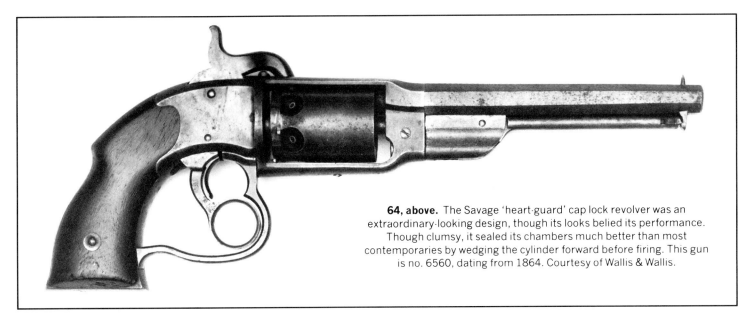

64, above. The Savage 'heart-guard' cap lock revolver was an extraordinary-looking design, though its looks belied its performance. Though clumsy, it sealed its chambers much better than most contemporaries by wedging the cylinder forward before firing. This gun is no. 6560, dating from 1864. Courtesy of Wallis & Wallis.

classified in the derringer class. It contained two charges, one on top of the other, which were to be fired by two hammers. In practice, unless the charges were carefully separated by greased wads, the first hammer fired both balls at once.

NORTH, SAVAGE AND ALSOP GUNS, 1856–65

The relationship between this collection of revolvers has been the subject of debate, largely because the frames of the so-called 'heart guard' Savage and the smaller Alsops resemble each other closely.

The revolver patented by Henry North on 17 June 1856 ('revolving firearm', 15,144) was made by Edward Savage and then Savage & North of Middletown, Connecticut, until an improved version was patented jointly on 18 January 1859 ('revolving firearm', 22,566) and 15 May 1860 (28,331). Both patents were assigned to the Savage Revolving Fire-Arms Company.

The first guns had an extraordinary ring-tipped actuating lever, which protruded from the frame below the trigger; a spur-like protector ahead of the operating lever gave the appearance of the number 8, a term by which these cap locks are now generally classified.

The clumsy ·36-calibre six-shot revolvers were about 14in long, had seven-inch barrels and weighed 56oz. They offered a pivoting rammer beneath the octagonal barrel and had a spur or saw-handle grip. A long-nose hammer, hung centrally, lay above the frame. One brass-frame gun was tested by the US Army Ordnance Department in June 1856, a hundred more being delivered in the late Spring of 1857. The second pattern had an iron frame a creeping rammer patented by Henry North in April 1858.

The third variation reverted to a brass frame, though its sides had been flattened and the spur on the back strap was rounded. The US Navy ordered three hundred revolvers in July 1858, and a 500-gun army order soon followed. Deliveries were painfully slow, as the navy contract was not fulfilled until the end of 1860. A very few fourth-model guns, with a flat iron frame and an improved 1860-patent cylinder adjustor, were made in 1860–1. Production of all the 'figure 8' Savages scarcely exceeded two thousand.

Despite their poor handling characteristics, the North & Savage guns had some advanced features. Pulling back on the operating lever revolved the cylinder and then cocked the hammer; releasing it allowed a wedge to press the cylinder forward until the chamfered chamber mouth rode over the end of the barrel—sealing the mechanism much more effectually against the escape of gas than in rival designs.

The improved 1859-patent revolver, made by the Savage Revolving Fire-Arms Company, shared the general lines of its predecessor. However, the butt-spur was greatly reduced and the trigger guard extended back to the base of the butt. The first sales of the new ·36-calibre 'navy'-type gun were made to the Federal government in August 1861, seven hundred for the navy and two hundred for the army. However, these had been acquired through retailers and Savage had had little success negotiating with the Ordnance Department. A 5,000-gun contract was eventually signed on 10 September 1861, but cancelled early in October owing to wrangling over payment of monies to entrepreneur Thomas Dyer, whom Savage had hired. However, another large contract was negotiated in mid-October, the last of five thousand guns being delivered by March 1862.

Offers to supply greater quantities had been declined by the Chief of Ordnance, Brigadier General James 'Old Fogey' Ripley, who regarded the Savage as 'not...a desirable arm for the service, and not such a one as I would supply, unless in case of emergency'. But another 5,000-gun order was forthcoming in November 1861.

The Federal government purchased 11,284 Savage Navy Revolvers from 1 January 1861 until 30 June 1866, apparently on behalf of the US Navy. It is suspected that few were acquired after 1863, as Savage began to make revolvers under contract to the Starr Arms Company.

The six-shot ·36 'heart guard' Savage & North system revolvers were no less clumsy than their predecessors, but shared the effectual gas-seal system and indexed their cylinders much more precisely than their contemporaries. Apart from the trigger guard, they had pivoting rammers instead of the original creeping pattern. They were sturdy and durable, though inexperienced firers often damaged the lock by attempting to pull the ring-lever and the trigger together; the lever had to be pulled to rotate the cylinder and cock the hammer before the trigger was pressed. A few guns were made for shoulder stocks patented by Charles Alsop in May 1860 (28,433) or Edward Savage in April 1861 (32,003).

The Alsop revolvers appeared to be sheath trigger diminutions of the perfected Savage & North pattern. They were made in a separate factory in Middletown, Connecticut, in 1862–3 even though members of the Alsop family held a stake in the Savage Repeating Fire Arms Company. Protected by patents granted to Charles R. Alsop between 17 July 1860 (29,213) and 21 January 1862 (34,226), the revolvers embodied a rotary cam that pressed the entire cylinder forward over the breech as the elongated hammer spur was thumbed back. This gas-seal was supplemented by movable chambers patented by Charles H. Alsop on 26 November 1861 (33,770).

Production was small: only about five hundred ·36-calibre six-shot guns, with round or fluted cylinders and barrels of 3½–6½in, were made before work concentrated on a six-shot ·31 with a four-inch barrel and a plain cylinder. However, less than 300 small-calibre guns were made before work ceased in 1863. They were simply too expensive to compete with the legions of conventional small-calibre cap locks.

CAP-LOCK REMINGTONS, 1856–65

Colts accounted for 39 per cent of the total government acquisitions in 1861–6, making them only marginally more numerous than the Remingtons (35 per cent).

Remington's earliest foray into the revolver market had been a five-shot ·31 pocket gun patented by Fordyce Beals, who had previously designed the 'Walking Beam' revolver for Whitney, on 24 June 1856 (15,167) and 26 May 1857 (17,359). Only about five thousand guns were made from 1857 until production ceased in favour of the Rider pattern described below, shortly before the Civil War began.

The first pattern had an external arm and pawl actuating the cylinder, the second version (1858–60) had a disc and pawl, and the otherwise similar third type had a lever rammer patented on 14 September 1858 (US 21,478). The third-model Remington-Beals revolvers also had four-inch barrels; earlier examples measured 3in. Weight ranged from twelve to 14oz.

The perfected ·31 pocket revolver was the subject of patents granted to Joseph Rider on 17 August 1858 (21,215) and 3 May 1859 (23,861). An odd little five-shot gun with a three-inch barrel, weighing about 10oz, it had a solid frame and an instantly recognisable 'mushroom' cylinder. The front sight was a small brass pin, the rear sight being a simple groove in the top of the frame. Offered in blue or nickel-plate finishes, with grips of gutta percha, ivory or pearl, the Rider revolvers were surprisingly popular: about 100,000 were made, the last examples remaining in the Remington warehouse into the 1880s.

The ·44-calibre six-shot single action Remington Beals Army Revolver was made by E. Remington & Sons of Ilion, New York, to Fordyce Beals' US Patent 21,478 of September 1858. It was a sturdy solid-frame gun with Beals' Patent Rammer, a brass trigger guard, an octagonal barrel and a small web beneath the rammer shaft. Unlike later Remington army revolvers, the attaching threads were invisible where the barrel abutted the cylinder face. The guns were 13·8 inches overall, had an eight-inch five-groove barrel, and weighed 46oz unladen. They were generally blued, and had case-hardened hammers. About two thousand were made (alongside 15,000 smaller ·36-calibre navy revolvers) before the basic design was superseded by the Model 1861 Army Revolver.

The comparative lack of success of the Beals pattern army revolver prompted Remington to substitute a rammer patented by William Elliot

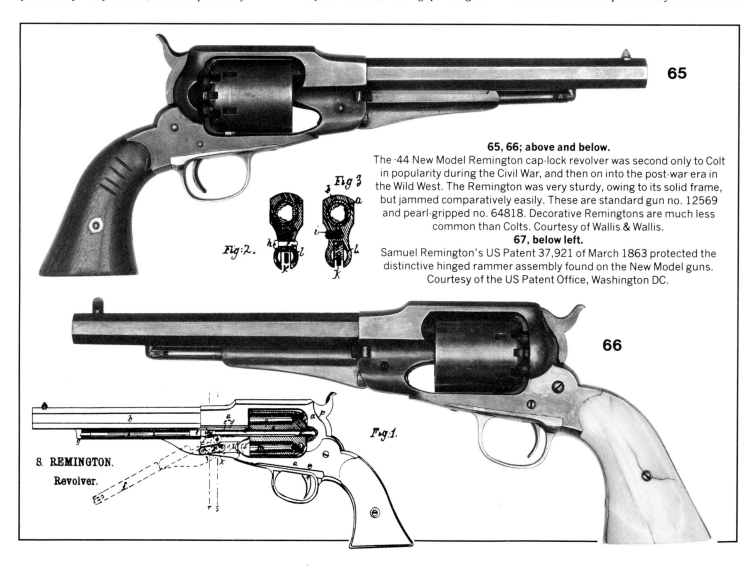

65

65, 66; above and below.
The ·44 New Model Remington cap-lock revolver was second only to Colt in popularity during the Civil War, and then on into the post-war era in the Wild West. The Remington was very sturdy, owing to its solid frame, but jammed comparatively easily. These are standard gun no. 12569 and pearl-gripped no. 64818. Decorative Remingtons are much less common than Colts. Courtesy of Wallis & Wallis.
67, below left.
Samuel Remington's US Patent 37,921 of March 1863 protected the distinctive hinged rammer assembly found on the New Model guns. Courtesy of the US Patent Office, Washington DC.

66

S. REMINGTON.
Revolver.

in December 1861 (US Patent 33,932). This supposedly permitted the cylinder axis-pin to be withdrawn without releasing the rammer catch, but the cylinder catch sometimes slid forward on firing and jammed the mechanism. Excepting the rammer, the 1861-model was practically indistinguishable from the earlier Beals type. Virtually all nineteen thousand ·44 M1861 weapons were purchased by the Federal Government, official-issue weapons displaying inspectors' initials in a cartouche on the outer surface of the left grip. About 7,500 smaller ·36-calibre navy revolvers were made in the same number sequence.

The ineffectual Elliott Rammer was replaced by an improved pattern patented by Samuel Remington in March 1863. New Model Army Revolvers had safety notches between the nipples and attachment threads visible where the barrel abutted the cylinder face. The army revolvers had brass trigger guards, were about 13·8in overall, had five-groove eight-inch barrels, and weighed 46oz. The legend NEW MODEL appeared on the octagonal barrel, while the walnut grips usually bore cartouched army inspectors' marks—e.g. 'BH', 'GP', 'OWA'.

From 1863 until 30 June 1866, Remington supplied the Federal government with 125,314 ·44-calibre guns, constituting almost the entire production run. There were also about 23,000 ·36-calibre, but otherwise similar 42oz Navy Revolvers. Generally comparable to the 1860 army Colt, the ·44 Remington cost only $13.02 against $17.70 for its rival.

Several small-calibre cap lock Remingtons were made in this period. They included about eight thousand ·36 six-shot New Model Belt Revolvers, with 6½-inch octagonal barrels and—to order—special fully fluted cylinders. The production runs favoured the double action guns, 4,500–5,000 of which were made. Finish could be blue or nickel, or, occasionally, a combination of a nickel-plated frame with a blued barrel.

The ·36 five-shot New Model Police Revolver was essentially similar to the Belt patterns, but had barrels of 3½–6½in and weighed 21–24oz instead of 36oz. About eighteen thousand were made in 1863–70, the last new guns being sold in the 1880s. The essentially similar ·31 five-shot New Model Pocket Revolver, 27,500 of which were made, was distinguished by its sheath trigger—though otherwise built on classically Remington lines. Offered in a variety of finishes with octagonal barrels of 3½- or 4½in, it weighed 14–16oz.

CARTRIDGE DERINGERS, 1857–66

Patented in 1857, the break-open Marston derringer had a monoblock containing three

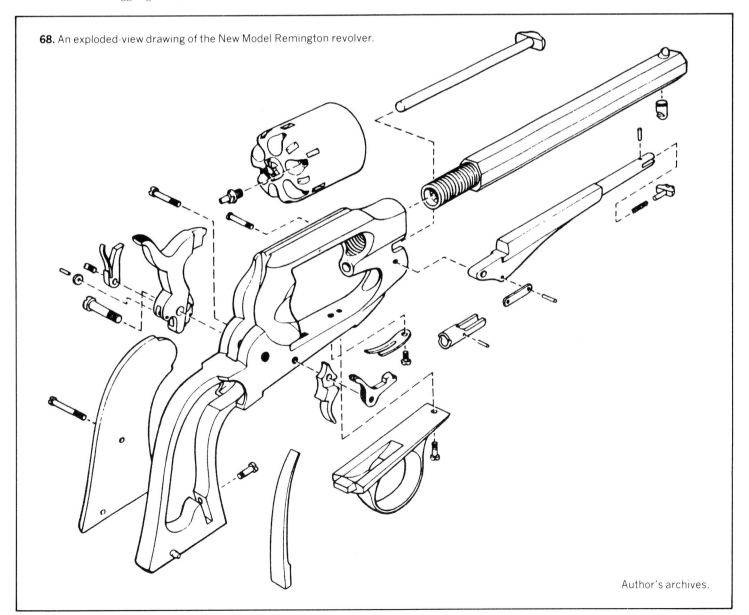

68. An exploded-view drawing of the New Model Remington revolver.

Author's archives.

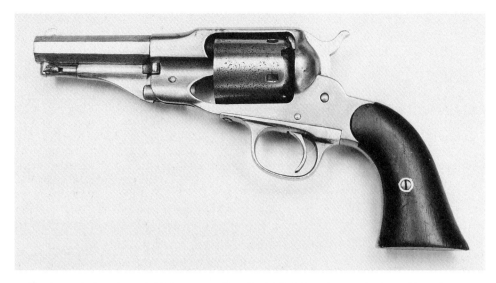

69, above. A short-barrel ·36 Remington New Model Belt Revolver, well polished but showing signs of hard use. Author's collection.
70, below. An ornate ·38 rimfire Sharps four-barrel cluster derringer. Courtesy of Ian Hogg.

rifled barrels. Chambering ·22 and ·32 rimfire cartridges, the mechanism had a travelling striker that fired the barrels sequentially from the bottom upward.

Christian Sharps made thousands of his distinctive four-barrel derringers between 1859 and 1874, when they were licensed to Tipping & Lawden in Britain and North American production ceased. The sheath-trigger Sharps guns were offered in ·22, ·30 and ·32 rimfire, their barrels measuring 2¼–3½in. They were 'cluster derringers', the barrels being arranged as two rows of two in a monoblock. Their barrel-group slid forward to give access to the breech after a catch had been released, while a rotating striker-plate—generally mounted on the hammer, but in the frame of some of those made by Sharps & Hankins—ensured that the

chambers are fired correctly. Frames were either blued iron or brass, usually nickel or silver plated; grips were walnut or gutta-percha, though ivory and mother-of-pearl examples will also be encountered from time to time.

The cluster derringer group also contained some ·22 rimfire five-shot sheath-trigger guns produced by the Continental Arms Company, which had a rounded barrel block resembling a small pepperbox.

Guns produced contemporaneously by the Bacon Arms Company, trading in Norwich, Connecticut, had a frame extending forward to the front of the elongated cylinder. The cylinder axis pin, which ran through an arbor on the frame-tip, doubled as an ejector rod when the cylinder had been revoved. Wheeler derringers, made by the American Arms Company in

1865–6, featured a two-barrel monoblock that rotated through 90° to give access to the breech. The guns were made in variety of calibres, including ·22, ·32, ·38 and ·45. Some had identically-chambered barrels; others had two different ones.

STARRS AND WHITNEYS, 1858-65

The idiosyncratic Starr revolvers accounted for only thirteen per cent of official purchases during the Civil War. Based on patents granted to Ebenezer Starr on 15 January 1856 ('revolving firearms', 14,118), the original ·36 revolver elicited impressive testimonials from government trials. The Starr Arms Company of Binghamton and later Yonkers, New York, made full use of opinions voiced by officers such as Lieutenant Colonel Alexander, of the Cavalry Bureau, who regarded the double action ·44 revolver as 'the best for Army use'; and Brigadier General Davies, who regarded the Starr's 'mechanical combination of parts…superior…to any revolver made'.

The revolver was described as a 'self-cocker' in promotional literature; though now generally labelled 'double action', it could be fired merely by thumb-cocking the hammer and then pressing the trigger, as this did not turn the cylinder. A 'cocking lever' (the front trigger) had to be pressed before the cylinder could be rotated manually.

If the sliding stop on the back of the cocking lever was upward, the gun could be fired simply by pulling through on the lever. At the end of the stroke, the cocking lever struck the sear-release set into the rear of the trigger guard and tripped the hammer. With the cocking-lever stop down, the hammer remained cocked until the firer released the cocking lever and consciously pressed the sear release. Though achieved at the expense of complexity, this 'hesitation cocking' action released the hammer with far less effort than simply pulling through on the cocking lever.

Federal purchases included a thousand six inch barrelled ·36-calibre guns for the US Navy in 1858 and about 1,250 for the army, the first authenticated issue being to the 7th New York Regiment of National Guard in April 1861. A 51oz ·44-calibre version with a six-inch barrel appeared at the end of 1861, more than 23,000 being purchased in 1862–3.

A simpler single-action eight-inch barrelled 47oz ·44 pattern was introduced early in 1864 to accelerate production. Much of the work is said to have been subcontracted to Savage (q.v.) and in excess of thirty thousand guns were made before the Civil War ended. The mechanism incorporated elements of the patents granted to Starr in December 1860

(30,843) and Thomas Gibson in April 1864 (42,435). A few guns incorporated a bar-type safety, mounted on the side of the hammer, which had been patentcd by Starr on 20 December 1864 (45,532).

The self-cocking Starrs were superior to the Colts and, therefore, widely liked. Their cylinders and axis pins were forged integrally, reducing the chance of cap fragments or propellant fouling jamming the cylinder, and adequate clearance was provided arund the nipple. They could be reloaded by unscrewing the prominent transverse bolt at the top rear of the frame, which allowed the barrel to move forward to release the cylinder. However, their manufacturer had neither the capacity nor the wide experience of Colt's Patent Fire Arms Manufacturing Company. By comparison, Starr revolvers were poorly made. Total government procurement in the period between New Year's Day 1861 and 30 June 1866 amounted to 47,952—comprising about 1,250 ·36 revolvers at $20 apiece, 23,250 ·44 double-action guns at $25, and then in excess of 20,000 ·44 single-action guns at $12 apiece. Thousands more had sold privately, or to state militia.

The first Whitney revolvers were inspired by the success of the Walker-pattern Colt, which had been made in the Whitneyville Armory. Whitney wished to make revolvers of his own, but was so hamstrung by the extension of Colt's 1836-vintage master patent that his earliest designs were inferior. They included a crude brass-framed gun with a bird's head butt and a manually-rotated cylinder with a distinctive guard. This was followed by a conventional gun, with a manually rotated cylinder locked by a trigger-like lever ahead of the square-back trigger guard. Production was meagre, surviving guns offering a selection of brass or iron frames, with straps and trigger guards of iron or brass.

Eli Whitney then patented a ring-trigger revolver on 1 August 1854 (11,447) in which the frame was made 'all in one piece, with a top bar, not only to strengthen the frame but also to serve as a foil with a comb of the hammer to strike against to prevent battering the cones [nipples]. Ironically, the inventor did not include the solid frame among the claims to novelty, losing the chance to make a fortune in royalties.

Only a handful of 1854-patent guns was made, production concentrating on an odd ring trigger revolver designed by Fordyce Beals and patented on 26 September 1856 (11,715). Known as the 'Walking Beam Whitney', this quirky design relied on an oscillating bar to rotate the cylinder. The mechanism was first cocked manually. Pushing the trigger lever forward rotated the cylinder; pulling it back again locked the cylinder in place and then released the hammer. Production of these distinctive solid-frame cap locks, with ring triggers and the oscillator housing on the left side of the frame (covering the lower part of the cylinder aperture) was never large. The ·28 version is particularly rare, most surviving guns being ·31-calibre with five-chamber cylinders.

The perfected ·36 Belt (or Navy) Revolver, which appeared after copies of the Colt Navy had been made, numbered among the more popular revolvers to serve during the Civil War. Safety notches appeared between each pair of nipples shortly after production began, while a modified maritime scene was soon rolled into the cylinder periphery. A rammer-locking wedge was substituted for a spring-loaded ball midway through the production run, the trigger guard was enlarged, and five-groove rifling replaced the original seven groove type.

Made in the Whitney factory in New Haven, Connecticut, the standard single action six shot Whitney 'Navy' revolvers measured 13·1in overall, had a 7·6-inch octagonal barrel and weighed about 41oz.

Federal purchases during the Civil War amounted to 11,214 for the army, 5,726 for the navy and 792 for the New Jersey State Militia, though others were purchased privately from a total production approaching 33,000. Ordnance records reveal that the Whitneys cost the Federal treasury $136,690.39.

Though Whitneys were still being sold after the end of the Civil War, their maker seems to have lost interest in them very quickly: cartridge conversions are very rare.

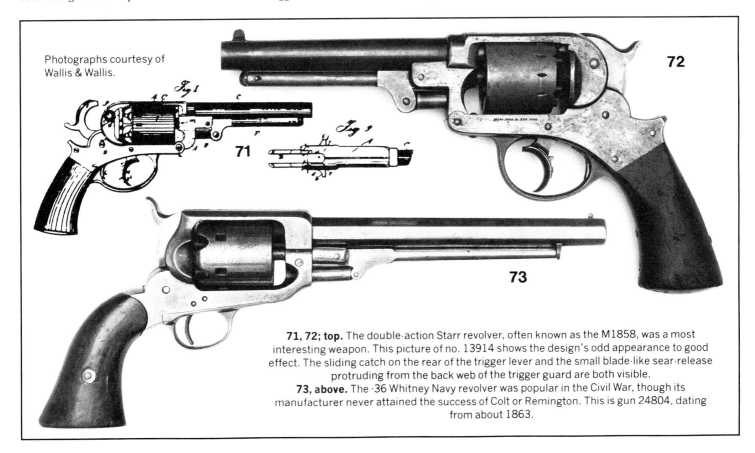

Photographs courtesy of Wallis & Wallis.

71, 72; top. The double-action Starr revolver, often known as the M1858, was a most interesting weapon. This picture of no. 13914 shows the design's odd appearance to good effect. The sliding catch on the rear of the trigger lever and the small blade-like sear-release protruding from the back web of the trigger guard are both visible.

73, above. The ·36 Whitney Navy revolver was popular in the Civil War, though its manufacturer never attained the success of Colt or Remington. This is gun 24804, dating from about 1863.

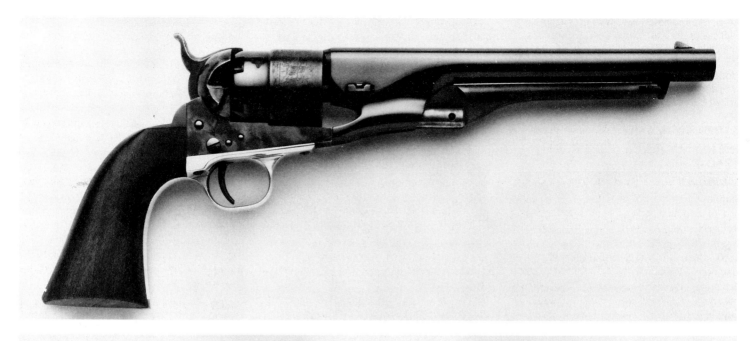

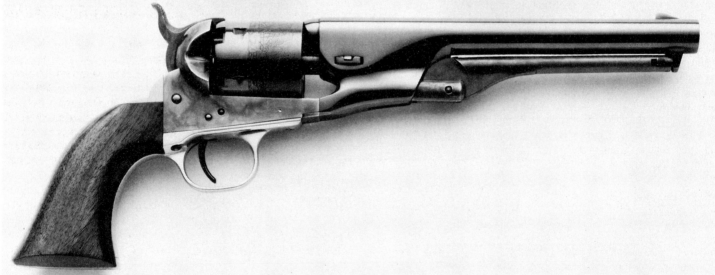

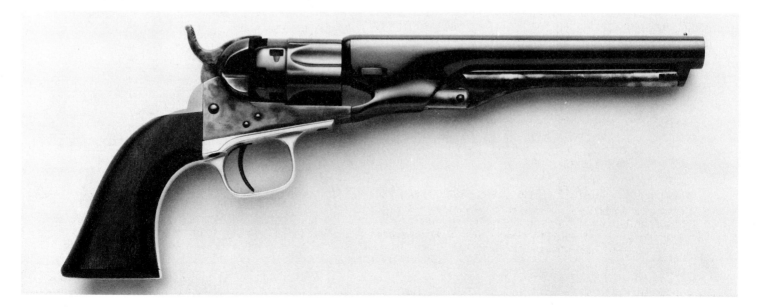

74–6, left and below left. Three Uberti-made replicas of the New Model Colt revolvers, specially commissioned by Colt Industries in the 1980s. These are the ·44 1860 Army Model (74), the ·36 New Model or M1861 Navy (75) and the ·36 Pocket Police (76). Courtesy of Colt Industries.

THE NEW MODEL CAP-LOCK COLTS, 1860–73

Samuel Colt died in 1862, but not before the first of a new series of streamlined cap-lock revolvers had appeared. The most important was the ·44 New Model Army Revolver, or Model 1860, which was a replacement for the ageing Dragoons. The culmination of experiments with lightened guns, the New Model Army was really little more than a ·36 Navy pattern with a longer grip, the front half of the cylinder enlarged to take the larger balls, a change to the frame to accommodate the new cylinder, and—most noticeably—an eight-inch barrel with a supremely elegant rammer shroud. Detachable shoulder stocks were introduced shortly after production began, whereupon a fourth screw was added through the frame and small (but instantly identifiable) cuts in the lower face of the recoil shields.

The ·44 army revolvers were made in several identifiable variants, barrels measuring 7½in and fully fluted cylinders being particularly sought; 55 special guns were made in c.1860 with short Navy-style grips, 7½-inch barrels, silvered grip straps and no capping recess on the recoil shield on the right side of the frame behind the cylinder. Other non-standard guns were made during the during the Civil War when army-style components periodically ran short. Back straps were iron; trigger guards were

normally brass. Ironically, the cylinder surface bore the same maritime scne as the ·36 Navy had done.

A Board of Officers appointed to consider the merits of the new revolver was impressed. Its president, Acting Inspector-General Joseph Johnston, reported that no doubt was left that:

"…the decided advantages which Mr. Colt has gained for his pistol by the introduction of his recent improvements…, with the 8 inch barrel, will make the most superior Cavalry arm we have ever had…"

The ·36 New Model Navy Revolver, now known as the Model of 1861, combined the small calibre and 7–inch barrel of the established navy pattern with the sinuous barrel shroud and creeping rammer of the ·44 1860-type army gun. Production amounted to 38,843 in 1861–74, about a hundred with fluted cylinders and a similar number with a shoulder stock.

The five-shot ·36 New Model Police and ·36 'New Model Pocket Pistol of Navy Caliber' appeared in 1861, though now generally known as the Models of 1862. Approximately 47,000 were made in a single number-series, Police guns being in a small majority. The guns are identical, though the Police variant had a fluted cylinder and a creeping rammer instead of the navy-style plain-surface cylinder and hinged rammer. Barrels measured 4½–6½in, though fifty 3½-inch rammerless barrelled Police revolvers were made in 1862 with a separate brass rammer to be pushed through the aperture in the barrel shroud.

Few Police or Pocket Navy revolvers were engraved, though a few highly decorative guns were made with the so-called Tiffany Grips. Cast from white metal to the designs of John Ward, and then often plated, most of these dated from the 1860s. The most popular patterns were eagle-and-justice, a Civil War battle scene, or US and Mexican eagles.

The Colts were marginally the most popular revolvers purchased by the Federal government during the Civil War, 129,730 examples of the ·44 "1860" or Army Model being acquired together with 17,010 ·36-calibre Navy Models. The army pattern also provided the basis for some of the most spectacular decorative Colts.

These included a matched pair presented in 1863 by Abraham Lincoln to kings Carl XV Gustav of Sweden and Frederik VII of Denmark, politically motivated acts intended to prevent sturdy Scandinavian spars gracing Confederate blockade runners. The Danish guns, 31904 and 31905, and the Swedish presentation pieces (31906 and 31907) were inlaid in gold by Gustave Young. Their American walnut grips were finely chequered, carved and inlaid with silver plates. Butt caps on the Swedish revolvers depicted the Great Seal of the USA.

MOORE, NATIONAL AND COLT DERRINGERS, 1861–1912

Moore's Patent Fire Arms Company and its successor, the National Arms Company of Brooklyn, made a derringer of its own design alongside the Williamson. Designed by Daniel Moore and patented on 19 February 1861 ('firearms', 31,473), the ·41 rimfire National Model No.1 'Knuckle Duster' single-shot pistol, brass framed but often nickel plated, had a sheath trigger and a barrel that pivoted laterally to gain access to the breech. It was a clumsy design, but very durable.

Several manufacturing patterns are known, the earliest being made before the patent had been granted. Later guns display a refined hammer and an improved breech catch. Some guns were made with blade-pattern extractors, others had none. The Model No.2 was very

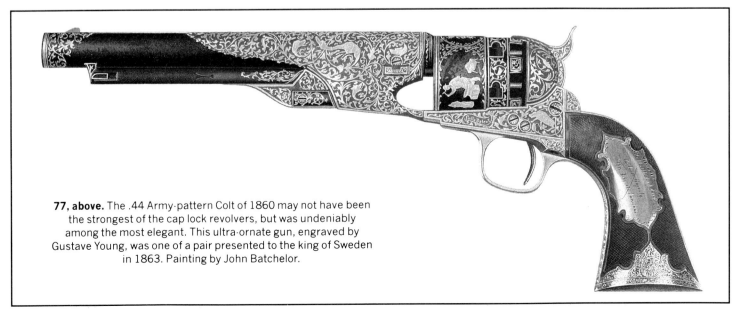

77, above. The .44 Army-pattern Colt of 1860 may not have been the strongest of the cap lock revolvers, but was undeniably among the most elegant. This ultra-ornate gun, engraved by Gustave Young, was one of a pair presented to the king of Sweden in 1863. Painting by John Batchelor.

similar, but the distance between the trigger and the grip was increased—it had been very cramped—and walnut or rosewood grips were fitted.

National was purchased by Colt in 1870, production of the No.1 and No.2 derringers continuing in the Hartford factory with no modifications other than changes in the manufacturer's marks. In addition to quantities of guns with National markings, and others assembled from Brooklyn-made parts before work in Hartford had commenced, Colt is estimated to have made about 6,500 No.1 and 9,000 No.2 derringers, sold in matched pairs with hand-cut scroll engraving.

The ·41 rimfire Colt No.3 derringer, designed by F. Alexander Thuer, was another single shot design. The barrel pivoted sideways to give access to the breech and had an automatic extractor. The No.3 Colts were made with walnut or rosewood bird's head grips, though ivory and mother-of-pearl could be obtained on order. A few were offered in ·41 centre-fire, while others differed in barrel length: 2½in was standard. There are several minor variants, the earliest guns having a pronounced bolster or reinforcement on the frame beneath the barrel; later guns had straight frames. Changes were made to the radius of the grip, and the hammer spur was raised at about the same time.

About 45,000 No.3 Colts had been made by 1912, when they were discontinued. Particularly desirable are later guns bearing a minuscule rampant colt motif and the letter 'C' for 'Colt'.

The Thuer derringer was an interesting design. Easily made, cheap and very popular, it was copied by many enterprising gunmakers. Among the legion of near-replicas were the O.K. and Victor pistols made by John Marlin of New Haven, Connecticut, and the differing XL patterns made by Marlin or Hopkins & Allen. Similar guns were available from Hopkins & Allen and their successors, Forehand & Wadsworth, as late as 1889.

LESSER MILITARY CAP-LOCK REVOLVERS OF THE CIVIL WAR

Only about 2,500 ·44-calibre revolvers were made by C.B. Hoard's Armory of Watertown, New York, to the designs of Austin Freeman of Binghampton, New York State. Freeman received US Patent 37,091 in December 1862 to protect a unique cylinder axis pin/locking catch assembly. This could be pulled forward to disengage the frame and allow the entire cylinder to be taken out of the left side of the gun. The earliest Freemans had a removable side plate; later examples had sturdier solid frames with fixed pivot-screws for the hammer and trigger.

COLT'S PATENT FIRE ARMS MANUF'G COMPANY,
HARTFORD, CONN.

COLT'S NEW PATENT DERINGER PISTOLS.

EXACT SIZE.

THIS BREECH-LOADING DERINGER can be Loaded and Fired more rapidly, and with less inconvenience, than any other kind.

Weight 6¼ ounces.

Cartridge, .41 cal.

Silver Plated Frames, Blued Barrels, $8.00 per pair.
Silver Plated Frames, Silver Plated Barrels, $9.00 per pair.

DIRECTIONS FOR USE.

TO LOAD.--Set the Hammer at half-cock, and swing the Barrel to one side; this opens the Breech. After firing, the empty shell may be expelled entirely by opening the Breech as far as possible.
The exploded shell need not be touched by the fingers.

THE NATIONAL DERINGER PISTOL,
(Formerly Manufactured by the NATIONAL ARMS CO., of Brooklyn, N.Y.)
Silver Plated Frames, Blued Barrels, $9.50 per pair.   Silver Plated Frames, Silver Plated Barrels, $10.50 per pair.

THESE PISTOLS ARE MADE WITH METAL OR WOOD STOCKS.

EXACT SIZE.

DIRECTIONS FOR USE.

TO LOAD.--Set the Hammer at halfcock; grasp the stock in the right hand, and drawing back the Steel Button with the fore-finger, rotate the Barrel toward you with the left hand. Holding the Barrel thus turned aside, introduce the Cartridge and then rotate it to its original position.

After Firing, the empty shell may be ejected by rotating the Barrel as directed for loading.

Weight 10 oz.
Calibre 41-100 inches.

No. 1.

TERMS CASH.

Manufactured by COLT'S PATENT FIRE-ARMS MF'G CO., Hartford, Conn.

ALL COMMUNICATIONS MUST BE ADDRESSED TO

Colt's Patent Fire Arms Manuf'g Company,
HARTFORD, CONN., UNITED STATES OF AMERICA.

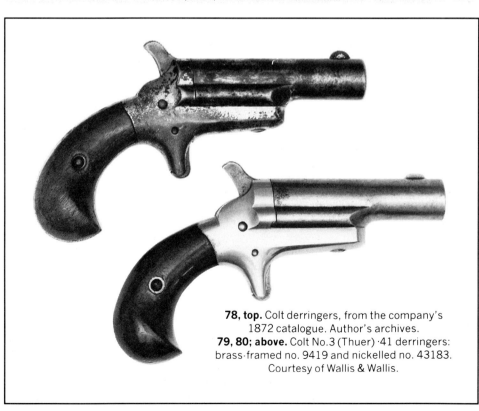

78, top. Colt derringers, from the company's 1872 catalogue. Author's archives.
79, 80; above. Colt No.3 (Thuer) ·41 derringers: brass-framed no. 9419 and nickelled no. 43183. Courtesy of Wallis & Wallis.

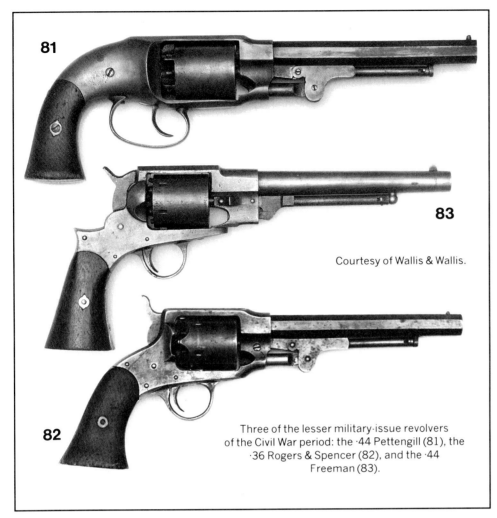

Courtesy of Wallis & Wallis.

Three of the lesser military-issue revolvers of the Civil War period: the ·44 Pettengill (81), the ·36 Rogers & Spencer (82), and the ·44 Freeman (83).

Hoard received a Federal government contract for five thousand revolvers on 8 May 1864, but none was ever accepted and the contract subsequently passed to Rogers & Spencer.

Six-shot ·44-calibre single action Freeman revolvers had a distinctive angular frame and a 'hump back' wooden grip. They were 12½in overall, weighed 45oz and had 7½-inch barrels with six-groove rifling.

Charles Pettengill of New Haven, Connecticut, received his first revolver patent in July 1856. As the trigger was pulled, a top-mounted cam rotated the cylinder through the 'combination lever' and put the mainspring under tension. When the cylinder had been indexed, the trigger-cam disengaged the sear from the hammer and the gun fired.

Made by Rogers & Spencer of Willowvale, New York State, the Pettengills also embodied a main spring and combination lever patented by Thomas Austin in October 1858 (21,730), and were finally simplified through a patent granted to Edward Raymond and Charles Robitaille in July 1858.

Rogers & Spencer obtained a Federal order for five thousand 'Army Caliber' (·44) Pettengills on 6 December 1861. These guns were simply enlargements of the ·34-calibre 'navy' model, but so many problems ensued that the US Army refused to accept any guns from the first batch. After modifications had been made to prevent fouling jamming the cylinder axis pin, and once the trigger patented by Henry Rogers in November 1862 had been substituted for the original cam type, the Ordnance Department finally accepted 2,001 modified revolvers. They were delivered between 20 October 1862 and 17 January 1863 at a cost of $40,287.10.

The odd-looking Pettengill could not be mistaken: its cylinder was an axial extension of the grip/frame unit, reminiscent of the earliest transitional designs that linked pepperboxes with classical revolvers exemplified by Colt, Remington, Starr or Whitney. It measured about 14in overall, had a 7½-inch six-groove barrel, and weighed 48oz unladen. The quirky double-action trigger generally exhibited a fearsome pull, discouraging accurate shooting.

The failure of the Pettengill, which had left Rogers & Spencer with thousands of unwamted components, was eased when the company obtained a 5,000-revolver contract that had once been given to backers of the Freeman (q.v.). The new Rogers & Spencer revolver, adapted to use as many old Pettengill parts as possible, was a conventional single-action six shot ·36-calibre cap lock measuring about 13½in overall and weighing 47oz unladen. Its most obvious feature was the shoulderless black walnut butt, which gave the gun a cramped appearance not unlike the later Colt Bisley.

Delivered into Federal stores in January–September 1865, at a cost to the US Treasury of $12 apiece, the Rogers & Spencer revolvers were never issued. They were eventually sold to Francis Bannerman & Sons, still in their original packing, for 25 cents each.

About 1,100 revolvers patented by Benjamin Joslyn of Worcester, in Massachusetts, were acquired by the Federal government during the Civil War at a cost of $24,793. The principal claim to novelty in the May 1858 specification was a 'spring clutch' and a cylinder-rotating mechanism embodying a ratchet.

The ·44-calibre five-shot single action Joslyn had a solid frame and an external side hammer which was cranked to allow the cylinder axis pin to enter from the rear of the frame. The guns displayed a conventional three-piece rammer, measured 14·4in overall, had five groove 8-inch octagonal barrels and weighed 49oz unladen.

Their first manufacturer—W.C. Freeman of Worcester, Massachusetts—contracted with the Chief of Ordnance on 28 August 1861 to provide five hundred guns at an extortionate $25 apiece (cf., Colt ·44 Army Model, $17.70). These Joslyns had plate-type butt caps retained by two screws.

Freeman claimed he subsequently refused to deliver an 'unserviceable design' to the US Army, but the first contract was terminated by the Federal government owing to non-delivery. Freeman's subsequent offer of revolvers was declined partly because the asking price was too high, but largely because 225 Joslyns had been purchased from Bruff, Brother & Seaver of New York in the winter of 1861.

Active service revealed faults serious enough to discourage additional purchases, and many unwanted guns were passed to the Ohio state militia at the end of 1861.

Joslyn subsequently made about 2,500 guns in Stonington, Connecticut. The first of these had iron trigger guards, instead of brass, and lacked butt caps; the Freeman-type cap reappeared after about 1,400 had been made. Approximately 875 Stonington Joslyns were delivered to the Federal government in 1861–2 and five hundred were acquired by the navy in 1862, displaying anchors on the butt strap or under the barrel.

An attempt was made to sell 675 guns to the 5th Ohio Military Cavalry in 1862, but the Ohioans rejected the entire consignment.

The archaic appearance of the Butterfield revolver belied its age. The principal novelty was a detachable tube of disc primers ahead of the trigger guard. Patented by Jesse Butterfield in 1855 (12,124), the mechanism positioned an individual primer above the nipple each time the prominent external hammer was cocked.

Butterfield believed that he had accepted a contract for 2,280 ·41-calibre Army Model guns, placed on behalf of the Ira Harris Guard of the 5th New York Cavalry, but the Ordnance authorities revoked the order on 24 June 1862. Probably no more than seven hundred guns had actually been completed by Krider & Co. of Philadelphia by the time work ceased. Many subsequently found their way into Confederate hands in circumstances that have never been explained.

The five-shot single action Butterfield Army Model Revolver measured 13·8in overall, had a seven-groove 7·1-inch barrel and weighed about 41oz.

LESSER COMMERCIAL CAP-LOCK REVOLVERS

The success of the cap lock Colts in the early 1850s persuaded many companies to market rivals. Among the most effectual were the Wesson & Leavitt revolvers, made by the Massachusetts Arms Company of Chicopee Falls. The guns were based on a manually rotated cylinder design patented by Daniel Leavitt on 29 April 1837 (US 182) and a mechanically-rotated version designed by Edwin Wesson. The latter had been patented posthumously in 1859, whereupon Wesson's heirs and assignees elected to produce the gun.

Original Wesson & Leavitt revolvers relied on a system of bevel gears to rotate the cylinder. The most impressive of the original guns had been the gigantic ·40-calibre six-shot army revolver, which, in its perfected version, weighed no less than 4lb 2oz and was nearly 15in long. The 7·1-inch barrel, hinged to the standing breech alongside the side hammer, was held to the substantial cylinder axis pin by a swivel-latch. Wesson & Leavitt revolvers could be reloaded simply by pressing the latch and raising the barrel and pulling the cylinder forward and off the axis pin. About 800 guns were made, together with a thousand ·31-calibre 3–7in barrelled six-shot Wesson & Leavitt Belt Models in 1850–1.

The guns were sturdy and effectual enough to attract the ire of Colt, fortified by an extension of his patent until 1857. After an historic trial, Colt won; the Massachusetts Arms Company, forced to pay substantial damages, was all but broken by the experience. Production

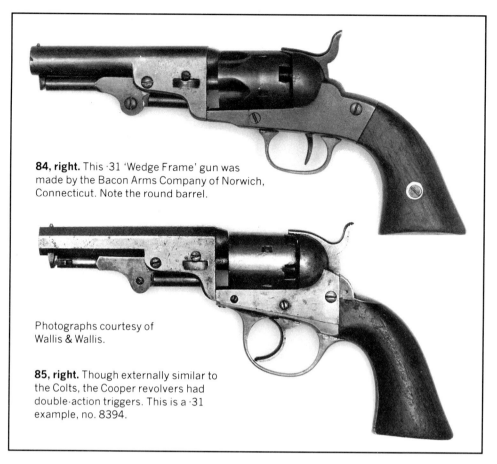

84, right. This ·31 'Wedge Frame' gun was made by the Bacon Arms Company of Norwich, Connecticut. Note the round barrel.

Photographs courtesy of Wallis & Wallis.

85, right. Though externally similar to the Colts, the Cooper revolvers had double-action triggers. This is a ·31 example, no. 8394.

of mechanically actuated Wesson & Leavitts ceased in favour of simpler ·31 Belt Model guns with manually-rotated cylinders locked by a latch in the trigger guard ahead of the trigger. Almost all were fitted with Maynard Tape Primers, while a few made after 1853 had a rammer patented by Joshua Stevens. Only about 1,000 ·31 guns were made in 1851–7. Two hundred were supplied to Abolitionists by the Massachusetts–Kansas Aid Committee in 1856, many eventually reaching John Brown.

The Massachusetts Arms Company also made ·28-calibre Pocket Model revolvers with 2½ or three-inch octagonal barrels, Maynard Tape Primers and a single frame-mounted nipple serving all six chambers. The first thousand guns had manually rotated cylinders, locked by a button inside the trigger guard. Attempts to circumvent Colt's patents came with a mechanism patented by Joshua Stevens in August 1853 (9,929). This required the hammer to be thumb-cocked, operating the Maynard primer; pressing the trigger unlocked, rotated and then secured the cylinder, finally tripping the hammer at the end of the stroke. It was replaced by an improved version patented on 2 January 1855 (12,189) in which the trigger rotated the cylinder before the hammer was cocked.

About fifty Belt and three hundred Pocket Model Massachusetts Arms Company revolvers

embodied the 1853 Stevens system, plus about 1,500 large-frame ·28 or ·31 Pocket Models with the later or 1855-type action. These had round or octagonal barrels measuring 3–3½in.

The expiry of Colt's master patent in 1857 allowed the Massachusetts Arms Company to revert to simple hammer-rotated cylinders. About two thousand guns were made in this guise, plus about 300 converted from the improved Stevens action.

Exasperated by its lack of success, the Massachusetts Arms Company negotiated a licence to make the British Beaumont-Adams revolver, but only about a thousand of the ·36-calibre six-shot Navy Model and less than 5,000 ·31 five-shot Pocket Models were made prior to the Civil War. They were protected by patents granted to Robert Adams on 3 May 1853 (9,694), Frederick Beaumont on 3 June 1856 (15,032) and James Kerr on 14 April 1857 (17,044). Amusingly, the ·36 revolvers showed the date of the Adams patent as 1858, while the ·31 version erroneously dated the patent protecting the Kerr rammer to 7 April. A few hundred American-made ·36 Beaumont-Adams revolvers were purchased by the Federals during the Civil War, survivors often bearing the marks of government inspectors William Thornton ('WAT') or Lucius Allen ('LCA').

The Springfield Arms Company made a series of revolvers resembling the Wesson & Leavitts, but incorporating a hammer-rotated cylinder patented by its superintendent James Warner on 15 July 1851 (8,229). The earliest guns were all-metal ·40-calibre six-shot 'Dragoon Pistols' with a distinctive nipple shield and a safety gate. Later guns had pivoting rammers and standard wooden grips.

Next came the so-called Jaquith Patent Belt Model, though acknowledgement of a patent granted to Elijah Jaquith on 12 July 1838 seems to have been nothing but a ploy to confuse Colt. The ·31-calibre six-shot revolvers had round barrels of 4–6in. They were superseded by the similar Warner Patent Belt Model, incorporating a modified Jaquith-pattern cylinder-rotating hand, with a separate locking bolt. A two-trigger pattern appeared in 1852. After the hammer had been cocked, pulling the front trigger indexed the cylinder and then pressed the rear lever to trip the hammer. Most guns were fitted with an early form of Warner's patent rammer.

A few ·36-calibre six-shot Warner Patent Navy Model revolvers were made in the mid-1850s, mostly with the twin-trigger mechanism. Apart from calibre, the principal differences from the ·31 belt patterns concerned the rammer, which was pivoted to the barrel lug instead of the cylinder arbor. Thus the barrel of the navy-type guns could be removed without detaching the rammer.

The ·28-calibre six-shot Warner Patent Pocket Models were made in bewildering variety, their cylinders being rotated by the hammer, a ring trigger or the perfected two-trigger system. Some were rifled, others were smooth-bores; there were several differing ratchet patterns and cylinder-arbor locks, even though production scarcely exceeded 1,500.

Warner made guns under his own name after the failure of the Springfield Arms Company in the early 1860s. The best-known revolver was a ·28 pocket model, originally made with a three inch octagonal barrel. A round barrel appeared after about a thousand guns had been made, and the calibre was changed to ·31. Made with round barrels of 2·6–4in, the ·31 gun was made until Warner's death in 1870. Total production approached ten thousand.

The sturdy solid-frame Allen & Wheelock revolvers ranged from tiny five-shot ·31 and ·34-calibre double-action bar-hammer guns, derived from pepperbox designs, to a perfected ·44 six-shot 'army' pattern.

The revolvers had a cranked side hammer to clear the axis pin, which entered the cylinder through the rear frame in the manner of the Root-model Colts; the unique rammer formed the major part of the trigger guard, but could pivot forward around the lower front of the frame. They also had a unusual method of

rotating the cylinder: a transverse bar in the recoil shield, revolved by the hammer, engaged a groove cut across the rear face of the cylinder.

Frames came in four sizes, a spring-loaded rammer latch replacing the original friction pattern during each production runs. Side hammer guns were made in ·28, ·31, ·34 (five shots apiece) and a six-shot ·36; barrels were octagonal, measuring 2½–8in. Total production amounted to perhaps four thousand, ·31 examples being marginally the most common.

Patented by Ethan Allen on 13 January 1857 (16,367) and 15 December 1857 (18,836), the gun had some excellent features, not least of which was the precision with which it indexed its cylinder. A third patent (21,400) added a projection on the cylinder to deflect propellant cases away from the cylinder-axis pin to reduce the effects of fouling.

Revised six-shot ·36 and ·44 centre-hammer guns with conventional cylinder axis pins were made in 1861, the Federal authorities taking 536 ·44 guns in 1861–2. The smaller 'navy' pattern had round barrels of 4–7½in, while the larger 'army' variant had a 7½-inch barrel. A sheath trigger ·36 single-action gun was also developed during the Civil War, allegedly for the police department of Providence, Rhode Island, though variations in barrel length (3–6in) suggest commercial acceptance.

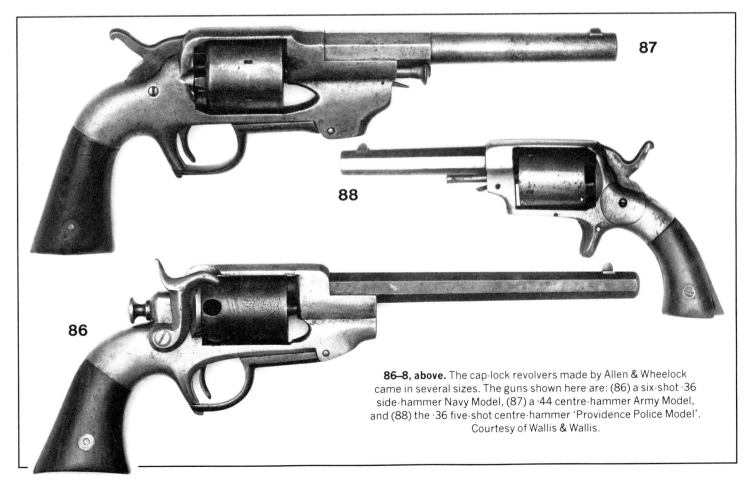

86–8, above. The cap-lock revolvers made by Allen & Wheelock came in several sizes. The guns shown here are: (86) a six-shot ·36 side-hammer Navy Model, (87) a ·44 centre-hammer Army Model, and (88) the ·36 five-shot centre-hammer 'Providence Police Model'. Courtesy of Wallis & Wallis.

A few centre hammer Allen & Wheelock revolvers were chambered for rimfire cartridges in the 1860s, though their bored-through cylinders infringed the Rollin White patent controlled by Smith & Wesson and action was soon taken to stop production.

The runaway success of the cap-lock revolver, evident from the earliest days of the Civil War, persuaded many companies to copy many of the best-known—particularly the Colts. The most notorious of these were ·31 pocket and ·36 navy-type revolvers made by the Manhattan Fire Arms Company of Newark, New Jersey, ostensibly under a patent granted to Joesph Gruler and August Rebety on 27 December 1859. This protected the inclusion of safety rebates on the cylinder between each pair of cylinder-stop notches.

Eventually, Colt managed to stop production in 1864, but not before five thousand ·31 and about 80,000 ·36 open-frame cap locks had been made. Some had been sold as products of the spurious London Pistol Company; virtually all ·31-calibre revolvers had detachable side plates, unlike the Colts, while all but ten thousand ·36 examples had five chamber cylinders.

The Bacon Manufacturing Company of Norwich, Connecticut, also made detachable side-plate guns. Thomas Bacon had worked for Manhattan during the period in which the latter's design was being perfected and had simply copied it, though his ·31 five-shot revolvers usually had a ball catch on the rammer-head in place of the Manhattan sliding wedge. Bacon revolvers often bore the marks of Fitch & Waldo; B.J. Hart & Brother; Tomes, Melvain & Company; Union Arms Company; or the Western Arms Company. Most of these were wholesalers, lacking facilities of their own.

Hopkins & Allen purchased Bacon's assets and liabilities in 1867, continuing to market the ·31-calibre side-plate cap locks (with a modified three-piece rammer) alongside a larger ·36 version christened 'Dictator'. Only about a thousand Dictators were made before the basic design was changed to handle ·38 rimfire ammunition. Total production, however, exceeded 6,000.

The Nepperhan Fire Arms Company of Yonkers, New York, also made ·31-calibre detachable side-plate revolvers in Civil War days. Nepperhan guns had brass trigger guards, dovetailed into the frame; the iron guards of rival Bacon and Manhattan revolvers were held by screws.

Colt-type guns were made by the Metropolitan Fire Arms Company of New York City, founded in February 1864 to capitalise on the disastrous fire that had destroyed much of Colt's Hartford factory and interrupted production. Periodic omissions of serial-number blocks make production difficult to assess, but it is believed that the company made six thousand copies of the six-shot ·36 Navy Model and New Model Navy Colt revolvers (the so-called M1851 and M1861) and about 2,750 based on the five-shot ·36 New Model Police ('M1862'). The principal difference concerns the rammer on New Model guns, which is pivoted rather than the creeping variety. Though many guns were unmarked, others bore their maker's name on top of the barrel, and at least one batch was made for H.E. Dimick & Co. of St Louis. Many also have the Battle of New Orleans (April 1862) rolled into the surface of the cylinder.

The Cooper revolver, though externally very similar to the contemporary ·36-calibre Colt pocket models, embodied a sophisticated double-action lock patented by James

Cooper of Pittsburgh, in Pennsylvania, on 4 September 1860 (29,684) and 22 September 1863 (40,021). The most obvious characteristic is the curved trigger lever set well forward in the guard.

After a hundred guns had been made in Pittsburgh, with a safety-notch system infringing that of Gruler & Reberty and the Manhattan Fire Arms Company, Cooper moved his factory to Philadelphia. Production of five-shot ·31 pocket and six-shot ·36 navy-calibre revolvers commenced immediately, barrels measuring 4–6in. Iron guards and straps were standard on the first few hundred, after which brass was substituted. The earliest ·36 guns had short smooth-surface cylinders, but these were soon replaced by a double-diameter pattern. The frame was cut away to accommodate the new cylinder and the barrel lug was changed to admit conical-ball ammunition. Finally, after more than 10,000 guns had been made, the ·31 pocket model was revised to accept a large diameter cylinder with a sixth chamber.

Perfected Cooper revolvers bore a selection of markings, including acknowledgements of patents granted to Stanhope Marston on 7 January 1851 (7,887) for the lock of a double action pepperbox; to Josiah Ells on 25 April 1854 (10,812), protecting the extension around the cylinder-axis pin); to Joseph Cooper on 4 September 1860 (29,864) and 22 September 1863 (40,021); and to Charles Harris on 1 September 1863 (39,771) to protect a modified cylinder-locking bolt. About 15,000 Coopers were made prior to the end of the Civil War.

The Bacon Arms Company, formed in 1864 by Thomas Bacon in Norwich, Connecticut, made about 2,000 sheath-trigger solid-frame ·31 cap lock revolvers. Occasionally encountered under the 'Union Arms Co.' name, the five-shot guns had a four-inch round barrel with a pivoting rammer and a Freeman-type cylinder latch. The latch was later replaced by a simple pin retained by a cross-screw.

A selection of Whitney-like guns was marked by W.W. Marston, the Phoenix Armory, the Union Arms Company or the Western Arms Company. Whitney probably supplied ready engraved cylinders and other parts to Marston; nipple recesses on the Union and Western guns are squared rather than rounded, which may confirm the supply of unfinished components.

Among the imports were nearly 13,000 Lefaucheux pinfires, plus a few British Beaumont-Adams, French Raphaels, and Perrins with their distinctive rimfire cartridges.

CONFEDERATE REVOLVERS

The Confederacy had a much poorer arms industry than the Federals, most resources

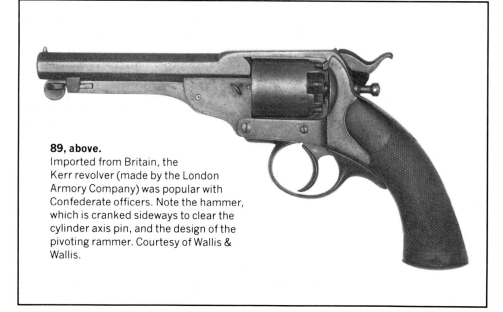

89, above.
Imported from Britain, the Kerr revolver (made by the London Armory Company) was popular with Confederate officers. Note the hammer, which is cranked sideways to clear the cylinder axis pin, and the design of the pivoting rammer. Courtesy of Wallis & Wallis.

90, 91: right and below.
The Le Mat revolver of the Civil War had a large-calibre smooth-bore barrel doubling as a cylinder axis-pin. This is a later pinfire version, which enjoyed a short heyday in Europe. Courtesy of Ian Hogg.
(Inset: the hammer-mounted selector on cap-lock guns.)

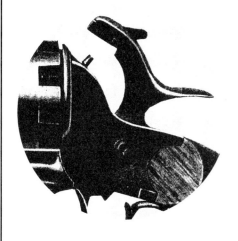

being concentrated north of the Mason-Dixon Line. The South was predominantly rural.

About a hundred copies of the ·36 six-shot Navy-model Colt were made by the Augusta Machine Works of Augusta, Georgia. They had octagonal 7·8in barrels and six (rare) or twelve cylinder-stop notches. The Columbus Fire Arms Company of Columbus, Georgia, founded by Louis & Elias Haiman in 1862, began to make copies of the ·36 Navy-type Colt a year later. Most guns had octagonal barrels, though a few apparently had the rounded pattern associated with the Dragoon Colts. Only about a hundred had been made before the factory was sold to the Confederate government and moved to Macon, Georgia.

Dance Brothers (or Dance Bros. & Park) of Columbia, Texas, made a modified Dragoon type Colt in ·36 and ·44. This lacked recoil shields behind the cylinder as well as an exploded-cap channel in the breech face. Production is estimated to have been five hundred guns, the ·44 version outnumbering the ·36 pattern by about two to one.

Tucker, Sherrard & Company of Lancaster, Texas, contracted with the State of Texas in April 1862 to make three thousand Colt-type revolvers. Deliveries had not even commenced when Labon Tucker withdrew to form Tucker & Son in nearby Weatherford. There he made about a hundred revolvers based on the ·36-calibre Navy Colt, but with round Dragoon style barrels.

Taylor, Sherrard & Company succeeded to the original operations, completing a few sets of parts before failing. Eventually, Clark, Sherrard & Company completed about five hundred guns—but only after the end of the Civil War.

None of these gunmakers contributed more than a few hundred serviceable weapons to the Confederate arsenal. However, Griswold & Gunnison of Griswoldville, Georgia, made 3,500 ·36 six-shot Colt Navy-type revolvers with brass frames and round Dragoon-style barrels. Production began in the summer of 1862 and ceased in the winter of 1864. Leech & Rigdon made a few ·36 Colt-type revolvers (with 7½-inch round barrels) in the Novelty Works in Columbus, Mississippi, before moving to Greensboro (Georgia) in the Spring of 1863. The partnership dissolved in January 1864, each partner continuing alone. About 1,500 guns were made with Leech & Rigdon marks, though the last batches had been completed by Rigdon & Ansley in Augusta, Georgia; Thomas Leech contributed an extra hundred revolvers, made in Greensboro after the split.

Spiller & Burr made about 800 brass-frame ·36-calibre copies of the Whitney navy revolver in 1863. The Confederate government bought the partnership's assets in January 1864, moving the plant to Macon, Georgia, where another 750 guns were made. Production ceased in November 1864, owing to the promximity of Federal army units.

Thomas Cofer of Portsmouth, Virginia, made more than a hundred copies of the ·36 Whitney navy revolver with a brass frame and a distinctive spurred trigger guard. These were originally designed for a special percussion cartridge patented by Cofer on 12 August 1861, though finalised guns accepted conventional ammunition.

The parlous nature of Confederate ordnance was best illustrated by the efforts of farmers such as Alfred Kapp of Sisterdale, Texas, who painstakingly hand-made about twenty Remington-Beals type revolvers.

The most interesting of the Confederate cap locks was the Le Mat revolver, patented by François Alexandre le Mat of New Orleans on 21 October 1856 (US 15,925) to protect the substitution of an extra barrel for the cylinder axis pin and a 'gun-cock with double hammer'. The essence of the guns used during the Civil War was a ·67-calibre shot barrel around which the nine-shot ·40 cylinder revolved.

The guns were made in small batches, apparently by several manufacturers in Britain and France; consequently, they vary greatly in detail. Though they share an open-top frame, some have octagonal barrels while others are half-octagonal. The rammers differ—some on the right side of the barrel, others on the left—while trigger guards may be oval or spurred. The Le Mat revolvers generally share lanyard rings on their butts, lengthy hammer spurs, single-action locks, and a selector on the hammer nose.

Popular with Confederate cavalry officers such as Jeb Stuart and Pierre Beauregard, Le Mats were large and heavy. However, though their rammers and selective-fire hammers were comparatively weak, they were generally very well made and gave better service than many handguns in Confederate service. François Le Mat patented a metallic-cartridge version on 14 December 1869 (97,780), and a selection of pin- or centre-fire guns was made in Europe in the early 1870s. Most emanated from Liége.

THE FIRST CARTRIDGE REVOLVERS

When Horace Smith and Daniel Wesson sold their interests in what became the Volcanic (q.v.), they did so in the knowledge that they had acquired the rights to a revolver designed by Rollin White. This gun was complicated and potentially very ineffectual, but its chambers were bored entirely through the cylinder. The existing cap-lock revolvers all had 'blind' chambers, with a closed rear surface into which the flash-channels were bored.

Wesson, still smarting from damage inflicted by Colt on the Massachusetts Arms Company some years previously, was well aware that Colt's master patent expired in 1857. In January 1858, therefore, Smith & Wesson announced the seven-shot Model No.1 ·22 rimfire revolver. This tiny weapon, initially scarcely seen as effectual, was a landmark in firearms history.

Demand prior to the introduction of an improved 'second pattern' No.1 in May 1860 was comparatively small, amounting to a little over eleven thousand guns. The advent of the Civil War benefited Smith & Wesson's operations tremendously, just as it gave a boost to many other manufacturers. By 3 April 1869, when the licensing agreement concluded with Rollin White ended on the expiry of his patent, 271,639 revolvers had been made. One irony was that White had received almost $68,000-worth of royalty payments on a design that had been very poor. A rich man, he retired from the arms business to pursue other goals—including, finally, the White Steam Car.

In spite of its small calibre and tiny cartridge, the Smith & Wesson was extremely popular with the Federal forces. It was widely favoured by officers, who were not normally issued with handguns, and also by the rank-and-file to reinforce the standard weapons.

Smith & Wesson, emboldened by success, were mindful of the ineffectiveness of the ·22 rimfire cartridge. Initially, however, the partners were unable to make copper cartridge cases strong enough to withstand anything more than the three grains of black powder the No.1 (·22) version contained. As the bullet weighed a mere 29–30 grains, the tiny Smith & Wesson revolver compared poorly with ·36 and ·44 service weapons.

By 1861, however, manufacturing problems had been solved well enough to permit a ·32 cartridge to be introduced. This contained about thirteen grains of powder and a 90-grain

bullet, a load which, though prone to excessive fouling, improved power beyond comparison with the earlier ·22. Six-shot ·32 Model No.2 revolvers, made with barrels of 4–6in, were joined in 1864 by the Model No.1½. The latter was a light five-shot ·32-calibre gun, made with 3½- and then 4-inch barrels. It filled a gap between the puny No.1 and the appreciably larger No.2.

When hostilities were over, Smith & Wesson refined the Nos. 1 and 1½ by the addition of cylinder fluting, cylindrical instead of octagonal barrels and the substitution of bird's head for conventionally flared grips. The changeover was gradual, owing to the existence of many old parts, and so an assortment of transitional weapons will be encountered.

Like Colt before them, Smith & Wesson were almost immediately faced with infringements of their licence with Rollin White. However, as a keystone of the agreement, White had agreed to take action against such infringers; though Smith & Wesson's vested interest was strong enough to persuade the company to pay at least part of the costs of the lawsuits, the latter ate heavily into White's royalties.

Alone among the major arms makers, Remington approached Smith & Wesson to reach agreement over a metallic cartridge conversion of its cap-lock revolvers. Consequently, a little less than five thousand ·44 Remington army revolvers were modified for a ·46 rimfire cartridge by the substitution of a new five-cartridge cylinder for the original six-shot percussion type. The cylinders of these guns were marked in recognition of the White patent. A one-dollar royalty was paid to Smith & Wesson on each gun, 25 cents of which were passed to Rollin White.

Smith & Wesson-type revolvers were made by the Rollin White Arms Company, originally legitimately; White had retained rights to make guns under his own patent. However, the Rollin White company soon passed into receivership and its assets were subsequently acquired by

the Lowell Arms Company. White had no financial interest in the Lowell business, so revolvers made after the reorganization were regarded as infringements of Smith & Wesson's rights.

The earliest Smith & Wessons were neither sturdy nor particularly effectual mechanically. By the time they appeared on the market, in the early part of 1858, Colt's master patent had expired. Smith & Wesson could have adopted some of the better features of the Colts, particularly the means of rotating and indexing the cylinder to ensure that the cylinder and the barrel-bore were in a straight line. Smith & Wesson's system was simultaneously more complex and less effectual than the well-tried Colt pattern.

In addition, the Smith & Wesson No.1 lacked a safety or half-cock notch on the hammer, causing accidents with loaded guns.

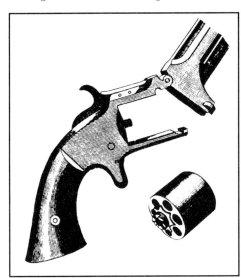

92, above; 93, below. The ·32 rimfire Smith & Wesson Model No.2, the first effectual metal-case cartridge revolver. Though lacking power, it was very popular during the American Civil War as a back-up or last-ditch weapon. Photograph courtesy of Ian Hogg.

SMITH & WESSON INFRINGEMENTS

Guns that transgressed the Rollin White patent were made in a wonderful selection of shapes and sizes.

Some of the most numerous were made by Lucius Pond of Worcester, Massachusetts, under a patent granted to Abram Gibson on 10 July 1860 (29,126, partly assigned to Joseph Hale), which had a Smith & Wesson-style barrel/cylinder assembly hinged at the top rear of the frame. The action was locked by a lever on the lower left side of the bottom strap. The sheath trigger Pond revolver had cylinder-stop slots towards the front of the cylinder surface; in addition, the cylinder-face was recessed in a recoil shield when the action was closed. Six-shot guns were made in ·32 and ·44 rimfire. The smaller guns usually had four-inch barrels and measured 8½in overall, while the larger or 'army' pattern had a 7¼-inch barrel.

E.A. Prescott of Worcester, Massachusetts, made an even closer Smith & Wesson facsimile in ·32 rimfire, with an iron frame and a sheath trigger. Prescott also made revolvers with a cylinder latch protected by his patent of 2 October 1860 (30,245). Introduced early in 1862, these included a ·38 six-shot rimfire 'navy' pattern with an eight-inch barrel, a conventional spurred trigger guard and a saw-handle grip. The seven-shot ·22 and six-shot ·32 rimfire sheath trigger pocket models generally offered four-inch barrels.

Revolvers made by Allen & Wheelock and its successor, Allen & Company (from 1863), were much more distinctive. Based on the Allen & Wheelock cap locks (q.v.), they had central hammers and a conventional cylinder axis pin entering from the front of the frame. They included ·32 and ·44 lip-fire 'evasions', which, though quite unlike the Smith & Wesson revolvers, still featured bored-through cylinders. However, Allen also made small-calibre side hammer guns in ·22 and ·32 rimfire.

William Irving of New York made distinctive ·22 and ·32 rimfire revolvers, introduced in the summer of 1862, with fixed barrels and a button in the tang that released the recoil shield on the right side of the frame; this swung up and back to permit loading, any convenient rod serving as an ejector. Owing to their rarity, production of Irving revolvers may have ceased after the Draft Riots of 1863. Irving also made convertible ·30 rimfire cartridge/·31 cap-lock solid-framed sheath trigger revolvers to a patent secured by James Reid on 28 April 1863. (US 38,336).

Samuel Cone, working in West Chesterfield, Massachusetts, made a six-shot ·32 rimfire solid-frame infringement with a hinged loading gate on the right side of the frame behind the cylinder.

James Warner of Springfield, Massachusetts, made a ·30 rimfire version of his cap-lock pocket revolver. This five-shot gun had a solid frame, a loading gate on the frame-side behind the cylinder, and a conventional trigger guard; but its bored-through chambers infringed the Rollin White patent. Warner had been one of the many sub-contractors employed by Smith & Wesson in the production of the Model No.1 pistol and would have been well aware of developments.

The Manhattan Fire Arms Company of Newark, New Jersey, made close copies of the Smith & Wesson Model No.1 in ·22 and ·32 rimfire, seven- and six-shot respectively. The octagonal barrels tipped upward around a pivot on the top rear of the frame, and were latched in much the same fashion as their prototypes. Smith & Wesson successfully sued Manhattan—among the most unscrupulous of the North American gunmakers—and removed the guns from the market.

The Bacon Arms & Manufacturing Company of Norwich, Connecticut, was just one of many making ·22 and ·32 rimfire infringements, often unmarked. Bacon also made substantial quantities of six-shot ·32 and ·38 'navy' rimfire revolvers embodying a swinging cylinder patented by Charles Hopkins on 27 May 1862 (35,419, part-assigned to Henry Edgerton).

Daniel Moore & Company of Brooklyn, New York, made a series of ·32, ·38 and ·44 rimfire revolvers based on a patent granted on 18 September 1860 (30,079). This protected an open-frame gun with a barrel/cylinder group that could be rotated laterally to the right to facilitate loading. Moore's revolvers had a conventional trigger guard and a spring-loaded ejecting rod under the barrel. They were among the most effectual and easily loaded cartridge handguns made prior to 1865.

Pepperboxes with bored-through cylinders, which could be classed as infringements, were made by Elliot, Rupertus and Sharps.

Virtually all these companies operated in the States of Connecticut and Massachusetts, the cradle of the North American gunmaking industry. Suits brought by Smith & Wesson against some of the principal transgressors began with an action against Herman Boker of New York (a well-known distributor) for selling revolvers with bored-through cylinders made by the Manhattan Fire Arms Company. The case was settled in favour of Smith & Wesson and Rollin White in 1862. Then came suits against Bacon, Moore, Pond and Warner, all of

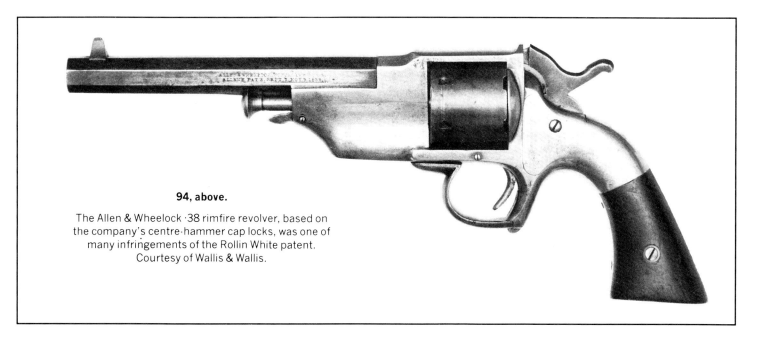

94, above.

The Allen & Wheelock ·38 rimfire revolver, based on the company's centre-hammer cap locks, was one of many infringements of the Rollin White patent. Courtesy of Wallis & Wallis.

which predictably resolved in Smith & Wesson's favour. However, the defendants were allowed to complete guns 'in the course of manufacture' provided royalties were paid to the owners of the Rollin White patent. These guns were marked 'April 3, 1855' in acknowledgement of the White patent.

Ironically, Smith & Wesson bought some of the infringing guns for re-sale. These included 3,299 assorted Moore-made revolvers, 1,437 ·30 rimfire Warners, 4,880 ·32 rimfire Ponds and 1,124 miscellaneous Bacons in ·22, ·32 and ·38 rimfire.

Smith & Wesson allowed the Rollin White Arms Company of Lowell, Massachusetts, to make ·22 rimfire revolvers, even purchasing ten thousand guns at a time when its own production was lagging. However, the Rollin White Arms Company then ousted the inventor, changed its name to Lowell Arms Company, and continued production. Smith & Wesson threatened to sue for infringement, whereupon 1,853 additional revolvers were surrendered and manufacture ceased.

SMITH & WESSON EVASIONS

In March 1862, a Patent of 'Improvement in Revolving Fire-Arms' was granted to C. Edward Sneider of Baltimore, Maryland. One of the earliest effectual evasions, this strange gun featured twin cylinders, one pointing towards the target and the other at the firer. An extended hammer-nose reached forward over the back cylinder to strike the rims of cartridges in the front one. When seven shots had been fired, the action was opened—it had a hinge at the bottom front of the frame—and the cylinders were reversed.

The Sneider revolver was never made in quantity; indeed, there is no evidence that anything other than a patent model existed. The same could not be said of the gun made by Plant's Manufacturing Company of Southington (1860–1), New Haven (1861–6), and then Plantsville and Southington, Connecticut (1866–8).

Patented by Willard Ellis & John White on 12 July 1859 (24,726) and 25 August 1863 (39,318), the Plant revolver fired a self contained 'cup primer' metal-case cartridge loaded from the front of the cylinder. Fulminate was contained in a longitudinal extension of the cartridge case instead of the conventional projecting rim. A small hole was bored in the rear of the cylinder-chamber to admit the nose of the hammer.

The first six-shot ·42 rimfire Plant revolvers resembled the contemporary Smith & Wesson No.1, which was no mere coincidence. They had plated bronze frames, blued octagonal

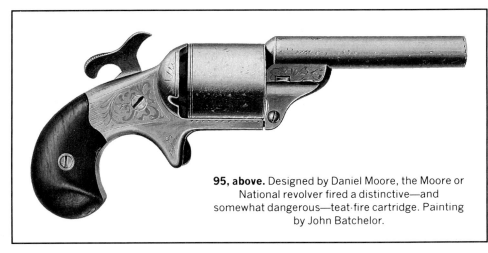

95, above. Designed by Daniel Moore, the Moore or National revolver fired a distinctive—and somewhat dangerous—teat-fire cartridge. Painting by John Batchelor.

barrels, and proved to be quite successful once the Civil War had begun. By 1863, however, the tipping-frame Plant had been replaced by a sturdier ·28, ·30 or ·42 solid frame pattern, which was then made on into post-war days. Most revolvers made after 1864 had improved ejectors patented by Henry Reynolds of Springfield, Massachusetts, on 10 May 1864 (42,688) and 22 November 1864 (45,176, reissued in May 1866). The improved weapon bore a selection of markings, including those of the Eagle Arms Company of New York; J.M. Marlin & Company of Rock Falls, New York; Merwin & Bray Fire Arms Company of New York; and Reynolds, Plant & Hotchkiss of New Haven, Connecticut.

Merwin & Bray was simply a distributor, while the Eagle Arms Company, incorporated in November 1865, was apparently an agency formed to sell Plant revolvers. Ebenezer Plant's own factory was razed by fire in 1866, whereafter Marlin made guns for him.

Plant, like James Reid, made convertible cap-lock/cartridge revolvers; Plant's had exchangeable cylinders, while Reid's guns had detachable screwed-in nipples. Cup-primer cartridges were also chambered in revolvers briefly made by the Connecticut Arms Company of Norfolk, Connecticut, after the end of the Civil War. The single-action sheath trigger ·28-calibre brass framed guns were based on patents granted to Stephen Wood on 1 March 1864 and 16 January 1866; break-open designs patterned on contemporary Smith & Wessons, they incorporated a spur-type extractor in the bottom strap.

Daniel Moore, an entrepreneur who fronted several companies during his active life, originally made a seven-shot rimfire revolver with a bored-through cylinder. These guns achieved a temporary popularity out of proportion to their sales, thanks to the book *The Twin Six Shooters* by Civil War veteran Major G.W. Manderson, but fell foul of Rollin White and Smith & Wesson. After losing a

lawsuit, Moore turned to a revolver firing a teat fire cartridge patented on 5 January 1864 by David Williamson, better known for his single shot cartridge derringer. The revolver was also made under the National brand, signifying a change in ownership in the mid 1860s.

Moore received a patent in 1863 for a ·32 teat-fire cartridge revolver with a hinged loading gate ahead of the cylinder. To his later chagrin, Moore did not claim any specific novelty either in the teat-fire system or the insertion of a cartridge from the chamber mouth. Consequently, he had to pay royalties to Williamson on ammunition he could have protected a year earlier.

Moore ·32 teat-fire revolvers had a six-round cylinder, an open-top frame with a sheath trigger, and a bird's head butt. Most of them acknowledge Williamson's patents of 17 May 1864 and 5 June 1864, protecting combination extractor/cartridge retainers found on the right side of the frame beneth the cylinder. Tiny numbers of ·45 solid frame enlargements, with a conventional trigger guard, were made in the dying days of the American Civil War.

Teat-fire revolvers—indeed, all similar front loaders—had a serious drawback. Fouling in the chamber itself, if it accumulated far enough, could make cartridges difficult to seat. If force was used, there was always a chance that the teat would crush and the fulminate ignite. Soon, a series of accidents occurred: eyes were damaged, fingers were lost. Speedily, the vulnerable teat fire passed into history.

Another successful evasion was the single action five-shot 'sliding sleeve' ·32 rimfire gun patented by Frank Slocum on 27 January (37,551) and 14 April 1863 (38,204), rights being assigned to the Brooklyn Firearms Company

Among the first of the cartridge revolvers to differ acceptably from the Smith & Wesson, Slocum's design featured detachable sliding sleeves or tubes in each cylinder. These were pushed forward to allow conventional rimfire cartridges to be inserted in the chambers and then returned to their original position to provide support during firing. Apart from a slot for the hammer nose, the chambers could not be considered as bored through, and thus avoided the ire of Smith & Wesson.

The revolver patented by Silas Crispin on 3 October 1865 (US 50,224) was another hinged frame design. Made by the Smith Arms Company of New York, its principal claim to novelty was a two-part cylinder, capable of revolving independently until loaded with a special cartridge with an annular priming band around the case; these odd rounds were loaded backwards through the front section of the cylinder, then fired by a striker acting down between the two halves of the cylinder unit. The ·32 Crispin never achieved success, owing to the poor distribution of its strange cartridge. Placing sensitive mercuric fulminate around the periphery of the case, as in the Crispin cartridge, was a bad idea: unlike conventional centre-fire cartridges, the Crispin primer was vulnerable to knocks.

One of the inventors whose guns had been adjudged guilty of transgressing White's patent, Lucius Pond, was responsible for an evasion revolver based on a patent granted to John Vickers on 17 June 1862 ('cartridge cases for revolving firearms', US 35,667); Pond was the assignee of Vickers' later patents in the revolving firearms category—47,775 of 16 May 1865 and 57,448 of 21 August 1866.

The guns had separate chambers, lining tubes or 'thimbles', containing conventional ·22 and ·32 rimfire cartridges, which were inserted from the front of the cylinder. The seven-shot ·22 and

96, below. Some of the drawings that accompanied the US patent granted to Freeman Hood in November 1864, embodied in the improved Pond revolver. Courtesy of the US Patent Office, Washington DC.

six-shot ·32 guns normally had brass frames with sheath triggers and blued steel barrels.

Improvements to the Pond revolver were patented by Freeman Hood of Worcester, Massachusetts, on 8 November 1864 (44,953). Guns made to this patent had a pivoting ejector or 'discharger', attached to the cylinder axis pin, which supposedly extracted the spent rimfire cases when the thimbles were withdrawn.

The Belgian Polain revolver, patented in the USA contemporaneously with Pond's, used a similar cartridge-loading system with a pierced disc to which the tubes were secured. This, an early quick-loading device, enabled the tubes to be inserted (or removed) simultaneously.

REMINGTON DERRINGERS, 1865–1917

About a thousand examples of a ·22 rimfire six-shot Elliott Zig-Zag derringer, patented on 17 August 1858 (21,188) and 29 May 1860

97, above. The Protector was one of the oddest pistols to be made in the period prior to the outbreak of the First World War.

(28,461), were made shortly before the Civil War began.

The standard Remington-Elliott derringer, patented on 29 May 1860 (28,460) and 1 October 1861 (33,362), had a multi-shot three-inch barrel cluster that tipped down for loading. It was fired by a revolving striker actuated by a ring trigger. The guns were generally blued, but could be obtained with a nickel-plated frame or full nickel finish. Grips were smooth gutta-percha or, alternatively, mother-of-pearl or ivory. About fifty thousand five-shot ·22 and four-shot ·32 examples were made in 1863–88 with cylindrical and squared barrel clusters respectively.

From 1865, Remington contributed the Vest Pocket Pistol, with a rolling-block type breech and a distinctive saw-handle grip. Made in two versions, chambering ·41 and ·22 rimfire cartridges (in addition to an extremely scarce ·32), the Vest Pocket Model was quite popular; production prior to 1888 has been estimated at 50,000.

The ·41 version (which bore an additional 15 November 1864 patent date) was 5½in long, had a four-inch barrel and weighed 11–12oz. It was supplied in blue or nickel finish, with an additional option of blued barrel and nickelled frame. Grips were lacquered or varnished walnut, ivory and mother-of-pearl being supplied to order. Decoration was extra.

Remington's 'Deringer Pistol', designed by William Elliott, to whom a patent was issued on 27 August 1867 ('hammer for breech loading firearms', 68,292), was a single-barrel ·41 rimfire pattern with a hammer that doubled as the breech block. Available from stock until 1888, It is highly unlikely that production was undertaken after the early 1870s. It measured 4·9in overall, had a 2½-inch barrel and weighed 7oz. In its standard blued form—with walnut bird's head grips—it cost $7 in 1876, compared with $3.75 for the large Vest Pocket Pistol and $8 for the over-under or Double Repeating Deringer Pistol (sic) designed by Elliott and the subject of US Patent 51,440, granted on 12 December 1865 to protect a 'many barrelled firearm'.

Introduced commercially in 1866, this gun sold amazingly well; when it was finally discontinued in the mid 1930s, about 150,000 had been made. The essential feature was a pair of superimposed three-inch ·41 rimfire barrels in a monoblock hinged to the frame. The barrel-block swung upward around a pivot at the top rear of the frame when the lever on the right side of the frame was pressed downward, allowing the gun to be reloaded. The firing pin fired the top barrel first, being re-set each time the frame was opened. Most of the guns were nickel-plated, although blued examples were produced in small numbers.

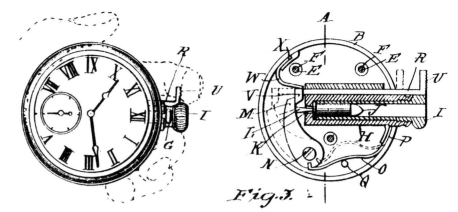

98, above. Drawings from the patent granted to Leonard Woods of St Louis, Missouri, in 1913, reveal one of the strangest pre-1917 hideaway weapons. Courtesy of the US Patent Office, Washington DC.

99, below right. Remington derringers, from original literature. Author's collection.

Their grips may be walnut or rosewood or, alternatively, chequered gutta-percha, mother of pearl, or even ivory. Double derringers were marked as the products of E. Remington & Sons until 1887, then by 'Remington Arms Company' or 'Remington Arms—UMC Co.'

The Remington Magazine Repeating Pistol, another product of the fertile imagination of Joseph Rider, was patented on 15 August 1871 (118,152). The pistol had a tube magazine beneath the barrel, holding four ·32 Extra Short rimfire cartridges; a fifth could be loaded directly into the chamber. The mechanism embodied a variant of the rolling-block action, relying on an elevator to convey cartridges into the breech. Guns were encountered with three inch barrels and weighed 10oz. Some were nickel plated, while others had colour case hardened frames; grips were varnished walnut, though ivory and mother of pearl were also available. About 15,000 of these interesting sheath-trigger guns were made in 1872–88.

KNUCKLE-DUSTERS AND PALM-SQUEEZERS, 1865–1906

Among the most interesting derringers was the Reid knuckle-duster revolver, which featured a flat frame with a prominent hole and a long cylinder contained within the frame. It was patented by James Reid of Catskill, New York, on 26 December 1865 (51,572), and marketed under the trade name 'My Friend'. About twenty thousand Reid revolvers were made from 1865 until about 1880, when they were supplanted by a version with a short barrel (1880–4).

My Friends were made in differing patterns, including seven-shot ·22, five-shot ·32 and five-shot ·41 examples. Sliding safety catches that locked the hammer between the chambers were fitted to some (but by no means all) the ·22 and ·32 guns, and almost always on the ·41—the rarest variant, production apparently totalling less than five hundred.

Another oddity was the turret-type palm pistol patented in the USA by Frenchman Jacques Turbiaux on 6 March 1883 (273,644). A patent of improvement was granted to Peter Finnegan of Austin, Illinois, in August 1893 (504,154). Marketed in quantity by the Minneapolis Fire-Arms Company and then by a successor, the Chicago Fire Arms Company, the seven-shot ·32 Short rimfire Protector was made by the Ames Sword Company of Chicopee Falls, Massachusetts. It comprised a flat disc-like magazine with a short barrel that protruded between the firer's fingers. The trigger was a spring-loaded plate at the back of the disc, which was simply pressed against the base of the firer's palm. The pistols are usually found with two or three finger spurs on the front surface, alongside the barrel.

The Minneapolis guns usually have a safety lever, while the Chicago guns use an automatic safety on the finger spur, which disengages when the trigger-lever is squeezed. Loading was effected by removing the side plate, which was retained by a small bolt. Catalogues issued by Hartley & Graham in 1892 indicates that the Minneapolis variant existed in three patterns, nickel-plated or blued, with rubber or pearl 'sides'.

A few Chicago-type Protectors will be found with a double-ring finger guard said to have been patented by John Norris of Springfield, Ohio, c.1900. This was developed to hold the fingers away from the muzzle of the ultra-short barrel, from which it may be deduced that accidents had occurred.

A single-barrel ·32 centre-fire squeezer pistol was patented by George Webber of Chicago in

May 1905 ('firearm', 788,866), but was never made in quantity. More successful was the Shatuck Unique, patented by Oscar Mossberg of Chicopee Falls, Massachusetts, on 4 December 1906 (837,867). The gun had a four-barrel block, which tipped down to load, and was fired by a slider-actuated rotary striker. The Unique was made in ·22 and ·32 rimfire, the iron frames being blued or nickel-plated.

One of the last of the squeezers was a single-shot pistol disguised as a pocket watch, patented by Leonard Woods of St Louis, Missouri, on 16 September 1913 (1,073,312). Belonging to the eccentric fringe of handgun design, it disappeared into history unnoticed.

CARTRIDGE DERRINGERS, 1866–75

Designed by Henry Hammond of Naubuc,

Connecticut, patented on 23 January 1866 and made until 1868 by the Connecticut Arms Company of Glastonbury, the Bulldog (or 'Bulldozer') derringer was an angular and unattractive weapon. It was offered during its short life in chamberings ranging from ·22 Short rimfire to ·50, though ·32 and ·41 rimfire were most common. The Hammond barrel, released by a catch on the breech-top, pivoted to the left to expose the chamber. A few long-barrel guns were made, complete with shoulder stocks to convert them into light (but very unsuccessful) carbines.

Patented on 2 October 1866, using a teat-fire cartridge patented by David Williamson in 1864, the Williamson derringer was a single shot convertible pattern capable of handling rimfire cartridges or, alternatively, powder and ball. The adaptor consisted of an iron tube, not unlike an empty cartridge case, with a nipple to

accept a conventional percussion cap. Once the hammer had been thumbed back to half cock and the barrel-locking catch pressed, the Williamson barrel slid forward to allow access to the breech. Ignition was supplied by a central hammer, with a blade to fire cartridges above a small projection to fire caps.

About five thousand Williamsons were made in 1866–7 by Moore's Patent Fire Arms Company. They measured 5¼in overall, had 2½-inch barrels and weighed about 9oz. The frames and trigger guards were brass castings, but were usually nickel or, more rarely, silver plated.

The Bacon Arms Company, after falling foul of Smith & Wesson and Rollin White, switched production from small-calibre revolvers to conventional single-shot ·32 rimfire swinging barrel derringers.

The Southerner derringer was made by the Merrimack Arms & Manufacturing Company of Newburyport, Massachusetts (1867–9), and by the equally short-lived Brown Manufacturing Company (1869–73). The Southerner, which was especially popular below the Mason-Dixon Line, originally had a 2½-inch barrel swinging laterally after a catch set in the frame had been released. Brown produced a handful of long barrel guns, with square-heel butts instead of the traditional Southerner bird's head, but they were never successful.

The derringer patented by Charles Ballard on 22 June 1869, made by Ballard & Fairbanks in Worcester, Massachusetts, was a ·41 rimfire single-shot pistol with barrel that tipped down to expose the chamber after the knurled catch on the barrel-block had been pushed forward to disengage the frame. Most guns had a distinctive ejector operated by a toothed rack in the frame. Ballards had brass or iron frames with a distinctively spurred back strap. The finish was generally nickel plate, grips being rosewood or walnut.

In the late 1860s, Franklin Wesson made a selection of two-shot ·32 derringers with a flat barrel block that rotated laterally to the right when the breech catch was released. He also made what he termed a 'Pocket Rifle', which was a ·32-calibre single-barrel pistol no more than 6in long. The barrel was released by a latch protruding beneath the frame ahead of the sheath trigger—a poor feature, as the barrel could often open accidentally in the confines of a pocket.

Forehand & Wadsworth's derringer was another ·41 rimfire single-barrel pattern, made in 1871–5 but available commercially as late as 1889. It resembled the Southerner externally, with a bird's head grip, but had a rounded fore-end.

Single-barrel pistols were very easy to make, encouraging companies with little previous

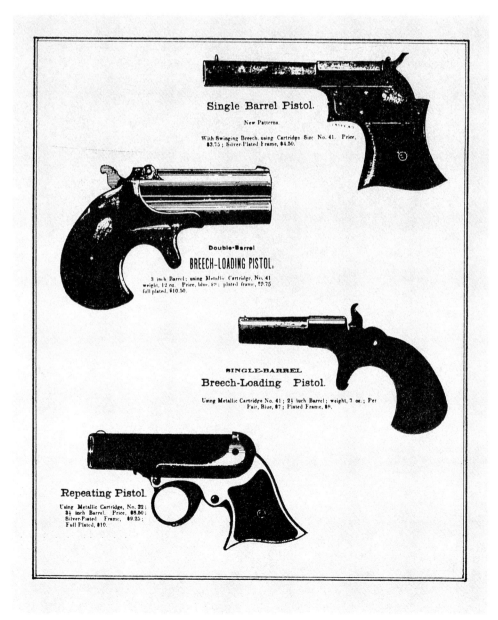

Single Barrel Pistol.
New Patterns.
With Swinging Breech, using Cartridge Size No. 41. Price, $3.75; Silver-Plated Frame, $4.50.

Double-Barrel
BREECH-LOADING PISTOL.
3 inch Barrel; using Metallic Cartridge, No. 41
weight, 12 oz. Price, blue, $9; plated frame, $9.75
full plated, $10.50.

SINGLE-BARREL
Breech-Loading Pistol.
Using Metallic Cartridge No. 41; 2¼ inch Barrel; weight, 7 oz.; Per Pair, Blue, $7; Plated Frame, $8.

Repeating Pistol.
Using Metallic Cartridge, No. 32;
3½ inch Barrel. Price, $8.50;
Silver-Plated Frame, $9.25;
Full Plated, $10.

experience of firearms production to try their hand in the hope of making a fortune. Morgan & Clapp made a sheath-trigger ·32 gun with a laterally swinging barrel—not unlike the Southerner (q.v.), but without a characteristic frame-step in the vicinity of the hammer. Joshua Stevens made some ·32 single-shot pistols that could be mustered in with the personal-defence weapons by stretching the imagination.

THE SUICIDE SPECIALS

The rise of the firearms industry in New England and, particularly, the perfection of small-calibre revolvers by Smith & Wesson and others, encouraged many manufacturing companies to participate.

With the exception of a few gunmakers who subsequently rose to prominence, most of the products were 'Suicide Specials'—a derogatory term that is now applied to small solid-frame guns with detachable cylinders, bird's head butts and sheath triggers. It may also be applied to a later group of cheap break-open auto ejectors.

Few of these weapons have much claim to novelty, though, particularly among the later group, some variety will be encountered in barrel-locking systems, ejectors and lock work.

Owing to the comparatively minor status of Suicide Specials in the West—their role in the supposedly civilised parts of the North America was more telling—it is sufficient to identify the most important brandnames.

Among the more interesting guns were those produced briefly by the American Arms Company of Boston, Massachusetts (1872–93), and then Milwaukee, Wisconsin (1893–1901). These were made to a patent granted to George Fox and Henry Wheeler on 11 March 1890 (422,930), which protected a hammer that could be rotated to full-cock and then released by a second pull on the trigger. The guns had a selector on the side of the frame to allow the firer to revert to conventional double-action at any time.

The Foehl & Weeks Manufacturing Company of Philadelphia, Pennsylvania, made a series of solid-frame and break-open revolvers under names such as 'Columbian' and 'Perfect' in 1891–4. Some included a removable cylinder system patented by Charles Foehl on 17 December 1889 (417,672). Foehl had been granted an earlier patent to protect the cylinder-rotating pawl incorporated in revolvers made briefly by Henry Deringer & Company of Philadelphia.

Though best known for its lever-action rifles, the Marlin Fire Arms Company also made substantial quantities of small-calibre revolvers. John Marlin's operations had begun in

New Haven in 1863, where single-shot rimfire pistols were made. These were modified by the addition of an ejector, patented in April 1870, and then supplemented by a selection of small revolvers. The XXX Standard, sometimes known as the 'Model 1873', was a five-shot tipping barrel gun chambered for ·30, ·32 and ·38 rimfire.

Marlin also made Smith & Wesson style top-latch ·32 and ·38 centre-fire double action revolvers in the 1880s. However, production of all handguns had ceased by the end of the century.

Andrew Fyrberg & Company of Hopkinton, Massachusetts, marketed a few double-action break-open revolvers under its own name—though they were probably made by Iver Johnson, for whom Fyrberg had designed part of the famous Hammer-the-Hammer system (q.v.). They embodied an improved barrel latch and cylinder retainer protected by US Patent 735,490 of 4 August 1903. The guns did not appear commercially until 1905 and lasted for no more than a couple of years.

The Meriden Firearms Company of Meriden, Connecticut, made five-shot ·32 and ·38 break open guns in conventional hammer and hammerless patterns in the years before the First World War, though little else is known of the company's operations.

Otis Smith of Middlefield and later Rock Fall, Connecticut, made a series of solid-frame sheath trigger revolvers incorporating his patent of 15 April 1873 (137,968), which protected a quick-release cylinder catch. The guns were superseded by a break-open auto-ejecting gun patented in collusion with John Smith on 20 December 1881 (251,306). These guns were marketed as Model 83 Shell Ejectors, with sheath triggers and bird's head grips. They were replaced by a conventional solid-frame hammerless gate-loading gun chambered for ·38 rim- or centre-fire cartridges. This five-shot weapon had a double-action trigger and an exposed cylinder stop that could be depressed by the thumb to allow the cylinder to rotate.

Model 1892 Smith revolvers were handled by the sporting-goods suppliers Maltby, Henley & Company of New York City, and may be encountered under several misleading manufacturer's names—e.g., Columbia Armory, Spencer Revolver Company or Parker Revolver Company.

Maltby, Curtis & Company and its 1889-vintage successor, Maltby, Henley & Co., also marketed a series of rim- and centre-fire revolvers under the 'Metropolitan Police' brandname. These were protected by patents granted to William Bliss of Norwich, Connecticut, between April 1878 and March 1885.

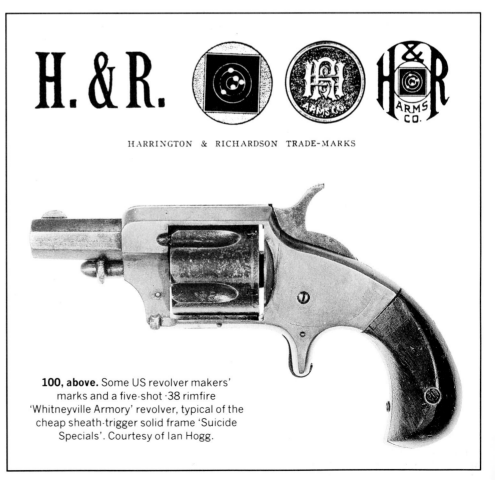

HARRINGTON & RICHARDSON TRADE-MARKS

100, above. Some US revolver makers' marks and a five-shot ·38 rimfire 'Whitneyville Armory' revolver, typical of the cheap sheath-trigger solid frame 'Suicide Specials'. Courtesy of Ian Hogg.

The company also promoted a double-action five-shot revolver with a brass frame cast integrally with its brass barrel shroud, relying on a rifled steel liner for strength and accuracy. This was patented by John Smith on 24 January 1889 (376,922) and 28 October 1889 (413,975).

Maltby, Curtis & Company's revolvers were made by the Norwich Pistol Company, formed in Norwich, Connecticut, in 1875. Operations ceased on liquidation in 1881, but the assets were retrieved by Maltby, Curtis & Company, business was reorganized, and production began again under the 'Norwich Falls Pistol Company' banner. Operations failed in 1887, no doubt linked with a decline in the sporting goods market that caused Maltby, Curtis & Company to enter a temporary eclipse.

The XL series, made by Hopkins & Allen from 1871, contained a superior brand of sheath trigger Suicide Special. The XL No.1 was a seven-shot ·22 rimfire; XL No.2 was a five shot ·32 rimfire; XL No.2½ was similar, but chambered for ·32 Short rimfire; and XL No.3 handled ·32 Long rimfire. By 1875, the series encompassed the XL No.4 in ·38 Short rimfire; XL no.5, apparently in ·38 Long rimfire; XL No.6 in ·38 centre-fire; and XL No.7 in ·41 rimfire.

CARTRIDGE REMINGTONS, 1868–88

Remington contracted with Smith & Wesson in February 1868 to convert ·44 cap-lock New Model Army revolvers to ·46 rimfire. These were subsequently despatched to Benjamin Kittredge & Company of Cincinnati (4,141 between 28 October 1868 and 1 April 1869), plus 400 to J.W. Storrs, 31 to M.W. Robinson & Company and a single example to Wexell & DeGress.

The guns were fitted with new five-round cylinders in Remington's Ilion factory, marked APRIL 3, 1855 in acknowledgement of the Rollin White patent, and shipped to Smith & Wesson for inspection. The first fifty were rejected, but these were followed by 4,524 guns that successfully passed their tests. Kittredge paid Smith & Wesson $3.36¼ per gun, a one-dollar royalty being deducted before the monies were passed to Remington. In time, the majority of the Kittredge guns went westward.

Remington made a ·38 centre-fire version of the old ·36 cap-lock New Model Navy Revolver until the demise of E. Remington & Sons, assembly ceasing in 1888. The gun was never widely distributed: its solid frame and single loading features were rooted too firmly in the tradition of its cap-lock precursors. Indeed, several of the original patterns were still being sold in 1888—an indication of the time it took for the metallic-cartridge guns to supplant the muzzle loaders in inaccessible districts of North America. Catalogues produced by E. Remington

& Sons in 1884 still offered the ·31 Rider and New Model pocket revolvers; plus the ·36 New Model Navy, Belt and Police revolvers. None of these were made in quantities that could challenge Colt and Smith & Wesson, and Remington's importance as a handgun maker steadily waned.

COMMERCIAL HOPKINS & ALLEN REVOLVERS, 1868–1915

Formed by S.S Hopkins, C.W. Hopkins and C.H. Allen in 1868, Hopkins & Allen began trading with cheap sheath-trigger guns disguised by names ranging from Acme to Universal.

Large numbers of revolvers were made for Merwin, Hulbert & Company (later Hulbert Brothers & Company), sporting goods dealers based in New York City from 1874-5; Hopkins & Allen-made, but Merwin & Hulbert marked revolvers were sold until Hulbert Brothers entered liquidation in 1896.

Solid-frame XL-series Suicide Specials (see above) were supplemented in the 1880s by the XL DA series, which had conventional triggers and trigger guards, folding-spur hammers and enlarged butts that offered a better grip. The XL No.3 DA was a five-shot 2½-inch barrelled gun chambering ·32 Short rimfire; XL No.6 DA was a similar six-shot ·32 and ·38 centre-fire weapon; and the XL Bulldog chambered ·32 or ·38 Merwin & Hulbert centre-fire ammunition.

The Forehand Model 1891 was made for Forehand & Wadsworth (q.v.) on the same machinery as the XL No.6 DA. Offered in hammer and hammerless forms, this five-shot ·32 or ·38 centre-fire revolver was a cheap solid-frame non-ejector. A safety catch on the back strap, preventing the hammer going to full-cock except when the trigger was pressed. The Acme, for Hulbert Brothers, duplicated the hammerless Forehand Model 1891.

The Automatic Model, dating from 1885, had a simultaneous ejector actuated when the barrel was tipped down. One praiseworthy feature of the gun was the effectual latch that locked the barrel/cylinder unit to the frame.

Hopkins & Allen reorganised in 1898 as the Hopkins & Allen Arms Company, surviving a disastrous fire in 1900 to acquire (in 1902) the assets of Forehand & Wadsworth—for whom Hopkins & Allen had been making revolvers under sub-contract.

The established H&A Automatic Model was replaced in 1907 by the Safety Police pattern, offered in ·22 rimfire, ·32 and ·38 centre-fire. This revolver shared the frame and ejection system of its predecessor, but its Triple Action Safety lock had been patented by John Murphy of Norwich, Connecticut, on 21 August 1906 (829,082).

The hammer was mounted on an eccentric pin. When the hammer was down, the pin raised the hammer tip to rest on an abutment in the frame. Pressing the trigger rotated the eccentric, changing the hammer-fall arc to strike the firing pin. The system was highly efficient, but production had hardly begun when the advent of lucrative military contracts in 1914 caused it to be abandoned. Finally, just before the USA entered the First World War, the Hopkins & Allen Arms Company was bought by Marlin, which had just become part of the Marlin-Rockwell Corporation.

THE FIRST CARTRIDGE COLTS, 1869–72

The purchase of the Rollin White patent of 1855 by Smith & Wesson, all but unnoticed by the other revolver makers, assumed paramount importance after the end of the Civil War. Though the patent supposedly expired in 1869, Smith & Wesson, through a series of appeals, managed to prolong its effect until 1872.

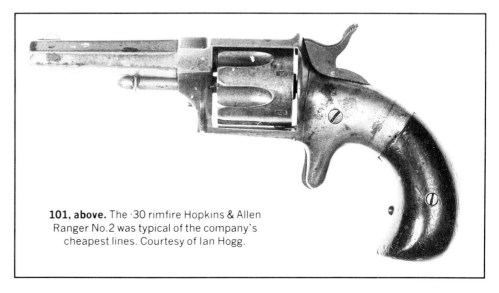

101, above. The ·30 rimfire Hopkins & Allen Ranger No.2 was typical of the company's cheapest lines. Courtesy of Ian Hogg.

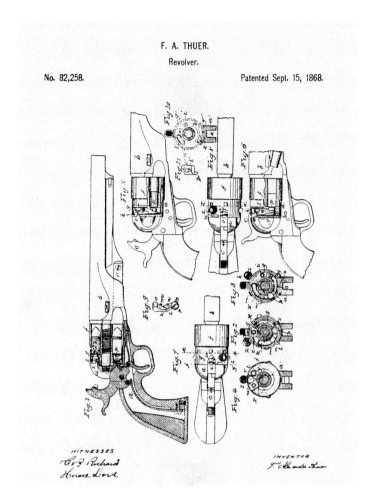

F. A. THUER.

Revolver.

No. 82,258.

Patented Sept. 15, 1868.

WITNESSES

INVENTOR

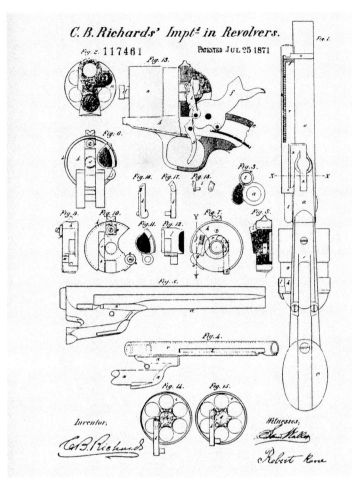

C. B. Richards' Impt. in Revolvers.

Fig. 2. 117461

PATENTED JUL 25 1871

Inventor,

Witnesses,

In November 1865, Brigadier General William Franklin, who had assumed the vice-presidency of Colt after the death of Elisha Root, attempted to purchase a license to the Rollin White patent. Negotiations continued until Smith & Wesson and Rollin White asked for $1·1 million and the project foundered. Franklin and his advisers calculated that this was too great an investment in a patent that had only three years to run.

The first successful Colt conversion system was patented by F. Alexander Thuer of Hartford, Connecticut, on 15 September 1868 (82,258). Marketed briefly in 1869–70, Thuer Transformation revolvers were converted from ·31 1849 Pocket, ·36 1851 Navy, ·44 1860 Army, ·36 1861 Navy, and ·36 1862 Police and Pocket (Navy) cap-locks. Production was apparently about five thousand, though no factory records were kept.

The standard cylinders were shortened or replaced to allow an auxiliary ring to be placed between the cylinder and the recoil shield. The chambers were bored completely through the cylinder, but were loaded from the front with unique tapered copper-case cartridges. The cartridges were fired by the nose of the original hammer striking a rebounding firing pin in the auxiliary ring. A thumb-piece on top of the unit allowed the Thuer guns to fire normally when turned to the right; rotated to the left, it allowed an ejecting arm in the auxiliary ring to expel either a spent case or a loaded cartridge each time the hammer was cocked and fired.

The ejector arm struck the side of the case head which—in theory at least—allowed a primed cartridge to be safely expelled. In practice, it carried more than a hint of danger.

Though the Thuer conversion could revert to cap-lock operation, requiring nothing other than a spare cylinder, it was comparatively ineffectual. Tested by the US Army in 1868–9, but unacceptable militarily, neither could it compete satisfactorily with the contemporary centre-fire Smith & Wessons. The Thuer system was abandoned in 1871.

About nine thousand examples of the Richards Transformation or "Colt's New Breech Loading Army Revolver" were built exclusively on 1860- or Army-pattern frames. Unlike the Thuer system, which was designed as an evasion of the Rollin White patent, Charles Richards used a conventional rimmed cartridge loaded from the rear. The Rollin White patent had expired and Colt could no longer be sued for infringement. Patented in the USA on 25 July 1871 (117,461), the system relied on a circular disc or 'Conversion Plate' inserted in the breech behind a shortened, but otherwise

102, above left. The drawings accompanying US Patent 82,258, granted to F. Alexander Thuer in 1868, show how the ·44 Colt Army Model was converted. Courtesy of the US Patent Office, Washington DC.

103, above right. The Thuer conversion was superseded by the Richards pattern, patented in July 1871. Note the new ejector case on the right side of the barrel. Courtesy of the US Patent Office, Washington DC.

standard cylinder. Unlike the Thuer disc, which could rotate laterally, the Richards pattern was held in place by the cylinder pin and a projection engaging the hammer channel. It contained a spring-loaded rebounding firing pin.

The original rammer of the cap-lock M1860 was replaced by an ejector case, attached to the right side of the barrel, while a pivoting gate—latched initially by an internal plunger and then by an external leaf spring—was incorporated in the conversion plate.

The conventionally loaded Richards system was much more effectual than the earlier Thuer evasion. It attracted sufficient US Army interest for the conversion of a thousand M1860 army revolvers to be approved by the Secretary of War in January 1871. On 21 April 1871, Brigadier General Alexander Dyer, the Chief of Ordnance, informed the officer commanding Springfield Armory that 1,153 revolvers had been sent to Colt from differing collection points and that 'with the fifty to which you were directed to apply the Locke Safety Notch [on] January 31st, 1871, will make 1203'.

Writing in 1873, William Franklin confirmed that 'Twelve hundred…[M1860 conversions] are now in service with the Cavalry, and we hear excellent reports from them'. Small numbers, apparently totalling 368, were subsequently converted on behalf of the US Navy in 1873–5. These included of 1851- and 1861-pattern ·36 navy cap-locks, which were altered to fire ·38 centre-fire cartridges.

The Richards-Mason Transformation was a variant of the Richards pattern with a better ejector patented by William Mason of Taunton, Massachusetts, on 2 July 1872 (128,644). The mouth of the ejector case lay nearer to the cylinder than the preceding Richards type. Mason-pattern guns also had an extended hammer nose instead of a rebounding hammer.

The use of newly forged barrels and the quantities involved—the production of Richards-Mason transformations is said to have exceeded thirty thousand guns—suggests that the Richards-Mason conversion was not simply a means of ridding the factory of old parts. The most important numerically was the ·38 version of the M1862 Police and Pocket Navy cap-locks, some 24,000 of which were made in a bewildering profusion of styles. In addition, similar conversions were undertaken elsewhere.

The first effectual cartridge revolver was an open-top ·44–23–200 rimfire embodying the classical Colt three-piece construction. Variously known as the New Model Army Revolver, 'New Model Holster Revolver', 'Model of 1872' or 'Open Top Frontier', it had a navy-style grip, a short cylinder with a roll-engraved maritime scene, and a cylindrical barrel with a flat-sided frame lug grooved to receive the Mason ejector case.

Only about seven thousand of the open-frame ·44 rimfire revolvers were made, variations being restricted to an occasional long or army-type grip, an eight-inch barrel instead of the standard 7½-inch variety, and brass (rather than iron) grip straps.

Most guns were sold in Mexico after the introduction of the perfected Model 1873 (q.v.). They are usually nickel plated and—much more rarely—have the ultra-ornate metal or ivory grips popular south of the Rio Grande.

THE MODEL NO.3 (AMERICAN) SMITH & WESSON, 1870–5

The first large-calibre Smith & Wesson revolver was the ·41 rimfire Model No.3, approximately fifty of which were made prior to the Paris exposition of 1867. The gun had a sheath trigger and a four-cartridge cylinder. It weighed only 17oz, but its weak construction attracted so much adverse comment in Europe that the project was abandoned.

The failure of the Model No.3 left Smith & Wesson without a large-calibre gun effectual enough to challenge the cap-lock Colts. With the White patent nearing the end of its life, Colt would clearly produce a revolver with a bored through cylinder as soon as practicable.

The first top-break Smith & Wesson revolver, with the hinge moved to the bottom front of the frame, appeared in 1868. A sturdy latch lay ahead of the hammer, while the new star plate extractor was attached to a hollow central tube containing a rack mechanism. This extracted spent cartridge cases when the barrel was depressed, allowing them to be shaken free. At the limit of the opening stroke, the extractor snapped back into place to allow the gun to be reloaded.

Mindful of problems that had arisen back in the days of the Massachusetts Arms Company, when a patent-infringement lawsuit brought by Colt had been so costly, Smith & Wesson's attorneys mounted a careful search of existing records. Early in 1869, therefore, the partners acquired rights to a simultaneous extraction system patented by William Dodge of Washington DC on 17 January ('cartridge retractor for many chambered firearm', 45,912) and 24 January 1865 (45,983); a ratchet integral with the extractor for rotating the cylinder, patented by Louis Rodier of Springfield, Massachusetts, on 11 July 1865 (48,775) and assigned to Samuel Morris; and a cylinder and barrel 'swinging away from the recoil shield', which had been patented by Abram Gibson of Worcester, Massachusetts, on 10 July 1860 (29,126) and assigned in part to Joseph Hale.

Acquiring these rights allowed Smith & Wesson to apply for a patent in the United Kingdom in April 1869, Letters Patent being granted to Robert Lake on 17 May 1869. A similar US patent, 94,003, was issued on 24 August 1869 to Charles King, Smith & Wesson's factory superintendent.

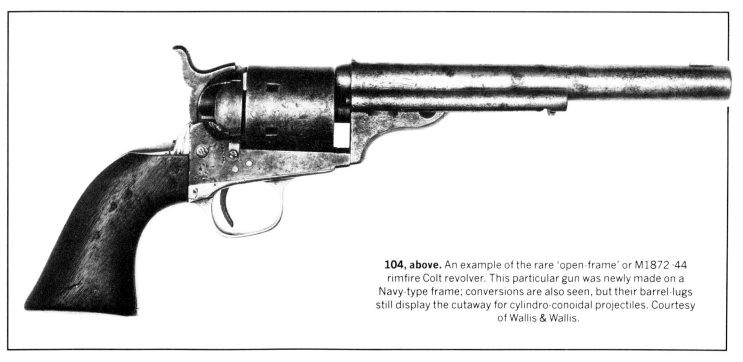

104, above. An example of the rare 'open-frame' or M1872 ·44 rimfire Colt revolver. This particular gun was newly made on a Navy-type frame; conversions are also seen, but their barrel-lugs still display the cutaway for cylindro-conoidal projectiles. Courtesy of Wallis & Wallis.

The first new Model No.3 revolver was despatched in May 1870 to a US Army Board of Officers convened in St Louis. The gun resembled the patent model, though a conventionally guarded trigger had been substituted for the original sheath pattern. Apart from recommending a change from rim- to centre-fire ammunition, the Board of Ordnance and Fortification considered the Smith & Wesson 'superior to any other…submitted'. A centre-fire cartridge was produced simply by adapting ·44 Henry rimfire to produce ·44/100.

The first US Army contract, signed on 28 December 1870, called for a thousand 'Model No.3 Army Revolvers', eight hundred to be blued and the remainder nickelled. The consignment was delivered in March 1871, the guns displaying a small 'U.S.' on the barrel rib and the mark of government inspector O.W. Ainsworth—a cursive 'OWA'—pressed into the left grip.

Smith & Wesson saw that considerable commercial potential lay in its new guns and shipped samples to its dealers in the summer of 1870; bulk shipments began late in the autumn.

The original Model No.3, known as the First Model No.3 American after the introduction of Russian-type guns, underwent many minor variations during the first years of its life. The most obvious change was the deletion of the oil hole in the extractor housing, in the region of gun number 1500. The revolvers were blued or nickel plated, and had barrels measuring six, seven or eight inches. Production continued after the acceptance of the Russian contract, described below, until the end of 1871. Smith & Wesson then saw the futility of making two separate ·44 revolver frames.

About 6,800 'American' guns had been made. Virtually all had chambered ·44 centre-fire cartridges, though two hundred were made in 1870 for ·44 Henry rimfire. These had a modified frame and hammer, but otherwise duplicated the centre-fire version.

The Second Model No.3 American replaced the First Model, about five hundred hybrid guns being made during the transition. These had eight-inch barrels, were offered in blue or nickel finishes, and numbered either in the Russian series (apparently 3200–3700) or interspersed with the first Second Model No.3 Americans.

The Second Model had, among other Russian-inspired revisions, a large-diameter trigger pin, a locking hammer and a revised barrel catch. Numbered from 6800 upward, these guns proved very popular in the West. The basic design was improved in the Spring of 1873, in the region of number 18000, when a modified lock was adopted. The new cylinder stop was actuated by the trigger rather than by the hammer as in the previous guns. A shoulder stock was an optional extra, locking into

grooves cut in the base of the butt; only 604 were made, compared with about 20,835 revolvers.

Second Model No.3 American Smith & Wesson revolvers were offered in blue or nickel finish, though some 'two-tone' guns were made. An eight-inch barrel was regarded as standard, though 5½, 6, 6¼, 6½ and 7in options were supplied on request. Some guns featured engraving of the highest order; others were plated with gold or silver. Chamberings were ·44/100 or ·44 Russian, though five hundred ·44 Henry rimfire guns supplied to Mexico in 1872 and an additional 3,014 rimfires were made for the commercial market. The earliest of these incorporated the original non-locking hammer. Rimfire ·44 revolvers were abandoned in 1874.

RUSSIAN MODEL SMITH & WESSONS, 1871–7

Shortly after the specimen gun had been sent to

the US Army, another was presented to General Aleksandr Gorlov. The Russian military attaché was supervising the acceptance of Colt-made Berdan rifles in the nearby Connecticut town of Hartford. After protracted negotiations, a modified revolver was accepted for the Russian army and an order for twenty thousand was signed on 1 May 1871. Deliveries of the original, first-pattern or 'Old Old Model' No.3 Russian revolver had commenced by Christmas 1871.

The Russians guns chambered a cartridge with a bullet that was appreciably smaller than

105, below. A ·44 Smith & Wesson 'New New Model' or Cavalry pattern, with a spurred finger-rest. Note the lanyard ring on the butt and the detachable side plate gaining access to the lock components. Courtesy of Ian Hogg.

106, bottom. A Russian Model Smith & Wesson copy made by Ludwig Loewe & Co. of Berlin in the late 1870s. Apart from markings, which are not visible in this view, it is practically impossible to tell the original and the copy apart. Courtesy of John Walter.

COLT'S PATENT HOUSE PISTOL

The Drawing gives the precise size of the Pistol.

PRICE $9.

This is a Breech Loading Revolving Pistol, four chambered, .41 Calibre, Weight 14 1-2 oz., Weight of ball 138 grains or 82 to the pound.

It carries a heavier ball in proportion to its weight than any other Revolver in the market, and is particularly adapted for house defence against burglars, or for the pocket. Care should be taken when the Pistol is not in use, or is carried in the pocket, to allow the hammer to rest *between the chambers.* By this arrangement the Pistol is made very compact.

COLT'S,
BREECH LOADING,
SEVEN SHOT REVOLVING PISTOL.

The Drawing gives the precise size of the Pistol.

PRICE $8.

.22 Calibre, Weight 8 oz., Weight of ball 27 grains or 260 to the pound. Can be used with Long and Short No. 22 Cartridges.

107, left. A page from Colt's 1872 catalogue showing the ·41 'Cloverleaf' and seven-shot ·22 rimfire revolvers.

Author's collection.

the case mouth. Consequently, each cartridge chamber had to be 'stepped' rather than merely bored straight through. An unexpected benefit of the change to the ·44 Russian cartridge, which contained 23–24 grains of powder and a 244-grain lead bullet, was a substantial increase in muzzle velocity and a marked improvement in accuracy. In addition, the Russians requested a larger trigger pin; a larger cylinder retainer; a limiting tooth in the extractor gear; a hammer that locked the frame shut when down; a firing-pin bush to protect the recoil shield when firing; and a more durable front sight.

Not all these changes were made immediately. The first three thousand revolvers, for example, were accepted with the old-style (small) trigger pin. About five hundred revolvers were rejected at inspection, salvaged, given replacement ·44/100 cylinders, and sold on the North American commercial market. The Cyrillic barrel-mark was ground away and replaced by the standard company inscription, but the weapons can be identified by the presence of

full serial numbers in several places. About 4,655 genuine commercial first-pattern Russian No.3 were numbered in the same range as the Second Model No.3 American. They were identical with the Russian military weapons, but had commercial-style serial numbers and the barrel-rib inscription showed no signs of refinishing. They were supplied in blue or nickel finish, had optional lanyard rings and—from March 1873—could be fitted with a shoulder stock. Barrel lengths varied from five to eight inches.

The grip of the second-pattern No.3 Russian revolver, subsequently known as the 'Old Model', was modified to prevent recoil shifting the muzzle upward in the hand; a prominent prawl or knuckle appeared on the frame behind the hammer. The hammer thumb-piece was enlarged and the barrel pivot modified to eliminate the barrel-pivot locking screw. The cylinder stop was actuated by the trigger, instead of by the hammer, and the barrel length was reduced from eight inches to seven. The

base of the butt was narrowed and rounded, and a distinctive spurred finger rest was added to the trigger-guard bow.

Though Smith & Wesson heartily disapproved the appearance of the modified revolver, it was adopted by the Russian government in December 1872. A contract dated 15 January 1873 requested 20,000 guns at a cost of $15·33 apiece; on 15 December 1873, after all but the last consignments of the January order had been shipped, the Russian authorities ordered an additional twenty thousand. Other contracts followed until May 1877, production of second pattern No.3 Russian revolvers for the Tsar's forces amounting to about 70,000. All displayed the Cyrillic barrel-top legend, amended in later orders to include the gun serial number.

Second-pattern No.3 Russian-pattern guns were popular in Japan and Turkey. The Turks ordered a thousand ·44 Henry rimfire guns on 12 August 1874, then ordered 7,000 additional weapons in panic during the Russo–Turkish War. About 6,200 commercial second or Old Model No.3 Russian Smith & Wessons were numbered from 32,800 upward. These had standard barrel inscriptions, with the additional RUSSIAN MODEL. Large quantities were bought by Schuyler, Hartley & Graham of New York City and marked with 'SH' in a diamond.

Continued development led to the third pattern or New Model No.3 Russian revolver, adopted in the autumn of 1874. A contract for 11,138 of these Cavalry Model guns was signed on 27 October 1874, the preceding second pattern thereafter being designated 'Infantry' in Russian service.

The cavalry revolver was the final variation to be ordered from Smith & Wesson. Its most obvious characteristics were a new spring loaded extractor catch, which pivoted out of gear to return the extractor to its closed position; a shorter extractor housing; and an improved extractor-gear train. The return spring lay inside the extractor, and the screw retaining the extractor return-spring rod was replaced by a catch. The changes allowed the cylinder to be removed without tools, which was a significant advance.

The subject of a patent granted to Daniel Wesson on 19 January 1875 (158,874), New Model No.3 Russian revolvers had 6½-inch barrels carrying integrally forged front sights. Contracts for ten thousand guns apiece were signed in October 1876, January 1877 and May 1877, but these were the last of the lucrative Russian orders. After the last contract had been completed, the Russians ordered 75,000 copies of the New Model Russian revolvers from Ludwig Loewe & Company of Berlin.

Ultimately, after a duplicate production line had been created, the Russians began making guns in the Tula arsenal.

COLT POCKET REVOLVERS, 1871–93

In addition to single-shot derringers (q.v.), Colt also marketed ·22 'Open-top' and ·41 rim fire four-shot Patent House Pistols, the first Colt to be specifically designed for metal-case ammunition, was a curious-looking design. Offered with barrels of 1½ or 3in, it is now known as the 'Cloverleaf' owing to the strange shape of its cylinder.

One of the most interesting features of the revolver, patented by Charles Richards on 19 September 1871 (US 119,048), was the counter-bored chambers. These enveloped the case rims in a way that has since been regularly hailed as an innovation. The ejector rod was contained within the cylinder axis pin, and the cylinder could be turned through 45° to allow the nose of the firing pin to enter a small hole cut between the chambers.

Owing to the narrowness of the frame, the cartridges could fall out of the two side chambers when the gun was being fired. This was prevented by a detachable side plate on the left side of the gun, and by a lug on a collar held in the frame by the cylinder pin.

Frames were bronze, often camouflaged by silver or nickel plating, and the triggers were sheathed. The hammers originally had a high spur, but a lower version was substituted after about 1874. Several non-standard variants were produced, generally with short barrels.

Towards the end of production, a modified pattern with a conventional five-shot cylinder appeared in answer to criticism. The ejector rods were omitted, 2·63-inch barrels were standard, and a tiny bead-type front sight appeared immediately above the muzzle.

The Open-Top and Cloverleaf revolvers were replaced after 1873 by "Colt's New Breech Loading Revolvers", subsequently advertised as the New Line. There were five major variants, each differing in chambering and frame size. The cylinder-locking bolt and loading gate were the subject of a patent issued to William Mason in September 1874. These were added progressively to the basic New Line design.

The ·22 version was followed, in ascending order of size, by ·30, ·32, ·38 and ·41, The three largest calibres were available in rim- or centre fire, the smaller weapons being rimfire only. Excepting the seven-shot ·22 pattern, all New Line guns had five-cartridge cylinders. A few weapons had non-standard loading gates on the right rear of the frame behind the cylinder.

A major change in the mechanism was made in 1876, when the slots on the cylinder periphery were moved to the rear face. The New Line guns all had solid frames, sheath triggers and bird's head butts. Excepting the smallest gun, which was made of bronze, frames were iron. The barrels, made without ejectors, usually measured 2¼in; however, a few ·30-calibre examples had 1·75-inch barrels while ·38 and ·41 examples could be found with four-inch barrels. Grips could be walnut, rosewood, gutta-percha, ivory or mother of pearl.

The ·22 rimfire was known as the 'Little Colt', the ·30 as the 'Pony Colt', the ·32 as the 'Lady Colt', the ·38 as the 'Pet Colt' and the ·41 as the 'Big Colt'. The names were bestowed by Kittredge & Company of Cincinnati.

The five-shot New House Pistol, announced in 1880, was a variation of the New Line with a long-flute cylinder, locking notches on the rear face of the cylinder, a lateral cylinder-pin lock, and a loading gate on the right side of the frame behind the cylinder. Offered in ·38 and ·41 centre-fire, with the standard 2¼-inch barrel, it was characterized by a squared butt heel. Grips were walnut, rosewood, or chequered gutta percha with COLT moulded into the neck.

The ·38 centre-fire New Police Pistol of 1882 was a variant New Line gun with a barrel ranging from a scarce ejectorless 2¼-inch pattern up to a six-inch version with a Lightning ejector case. Owing to the design moulded into the gutta-percha grips, the New Police revolver is often known as the 'Cop-and-Thug' model. This nickname was never official.

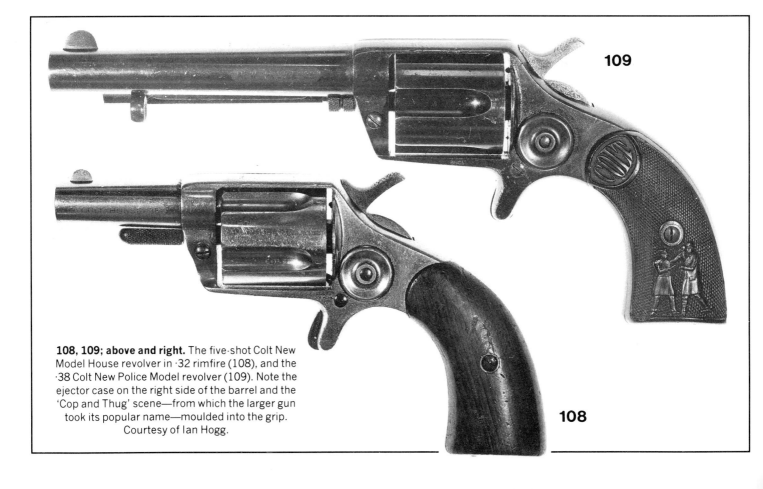

108, 109; above and right. The five-shot Colt New Model House revolver in ·32 rimfire (108), and the ·38 Colt New Police Model revolver (109). Note the ejector case on the right side of the barrel and the 'Cop and Thug' scene—from which the larger gun took its popular name—moulded into the grip. Courtesy of Ian Hogg.

IVER JOHNSON REVOLVERS, 1871–1917

Norwegian-born gunsmith Iver Johnson arrived in Worcester, Massachusetts, during the Civil War and eventually set himself up in a small workshop at 244 Main Street. In 1871, in partnership with Martin Bye, he formed Johnson & Bye to make revolvers.

The earliest identifiable guns were the Favorite and Tycoon, introduced c. 1873. These were cheap single action sheath-trigger revolvers with octagonal barrels, offered in calibres ranging from ·22 to ·44. They were soon joined by the Encore and Favorite Navy, which had plain cylindrical barrels. The 1875-vintage ·22, ·32, ·38 and ·41 rimfire Smokers, similar to their predecessors, had fluted cylinders and a 'Russian Handle'.

The contemporary sheath trigger ·22 rimfire, ·32 or ·38 Defender had an octagonal barrel, a 'Saw Handle' and a partially fluted cylinder (the fully fluted cylinders were optional in ·38 only).

The Old Hickory series, introduced in 1877, included solid-frame double action revolvers with conventional trigger guards as well as single-action sheath-trigger patterns. The double-action guns were made as seven-shot ·22 Long or six-shot ·32 Long rimfires, with 2½ or 4½-inch barrels, nickel plating and rubber grips. The sheath-trigger guns included a five-shot ·32 Long centre-fire version, generally encountered with a round barrel and a rubber gripped saw handle. However, fully-fluted cylinders, octagonal barrels, and grips of pearl or ivory could be obtained. The standard guns cost between $35–60 *per dozen* in 1881.

In 1879, Johnson & Bye began identifying their guns with their own name. The first new gun to be affected was the Eagle, a double-action ·38 centre-fire six-shot solid-frame revolver with a three-inch barrel. This was joined in 1881 by the British Bull Dog, a rarely-encountered double-action pattern, and then a year later by the American Bull Dog. The latter was another double-action design, with a five-round cylinder, an octagonal barrel and nickel plating. It could be obtained in ·32 and ·38, rim- or centre-fire.

Iver Johnson & Company was created in 1883, becoming 'Iver Johnson Arms & Cycle Works' within a year. The Model 1879 revolver, despite its designation, appeared on the market at about this time. Initially chambered only for ·38 Smith & Wesson cartridges, it was the first American-made double-action revolver with a laterally swinging cylinder. The action was protected by patents issued to Andrew Hyde of Hatfield, Massachusetts, on 4 November 1879 (221,171) and 6 March 1883 (273,282). Unfortunately, it was expensive for an Iver

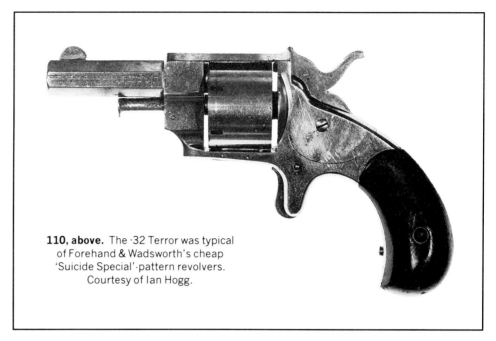

110, above. The ·32 Terror was typical of Forehand & Wadsworth's cheap 'Suicide Special'-pattern revolvers. Courtesy of Ian Hogg.

Johnson product and failed to find substantial enough markets to remain in production for more than a few years.

The Boston Bull Dog, introduced in 1887 in ·22 rimfire, ·32 and ·38 centre-fire, was a minor adaption of the double-action American Bull Dog of 1882. The Improved Defender of 1889 was a single-action solid-frame gate loader, almost always displaying DEFENDER 89 on the top strap above the cylinder. The Swift was the last revolver to be introduced before Iver Johnson moved to Fitchburg, Massachusetts, in 1891. It was a double-action ·38 centre-fire pattern, made in hammer and hammerless versions.

The first of the 'Hammer-the-Hammer' guns appeared in 1892–3, though the catchy slogan was not used until c.1904. The safety system relied on a spacer between the hammer and the firing pin to transmit a blow only when the trigger was deliberately pulled. It was so effectual that the hammer could be struck in perfect safety. Introduced in ·32 and ·38 centre fire, the revolver was joined by a Safety Hammerless Model in 1894.

The Model 1900 was a solid-frame double action revolver with a 4½- or six-inch octagonal barrel, available in ·22 and ·32 Short rimfire and ·32 centre-fire. The Cycle of 1901 was another of the special safety designs—hammer or hammerless—originally made only in ·32 with a two-inch barrel, but subsequently also in ·22 rimfire and ·38 centre-fire.

A refined Hammer-the-Hammer mechanism was introduced in 1908. Coil springs replaced leaf patterns, the main spring had an adjustable tension bar, and a ball-and-socket joint connected the mainspring plunger to the hammer. Together with other improvements in

the action, Iver Johnson had managed to produce a most effectual revolver. Chambered for ·32 Short or ·38 Short centre-fire cartridges, with barrels of 4–6in, the safety guns were unbelievably successful: by 1910, when a ·22 rimfire version appeared, Iver Johnson was making more revolvers than all the leading American manufacturers added together.

1910 also saw the introduction of the U.S. Double Action, a simplified variant of the standard Iver Johnson revolvers without the safety mechanism. Hammer models in ·22 rimfire, ·32 Short and ·38 Short centre-fire were sold alongside hammerless ·32 and ·38 models, all being marked as products of the imaginary 'U.S. Revolver Company'.

FOREHAND & WADSWORTH REVOLVERS, 1872–1902

Sullivan Forehand and Henry Wadsworth joined Allen & Wheelock in the 1850s. When Wheelock died in 1863, business passed to Ethan Allen—Forehand's and Wadsworth's father-in-law. Ethan Allen & Company made ·22 rimfire single-shot 'Allen' target pistols in a factory adjoining South Worcester railway station until production of cheap solid-frame revolvers began.

Ethan Allen died in 1871, allowing Forehand & Wadsworth to be incorporated in 1872. Its first products were solid frame five-shot pocket revolvers, chambered for ·32 or ·38 rim or centre-fire cartridges. Patented on 24 July 1877 (193,367) to protect the detachable side plate, these guns had round barrels. Octagonal barrels appeared only in Forehand Arms Company days.

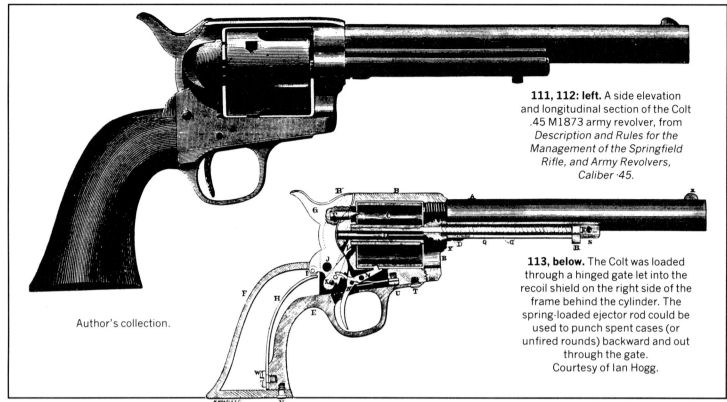

Author's collection.

111, 112: left. A side elevation and longitudinal section of the Colt .45 M1873 army revolver, from *Description and Rules for the Management of the Springfield Rifle, and Army Revolvers, Caliber ·45.*

113, below. The Colt was loaded through a hinged gate let into the recoil shield on the right side of the frame behind the cylinder. The spring-loaded ejector rod could be used to punch spent cases (or unfired rounds) backward and out through the gate. Courtesy of Ian Hogg.

A ·32 Russian Model was made to capitalise on the esteem in which the Smith & Wesson Russian Model was held. Nothing more than a small-calibre sheath-trigger Bulldog (q.v.), it was sold with a rounded butt, bone grips and a 2½-inch barrel. Most surviving specimens are lightly engraved.

The Forehand & Wadsworth Bulldog was marketed from 1877 as the British Bull Dog, Swamp Angel, or Terror. It was originally a ·38 five-shot single-action solid frame pocket revolver with a hexagonal barrel and a sheath trigger. Based on patents granted to Ethan Allen in October 1861 (33,509) and Forehand & Wadsworth in April 1875 (162,162), it cost $4·75 in 1881.

Later Bulldogs were ·44 calibre five-shot revolvers with longer butts, trigger guards and double-action lock work. Many appear to have been made for Hopkins & Allen (see above). The final version was a ·38 gate-loading hand ejector, with a bird's head butt and the legend BRITISH BULL DOG on the top strap above the cylinder.

The ·44 Forehand & Wadsworth Russian Model was a large six-shot single-action gun marketed briefly from 1877. It had a solid frame, a loading gate, and a spring-loaded ejector rod beneath the barrel. It weighed about 40oz and measured 13½in overall.

Sullivan Forehand and Henry Wadsworth died in 1898 and 1892 respectively. Manufacturing activities had gradually reduced in the 1880s, revolvers being purchased from Hopkins &

Allen. Finally, in 1902, the Forehand Arms Company was acquired by Hopkins & Allen and the once-famous name disappeared.

SOLID-FRAME ARMY COLTS, 1873–1902

The open-top frame of the New Model Army Revolver was weak, even by the standards of the day. The improved Single Action Army Model, 'Peacemaker', 'Model P' or 'Model 1873' was its successor. Though technically inferior to the contemporary Smith & Wesson Russian Model, the Colt was simpler, stronger and virtually impossible to wreck.

The Peacemaker appears to have been the work of William Mason, who astutely combined traditional Colt features—most importantly, the single-action lock—with a new solid-top frame suited to the increasing power of handgun ammunition.

In 1873, after protracted trials, the US Army adopted the new Colt as the Model of 1873. Captain John Eadie, President of the Board of Officers, reported that he had 'no hesitation in declaring the Colt revolver superior in most respects, and much better adapted to the wants of the Army than the Smith & Wesson'. Subsequently, however, only 37,063 guns were acquired by the army in 1873–91. Fewer still were issued.

Army-issue weapons had 7½-inch barrels marked COLT'S PAT. F.A. MFG. CO. HARTFORD CT.

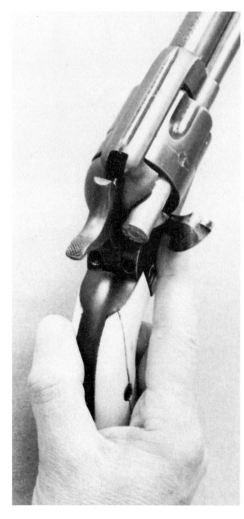

U.S.A., chambered ·45 Long Colt cartridges and displayed 'U.S.' on the left side of the frame behind the acknowledgement of US patents issued to Charles Richards on 19 September 1871 (119,048); to William Mason on 2 July 1872 (128,644); and—eventually—another granted to Mason on 19 January 1875 (158,957).

Patent marks took differing forms, depending on age, being joined on commercial guns by a rampant colt motif. Inspectors' marks were to be found on the left grip, often accompanied by the date of inspection (e.g., '1880' above 'DAL' in a cartouche on gun 55407). Among the inspectors were Rinaldo Carr (RAC), Daniel Clark (DFC), Frank Hosmer (H) and David Lyle (DAL).

In 1902, the US Army ordered 4,600 of the so-called Alaskan Model of the Double Action Army & Frontier revolver, with special deep trigger guards to allow either two fingers or a thickly gloved finger to be used. They were probably acquired while a new ·45-calibre handgun was developed; the enlarged trigger guard arose simply because cavalrymen saw duty in some very cold areas—northerly states such as Oregon or Alaska, for example. The ·45 revolvers are best known as the Model of 1902. They had walnut grips, lanyard rings on the butt heel, inspector's marks applied by Rinaldo Carr ('RAC') and 'U.S.' property markings.

COMMERCIAL COLT PEACEMAKERS, 1873–1917

The Colt Single Action Army Revolver was very popular commercially, though the notion that it was touted by every outlaw, lawman and frontiersman is far from the truth.

In the truly lawless days of the West, the Colt was simply one of many cap lock or cartridge guns on offer. The myth of its supremacy is attributable to Hollywood's love affair with the Colt revolver and Winchester lever-action rifle.

A combination of blued and case-hardened parts was standard, grips were walnut, and the back sight was a groove milled longitudinally in the frame-top. The length of ejector-case barrels varied between 4·75 and 16in, while those lacking ejectors ranged from two to 7·5in. Gutta-percha, ivory or mother of pearl grips were to be found, while decoration ranged from the most elegant damascening to pure vulgarity.

Few Colts were as attractive as the eighteen Single Action Army Models made as part of a 300-gun panoply for the 1876 Philadephia Centennial Exposition. These were engraved with scroll work, featured gold and silver plating, and had plain ivory grips. One of them, no. 11088, made in 1874, served as the company exhibition gun until sold in 1894.

Theodore Roosevelt owned two specially decorated ·44–40 Single Action Army revolvers. Gun no. 92248 was supplied by Colt to Hartley & Graham in May 1883 and sent to the celebrated engraver L.D. Nimschke. A 'TR' monogram was carved in high relief on the left grip, a bison's head appearing on the right; both grip-plates were made of ivory. The monogram was repeated on the left side of the recoil shield, and the gun was lightly scroll engraved overall. The other Colt, no. 92267, shipped in June 1883, was completed as a near-duplicate; however, the ivory grips bore only a facsimile of Roosevelt's signature on the right.

114, below. A 5½-inch barrelled M1873 Colt revolver, with the original screw-retained cylinder axis pin. The screw head is just visible on the angled front surface of the frame beneath the ribbed axis-pin head. Most army guns originally had seven-inch barrels, but many were shortened for issue to the artillery when the ·38 M1892 revolver appeared. Courtesy of Ian Hogg.

115, bottom. The Younger brothers were among the more notorious exponents of the Colt Peacemaker. This photograph of (left to right) Jim, Cole and Bob Younger with their sister was taken some time after the raid on Northfield, Illinois, in which the three desperadoes were captured. Author's collection.

Among the horrors was a gun used by Jack Sinclair, Bandmaster in Buffalo Bill's Wild West Show. Embossed plates on the grips encircled the barrel, the cylinder was gold plated over scroll work, while the silver-plated frame was engraved with shapeless flower-and-leaf motifs—the centre of each flower-head being a small jewel. The 'weapon' was apparently used as a baton, firing blanks to mark time.

Surprisingly few mechanical changes have been made in the M1873 action. A few rimfire guns were made from 1875, numbered in a separate sequence. With a mere handful of exceptions, they chambered ·44 Henry; total production amounted to less than two thousand, substantial numbers of which were sold in Mexico.

Minor variations were to be found in the design of the ejector assembly, the ejector rod and the ejector-rod head. The most obvious external change concerned the cylinder-pin retainer, originally a pointed screw running diagonally up under the pin. On 15 September 1874, William Mason patented an improved pin retainer embodying a transverse bolt locked by a spring. This was added to the Single Action Army Model at the end of 1893, in the region of no. 153000, and added gradually until incorporated in all guns numbered above 165000 (1896).

In addition to a minor target-shooting 'Flat Top' derivative (c.1888–95), which had a special open back sight on a raised strap above the cylinder, Colt made a target version known as the Bisley (1894–1915) with barrels of 4·75–7·5in. The grip was moved upward to bring the axis of the barrel nearer the hand, enabling the sights to be brought back onto the target after each shot with minimal trouble.

Bisley guns—occasionally made with flat-top frames—also had a special hammer with a lower spur. This enabled the sights to be seen; on the normal Single Action Army revolvers, other than the Flat Tops, the tip of the hammer served as the back sight.

The short-barrel ejectorless gun, often known as the Sheriff's or Bartender's Model, was introduced in the early 1880s. Widely favoured for personal defence, on both sides of the law, these Single Action Army revolvers usually had barrels of 3–4in.

The 'Buntline Special' was largely created by myth. No trace has been found of an order for five special long-barrel revolvers placed by Edward Judson, a write of pulp fiction and a dubious biography of Wyatt Earp under the pseudonym 'Ned Buntline'. These guns were allegedly presented early in the twentieth century to leading lawmen: Bat Masterson, Earp, Charlie Bassett, Neal Brown and Bill Tilghman. A few long-barrel Single Action Army revolvers had been made shortly after the 1876 Philadelphia Centennial Exposition, but they were considered as light carbines or 'Buggy Rifles' and had skeletal wire stocks.

Peacemaker chamberings varied from tiny ·22 Short to huge ·476 Eley. The *Single Action Army Model* (total production 310,386 in 1873–1940) was most commonly encountered in ·45 Long Colt (150,683) and ·44–40

(64,489); the rare *Flat Top Target Model* (914, c.1888–95) in ·38 Colt (122) and ·45 Long Colt (100); the standard *Bisley* (44,350, 1894–1915) in ·32–20 (13,291) and ·38–40 (12,163); and the rare flat-top *Bisley Target* (976, c.1894–7) in ·455 Eley (196) and ·32–20 (131).

Among the most popular chamberings were ·32–20, ·38–40 and ·44–40 Winchester, allowing purchasers, including many Westerners, to have an identically-chambered rifle and revolver. This was paramount where communications were very poor. By the time production ceased in 1940, approximately 357,859 revolvers had been made; serial numbers had reached about 335500 by April 1917.

Some commercial guns chambering ·44–40 were marked COLT FRONTIER SIX-SHOOTER; others bore the address of the London sales office, 14 Pall Mall.

REMINGTON POCKET REVOLVERS, 1873–88

Like Colt, Remington introduced a series of New Line cartridge revolvers in the 1870s. They embodied a lock patented by William Smoot on 21 October 1873 (143,855); solid frames, sheath triggers and bird's head butts were standard.

The New Line No.1 of 1873 chambered ·30 Short rimfire cartridges and offered a five-round cylinder. The barrel was octagonal, 2·8in long, and had an ejector rod on the right side of the frame web. The rarely encountered New Line

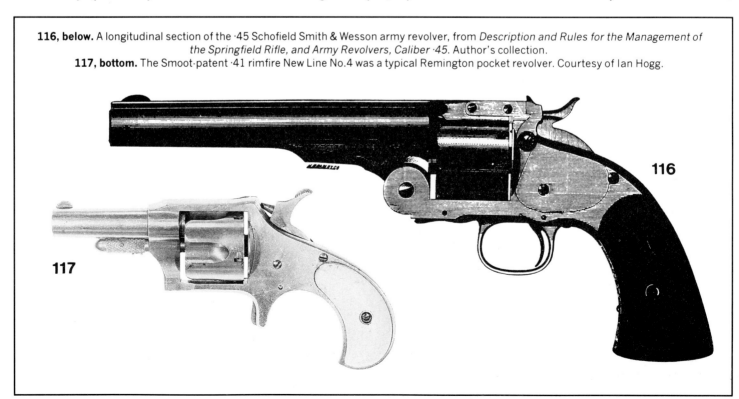

116, below. A longitudinal section of the ·45 Schofield Smith & Wesson army revolver, from *Description and Rules for the Management of the Springfield Rifle, and Army Revolvers, Caliber ·45.* Author's collection.
117, bottom. The Smoot-patent ·41 rimfire New Line No.4 was a typical Remington pocket revolver. Courtesy of Ian Hogg.

No.2 was identical, excepting that it chambered ·32 Short rimfire. The 1875-vintage five-shot New Line No.3 resembled No.1 and No.2, but fired ·38 Short rimfire cartridges. It had a sizable 3¼-inch octagonal barrel—out of proportion with the comparatively small grip—and weighed about 15oz. The 1877-vintage No.4 chambered ·38 Short centre-fire cartridges and had a 2½-inch round barrel. Unlike the other guns in the series, it lacked an ejector rod; the elongated cylinder axis pin was used to punch spent cases out of the detached cylinder.

The seven-shot ·22 rimfire Iroquois was similar to the No.4, though much more lightly built. It weighed a mere 7½oz: half as much as the ·38.

About 100,000 Smoot-type revolvers were made from 1873 until the demise of E. Remington & Sons in 1886, more than half the total being rimfire Iroquois.

SCHOFIELD SMITH & WESSONS, 1873–82

Though the Peacemaker had beaten its rivals in the US Army trials of 1872–3, including several guns submitted by Smith & Wesson, the appearance of a gun modified by Major George Schofield of the 10th Cavalry presented a serious threat. Patented on 20 June 1871 (116,225) and 22 April 1873 (138,047), the Schofield Smith & Wesson had a simplified extractor and a latch on the standing frame instead of the barrel extension. The changes were aimed specifically at cavalrymen. There were two models, as alterations were made to the locking latch assembly after production began.

After a trial in which the Schofield revolver was declared equal or superior to all its rivals, including the Colt, the army ordered three thousand as the Model of 1875. However, respondents who considered the Schofield superior technically were countered by others who considered the Colt simpler and more durable. Supporters of Colt may have gained an upper hand had not Schofield's brother been a general.

By the end of 1879, purchases amounted to 8,285 Schofield Smith & Wessons compared with 20,073 Model 1873 Colts.

Disaster at the Battle of the Little Big Horn led to claims that, as S&W Schofields were easily loaded, the outcome of the battle could have been different had cavalrymen been issued with them. One test showed that an experienced cavalryman could reload the Schofield in less than thirty seconds even at a gallop, while the Colt took a minute of undivided concentration.

Unfortunately, the Schofield Model S&W chambered a special short cartridge generating less power than the ·45 Long Colt. Colt revolvers would fire both rounds, whereas the S&W could not. Problems arose as soon as Colt cartridges were issued to Schofield-armed units, forcing the army to standardise the Model P. The Schofield was abandoned.

By a quirk of fate, the inventor took his life with one of his own revolvers in 1882.

HARRINGTON & RICHARDSON REVOLVERS, 1874–1917

Gilbert Harrington had been employed prior to 1870 by Ballard & Fairbanks, manufacturers of rifles, single-shot pistols and pocket revolvers, but had then joined his uncle Franklin Wesson.

William Richardson—another former Ballard & Fairbanks man—was enticed to become the factory superintendent, until Harrington bought his uncle's share of the business and formed Harrington & Richardson in 1874. The original ejector revolver soon found a niche, selling well enough for Harrington & Richardson to begin a steady expansion. The little gun was finally discontinued in 1878.

By 1876, a revolver with a removable cylinder axis pin had appeared; it was extremely simple and easily made. The first double-action gun was introduced in 1878 and, by 1908, three million revolvers bearing the Harrington & Richardson trademarks had been made.

Introduced c.1897, H&R's Automatic Ejecting Model—a break-open pattern resembling the contemporary Smith & Wessons—was made as a five-shot ·38 or a six-shot ·32. Guns were offered with barrels measuring 2½–6in and blue or nickel-plate finish. The grips were moulded gutta-percha, bearing the H&R pierced target trademark registered in 1889.

The otherwise identical Police Automatic had a spurless hammer patented by Homer Caldwell of Worcester, Massachusetts, on 4 October 1887 (370,926). It was possible to thumb-cock these guns, but only after the trigger had been pulled to raise the hammer to half-cock. H&R also made a truly hammerless gun in two forms: a small-frame five-shot ·32 weighing a mere 13oz, with barrels ranging from three to 6in, and a larger gun (offered as a six-shot ·32 or a five shot ·38) with barrels of 2½–6in.

The ·22 or ·32 Premier double-action revolver was another break-open pattern, locked by a latch at the rear of the back strap. Finished in nickel or blue, with a choice of 3–6in barrels, it weighed a mere 12oz. The Police Premier was essentially similar, but made with a spurless 'Safety Hammer'. The Bicycle Revolver—a seven-shot ·22 or a five-shot ·32—was made with a two-inch barrel, though otherwise following the standard H&R double-action simultaneous ejecting pattern. The Police Bicycle Model simply had a spurless hammer.

One of the stranger variants of the ·32 or ·38 Automatic Ejecting Model even had a folding knife blade beneath its four-inch barrel.

The American double-action revolver had a solid frame and a pivoting loading gate behind the cylinder. Offered in ·32 (six shots), ·38 and ·44 (five shots each), the guns were sold in blue or nickel with barrels of 2½–6in. The 'Safety Hammer American' had a spurless hammer, while the ·22 or ·32 rimfire Young America (with an optional Safety Hammer) was another similar gun with barrels of 2–6in.

Vest Pocket revolvers had spurless hammers and ultra-short barrels of 1·13 or 2in. They weighed merely 8–9oz depending on barrel length.

Other guns available in 1908 included the Young America Bulldog, a five-shot ·32 with a two-inch barrel; the H&R Bulldog, a compact double action pattern with a 2½-inch barrel

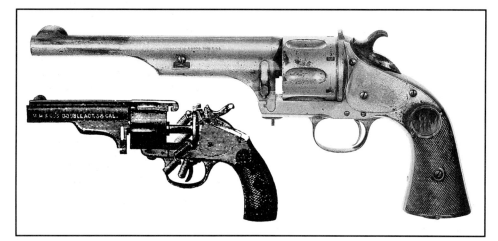

119, left. The ·45 Model 1875 Remington was offered to the US Army, but did not have sufficient merit to displace the Colt. The web under the barrel is most distinctive. Courtesy of Ian Hogg.

120, below left. The 1877-model Merwin & Hulbert revolver, made by Hopkins & Allen, featured a simultaneous ejector operated by unlatching the barrel and then drawing the cylinder forward. Though effectual enough, the gun had a comparatively weak open frame. Courtesy of Ian Hogg.

chambering ·32 (six shots) or ·38 (five); and three similar-looking models introduced in 1904–6. Generally made with barrels ranging from 2½ to 6in, these were apparently chambered for ·32 or ·38 (M1904), ·32 (M1905) and ·22 rimfire (M1906).

MILITARY REMINGTONS, 1875–90

The Model 1875 revolver, chambered for ·44 Remington centre-fire, ·44–40 or ·45 Colt, was another of the many guns developed in the hope of attracting US Army orders. It was offered to the government twice during the mid 1870s, but the authorities retained the Colt as the Remington had little extra to offer.

The M1875 had a 7½-inch round barrel and weighed 44oz. It was blued or nickel plated, except for colour case-hardening on the hammer and loading gate, and had oil-finished walnut grips. Decorative examples with ivory or mother of pearl grips were made to order.

The revolver resembled an amalgam of the Remington ·44 New Model Army cap-lock and the 1873-pattern Colt. It had a prominent web beneath the barrel and a lanyard ring on the butt. About 25,000 were made from 1875 until the demise of E. Remington & Sons in 1886. The M1875 was followed by the improved

Model 1890, differing principally in the removal of the under-barrel web. Indeed, the 'new gun' may simply have been a way of ridding the newly formed Remington Arms Company of many 1875-pattern components. The M1890 also underwent military trials, emerging most favourably, but gate loading was being challenged by the swinging cylinder; assembly ceased in 1894 after little more than two thousand had been made.

MERWIN & HULBERT REVOLVERS, 1876–96

Hopkins & Allen's solitary contribution to the large-calibre military revolver market was the Model 1877, based on patents granted to Benjamin Williams of New York in April 1874 (150,120); Daniel Moore in December 1874 (157,860, assigned to Merwin, Hulbert & Co.); and William Hulbert of Brooklyn, New York, in March 1877 (187,975).

The guns were marketed exclusively by Merwin, Hulbert & Company and then their successors, Hulbert Brothers & Company, sporting-goods distributors of New York City.

The revolver barrel, integral with the upper part of the frame, was attached to the standing breech by the cylinder axis pin and a lock on

the frame ahead of the trigger guard. When the catch was released, the barrel could be swung laterally and drawn forward. This pulled the cylinder forward until a star-plate extractor, attached to the breech, pulled spent cases (but not unfired rounds) out of the cylinder until they fell clear. A sliding gate on the right side of the frame beneath the hammer permitted reloading.

A ·44 centre-fire gun with a seven-inch barrel was tried by the US Army in 1877, but the comparatively weak open frame was unfit for service—though small quantities were bought by Kansas. Merwin & Hulbert military revolvers are scarce. Most of them chambered either ·44–40 WCF, being marked CALIBRE WINCHESTER 1873, or ·44 Merwin & Hulbert. The latter rarely bore marks.

The first top-strap M&H revolver, a five-shot ·38 centre-fire pattern, with a sheath trigger, appeared in 1879–80. It was followed by the ·44 Pocket Army Model, with a 3¼-inch barrel and a bird's head butt. The earliest Pocket Army revolvers lacked the top strap, probably to use existing components, but a revised pattern was available by 1882.

The first double-action gun was announced in the Spring of 1883. By 1884, the range included a ·44–40 Double Action Army revolver, with a seven-inch barrel and a weight of 41oz; the ·44–40 Double Action Pocket Army weighing 36oz; and the ·38 S&W-chambered Triumph, a five-shot gun with barrels of 3½ or 5½in. The Army pattern had a conventional lanyard ring on the butt heel, while the Pocket Army had a lanyard hole bored through the extended bird's head butt beneath the grips. Pocket Army revolvers could be converted to Army length simply by substituting the barrel and top-strap assembly, while later Triumph-type examples may be encountered with a folding hammer.

The effectual Merwin & Hulberts were all available in blued or nickel-plated forms, and had chequered gutta-percha grips. Made under contract by Hopkins & Allen, they offered much better quality than the manufacturer's own guns–many of which were anchored in the 'Suicide Special' category.

SINGLE-ACTION SMITH & WESSONS, 1876–1911

A top-break adaption of the original S&W Model No.1½ was made experimentally in 1870, but had no lasting influence. Work began again in 1874 on the basis of the highly successful Russian Model No.3. The new gun, chambering a new centre-fire cartridge, was known as the ·38 Single Action or 'Baby Russian'. After the introduction of modified designs, it became the '·38 Single Action First Model'.

The rack-and-pinion extractor of the Model 3 Russian was retained, but sheathed triggers were standard. The first ·38 Single Actions were supplied to distributors in the Spring of 1876; barrels were originally 3¼ and 4in, a five inch variant being added in 1877. They were accepted instantaneously and nearly thirteen thousand had been made by the end of 1876; 9,023 of them were nickel-plated, the remainder being blued. The most popular grips were chequered gutta-percha with 'S&W' moulded into a cartouche at the neck. Only fifteen sets of ivory or mother-of-pearl grips were made in this period. The original ·38 Single Action was modified in 1877 to simplify machining and reduce cost. Most importantly, the extractor

mechanism and the cylinder retainer were modified. The retainer was patented by Daniel Wesson and James Bullard in February 1877.

Production of the ·38 New (or Second) Model Single Action began immediately, the first guns being assembled in July 1877. Numbers reverted to 1, work on the earlier model ceasing after 25,548 had been made. The New Model was a success, production in 1877 alone amounting to twelve thousand. Nickel plating and chequered gutta-percha grips were preferred, the supposedly standard wooden grips being discontinued in 1879.

Few changes were made to the New Model prior to its demise in 1891, apart from the substitution (in 1881) of a slide-bar extractor cam actuator patented in May 1880. 108,225 New Model ·38 Single Actions were made.

The third ·38 SA Smith & Wesson, the Model 1891 or 'New New Model', was a particularly handsome gun in its long-barrel forms. The greatest external change was the reversion to a conventional trigger guard. Barrels ranged from 3¼ to 6in, finishes remained blue or more popular nickel-plate, and the grips were moulded gutta-percha with a decoratively bordered chequer panel.

The elegant appearance of the new gun did not accelerate sales, owing to a steady rise in enthusiasm for the newest double-action

revolvers. Accordingly, only 28,107 were made in 1891–1911. Many post-1893 examples were completed as single-shot target pistols and, amusingly, the company even had to develop an optional sheath-trigger unit—known as the 'Mexican Model' after the market in which it was most favoured.

The success of the ·38 Single Action inspired development of a ·32 version, embodying a rebounding hammer patented by Daniel Wesson and James Bullard on 18 December 1877. The first ·32 Single Action revolvers were completed at the beginning of 1878. Moulded gutta-percha and plain walnut grips were offered during the first year, but wood was abandoned during 1879. More than ninety per cent of the guns produced in 1878–81 were nickel plated rather than blued.

The ·32 revolvers had barrels ranging from three to 10in, the longest options (eight and 10in) being used sparingly. Production ceased in 1892, after 97,599 guns had been made.

121–3: below. The ·45 Double Action Army & Frontier Model Colt of 1878 (121), together with the smaller ·38 and ·41 Lightnings (122, 123), was very popular. Though its lock components were delicate by comparison with the Peacemaker, it was easier to use with one hand. Courtesy of Ian Hogg.

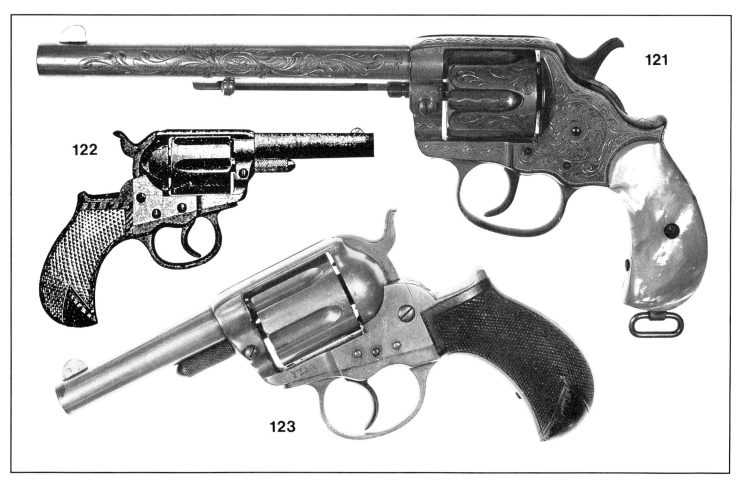

FAVOURITE WESTERN CARTRIDGES

All dimensions in inches and thousandths of an inch.

¶ •22 Long Rimfire

29-grain lead bullet; ·615 straight rimmed case. 1,055 ft/sec⁻¹, 72 ft-lb. Adapted from ·22 Short in the late 1860s. Unfortunately, ·22 Long had neither the accuracy of ·22 Short nor the hitting power of ·22 Long Rifle.

¶ •22 Long Rifle Rimfire

40-grain bullet; ·615 straight rimmed case. 1,150 ft/sec⁻¹, 117 ft-lb. Allegedly developed for or by the Stevens Tool & Arms Company in 1886–7.

¶ •22 Short Rimfire

29-grain bullet; ·420 straight rimmed case. 1,040 ft/sec⁻¹, 70 ft-lb. Introduced by Smith & Wesson in 1857 and widely copied by the mid 1860s. Very weak by current handgun standards.

¶ •25–20 Winchester (•25–20 WCF)

86-grain bullet; 1·330 necked rimmed case. 1,460 ft/sec⁻¹, 407 ft-lb. Introduced for the short-action Winchester Model 1892 rifle in the mid 1890s, comparatively low power restricted effective range to about 150 yards.

¶ •30 Long Rimfire

75-grain bullet; ·615 straight rimmed case. 750 ft/sec⁻¹, 94 ft-lb. An elongated ·30 Short rimfire, sharing many of the same vices, this cartridge originated in the late 1860s.

¶ •30 Short Rimfire

58-grain bullet; ·515 straight rimmed case. 685 ft/sec⁻¹, 60 ft-lb. Introduced in the 1860s for the Sharps four-barrel derringer and other close-range defence weapons. Confined to roles in which low power was no handicap.

¶ •30[-06] Springfield

165-grain bullet; 2·495 necked rimless case. 2,800 ft/sec⁻¹, 2,873 ft-lb. Adopted by the US Army in 1906, replacing the M1903. Many military and sporting loads have been made, though few appeared prior to 1917.

¶ •30–30 Winchester (•30–30 WCF)

150-grain bullet; 2·010 necked rimmed case. 2,415 ft/sec⁻¹, 1,943 ft-lb. Introduced commercially in 1895, this is still one of the best-known US sporting rifle cartridges. Widely used throughout North America against medium game, but not particularly powerful.

¶ •30-40 Krag

180-grain bullet; 2·215 necked rimmed case. 2,470 ft/sec⁻¹, 2,439 ft-lb. The US Army's first small-bore cartridge, adopted in 1892, this has since built a lasting reputation for accuracy—but only when loaded to moderate pressures. Inferior in almost every respect to ·30–06, it is considerably better than ·30–30.

¶ •32–20 Winchester (•32–20 WCF)

100-grain bullet; 1·215 necked rimmed case. 1,700 ft/sec⁻¹, 642 ft-lb. Introduced for the Model 73 lever-action rifle in 1882. Its low power was useful in urban districts.

¶ •32–40 Ballard (•32–40 WCF)

165-grain bullet; 2·130 straight-tapered rimmed case. 1,440 ft/sec⁻¹, 760 ft-lb. Introduced in 1884, this was soon appropriated for Winchester and Marlin lever-action rifles. Ammunition was loaded until c.1942.

¶ •38–55 Ballard (•38–55 WCF)

255-grain bullet; 2·130 straight-taper rimmed case. 1,320 ft/sec⁻¹, 987 ft-lb. Introduced for the Ballard No. 4 target rifle in 1884. Marlin and Winchester subsequently produced guns chambering it, while Remington adapted the Lee bolt-action rifle. ·38–55 had lost favour completely by 1940.

¶ •40–50 Sharps

1·720 necked rimmed case. 1,460 ft/sec⁻¹, 1,260 ft-lb. Among the shortest of the Sharps cartridges, dating from c.1875, this originally chambered in Sharps, Remington and similar single-shot rifles. Powerful enough for use on small or medium game.

¶ •40–60 Winchester (•40–60–210 WCF)

210-grain bullet; necked rimmed case. 1,560 ft/sec⁻¹, 1,135 ft-lb. Introduced with the M1876 lever-action rifle to provide a better game cartridge than ·44–40 WCF. Loaded as late as 1934. Also known as '·40–60 Marlin'.

¶ •40–70 Sharps (•40–2¼)

330-grain bullet; 2·250 necked rimmed case. 1,470 ft/sec⁻¹, 1,482 ft-lb. Introduced in the 1870s, popular among buffalo hunters and target shooters alike—combining excellent accuracy and with an acceptable punch. '·40–70 Remington' cartridges would interchange.

¶ •44 Henry Rimfire

216-grain bullet; ·815 straight rimmed case. 1,125 ft/sec⁻¹, Introduced for the Henry rifle in 1860, remaining in production as late as 1934. Very weak by post-1870 rifle standards, though a comparatively powerful rimfire.

¶ •44–40 Winchester (•44–40 WCF)

200-grain bullet; 1·305 necked rimmed case. 1,310 ft/sec⁻¹, 762 ft-lb. Introduced to accompany the Winchester Model 1873 lever-action rifle, and subsequently also chambered in the Colt Peacemaker revolver, this holds a special place in the history of the Wild West—though weak by modern rifle standards.

¶ •44–90 Sharps

520-grain bullet; 2·630 necked rimmed case. 1,270 ft/sec⁻¹, 1,863 ft-lb. Introduced in 1873 for the Sharps Creedmoor rifle, but made only until c.1905.

¶ •45 Long Colt

255-grain bullet; 1·285 straight rimmed case. 795 ft/sec⁻¹, 358 ft-lb. Introduced for the Colt Peacemaker revolver in 1872–3, this round was accurate and a good man-stopper. It was amongst the most powerful handgun cartridges available prior to 1917.

¶ •45–70–405 (•45–70 Government)

405-grain bullet; 2·105 straight rimmed case. 1,300 ft/sec⁻¹, 1,520 ft-lb. Adopted by the US Army in 1873 for the 'Trapdoor Springfield' rifle, replacing ·50–70 (q.v.). A weaker carbine load was also made.

¶ •45–120 Sharps

500-grain bullet; 3·250 rimmed straight case. 1,520 ft/sec⁻¹, 2,566 ft-lb. One of the longest cartridges in its class, this was introduced for the Sharps-Borchardt rifle in 1878–9; however, few guns and only a handful of cartridges were made. Owing to the great weight of its bullet, ·45-120 proved satisfactory against all but the largest soft-skinned game.

¶ •50–70 Government Musket

450-grain bullet; 1·750 rimmed case. 1,260 ft/sec⁻¹, 1,587 ft-lb. The official US Army service cartridge in 1866–73, developed into ·45–70 (q.v.). The original cases had a slight-but-perceptible neck, but later examples were virtually straight-sided.

¶ •56–50 Spencer Rimfire

350-grain bullet; 1·155 straight rimmed case. 1,225 ft/sec⁻¹, 1,167 ft-lb. A US Army-designed variant of the original ·56–56 round, introduced in 1865 and offered by Remington–UMC as late as 1920.

Below: a selection of the most important pre-1917 handgun and rifle cartridges.

124, right. A second-pattern Smith & Wesson New Model ·38 double-action revolver. The design of the trigger lever is typical of these early guns. Courtesy of Ian Hogg.

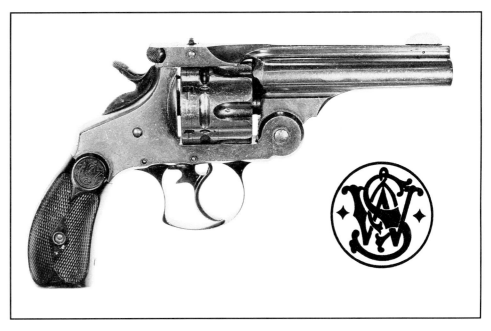

COMMERCIAL DOUBLE-ACTION COLTS, 1877–1909

On 1 January 1877, Colt announced the introduction of a ·38 Double Action Revolver. Now generally known as the 'Lightning'—a trade name originally applied by Benjamin Kittredge & Company of Cincinnati—this was soon followed by a ·41-calibre version known as the 'Thunderer'. An improved ·45 derivative, built on a differing frame and generally known as the Double Action Army & Frontier Model of 1878 or 'Omnipotent', appeared a year later. These guns had an entirely new lock credited to William Mason.

The delicate appearance of the Lightning, which had a frame not unlike that of the Single Action Army matched to a slender bird's head butt, was complemented by the delicacy of its action. A range of finishes was offered, though many surviving guns are nickel-plated. Grips were made from a single piece of rosewood or, alternatively, chequered gutta-percha. Barrel lengths varied from 1½ to 10in, ejectors being omitted from guns with barrels shorter than 4½in and, on request, from some of the longer examples. In addition, a few revolvers were chambered for ·32 instead of the more popular ·38 or ·41.

Accepting a variety of cartridges—including ·32–20, ·38–40 and ·44–40 Winchester, ·450, ·455 and ·476 Eley—the Double Action Army & Frontier Model was very similar internally to the Lightning. However, minor changes had been made in accordance with William Mason's patents of 20 September, 4 and 11 October 1881 (247,374 and 247,379, 247,938 and 248,190), and the rear of the frame differed greatly; the classical outline of the Single Action Army was replaced by a sinuous curve sweeping into the top strap, which gave a heavier appearance.

Standard guns were blued, with walnut grips; options included nickel plating with rubber, ivory, or pearl grips. Barrels ranged from three to 7½in, short-barrel examples lacking the ejector case. A few guns—usually the short-barrel ejectorless "Sheriff's" or 'House' patterns—were also made with spurless hammers; these could not be thumb cocked, but were less likely to snag on clothing.

The lock of the Lightning and Thunderer was fragile by comparison with the robustness of the Single Action Army; however, in the hands of an experienced firer who had adapted to the additional effort required to pull through on the trigger, double-action revolvers often paid dividends. Not surprisingly, they were favoured by many famous Westerners—and some noted more for infamy.

Persistent criticism has been levelled at these Colts, overlooking that they were surprisingly successful: 166,849 ·38-calibre Lightnings and ·41 Thunderers were made from 1877 until 1909, plus 51,210 ·45 Double Action Frontier Revolvers (1878–1905). A total approaching 220,000 compared favourably with production of Single Action Army revolvers, approximately 270,000 of which were made from 1878 until the end of 1909.

COMMERCIAL DOUBLE-ACTION SMITH & WESSONS, 1880–1917

In spite of experimentation, no double-action Smith & Wesson was made in quantity until the Colt pattern appeared early in 1878. Daniel Wesson and James Bullard then strove to perfect a rival, Bullard completing the design of a ·32 revolver in February 1879 and a ·38 in October.

As the Colt was available in ·38 and ·41, Smith & Wesson initially concentrated on the ·38 Double Action. The company's 1880 catalogue offered the new five-shot ·38/100 revolver, which weighed 18oz, with barrels of 3¼, four and 5in; six, eight and ten-inch options were added at later dates. Blue or nickel finish was available, the latter, which was much preferred, having the trigger guard and barrel latch in blue. Moulded black gutta-percha grips were standard, a red pattern being optional.

The detachable side plate fitted to the original Double Action revolver ran completely across the frame, weakening it perceptibly. After about 4,000 guns had been made, the frame was changed to accept a smaller side plate. This second pattern was extremely successful, about 115,000 being made in 1880–4.

The third pattern had an improved cylinder stop, which eliminated the double row of cylinder-stop slots. About 203,700 had been made by 1895. The fourth variation (1895–1909) was similar externally to its predecessor; internally, however, the sear had been redesigned to improve its efficacy. 216,300 were made.

The final, or fifth model, made only until production ceased in 1911, had a squared barrel catch and a front sight forged integrally with the barrel instead of pinned in place. These guns were obsolescent by 1910, so only about fifteen thousand were made.

The so-called Perfected Model ·38 double action Smith & Wesson, designed by Joseph Wesson and introduced in 1909, was a top break derivative of the contemporary ·32 Hand Ejector (q.v.). The guns had a conventional oval trigger guard instead of the reverse-curve pattern associated with the earlier ·38 DA. In addition, unlike its predecessors, the Perfected Model had a sliding thumb-latch on the frame behind the recoil shield, providing extra security. No longer could the gun be opened simply by grasping the latch.

The Perfected Model was discontinued soon after the end of the First World War, when nearly sixty thousand had been made. It had been offered in blue or nickel finish, with barrels ranging from 3¼ to 6in.

The first eleven ·32 Double Action revolvers were assembled in May 1880, production of the five-shot 14oz guns amounting to 9,881 by the end of the year. The original barrel-lengths were three or 3½in, a six-inch option being offered in 1882; eight and ten-inch barrels were available from 1888 for a short period. Nickel plating was even more popular than on the larger ·38, less than two hundred blued ·32 guns being made in the first year.

The first pattern, only about thirty of which were made in the summer of 1880, had a full width side plate. This was abandoned as soon as it was realised that it weakened the frame. The second variation had the smaller plate, about 22,140 guns being made in 1880-2. The action of the third model included an improved cylinder stop, but its life was short: 21,230 guns were made in 1882–3.

The major change in the fourth pattern, introduced in the summer of 1883 and made until 1909, was the substitution of the oval trigger guard for the original reverse-curve design. The cylinder stop and sear were modified, though this could not be detected

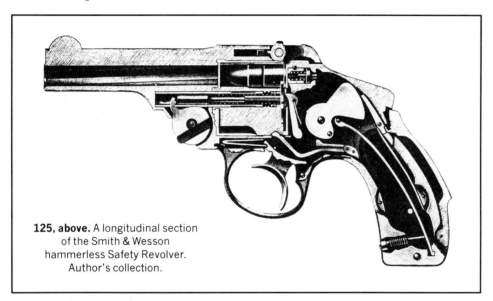

125, above. A longitudinal section of the Smith & Wesson hammerless Safety Revolver. Author's collection.

externally. The fourth model was by far the most popular, 239,600 being made. It was replaced by the fifth variation, with an integral front sight. This lasted until 1919, total production amounting to about 44,640.

Production of the top-break double-action Smith & Wessons amounted to more than 940,000 by the time assembly ceased in 1920. Though the ·32 type was ineffectual compared even with the ·38—itself no great performer— many thousands of both patterns served the West well.

A ·44 Double Action revolver (originally known as the 'New Model Navy No.3') was made from 1881 until 1913; 54,700 guns were made in their own number sequence. Offered in blue and nickel, they weighed 2lb 3oz and had barrels of 4–6in. Later options included 3½ and 6½in, but no major mechanical changes were made during their production life. The only clue to date, excepting the serial number,

was a change in the cylinder length about 1900. Original cylinders measured 1·44in, whereas later ones were 1·56.

About 1,170 examples of the so-called ·44 Favorite revolver, numbered in the same series as the standard ·44, were made in 1882–5. Efforts were made to lighten the weapon by tapering the barrel, reducing the diameter of the front part of the cylinder and thinning the frame and side-plate walls. The grips were generally chequered wood, finish invariably being nickel plate.

The ·44–40 Double Action Frontier pattern was introduced in 1886 to persuade purchasers of rifles chambering Winchester ammunition to buy a Smith & Wesson revolver. By the time it was discontinued in 1913, however, only 15,430 had been made. Offered in blue or nickel, with a 1·56-inch cylinder, DA Frontiers had barrels of 4–6½in. There was also a ·38 Winchester Double Action, but only 276 were made in 1900. Sales were so poor that guns were still being offered in Smith & Wesson catalogues as late as 1910; available in blue or nickel, they had barrels measuring 4–6in.

HAMMERLESS SMITH & WESSONS, 1886–1917

Developed by Joseph Wesson, these were based on the contemporary double-action guns. The hammer was concealed entirely within the frame, which was raised at the rear to envelop it. The finalised design, dating from 1886, also featured a spring-loaded safety plate set into the back strap and an inertia firing pin.

A ·44 version was abandoned after prototypes had been made, the first to be made in quantity being the ·38 Safety Hammerless. The first nickel-plated samples dated from midsummer

1886. The first pattern had a Z-bar latch in the top strap above the cylinder. About 5,250 guns were made in 1886–7. The second variation had an improved barrel latch on the top rear of the frame. Production continued until about 1890, reaching 37,230, but perpetual problems with the barrel-latching system led to the third Safety Hammerless revolver. This had a knurled thumb piece pinned into the top strap and an auxiliary safety to prevent the gun firing as it was being opened. About 73,520 were made in 1890–8.

The fourth model of 1898–1907 had a knurled-head barrel latch. About 104,000 guns were made in this pattern, the most common of the five ·38 variants. The fifth variant was identical with its predecessor, excepting that the front sight was integral with the barrel and some minor adjustments were made internally. The last ·38 Safety Hammerless revolvers were not shipped until 1940, though sales had slowed after 1918. Production totalled 41,500.

The ·32 Safety Hammerless model, also known as the 'New Departure' or 'Lemon Squeezer', appeared in the Spring of 1888. It was little more than a reduced-scale ·38, sharing similar characteristics. The first pattern resembled the third-model ·38 (see above), though lacking the internal safety. A small button-type barrel latch protrude from the top strap. Production was confined to 1888–1902, 91,417 revolvers being made in their own series. Available in blue or nickel, the latter predominating, they had been originally offered with gutta-percha grips. Barrels measured 3in and 3½in until a two-inch option was introduced in 1902 and a six-inch version in 1904.

The second pattern used the standard T-latch, with knurled-head buttons, while the otherwise similar third model had a forged front sight and (ultimately) minor internal adjustments. Confined to 1902–9 and 1909–37, production totalled 78,580 and 72,980 respectively.

MILITARY SWINGING-CYLINDER COLTS, 1889–1917

The earliest double-action Colts were not durable enough to attract military interest. As the contemporary hinged-frame auto-ejecting revolvers were far more advanced technically, Colt determined to develop a gun that offered the advantages of the Smith & Wessons without their comparative fragility.

The project was entrusted to William Mason, who received patents on 6 December 1881 (250,375) to protect a solid-frame revolver with a cylinder that swung out laterally. Tests with the earliest prototypes suggested several improvements: Mason's simplified hammer and spring mechanism was patented on 29 August 1882; Jean Warnant's lever ejector on 8 July

1884; Carl Ehbets' improved star-pattern ejector plate on 5 August 1884; and Horace Lord's improved cylinder retainer on 5 August 1884. These were followed by a minor improvement granted to Ehbets in October 1884, and then by the second major patent protecting the Colt swinging-cylinder revolver: 6 November 1888.

Five thousand ·38-calibre Navy Model 1889 revolvers were ordered after a series of competitive trials. These were made with the long-fluted cylinder that had characterised the Lightning (q.v.), lacking external locking notches. The cylinders were carried on a yoke, unlocked by retracting the recoil shield on the left side of the frame. When the cylinder had been pulled out of the frame to the left, backward pressure on the cylinder axis pin, to which the extractor plate was anchored, expelled the spent cases. Externally, the guns were similar to the preceding ·45 Double Action

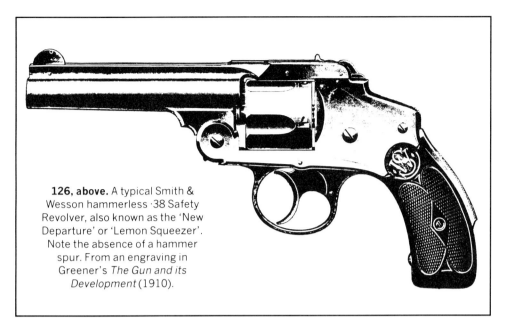

126, above. A typical Smith & Wesson hammerless ·38 Safety Revolver, also known as the 'New Departure' or 'Lemon Squeezer'. Note the absence of a hammer spur. From an engraving in Greener's *The Gun and its Development* (1910).

127, 128. The M1892 Colt New Army revolver introduced the laterally-swinging cylinder to the company's inventory. This is a commercial gun (left) with moulded gutta-percha grips. The drawing (below left) shows how the yoke-mounted cylinder swung out to the left, to expel spent cartridges simultaneously when the cylinder axis-pin head was pressed backward. Photograph by courtesy of Ian Hogg.

Army & Frontier model, though they lacked the ejector case and had straight-bottom frames. Navy revolvers were made with six-inch barrels and wood grips, though commercial examples of the 'Double Action Navy Model Revolver' had barrels of varying length.

Unfortunately, the cylinder of the 1889-pattern navy revolver rotated to the left. As the cylinder yoke also swung leftward, wear eventually loosened the action until the bore and chambers no longer aligned satisfactorily.

In 1890–1, a hundred Navy-pattern revolvers was tested by the US Army against a similar quantity of ·38 Smith & Wesson Safety Hammerless auto-ejectors. The trial board, while appreciating the safety features of the Smith & Wesson, had expressed concern about its complexity; though the Colt had failed the dust test, which its rival had negotiated easily, the S&W had been completely disabled by rust.

The rebound spring of the Colt was strengthened, and the trigger was combined with the cylinder bolt. A separate cylinder lock was added to prevent the cylinder rotating with the hammer down, removing the principal objections of the trial board.

Cavalrymen had asked for a cylinder that swung to the right for loading. Mounted men were taught to hold their reins in the left hand, making it easier to transfer the gun to the left

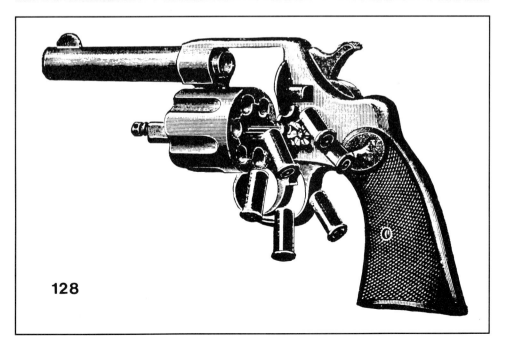

128

hand for loading than switch the reins to the right. The request was rejected and the first of orders for 68,500 M1892 army revolvers was received by Colt in the summer of 1892.

The new short-flute cylinder had two sets of locking notches, preventing the cylinder rotating when the gun was holstered.

Model 1892 revolvers were acquired by the US Army and the US Navy, differing only in their markings. Navy guns displayed 'U.S.N.' over an anchor on the butt strap, together with the calibre, serial number, inspector's initials and the year of acceptance—e.g., '38 DA', 'No.2332' and 'P' over 'WWK' over '1889'. Army guns bore marks such as 'US', 'ARMY', 'MODEL', '1896', '14436' and 'LW' in six lines. Original guns acknowledged the patents granted on 5 August 1884 and 6 November 1888, but subsequently also those of 5 March 1895 and 9 April 1901.

It was soon discovered that the Model 1892 could be fired before the cylinder locked into the frame. A Colt engineer, Frederick Felton, developed a special interlock to release the trigger only when the cylinder latch was properly seated, creating the Model 1894. However, 7,490 M1892 guns were rebuilt to 1894 standards at Springfield Armory in 1895–6, complicating identification. Additional changes were made in 1901, when the rotation of the cylinder was reversed, and a reduction in the diameter of the bore occurred in 1903.

There were also 926 Model 1905 revolvers, eight hundred of which were delivered to the Marine Corps in 1905–9. These differed from

129, right. A broadsheet advertising Colt double-action revolvers, dating from the period of the First World War. Author's collection.

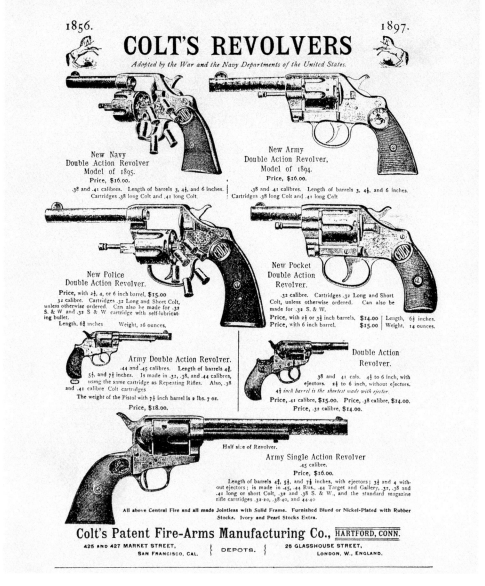

the contemporary army and navy patterns solely in their rounded-heel butt. Service guns had lanyard rings and chequered walnut grips; commercial equivalents, in blue and nickel finishes, generally had black gutta-percha grips. Issue weapons displayed butt-strap marks such as 'US' over 'MC', above a serial number.

New Service revolvers delivered to the army, navy and marine corps—nearly fourteen thousand Model 1909 guns were ordered by the army in 1910 alone—almost always had lanyard rings and plain walnut grips.

Though introduced after the end of the period with which this book deals, similar guns were issued in great numbers during the First World War to supplement M1911 Colt-Browning pistols. The US Government bought 150,700 ·45 New Service revolvers in 1917–18, the guns—with essentially similar Smith & Wesson Hand Ejectors—being known as 'Model 1917'. They chambered rimless ·45 pistol cartridges and

needed the so-called Half-Moon Clips (q.v.) to operate satisfactorily.

COMMERCIAL SWINGING-CYLINDER COLTS, 1889–1917

Commercial 1889- and 1892-type revolvers had barrels of varying length. The most popular variant was the Target Model, with chequered walnut grips, a special flat-top frame and adjustable sights. The last guns of this type were made in 1908. Many had been offered as 'New Model Double Action Navy' and 'New Model Double Action Army' revolvers, but some had gone to the Cuban gendarmerie (marked GUARDIA RURAL) and others to the Argentine navy (ARMADA ARGENTINA).

Army patterns had chequered gutta-percha grips with COLT in an oval, while the navy commercials displayed an additional rampant

colt motif. In addition to the regulation ·38, these revolvers were also offered in ·41 with barrels of 3in or 4½in.

The New Service Revolver, which appeared in 1897, was an improved New Model Double Action Army pattern. The name was registered with the US Patent Office in February 1899 and appeared on early guns, encircling a rampant colt motif on the left side of the frame. A reversion to clockwise cylinder rotation was made, the frame was enlarged to accept ·45 Colt or ·476 Eley cartridges, and the grip was suited to a large hand. Standard frames had sighting channels cut in the strap above the cylinder; rarer Target Models had flat-top frames with adjustable back sights.

Several changes in the trigger mechanism were made during the lengthy production life of the New Service revolver (1897–1943), the Positive Safety being added in 1905. Most other variations concern barrel length, finish or decoration. Revolvers purchased by the armed services almost always had lanyard rings and plain walnut grips, while pre-1918 commercial models had chequered gutta-percha patterns with COLT moulded into them. A scarce 'New Service Marine Corps Revolver' (c.1910–20) was offered commercially with a narrow round-heel butt and chequered walnut grips.

The standard military barrel-length was 5½in, though options ranging from 4in to 7½in were available to order. Pre-1917 barrel-top markings acknowledged patents up to 4 July 1905, though an October 1926 date was subsequently added.

The New Model Double Action Army revolver was replaced in 1908 by the Army Special (renamed 'Official Police' in 1928), initially offered only in ·32–20, ·38 Special and ·41 Colt. The standard barrels measured 4½ and 6in, though four and five-inch options were added in 1911. Finish was blue or nickel, clockwise rotating cylinders were used, and the readily detachable side plate lay on the right of the frame instead of the left. The Positive Lock was fitted in the trigger mechanism, while minor improvements were made to the cylinder latch and a single row of locking notches appeared. The standard chequered gutta-percha grips had serpentine bordering and a large decorative 'C' around the stock-screws. Standard 4in-barrel revolvers weighed about 34oz.

Though overlooked by the US military authorities, Army Special Colts were popular with police and militia units across North America. The Greek government bought 25,500 in 1912, shortly before the Second Balkan War.

Introduced in 1904, with anti-clockwise cylinder rotation, the Officers' Model revolver originally featured a cylinder-locking system in which the notches between the cylinder flutes (preventing rotation when the hammer was down) were supplemented by grooves into which a second bolt could lock when the hammer was fully cocked. The 1908 pattern substituted a conventionally latched clockwise rotating cylinder with only one set of locking notches.

Guns were offered only in ·38 Special, with six-inch barrels. A 7½-inch barrel was available from 1908 onward, and others were added after 1917. The goal of the Officers' Model was high quality, special attention being paid to the fit of the parts and the trigger mechanism.

The earliest guns had chequering on the trigger and back strap, and a beautiful lustrous blue finish. They were normally sold with an adjustable back sight patented by James Peard of Hartford, Connecticut, in April 1901 (671,609) and June 1904 (761,706). The guns also had hand-chequered walnut grips.

SMALL-CALIBRE DOUBLE-ACTION COLTS, 1893–1917

Colt introduced the first of its modern double action pocket revolvers in 1893. The ·32-calibre six-shot New Pocket Model, chambered for ·32 Colt, ·32 Smith & Wesson or ·32 New Police, filled the void left when the company's management declined to compete with the legion of 'Suicide Specials' and abandoned the New Line series entirely. The New Pocket Model shared many features with the contemporary ·38 Double Action Army Revolver (M1892), though its six-round cylinder rotated clockwise. Only 31,000 were made prior to 1905. The guns had small frames and barrels measuring 2½–6in. Few changes were made during their life, apart from minor improvements in the lock, the advent of reeded ejector-rod heads and a new chequered cylinder latch. The original walnut grips were soon replaced by chequered gutta-percha with COLT moulded into the neck.

The New Pocket revolver was superseded by the ·32 Pocket Positive Model, embodying the Colt Positive Safety Lock. This interposed a bar between the hammer and the cartridge-head until the trigger was pressed.

Many early Pocket Positives incorporated New Pocket parts, as supplies of frames were not exhausted until 1909. The last of about 130,000 Pocket Positive revolvers was assembled in 1943. Many had gone to police departments scattered throughout North America, and others to agencies such as the Caracas police in Venezuela.

The New Police Model, allegedly introduced in 1896 to satisfy Theodore Roosevelt and the New York Police Department, was a variant of the New Pocket model with a longer grip; almost fifty thousand were made in 1896–1907. Chambering the same variety of ·32 centre-fire cartridges as the New Pocket Model, the New Police Model had plain walnut or—later—chequered gutta-percha COLT grips. A rare New Police Target Model had a flat-top frame with an adjustable back sight.

The New Police Colt displayed its name on the left side of the frame beneath the hammer, curved around a rampant colt motif. This was eventually changed to the colt backed by the letter 'C', and then simply to the colt itself—a mark applicable to all Colt guns.

Discontinued in 1943 after almost 200,000 had been made, the Police Positive Model replaced the New Police Model after 1905. Incorporating the Positive Lock safety mechanism, it was made in standard and target versions—the latter ('Model G') being offered from 1911 in ·22 Long Rifle and Winchester rimfire.

Police Positives were light and handy, weighing only 16-21oz; barrels ranged between 2½ and 6in. Grips were originally chequered gutta-percha, with COLT moulded into the neck, but these were replaced by a more decorative pattern with a stylised 'C' surrounding the retaining screws. The grip was lengthened soon after introduction, an enlargement of the frame occurring in 1925. Finish was originally blue or nickel, though the latter had been discontinued by the early 1920s.

Police forces began clamouring for more powerful guns once ·32 had proved ineffectual. Consequently, the Police Positive Special Model of 1907 chambered ·38 Special—·32–20 was optional—and had a cylinder measuring 1·63in instead of 1·25in. The barrels were four, five or 6in, a two-inch option being added in 1926.

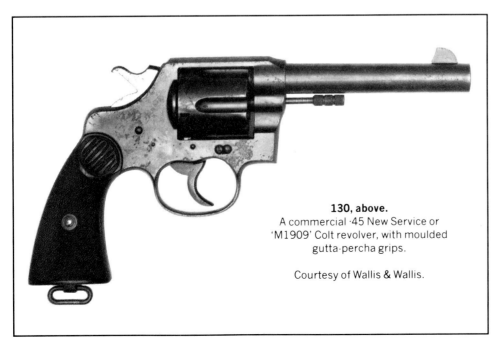

130, above.
A commercial ·45 New Service or 'M1909' Colt revolver, with moulded gutta-percha grips.

Courtesy of Wallis & Wallis.

The highly successful Police Positive Special was only slightly heavier than its ·32-calibre predecessor, weighing about 21oz with a four inch barrel. A ·38 New Police chambering was offered with the standard Police Positive in 1911, but was less effectual than ·38 Special and never popular.

SMALL-FRAME S&W HAND EJECTORS, 1896–1917

The introduction of Colt swinging-cylinder revolvers did not concern Smith & Wesson greatly, as sales of double-action break-open revolvers were booming. When the US Army adopted the ·38 Colt in 1892, Smith & Wesson were forced to act.

The ·32 Hand Ejector Model and its 32 ·S&W Long cartridge were introduced in 1896. A split-spring cylinder lock was let into the top strap above the six-chamber cylinder, which swung out to the left of the solid frame after the head of the ejector rod had been pulled forward to release the yoke. Finish was blue or nickel; barrels measured 3¼–6in. Adjustable target-pattern sights could be supplied to order, while the maker's marks lay between the flutes of the cylinder. The new Hand Ejector was not an instantaneous success, partly owing to Colt's lead but also to the enthusiasm with which the break-open Smith & Wessons were still received. Sales were stimulated by orders from the Philadelphia police, but only 19,712 guns had been made by 1903.

The improved ·32 Hand Ejector Model 1903 had an additional thumb latch on the left side of the frame, behind the recoil shield, locking the cylinder at both ends of the ejector rod. The top-strap cylinder stop system was replaced by an improved version mounted in the bottom of the frame above the trigger, and a round barrel with an integral front sight was substituted for the older ribbed version. Blue and nickel finishes were available, with barrels of 3¼–6in.

Numbers had reached 19,425 when the first major change was made. As most revisions concerned the lock, the interested reader is directed to *Smith & Wesson 1857–1945* for detailed descriptions. The first change (1904) was betrayed by longer stop slots in the cylinder surface; the second change of 1906 added a rebound slide in the action; the third and fourth changes, in 1909 and 1910 respectively, concerned the lock; and the fifth change of 1910 was revealed only by the solid ejector-rod knob and two pins retaining the ejector in the cylinder.

Production of the M1903 ceased in 1917, after about 263,000 had been made. The new Third Model Hand Ejector, similar externally to the fifth change M1903, had an additional hammer block safety in the lock.

The similar ·32 Regulation Police and ·38/32 Regulation Police revolvers of 1917 (the latter being a ·38-calibre gun built on the small I frame) were both derived from the ·32 Hand Ejector design, differing from the contemporary Third Model largely in their noticeably enlarged square-heel butts.

There were also seven-shot ·22 Hand Ejectors, 26,154 of which were made in three patterns in 1902–19, and a ·32–20 Hand Ejector built on the medium frame shared with ·38 Military & Police revolvers (q.v.). Popular with sportsmen who purchased similarly chambered rifles, only 65,700 ·32–20 revolvers had been made by the time the fourth change finally appeared in 1915.

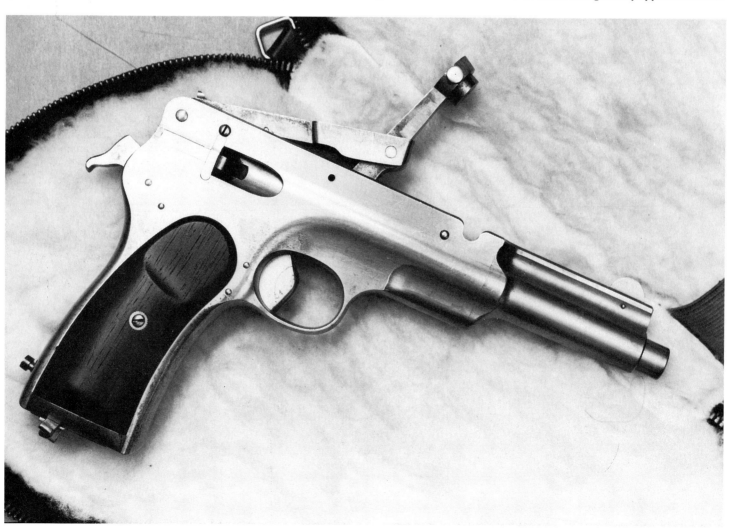

132, above. The Mauser-Selbstladepistole C/96, offered commercially from 1898, was a popular early import; small numbers had reached the West by 1900. This ten-shot gun, shown with its charger, is marked by Von Lengerke & Detmold of New York City. Its serial number dates it to about 1906.

131, left. Among the earliest US semi-automatic pistols was this quirky blow-forward pattern credited to Carl Ehbets. Designed in 1895, it was patented in April 1897. Only a handful of prototypes was made. Courtesy of Lieutenant-Colonel W. Reid Betz, John M. Browning Museum.

THE FIRST AUTO-LOADING PISTOLS, 1895–1900

The end of the twentieth century coincided with the commercial introduction of effectual auto-loading pistols. By 1905, sufficient were in circulation to reach the West. Many of these were exotic imports—Mausers and Lugers from Germany, or Brownings made in Belgium by Fabrique Nationale d'Armes de Guerre.

Few North American inventors produced truly viable designs prior to 1897, though Carl Ehbets patented a gas-operated pistol (US 570,388) and an aberrant blow-forward gun (580,935); at least one prototype of each was made, but the advent of simpler and more conventional Brownings halted progress.

By 1895, John Browning of Ogden, Utah, had constructed a prototype blowback pistol chambering a ·32 semi-rimmed cartridge made by Winchester. The pistol was successfully demonstrated to representatives of Colt in the summer of 1895 and a patent application was filed in September. It was eventually granted on 20 April 1897.

In May 1896, Browning delivered three more guns to Colt—a modification of the 1895-type blowback, a recoil-operated gun locked by dropping the barrel on two swinging links, and a third locked by rotating the barrel.

The rotating-barrel gun (US Patent 580,925) was abandoned after a prototype had been made. The small blowback was rejected by Colt after Browning had sought what became British Patent 22,455/98 of 25 October 1898. Colt apparently doubted the virtues of small calibre and an unlocked breech. The gun was promptly offered to Fabrique Nationale d'Armes de Guerre by Hart Berg, Colt's European representative: small calibres and low power were not the inhibition to sales in Europe they may have been in the Wild West.

MEDIUM-FRAME S&W HAND EJECTORS, 1899–1917

Smith & Wesson soon realised that the first ·32 Hand Ejector could be improved. A few experimental guns made in 1896–9 allowed

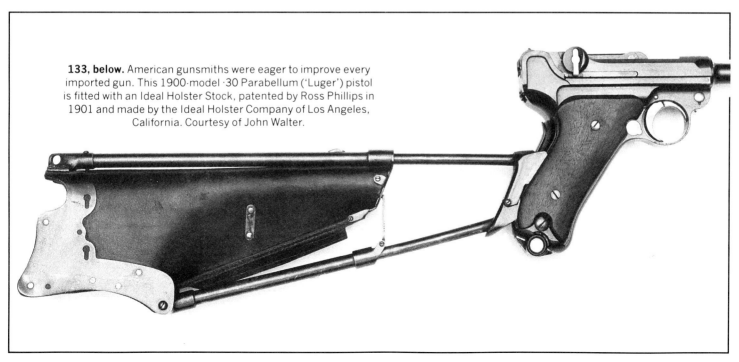

133, below. American gunsmiths were eager to improve every imported gun. This 1900-model ·30 Parabellum ('Luger') pistol is fitted with an Ideal Holster Stock, patented by Ross Phillips in 1901 and made by the Ideal Holster Company of Los Angeles, California. Courtesy of John Walter.

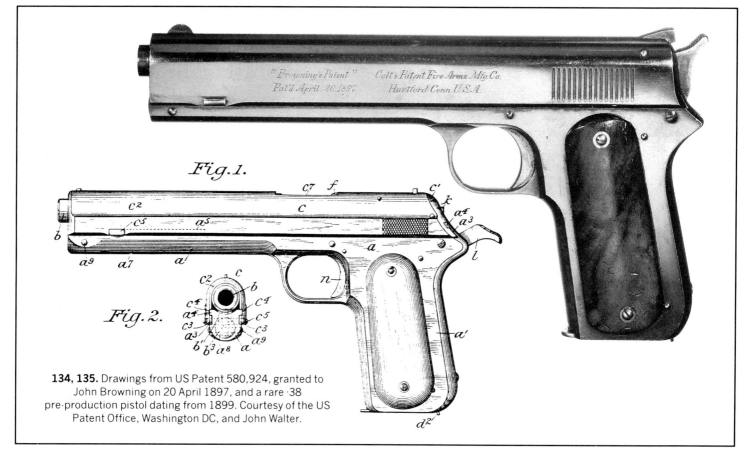

134, 135. Drawings from US Patent 580,924, granted to John Browning on 20 April 1897, and a rare ·38 pre-production pistol dating from 1899. Courtesy of the US Patent Office, Washington DC, and John Walter.

the ·38 Hand Ejector Model, built on the K-pattern frame, to be introduced in 1899. The most important change was the addition of a thumb latch for the cylinder which, unlike the earlier ejector-rod lock, locked the cylinder at both ends. This provided sufficient security for comparatively high-powered cartridges. The ·38 S&W Special cartridge was loaded with a 158-grain bullet and 22 grains of powder, compared with 150 and eighteen in the ·38 Colt pattern.

Also known as the 'Military & Police', or Model of 1899, the ·38 Hand Ejector was offered in ·38 and ·32–20, the two being numbered separately.

The first ·38 Military & Police guns were released commercially in 1899. The US Navy purchased a thousand guns on 25 June 1900, the US Army placing a similar order in February 1901. However, these were the only military purchases prior to 1917, as they coincided with the rejection of ·38 as a viable man-stopper.

The first guns were offered with barrels ranging from 4in to 8in, with blue or nickel finish, and rounded gutta-percha grips. They were made until 1902, when the first of several mechanical changes was made. Guns are now classified as the Model 1902, plus a single change made in 1903, or Model 1905 (and four changes). Periodic revisions were made among barrel-length options, though blue and nickel plate finishes were offered throughout the entire period. A square butt was introduced as standard in 1904. By 1915, when the fourth change was made to the 1905-pattern guns, production of ·38 M&P revolvers had reached 241,700.

A solitary target-shooting version of the ·38 M&P revolver, the '·38 Hand Ejector Target' or '·38 Military & Police Target' was numbered within the same series—being simply a long barrelled Hand Ejector with adjustable sights.

MILITARY ·38 COLT PISTOLS, 1900–5

Browning's second successful 1897 patent (580,924) protected a 'parallel ruler' system, the first example of which was shown to Colt representatives in Hartford in May 1896. Though it chambered ·38 rimmed revolver cartridges, it worked well enough to show its considerable promise.

When the pistol fired, recoil moved the slide and barrel backward while still securely locked together; once pressure in the system had dropped sufficiently, the links, rotated by the rearward movement of the slide, began to pull the barrel down until its lugs disengaged corresponding locking recesses in the inner top surface of the slide. The barrel block stopped against the frame, allowing the slide to run back alone to the limit of its travel; the coil-type main spring then pushed the barrel forwards again, stripping a new cartridge out of the magazine and raising the barrel lugs into the slide recesses.

The guns were not only simple and amazingly durable, but also efficient enough to allow Colt to approach the US Army—a suitable prototype being exhibited on 9 November 1898. A special ·38 smokeless semi-rim cartridge had been substituted for the rimmed revolver pattern, improving reliability.

European pistols were being tried by the authorities by this time, though experiments centred on their suitability as light automatic carbines. A Board of Officers convened at Springfield Armory in November 1899 to test Mauser, Mannlicher and Colt pistols, though only the Mauser was available. The Colt arrived in January 1900.

Testing revealed that it had great potential, but also some weaknesses—the barrel was exchanged once, while the rear barrel-link pin failed three times. However, the Mannlicher action had burst and the Mauser was very unpopular.

Eventually, the army bought 200 Colt and then 1,000 Parabellum (Luger) pistols for field trials. The Colts were delivered between July 1900 and April 1902, but the trials coincided with doubts that small-calibre bullets had sufficient stopping power. The 7.65mm (·30) Parabellum and the ·38 Colt were rejected when ·45 was set as the acceptable minimum.

Contemporary army Colts bear the marks of Rinaldo Carr ('RAC') in a cartouche on the grip. About fifty were acquired by the US Navy, displaying 'USN 1' to 'USN 50' in addition to the factory serials.

The earliest guns weighed 36oz unladen, accepted a seven-round box magazine and had six-inch barrels rifled with six grooves. The straight-case rimless cartridge, developed by Winchester, fired a 105-grain bullet at about 1,275 ft/sec.

The guns looked clumsy, with little overhang behind the butt. Sixteen retracting grooves lay above the grip on the earliest examples, but were soon moved to the front of the slide to facilitate cocking with the left hand. There was a spur hammer, the plain grips soon became chequered walnut with rounded ends, and the back sight doubled as a safety catch.

An improved version appeared a year later, when a fixed back sight replaced the original combination safety-sight.

The 1902-pattern gun, known to Colt as the ·38 Military Model, had a latch that held the slide back after the last round had been fired and ejected. Granted to Browning in September 1902, US Patent 708,794 protected a bar moving vertically in a channel in the frame ahead of the left grip.

In addition, the butt had been lengthened to contain an eight-round magazine and a lanyard ring was added to the bottom left side. The slide-retracting grooves were replaced by a chequered panel.

The new pistol impressed the army sufficiently for the purchase of two hundred Colt-Brownings to be authorised on 11 January 1902. They had all been delivered to Springfield Armory by 30 June 1903, at $20 apiece. Marks applied by Captain John Thompson ('J.T.T.') and Rinaldo Carr ('RAC') were struck into the left side of the frame and the right side of the trigger guard respectively.

The field trials were not successful, owing to the hostility of the cavalry units and the proven inadequacy of the ·38 cartridge. Surviving guns were sold at auction in 1906.

COMMERCIAL COLT PISTOLS, 1900–17

Colt revealed the new 'Automatic Colt Pistol, Browning Patent' at the Sportsman's Show in New York in March 1900. It was immediately touted commercially, being renamed the '·38 Sporting Model' in 1902 after about 3,500 had been made. The guns were essentially similar to the military pattern (q.v.), but had chequered rubber grips. Sales were slow, as only about two

thousand had been sold by the summer of 1901.

Improvements were made to the basic design in 1901, when the original safety-sight was replaced by a fixed open-block back sight, while chequered grips bearing COLT and an encircled rampant colt appeared. A new rounded hammer replaced the earlier spur at this time, and a reversion to conventionally placed slide-retracting grooves was made late in 1906.

Production of ·38 Sporting Models (M1902) continued until 1907, when the supply of parts was exhausted; serial numbers had reached 10,999. The last guns were assembled in 1908 in the block 30000–30190.

The ·38 Sporting Model was supplemented from 1902 by the commercial ·38 Military Model. The latter had a slide latch, an eight round magazine, a lanyard ring anchored in the bottom left side of the squared-heel butt, a rounded hammer and—except on post-1906 examples—chequer-panel retraction grips. Marked MODEL 1902 on the right side of the slide by the ejection port (at least until 1906), the guns were apparently numbered 15001–15200 and then backward to 11000 to use numbers omitted when production of the ·38 Sporting Model ceased. The Military Models

were subsequently numbered from 30200 to 47100. When the guns were discontinued in 1929, about eighteen thousand had been made. Conventional retracting grooves had appeared on the slide of the Military Model in 1906 and a spur hammer was fitted from 1907–8. When round-head hammers replaced the spurs on ·38 and ·45 Military Models later in 1908, the original 1900-type ·38 Sporting Model had been discontinued and was not affected.

1903 was marked by introduction of the ·32 and ·38 Pocket Models. The small-calibre gun was an adaption of the contemporary 7·65 or 9mm 1903 'Grand Modèle' FN Browning, developed to interest European governments seeking a suitable small-calibre service pistol. It contained a detachable barrel, held inside the full length slide by a series of ribs beneath the chamber engaging a block on the frame. The gun had an enclosed hammer lock, a mechanical safety, and a recoil spring beneath the barrel.

The subject of a patent granted to Browning on 22 December 1903 (747,585), the finalised ·32 Colt was smaller and lighter than the Belgian pattern and lacked the lanyard loop on the lower left side of the butt. Marketed commercially from the summer of 1903, the Colt had a 4in barrel (reduced to 3·75in on the

136

Photograph courtesy of John Walter; painting by John Batchelor.

137

136, 137. The .38 Pocket Model Colt (136) of 1903 was a variant of the Sporting Model. No. 34641, shown here, was made towards the end of production. It should not be confused with the .32 Pocket Model (137), a variant of the FN-Browning Mle 1903.

introduction of the ·380 version in 1908), an eight-round magazine and weighed 23–24oz. Grips were hard rubber, moulded with COLT and the rampant colt motif. Ten thousand sold in the first year of production, making the gun an instant success. Most were blued, though nickel plating was popular and engraved versions are known. Excepting changes in the slide legend, modifications made to the slide retracting grooves in 1905–6 and elimination of the barrel bush in 1910, no changes were made to the basic design during its production life; 572,215 were made prior to 1945.

The ·38 Pocket Model, which entered production in the autumn of 1903, was simply a short-barrelled Sporting Model with a round hammer and conventional slide retracting grooves above the moulded grips. The form of the grooves changed perceptibly in 1908, when they became deeper and closer together, and a spur hammer replaced the earlier rounded pattern at much the same time. The ·38 Pocket Model was finally discontinued in 1929, when numbers had reached about 47100. They ran from 16000 to 30199 and then, mixed with the ·38 Military Model, up to about 47100.

By the Spring of 1906, Colt was able to market the effectual '·45 Military Model' (or M1905) commercially. The guns were identical with the US Army trials pattern. A few accepted shoulder stocks, though stocks were never common. Production continued until 1911 when, at about gun no. 6100, manufacture was discontinued in favour of what subsequently became the M1911-type ·45 pistol.

The blowback ·380 Pocket Model of 1909 chambered a rimless cartridge developed by John Browning in collusion with William Thomas of the Union Metallic Cartridge Company. The gun was a modification of the original ·32 Hammerless Pocket Model, indistinguishable apart from calibre marks. The extractor was modified so that it could be used with ·32 or ·380 guns interchangeably, and the magazine capacity was reduced to seven rounds. Changes to the barrel and the slide, eliminating the barrel bush, were made in 1910. These revisions shortened all barrels by a quarter-inch.

The ·380 pistol was moderately successful, assembly continuing into 1945–6, but could not compare with the ·32 version. The terminal serial number is believed to have been 138009.

The ·25-calibre Hammerless Pocket Pistol had been developed in 1904–5 and placed in production in Belgium in 1906. During 1907, with assistance furnished by Fabrique Nationale, Colt readied a North American production line. The prototypes featured an internal hammer, but this was considered to be too complicated for so small a gun and a duplicate of the FN striker mechanism—with

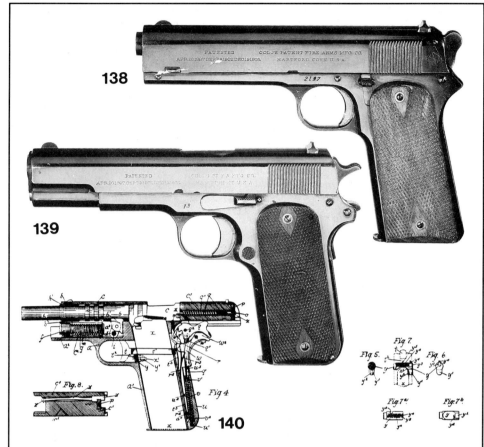

138–40. The ·45 M1905 Colt-Browning (138) was tested by the US Army in 1906–7, proving the best of the several guns under review. This gun, no. 2197, dates from the trial period. Note the rounded hammer. Only a few M1909 Colt-Brownings (139) were made, this example being no. 13. These were the first guns in which the twin-link barrel-depressor system was replaced by a single link. The patent drawings (140) show the basic action. Photographs courtesy of John Walter; drawings courtesy of the US Patent Office, Washington DC.

an additional manual safety—was eventually substituted.

Production began in 1908, 409,061 guns being made by 1941. They acknowledged patents granted to Arthur Wright in August 1896 in addition to Browning's of April 1897 and December 1903—even though nothing of Wright's abortive pistol was used. The safety, which could lock the sear or retain the slide in its open position, was the subject of Browning patent 947,478, granted on 25 January 1910.

The guns had moulded rubber grips bearing COLT and the usual motif. They had a grip safety, an external extractor, and a magazine release catch under the butt. Pistols made after 1916, when numbers had reached 141000, had an additional magazine safety patented by George Tansley (1,234,961 of 31 July 1917).

Modifications to the commercial blowbacks were made in the years preceding the First World War, and a new ·45 Military Model—the army's Model 1911—superseded the earlier 1905 and 1908 patterns. The perfected ·45

pistol proved very popular commercially, the guns being identical to military issue with the exception that they featured commercial-grade finish and C-prefix serial numbers. Numbers had reached about C85000 by April 1917.

A quantity of ·455 M1911 pistols with W-prefix numbers (W10001–W21000) went to Britain in 1915–16, apparently to supplement dwindling supplies of .455 Webley pistols in the Royal Navy and the Royal Flying Corps. Others went to Russia—paid for by British money, as a result of which they were marked 'English Contract' in Cyrillic. The Anglo-Russian guns appear to have been selected at random from commercial production, as their numbers suggested delivery of far larger quantities than the actual 14,500.

MILITARY ·45 COLT PISTOLS, 1905–17

Colt began work on a ·41 pistol in 1903, but the project was abandoned after a prototype or two had been made. Though the British were willing to adopt any pistol with a calibre greater than ·40, provided all other criteria had been met, the US Army had insisted on ·45.

The first ·45 Colt was adapted from a ·38 Military Model frame and slide, strenuous attempts to improve the twin-link barrel depressor delaying progress. Perfected guns were readied in the summer of 1905. External extractors replaced the earlier internal patterns, while the chequered wood grips extended down to cover most of the butt-frame. Modifications were made to the slide latch and the recoil-spring system; and though the guns still resembled short barrelled .38 Military Models, they had conventional retraction grooves on the rear of the slide above the grip.

The M1905 ·45 Colt was 8in long, had a five inch barrel and weighed 33oz unladen. It accepted a seven-round box magazine and attained a muzzle velocity of about 900 ft/sec. Guns supplied to the US Army for field trials had a flat-sided spur hammer with half- and full-cock notches, subsequently adopted for all exposed-hammer Colts.

Military trials began in January 1907. The Colt performed best, gaining recommendation over the Savage and the Parabellum (Luger). The Board of Ordnance and Fortification approved the purchase of two hundred Colts and two hundred Savage pistols, but the Savage Arms Company declined and its order was passed to DWM. The promoters of the German weapon then refused to make large-calibre Parabellums in such small quantities, allowing Savage a change of heart in time to deliver two hundred ·45 pistols in the autumn of 1907. The 1907-type 'Field Trials' ·45 Colts embodied features

recommended by the ordnance department. These included a loaded-chamber indicator in the top surface of the slide, patented by James Peard on 23 June 1908 (891,438), together with a grip safety adapted from designs of George Tansley (891,510, 23 June 1908) and Carl Ehbets (917,723, 6 April 1909). The ejection port was extended up over the slide and a long extractor was let into the right side of the slide, cutting through the retraction grooves. The contract guns—200 in two slightly differing batches of a hundred apiece—were despatched to Springfield Armory in mid-March 1908.

The Savages were delivered in November 1908, several months behind schedule, but were immediately rejected. Only 128 guns reappeared at the factory, the others vanishing en route; not until March 1909 were two hundred acceptable Savages available for trial.

Problems with defective sears dogged the early trials with the Colts, but ceased when the manufacturer supplied improved components. The Savages were decidedly inferior in the endurance test, and had an unpleasant recoil.

At least five Colts were made with Powell's Cartridge Indicating Device, a mica-covered slot being cut in the left grip to expose the magazine follower, but the cavalry was still vehemently opposed to auto-loading pistols.

On 14 February 1911, Browning received US Patent 984,519 to protect an improved breech locking system with only a single pivot at the breech, the muzzle being supported in the slide-mouth. This system had been perfected eighteen months previously, the patent application being filed in February 1910.

The new 'M1909' was 8in long, had a five-inch barrel and weighed 43oz loaded. Its magazine held seven rounds, though an eighth could be placed in the chamber. It was replaced by the Model 1910, the prototype being exhibited at Fort Myer on 9 February 1910. The gun suffered persistent ejection failures, but reappeared successfully on 14 February. Colt then made eight improved guns to the same design, one being satisfactorily tested at Springfield Armory in March. However, the Cavalry Board remained obdurate, remarking that '...the sentiment of cavalry officers is generally against the adoption of an automatic pistol...'

Trials so impressed the Board of Ordnance and Fortification that the perpetual dissent voiced by cavalrymen was ignored. Colt was asked to add a manual safety to lock the sear when the hammer was cocked.

On 4 November 1910, a Board of Officers convened at Springfield to test any ·45 pistols that were submitted. There were just two: the improved M1910 Colt and an improved 'Model H' Savage. The Colt proved more accurate and durable, registering thirteen stoppages in the 6,000-round endurance trial compared with 43 for the simpler, but less accurate Savage. Both guns had suffered broken parts, whereas the ·45 revolver used as a control weapon had merely jammed twice. The consensus was that the Colt was the better pistol, but remained inferior to the revolver.

Colt and Savage worked to improve their guns in time for trials in March 1911, where the modified Colt finally proved superior. In the 6,000-round endurance trial, indeed, there were no stoppages and no parts breakages.

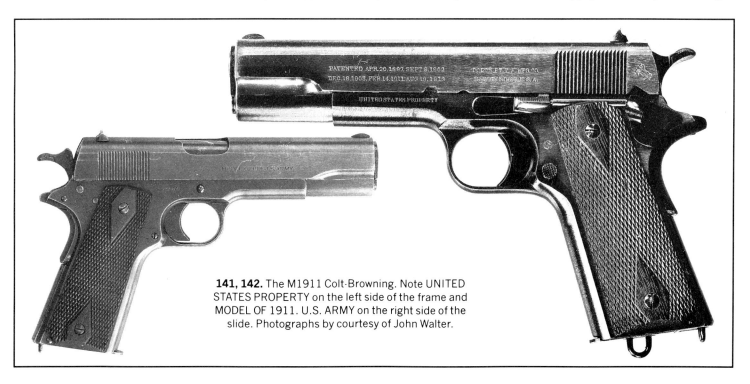

141, 142. The M1911 Colt-Browning. Note UNITED STATES PROPERTY on the left side of the frame and MODEL OF 1911. U.S. ARMY on the right side of the slide. Photographs by courtesy of John Walter.

The Savage was still comparatively unreliable. On 29 March 1911, the perfected Colt pistol was adopted by the US Army.

The differences between the M1910 and the M1911 were comparatively minor, though the latter had locking lugs on top of the barrel (instead of milled entirely around it), a mechanical safety, and a tubular housing containing the safety- and slide-lock plungers. The manual safety mechanism and the plunger-tube were subsequently patented by John Browning on 19 August 1913 (1,070,582).

An order for 31,344 guns went to Colt on 5 May 1911, and a licence was negotiated to allow production to begin in Springfield Armory once 50,000 pistols had been ordered. By the

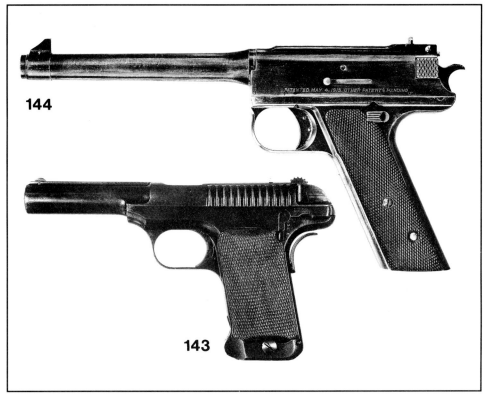

143, 144: right. The ·45 Savage pistol (143), designed by Elbert Searle, proved an effectual rival for the Colt-Browning. However, Savage had neither the experience nor the capacity to compete with Colt. Right at the end of the period under review, Grant Hammond produced a gun for consideration. Patented in May 1915, the weapon (144) did not prove effectual. Photographs courtesy of John Walter.

time the US Army entered the First World War, more than 75,000 M1911 pistols had been delivered by the two manufacturers.

LESSER AUTO-LOADING PISTOLS, 1905–17

The announcement of the US Army pistol trials of 1906 inspired the submission of indigenous auto-loading pistols. The best known was the Savage, patented by Elbert H. Searle of Philadelphia on 12 November 1905 (804,985). The patent was partly assigned to William Condit of Des Moines, Iowa, which has led to the Savage being credited to 'Searle & Condit patents'; Condit appears to have been a financier.

Improved guns in ·45, made in accordance with patent granted in 1909 (but sought in January 1907), were submitted to the US Army. They put up a creditable showing and were ultimately accepted for comparative field trials after the Parabellum (Luger) was withdrawn by its backers. Ultimately, the Savage failed—but only after it had provided Colt with an effectual competitor. At least 277 pistols were supplied to the US Army, though 105 were sold to Tryon of Philadelphia as late as 1922. The Tryon guns may have been army trials pistols returned to (or bought back by) their manufacturer.

Savage also made a 7·65mm pocket pistol incorporating the same marginally effectual rotating barrel lock, and parts that interlocked

without screws. The first gun was assembled in the company's Utica factory on 22 March 1908, chambering the '·32 ASP' (Automatic Savage Pistol) cartridge—the proven ·32 ACP or 7·65mm Browning.

The M1907 Savage was a diminutive of the ·45 guns developed for the US Army trials, but had a ten-round magazine allowing the slogan 'Ten Shots Quick' to be coined. They had moulded plastic grips and, originally, a round hammer protruding from the top of the slide. A spur hammer appeared on many guns assembled after the end of the First World War.

The retraction grooves were originally very broad, but a more conventional narrow pattern was soon substituted. The original ridged safety was exchanged at the beginning of 1909 for a chequered-head pattern; this was superseded in 1912 by a special pattern amalgamated with a Lang Patent trigger-lock bar (US 1,082,961 of December 1913). The magazine-release catch in the front of the butt was revised in the middle of 1912, and a loaded-chamber indicator—patented on behalf of Charles Nelson on 30 December 1913 (1,082,969)—was added after 27 November 1912.

At about gun 130000, the modified ·32 M1915 appeared with a concealed hammer and a grip safety system based on a series of patents granted to Charles Nelson and William Swartz. M1907 numbers then continued from 150000 (in 1916), though the basic gun had been superseded by the ·32 Model 1917. However, owing to war and existing parts, the basic

·32 1907-pattern Savage was not discontinued until April 1920. Production apparently totalled 208,800, making the Savages second only to Colt on the North American market.

The larger-calibre ·380 Savage Model 1907 pistols appeared in May 1913, their numbers beginning at B2000. After a few hundred had been made, the prefix became a suffix and continued up to 9999B. A block was then left for ·380 M1915 guns before recommencing at 13903B and terminating in 1920 at 15748B; consequently, ·380 guns are far rarer than the ·32 varieties. Small numbers of Savages went to France and Portugal during the First World War, while a few will be found with the marks of North American police forces.

The Smith & Wesson pistol was based on the Belgian Clément, which had been patented in the USA on 13 September 1910. Joseph Wesson added a grip safety in accordance with a patent of December 1910, and a disconnector for the recoil spring (a laterally sliding block) followed on 30 July 1912.

The first seven-shot 3½-inch barrelled guns were assembled in May 1913. They chambered a unique ·35 cartridge, loaded with a bullet with a half-jacket of cupro-nickel over a protruding lead core. Sales were encouraging, though production halted in April 1915 to concentrate on war-work for Britain. It resumed in the summer of 1916, but stopped again at the beginning of 1918. When the dated-looking ·35 pistol was put back into production in February 1919, the markets were glutted with war-surplus guns. The last ·35 pistols were completed in July 1922, production totalling a little more than eight thousand. Major changes included altering the magazine catch to work longitudinally instead of laterally, early in 1914, and the subsequent deletion of the separate guide-block for the breech assembly.

The Warner Arms Company of Brooklyn, New York, marketed the Schwarzlose blow-forward pistol in 1912–13, allegedly after buying up the remaining German stock, tools and dies. After the failure of the project, Warner purchased rights to an auto-loading pistol patented by Andrew Fyrberg on 28 July 1914 and 9 March 1915, though the application had been filed in March 1913. Production of the ·32 blowback 'Infallible' began in Norwich, Connecticut, in 1915; in 1917, Warner merged with N.R. Davis & Sons of Assonet, Massachusetts, to create the Davis-Warner Arms Corporation.

Work on the Infallible ceased in 1919, when Davis-Warner moved back to Norwich. About 1,500 had been made, distinguished by tip-up barrels to facilitate cleaning, and a fragile safety lever on the left side of the frame behind the trigger.

Harrington & Richardson made a few Webley inspired self-loading pistols, refinements being patented in the USA in 1907–9. Production prior to 1917 was painfully small; despite their excellent quality, the guns were too expensive to compete with the small Colts. About 17,000 guns are said to have been made prior to the US entry into the First World War. The ·25 H&R pattern was made only in 1912–15, the ·32 version, which had an additional grip safety, lasting from 1916 until 1940.

LARGE-FRAME S&W HAND EJECTORS, 1908–1917

Outcome of experiments commencing in 1905, the ·44 Hand Ejector Model Smith & Wesson, built on the N-pattern frame, was introduced commercially in 1908. The barrel marks acknowledged patents issued on 27 March 1894, 21 May 1895, 4 August and 22 December 1896, 8 October and 3 December 1901, and 6 February 1906.

A third locking point, between the cylinder yoke and the distinctive shroud for the ejector rod, gave the gun its sobriquet 'Triple Lock'—though also known as the 'New Century' and (to modern collectors) 'Gold Seal'. Introduced in blue or nickel, with a barrel of five or 6½in chambering ·44 S&W Russian or ·44 S&W Special, the revolver was not an immediate success. Small numbers were made in ·38–40, ·44–40 and ·45 Colt, usually to special order, but only 15,375 commercial guns had been made by 1915.

Substantial quantities of ·455 Triple Lock revolvers were made for the British armed forces, the first being assembled in September 1914. Work continued until mid-January 1915, when a revised version without the heavy ejector-rod shroud and the third lock was approved. The second model proved quite able to handle the pressures involved and was appreciably cheaper to produce.

Production began immediately, guns being offered in blue or nickel finish, with barrels ranging from four to 6½in. A special target version was available with a 6½-inch barrel and adjustable sights. Standard chambering was ·44 S&W Special, though substantial numbers were made in ·44–40 and ·45 Colt. Production stopped on 22 October 1917, when the factory was put on war production, and began again in December 1920.

Though only 17,510 commercial guns had been made by 1940, roughly 69,775 similar ·455-chambered guns had been made for the British authorities during the First World War (January 1915 onward) and 724 examples chambering ·45 Colt cartridges had been sent to Canada in February 1916. The most important variation, however, had been the ·45 Hand Ejector Model of 1917, adapted to fire US ·45 ACP cartridges; 163,476 guns were made during the First World War.

They required a special Half-Moon Clip, designed by Joseph Wesson, to locate the rimless pistol cartridges in the chambers and extract satisfactorily. The only major change necessary in the gun was to shorten the cylinder to accommodate the additional width of the clip.

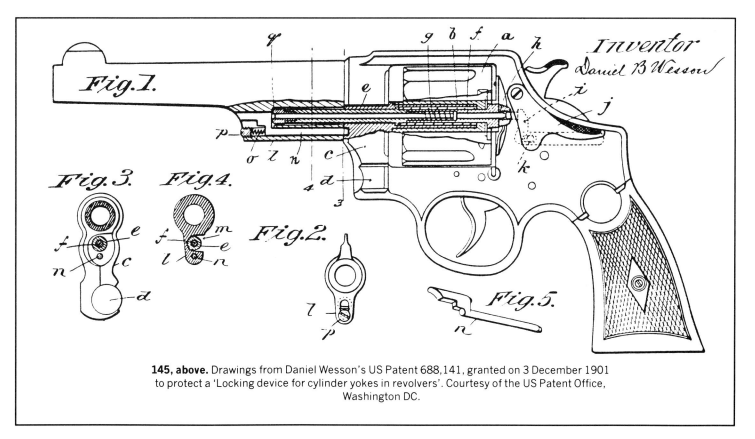

145, above. Drawings from Daniel Wesson's US Patent 688,141, granted on 3 December 1901 to protect a 'Locking device for cylinder yokes in revolvers'. Courtesy of the US Patent Office, Washington DC.

GUN PERFORMANCE
From smooth-bore to small-bore, 1850-1910

LONGARMS

The guns available in 1850 were uninspiring: almost all were slow firing, and—unless carefully loaded—capable of no great accuracy.

¶ Smooth-bore muskets had changed little since the War of Independence. Trials undertaken in France early in the nineteenth century had shown that the probability of hitting a man-size target with such guns was 23 per cent at 100 metres, yet still the military clung to them.

¶ A ·45-calibre Long Rifle tested by the University of California in 1935 attained a muzzle velocity of 2,100 ft/sec^{-1} with a hundred-grain charge and a 135-grain ball wrapped in a greased patch. Velocity declined rapidly until, at 500yd, the projectile was moving at only 550 ft/sec^{-1}; the experimenters concluded that there was a good chance of a hit at 300 yards only in calm conditions.

¶ Trials at Washington Arsenal in 1843–4, with a ballistic pendulum, revealed that the regulation ·69 flintlock (M1835) and cap-lock (M1842) muskets developed muzzle velocities of 1,500 ft/sec^{-1}. As the balls weighed about 400 grains, muzzle energy approached 2,000 ft-lb. However, the poor ballistics of the ball and the absence of rifling-induced spin prevented the initial velocity being retained; at 500yd, it had declined to 385 ft/sec^{-1}.

¶ Within a decade, however, tremendous strides had been made. In 1860, as the United States teetered on the brink of Civil War, the standard longarm was the effectual M1855 rifle-musket. Though still a single-shot weapon, fired by an external cap lock, the rifle-musket extended the range of the old smooth-bores by what contemporary observers regarded as a giant leap. Accuracy also improved dramatically. Though muzzle velocity was only about 1,000 ft/sec^{-1}, the M1855 rifle-musket retained much of its accuracy out to 500 yards, where velocity was still about 670 ft/sec^{-1}. Fifty shots at this distance returned a mean absolute deviation of 15·9in, or a potential group diameter of about 72in.

¶ Military rifles underwent a comparatively gradual improvement, concerned mainly with reduction in calibre to allow soldiers to carry more ammunition. In the US Army this led to the ·45 M1873 or 'Trapdoor' Springfield rifle, precursor of a series of similar weapons produced as late as 1889. The ·50–70–450 Government cartridge, loaded with seventy grains of black powder and a 450-grain lead bullet, compared well with contemporary European equivalents. The official handbook for the 1870-pattern Remington Navy Rifle indicates an Absolute Deviation (i.e., Figure of Merit) of 7·04in at 300yd and 32·7in at 1,050yd. These equate to group diameters of about 32in and 148in respectively.

¶ The velocity of the ·5 projectile, 1,240 ft/sec^{-1} at the muzzle, had declined to 912 ft/sec^{-1} at 300yd and 641 ft/sec^{-1} at 1,050yd. Like most cartridges of this period, the ·50–70 had a high trajectory, which made accurate range-gauging essential to achieve hits. With the sights set for 300yd, the bullet was 35·5in above the line of sight at 150yd; with the sights set for 1,050yd, the corresponding height at 700yd was about 87 *feet!*

¶ In 1886, the French produced the first small-calibre service cartridge to be loaded with smokeless powder, heralding a revolution in smallarms technology; overnight, everyone else's equipment was obsolescent. The great merits of the French ammunition, apart from minimal propellant smoke, were increased velocity and flatter trajectory. However, the small bullet required a hardened metal jacket to cope with vastly increased friction.

¶ The official handbook for the ·30 M1903 Springfield indicates an Absolute Deviation (i.e., Figure of Merit) with M1906 ammunition of 3·4in at 300yd and 24·8in at 1,500yd, equating to groups measuring 15in and 112in respectively. Velocity, 2,700 ft/sec^{-1} at the muzzle, had declined to 1,846 ft/sec^{-1} at 300yd and 852 ft/sec^{-1} at 1,500yd.

¶ Trajectory was greatly flattened compared with the Navy Remington; with the sights set for 300yd, the bullet was 7·14in above the line of sight at 157yd; with the sights set for 1,500yd, the corresponding figure was nearly 53ft at 885yd.

¶ Initially, North American sportsmen were unconvinced by the small-calibre revolution. Too many hunters remembered the days of the buffalo, where great smashing power was needed to offset the comparatively low velocities generated by black powder sporting cartridges. Among the ultimate long-range sporting rounds was the ·50–140 Sharps of *c*.1880, which offered sufficient hitting power to down the largest North American game at the expense of prodigious external dimensions. The case, 3·25in long, contained 140 grains of black powder and a 473-grain lead bullet. The muzzle velocity of 1,580 ft/sec^{-1} gave an energy of 2,520 ft-lb; mid-range trajectory at a range of 200yd was about 11·5in.

¶ Though the US Army accepted ·30 Krag-Jørgensen and then Springfield rifles, US sportsmen continued to resist small-calibre/high power cartridges to the very end of the period under review. Only when men came back from the First World War, with combat experience of the bolt action, did the balance shift perceptibly.

¶ The contrast is emphasised by comparing the ·256 Newton cartridge of 1913 with the ·40–82–260 Winchester pattern, dating from the 1880s. The Newton fired a 123-grain jacketed bullet at a claimed 3,100 ft/sec^{-1}, compared with only 1,490 ft/sec^{-1} for the 260-grain lead Winchester bullet; at a thousand yards, the Newton bullet was still travelling at 1,380

ft/sec^{-1} compared with only 560 ft/sec^{-1} for its rival. Judged by energy figures, the margin of superiority favoured the Newton by a factor of roughly two at the muzzle and three at 1000yd. The ·256 bullet took 1·46 sec to reach 1000yd; time of flight for the ·40–82–260 was 3·63 sec. Mid-range trajectory above the bore axis, with sights set for 200yd, was 2·7in and 11in respectively. The Newton seemed vastly superior. So why did it fail to prosper?

¶ High velocity was greatly appreciated by hunters of fleet-footed game to whom flat trajectory and low bullet-flight time were all-important, but much less to the man whose goal was to stop a moose or a grizzly bear. Small-diameter fully jacketed bullets often caused piercing wounds that minimised the rate of energy loss and, consequently, reduced shocking effect. This alarmed advocates of the 'Big Hit' theory, who preferred the devastating effect of a large-diameter lead projectile surrendering virtually all its energy very quickly.

¶ In more recent times, with restrictions placed on game-hunting and the increased popularity of 'varminting', the gulf between the proponents of high velocity or shocking power has lost much of its importance. But this was not so prior to 1917.

HANDGUNS

Derringers, pepperboxes and the earliest revolvers rarely offered much in the way of hitting power. The ·44 Walker Colt was an exception, capable of propelling a 200-grain ball at 1,300 ft/sec^{-1} with 57 grains of black powder—assuming the weak-walled cylinder survived the high pressures involved.

¶ Perfected cap-lock revolvers were capable of surprisingly good shooting. In addition, most ·44-calibre guns could down a man with a single hit. Accuracy was amazingly good, the biggest drawbacks being the tedious loading process and clouds of smoke accompanying each shot—a problem that was not solved until the end of the nineteenth century. Modern trials with original and replica cap-lock revolvers have often returned ten-shot groups bettering five inches as fifty yards.

¶ Accounts of life in the Wild West reveal many 'gunslingers' to have been poor performers. Even allowing the affects of fear, many shots were often necessary before participants were disabled. One reason was the universally low power of all but the largest cap-lock revolvers, and the frequency with which guns of ·31 or even ·28-calibre featured in confrontations.

¶ Though the effects became less notable as standards of metallurgy improved, rim- and centre-fire Suicide Specials far outnumbered Colt Peacemakers and Smith & Wessons on the Frontier. The trend finally became evident in the US Army, where the ·38 Colt revolver was adopted in 1892; however, adverse reports from the Philippine Insurrection (1900–2) soon led to the acceptance of ·45 as the minimum effectual man-stopper.

¶ The ·25 ACP round is now considered to be only marginally effectual for personal defence. Yet even this insipid little pistol cartridge develops more energy (73 ft-lb) than many rimfire cartridges popular in the 1870s, such as ·30 Short (62 ft-lb) and the robust-sounding ·41 Short (52 ft-lb).

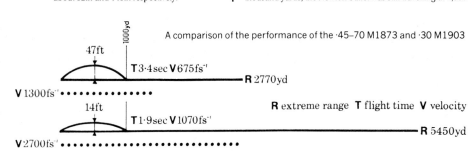

A comparison of the performance of the ·45–70 M1873 and ·30 M1903

47ft — 1000yd
T 3·4 sec **V** 675fs^{-1} — **R** 2770yd
V 1300fs^{-1}

14ft — 1000yd
T 1·9 sec **V** 1070fs^{-1} — **R** 5450yd
V 2700fs^{-1}

R extreme range **T** flight time **V** velocity

THE LONGARMS

CAP-LOCK BREECH-LOADERS, 1811–57

On 21 May 1811, John Hall of Portland, Maine, patented a breech-loading flint-lock rifle. The gun soon attracted the interest of the army, the US Treasury spending $150,000 on perfecting it in 1819–34 alone. Prior to his death in February 1841, Hall had received $17,333 in royalties and $20,200 for the use of his patents.

The Model 1819 Hall rifle had a ·52-calibre 32·7in barrel, measured 52½in overall and weighed about 10¼lb without its socket bayonet. The barrel was rifled with sixteen grooves, the clockwise or right-hand twist making a turn in 96in. However, the muzzle was reamed out for 1½in to give the appearance of a smooth bore.

A hundred-grain powder charge fired a ·525-diameter ball weighing about ½oz. Priming was ten grains of fine powder.

The first contract of 19 March 1819 permitted the US Government to make a thousand Hall system rifles, the work being undertaken in Harper's Ferry armoury. Even though John Hall was employed to oversee the contract, the initial order was not completed until 1824. Work on another thousand began immediately, a third contract, for 6,000, following on 22 April 1828.

The meagre facilities in Harper's Ferry could not unable to satisfy individual states, so, in accordance with the Militia Act of 1808, the US Government ordered Hall rifles from Simeon North. The last of North's five thousand guns was delivered by 1836.

The Hall Carbine, introduced in 1833, was a smooth bore with a 23-inch barrel. The first cap lock issued in the US Army, it was 43in over-

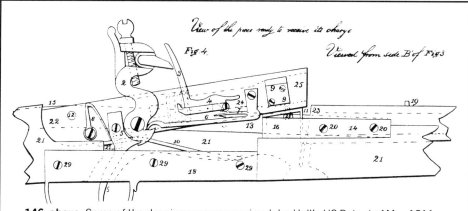

146, above. Some of the drawings accompanying John Hall's US Patent of May 1811. Courtesy of the US Patent Office, Washington DC.

all and weighed 8lb 3oz. It also introduced a sliding rod bayonet in the fore-end beneath the barrel. It had two barrel bands, and a large sling ring beneath the under-edge of the butt in the extremity of the trigger-guard. Some carbines had a patch box let into the butt.

1,026 ·69 smooth-bore carbines were made for the Regiment of Dragoons in 1834; later guns, however, were ·52-calibre.

The ·69 1836-model Hall Carbine, sometimes erroneously listed as the 'model 1837', was ordered for the Second Dragoons. The cap lock guns incorporated old flint-lock stocks and other components as an expedient. They were similar to their predecessors, retaining the rod bayonet, but had shorter barrels, an eye bolt through the stock-wrist to retain a sling, and a hole bored through the hammer.

There was also apparently a ·52-calibre rifled Hall carbine, formerly listed as the Model of 1836; this is believed to have been supplied to the Alabama State Militia in the late 1830s.

The 1840-model Hall Carbines were made in two patterns, one with a folding elbow- or L-shape breech lever and its successor with a fishtail pattern—designed by government arms inspector Nahum Patch and Captain James Huger of the US Army respectively.

On 3 March 1840, the Secretary of War approved a 21-inch carbine barrel and the substitution of a ramrod for the ineffectual rod bayonet. Five hundred Model 1840 carbines had been delivered by 2 May, but the elbow lever was disliked; from August 1840 until June 1843, therefore, six thousand were made with the Huger lever mechanism.

After Hall's death in 1840, a few improved Model 1841 cap-lock rifles were made at Harper's Ferry. Their receivers lacked a flash guard; the catch plate was integral with the trigger guard; a Huger-type breech lever was used; and the barrel was rifled with seven grooves extending to the muzzle. Production apparently exceeded 2,500 in 1841–3, though

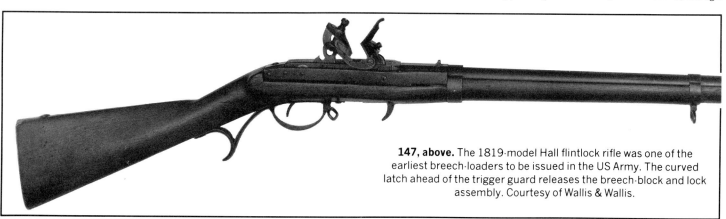

147, above. The 1819-model Hall flintlock rifle was one of the earliest breech-loaders to be issued in the US Army. The curved latch ahead of the trigger guard releases the breech-block and lock assembly. Courtesy of Wallis & Wallis.

documentation is lacking. The last of the regulation-pattern Halls was the ·52-calibre Model 1842 Carbine, a thousand of which was made in 1842–3. These had Huger-pattern breech levers; in addition, the design of the trigger-guard bow and the brass furniture differed from earlier guns.

Production of Hall-type guns was surprisingly large, even though manufacture was exacting by the standards of the day and several gunmakers proved unequal to the task. By 1842, when production ceased, about 23,500 rifles had been made by the government armoury at Harper's Ferry and gunmakers such as Henry Deringer, R. & J.D. Johnson, Reuben Ellis and Simeon North. Production of carbines had amounted to 13,684 by 1842, though orders were still being fulfilled.

The Hall-North carbines, the 'Improved Model of 1840' (or M1843), had a side-mounted breech lever eventually patented by North & Savage in July 1844 (US 3,686). About 11,000 carbines were made in 1842–50, without rod bayonets. They were ·52-calibre smooth bores, measured 40in overall and had 21-inch barrels. A sling bar and ring ran from the second barrel band back along the left side of the receiver.

Simeon North was asked to supply a thousand carbines of the original model (with the Huger fish-tail lever) in 1843, together with five hundred guns with the North & Savage lever. Subsequent batches of improved guns, at the rate of 500 every six months, were to be made until 3,000 had been delivered by 1 July 1846.

Hall's invention had a removable breech chamber embodying the lock. Though this permitted a tighter-fitting bullet and enhanced accuracy, gas leaked from the poor seal between chamber and bore. Improvements made in the basic action by North & Savage were too few to allow the Hall to compete effectually with the first rifle-muskets.

The best feature of the Hall rifle was the speed with which it could be fired, tests in 1826 showing that for each of its hundred shots the standard flintlock rifle could only fire 43 and the musket merely 37.

Unfortunately, Hall rifles required greater powder charges than the muzzle-loaders, even though their power was appreciably less. Experiments at West Point in 1837 revealed that penetration in oak at 100 yards was one inch for the muzzle-loading musket, ·93 for the muzzle-loading rifle and only ·34 for the cap-lock Hall. The muzzle velocity of the Hall-North carbine proved to be only 1,240 ft/sec compared with 1,687 ft/sec for the Jenks, which fired the same 70-grain charge and had a barrel of comparable length.

Though Hall and Hall-North guns remained serviceable until the Civil War, they had long since been declared obsolescent. However, according to ordnance records, 1,575 Hall rifles and 3,520 Hall carbines were bought back into Federal store from state reserves. At least a few saw service during the war, together with others remaining in the hands of state militia and volunteers. A few even served the Confederacy.

In the summer of 1861, five thousand 1843 pattern Hall carbines were sold from New York Arsenal to Arthur Eastman of Manchester, New Hampshire, for $3.50 apiece. The guns were re-sold to Simon Stevens of New York, rifled, re-chambered, and offered to Major General Fremont. The general, commanding the Army Department of the West, needed usable weapons so desperately that he paid $22.00 for each gun.

News of the circuitous deal reached the US Treasury and an outraged Congress authorised an immediate investigation. Collusion between Eastman, Stevens and Fremont was never proven. However, it was discovered that Eastman's original offer to rifle and refurbish the guns for the government for a dollar apiece had been rebuffed!

The principal challenger to the Hall system in North America initially came from the first Colt revolver rifles. These, protected by Samuel Colt's master patent of 25 February 1836, were tested in the summer of 1837. The board of officers responsible for trials of Colt, Hall, Cochrane and 'Baron Hackett' guns reported on 19 September that the Colt was complicated, much too prone to accidents, and totally unsuited to service.

The hammerless Model 1836 Colt-Paterson had a ring-type cocking lever ahead of the trigger; the improved Model 1837 had an external hammer and a small detachable rammer to seat the bullets in their chambers. When the Second Seminole War began in

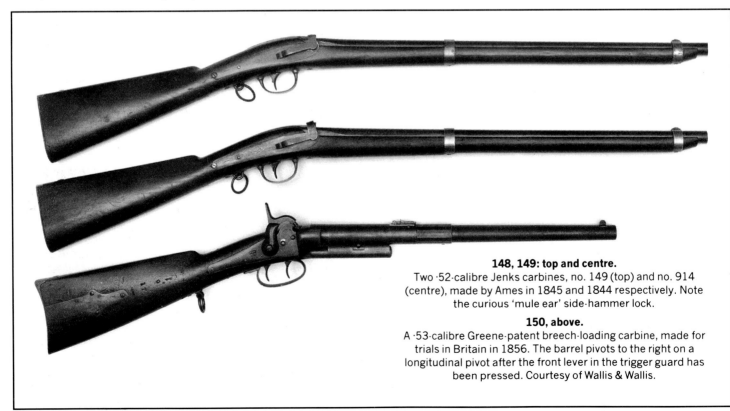

148, 149: top and centre.
Two ·52-calibre Jenks carbines, no. 149 (top) and no. 914 (centre), made by Ames in 1845 and 1844 respectively. Note the curious 'mule ear' side-hammer lock.

150, above.
A ·53-calibre Greene-patent breech-loading carbine, made for trials in Britain in 1856. The barrel pivots to the right on a longitudinal pivot after the front lever in the trigger guard has been pressed. Courtesy of Wallis & Wallis.

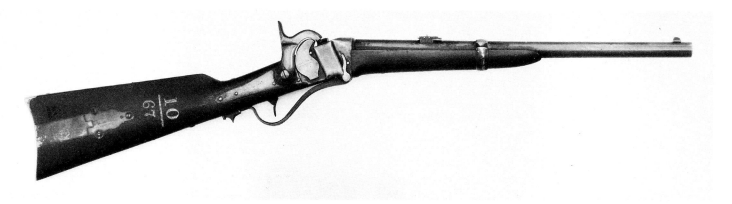

Florida in 1838, Colt deliberately exhibited examples of his revolver rifles in Charlestown, South Carolina. On 9 March 1838, a Board of Officers convened at Fort Jupiter in East Florida to examine them. It recommended that enough guns be acquired to partially equip a dragoon regiment. This was duly approved by the commander of the US Army in Florida, Major-General Jessup, and fifty rifles were ordered from Colt.

They were complicated and delicate, but worked reliably if loaded with care and were considerable improvements over the regulation flint-lock muskets. Unfortunately, more than half the consignment was lost in a skirmish at Caloosahatchie; the remainder entered ordnance stores in Baton Rouge, Louisiana, in 1843. Thus the Colt revolver rifles had little chance to prove their worth in battle.

Samuel Colt received a patent in August 1839 (1,304) to protect a loading lever mounted permanently on the gun. The M1839 rifle, therefore, was simply an improved 1837 pattern with the new rammer. Encouraged, Colt once again sought military interest.

In May 1840, a navy trial board reported that the advantages of the eight-shot cap-lock Colt-Paterson revolver rifles could not offset unreliability. They were still too complicated and delicate to withstand rigorous service, and tended to chain-fire. Purchase of a few guns to arm boat expeditions was recommended, as the Colts were clearly much more effectual than single-shot flint-locks, but this fell far short of Colt's aspirations.

A Board of Officers convened in the summer of 1840 at the Dragoon School of Practice in Carlisle, Pennsylvania, to reconsider the 1839-model Colt. Yet again, purchase of a few carbines was approved: 160 had been delivered by July 1841 at $45 apiece. They, too, were found wanting in service.

The later 1855 or Root Model side-hammer guns, with the action of the contemporaneous small-calibre revolvers, were purchased during the Civil War; Federal ordnance records show the acquisition of 4,612 "Colt's Revolving Rifles" for $204,487 in 1861–6.

The single-shot carbine patented by William Jenks of Columbia, South Carolina, in May 1838 (US 747) was more effectual than either the Hall or the Colt. The first flint-lock musket was tried in 1838, to be followed by a hundred ·64 smooth-bore 19½-inch barrelled carbines. Concurrently, the US Navy bought a few Model 1839 ·54 cap-lock muskets, with 36-inch barrels and a length of 52½in. This lightly built gun had three brass barrel bands, brass furniture, and weighed only 7lb 10oz.

The army's flint-lock carbines were soon supplemented by forty cap-locks, twenty based on the guns supplied to the navy and twenty specially rifled 'for the dragoons'. Ten each of the latter were issued to Companies A and D of the First Dragoons.

Trials in 1841 confirmed the Jenks' potential, and an endurance test at Fort Adam ceased only when the nipple split after 14,813 shots had been fired. There had been no serious problems.

A Board of Officers, meeting at Washington arsenal on behalf of the army and navy in 1845, recommended adoption; unfortunately, troop trials proved catastrophic. Attempts were made to load the large Hall cartridge into the small Jenks chamber; or, alternatively, to insert standard musket cartridges when the Jenks was specifically designed to receive loose powder and ball.

The perfected cap-lock Jenks had a very distinctive side hammer, quickly earning it the sobriquet 'Mule Ear'. Its toggle-type breech was opened by an elongated breech cover pivoted at the back of the action. Raising the lever broke the lock and withdrew the breech block from the chamber to permit reloading. The mechanism sealed effectually, as the breech lever deflected blast down and away from the firer's face.

The failure of the Jenks Carbine opened the way for the breech mechanism patented by Christian Sharps in September 1848 (US 5,763), in which a block that slid downward in a substantial receiver. The original combustible cartridge was ignited by a conventional side hammer striking a cap.

151, above. A ·55-calibre 1855-pattern Sharps 'slant breech' carbine with a Maynard Tape Primer, made for trials in Britain in the mid 1850s. Courtesy of the Board of Trustees of the Royal Armouries, HM Tower of London.

An initial test, in 1850, was highly satisfactory; later trials (1851–3) showed that early Sharps carbines leaked gas alarmingly. Attempts had been made to insert a platinum bush in the face of the breech block but, though durable, this minimized leaks instead of preventing them.

The first Conant seal was fitted in the bush aperture from 1853 in the hope that gas would expand it against the breech. Even the earliest Conant seals were improvements, but not until Richard Lawrence modified the design in 1859 was the problem solved. By 1860, the Marine Corps was able to report that 'all the earlier troubles encountered with Sharps Carbine' had been corrected. Though only 5,540 guns had been acquired prior to 1861, no fewer than 89,653 were officially purchased by the Federal government during the Civil War.

Trials of an 1853-model Sharps Carbine, undertaken in 1854, revealed that accuracy was poor. However, penetration of more than seven inches of pine at thirty yards showed the Sharps to be appreciably more powerful than Hall or Jenks patterns.

MILITARY CAP LOCKS, 1848–65

The history of the firearms of the US Army in the 1848–60 period parallelled that of most European states—a gradual diminution of calibre, the rifling of many obsolescent weapons, and the adoption of rifle-muskets firing self-expanding projectiles.

The first regulation cap lock, a ·57 cadet musket, was authorised in February 1841. It was followed by the ·54 Model 1841 rifle, the ·69 Model 1842 musket, and a ·54-calibre Model 1842 pistol made in Middletown, Connecticut, by Henry Aston. The M1841 rifle was about 48·8in long and weighed 9lb 12oz. It had a

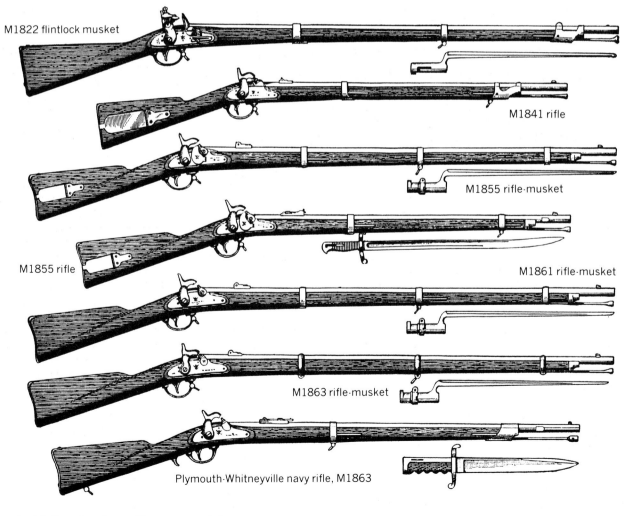

152, above. The Lindsay double rifle-musket, from a contemporary broadsheet. Author's collection.

153–9, below. A selection of the standard US regulation firearms.

160, right. A coloured engraving of Ellsworth's Zouaves, one of many Federal units to adopt French colonial-style uniforms. They are armed with 1855-model rifle-muskets, with Maynard Tape Primers. Courtesy of Philip J. Haythornthwaite.

M1822 flintlock musket

M1841 rifle

M1855 rifle-musket

M1855 rifle

M1861 rifle-musket

M1863 rifle-musket

Plymouth-Whitneyville navy rifle, M1863

Drawings by J.E. Coombes, from a Bannerman catalogue.

conventional cap lock, a walnut stock with a brass patch box, and two brightly polished brass bands. The trigger guard was also brass. The 33-inch barrel, rifled with seven grooves, had a standing back sight for fifty yards. Known as the Mississippi or Yaeger Rifle, it was made at Harper's Ferry (25,296 in 1846–55) and by an assortment of private contractors—E. Remington & Sons of Ilion, New York, who took over an abortive contract granted to John Griffiths of Cincinnati; Robbins, Kendall & Lawrence and its successor, Robbins & Lawrence of Windsor, Vermont; Edward Tryon & Company of Philadelphia; and Eli Whitney of Whitneyville, Connecticut.

The ·69-calibre M1842 musket was essentially similar to the last of the regulation flint-locks,

guard ring could locked on the muzzle by a thumb screw. Guns converted after 1859 usually accepted socket bayonets.

The Musketoon Model 1847 was adopted for cavalry, artillery and sappers on 12 March 1847, production continuing until 1856. The original guns had standing-block back sights and swivel rammers; post-1851 examples had chain rammers and an improved sight with holes for 300 yards and 500 yards in the leaf, plus a 700-yard notch on the leaf edge. A sling bar and ring ran back from the second barrel band to the breech. After the M1855 rifle carbine had been approved for cavalry, 1847-pattern musketoons were made exclusively for artillerymen and sappers. Guns destined for the artillery were issued with socket

Its rammer was retained by a swivel and a large sling ring pierced the trigger guard. Unlike others in the series, the rifle-carbines lacked tape primers.

The ·58 rifle-musket was the principal infantry weapon at the beginning of the Civil War. It was typical of its genre, firing a self-expanding Minié ball from a forty-inch barrel in which three grooves made a turn in 72in. It was 56in long, weighed 9lb 2oz and had iron furniture.

Backed by the enthusiasm of Jefferson Davis, the Secretary of War, the Maynard Tape Primer was adopted for all 1855-type guns excepting the rifled cavalry carbine. The US Ordnance Department was less certain, but the Maynard system had performed well enough on trial to allay the worst fears.

The endorsement in July 1855 approved ·58-calibre for all smallarms. It noted that the "present rifle, modified by the adoption of the new calibre and primer lock, will be...issued to the sappers instead of the sappers' musketoon...manufacture of which will be discontinued". The single-shot pistol carbine was to be used 'as a carbine by light artillery and mounted troops'. It was universally disliked, as it was far inferior to the Colt Dragoon revolvers.

Changes made to the basic M1855 musket included the adoption of a simple two-leaf back sight in 1858, plus substitution of an iron fore-end tip for the older brass pattern and the addition of a butt-side patch box in 1859.

The cadet rifle of 1858, 2,501 of which were made at Springfield Armory in 1858–60, was a variant of the M1855 rifle-musket with a 38-inch barrel and a bayonet with a 16-inch blade.

The Model 1855 rifle was a two-band variant of the musket, its 33-inch barrel accepting a sabre bayonet. Measuring 49·4in overall and weighing about 10lb without its bayonet, it had iron furniture. It was originally equipped with a detachable cross-hair front sight, held against the existing sight block by a binding screw to facilitate accurate shooting. This delicate component was normally carried within the patch box.

Breech-loading trials guns included a carbine designed by Lieutenant Colonel James Durrell Greene of the US Army.

Greene had devised an unsuccessful pivoting barrel carbine in 1852–3, before progressing to an under-hammer bolt-action rifle (US Patent 18,634 of November 1857). Purchase of a hundred 'Bolt Guns' was officially authorised on 5 August 1857, but Greene refused to supply them as the costs of tooling could not be recovered from a small order. He preferred to travel to Europe, where a 3,000-gun order was obtained from Russia.

The purchase of two hundred cap-lock carbines made to the patent of John Symmes of

but had a cap lock and a bolster on the right side of the breech to accommodate the nipple. It was 57·7in long, had a 42-inch smooth-bore barrel and weighed 9lb 3oz. Furniture was iron. Most survivors were rifled after the introduction of the M1855 rifle-musket; 14,292 were adapted in 1856–9, though not all were given new Minié ball sights. The revised back sight had a single leaf with a slider, graduated to 900 yards.

Surviving M1841 rifles were altered at the same time, their bores being reamed-out to ·58 and re-rifled to handle conical bullets. They were also given new long-range sights. The original 1855 rifle-musket pattern had a single leaf with a slider and a stepped base, but was replaced in 1858 by a simpler pattern with two small folding leaves. Some guns were subsequently fitted with a screw-adjustable back sight of superior performance.

A new sabre bayonet was attached either by a conventional spring, groove and stud, or by a cumbersome system of rings. Some bayonets relied on split rings while others had a pommel ring sliding over the front sight until the

bayonets; sapper issue took sabre bayonets, and had swivels under the butt and band.

Many old flint-lock muskets were modernised at Springfield Armory, 30,431 Model 1822 and 26,841 Model 1840 guns being fitted with cap locks in 1851 alone. Some of the best survivors were rifled and re-sighted for expanding-ball ammunition in the late 1850s.

Remington converted about 5,000 Model 1816 muskets by exchanging the old flint-locks for cap locks with Maynard Tape Primers, and many flint-locks that survived into the early days of the Civil War were converted in 1861–2. These simply had the old breech cut away and a plug carrying the nipple-bolster screwed into the barrel.

The advent of the Minié expanding ball brought small-calibre weapons. Approved on 5 July 1855, the series comprised a rifle-musket, a rifle, a rifle-carbine and a pistol-carbine.

The rifle-carbine was intended to arm several new cavalry regiments, 1,020 being made at Springfield in 1855–6. The perfected gun had a single barrel band and a vestigial nose-cap.

Watertown Arsenal, Massachusetts (22,094 of November 1858), was approved on 21 April 1856, though only twenty had been made by March 1857. Symmes' rotating breech block had an 'elastic lip' gas-seal around the chamber. When the action was opened, a hole through the block gave access to the chamber.

The conversion of two thousand muskets to the Morse system (q.v.) was authorised in September 1858, but progress was so slow that only sixty had been completed by the end of 1859. Work dragged on so long that very little had been done when Confederate forces seized Harper's Ferry Armory in April 1861. The few existing Morse-system conversions spent their time in the Federal stores, apparently without seeing service.

Ten thousand Morse transformations of ·69 Model 1842 muskets were ordered in 1860 from the Muzzy Rifle & Gun Manufacturing Company of Worcester, Massachusetts, but few—if any— were completed.

A breech-loading rifle designed by William Montgomery Storm, patented in the USA on 8 July 1856 (15,307), was tested by the Ordnance Department prior to the Civil War. The weapon had sufficient potential for the conversion of two thousand Model 1842 muskets to be authorised in September 1858, though little was ever achieved. The Storm breech block, which swung up and forward over the barrel, was locked by a sliding bolt as the hammer fell.

COMMERCIAL CAP LOCKS, 1848–65

The percussion cap retained its popularity far longer in the West than in military service, lasting almost into the twentieth century in remote parts of Northern America. Its popularity was due to comparatively poor distribution of metal-case ammunition, persuading men whose livelihood depended on firearms to be wary of innovation.

The single-shot rifle had a lengthy pedigree, descending through the Trade Guns supplied to settlers and Indians alike during the eighteenth century, to the indigenous Long Rifles. The market for trade guns was exemplified by the Hudson's Bay Company Fuke (or 'Fusil'), a short smooth-bore of ·65–·75 calibre, with an enlarged trigger guard for gloved fingers. By the 1840s, however, the markets had changed. Cap locks were finding increasing favour not only among gunmakers, but also with hunters who ventured into the Great Plains in pursuit of buffalo.

Development of the traditional Plains Rifle is usually credited to the brothers Jacob and Samuel Hawken of St Louis, Missouri. Taking the regulation US Model 1803 flintlock rifle as a pattern, and aware that long barrels were a

handicap in brush, the Hawkens gradually refined their guns until a typical example had a calibre of ·32–·38, a 35–40in barrel and weighed about 11lb. Most had a cap lock, and a patch box let into the butt side. Decoration was kept to a minimum on what were often sold as 'Plain Rifles'—from which their modern name seems to have been corrupted.

The supremacy of the Hawken rifle passed with the Civil War, in the face of competition provided by the Sharps and Remington breech loaders. Jacob Hawken died in May 1849, at a time when his products were already being challenged by similar guns made by Diettrich and Dimick of St Louis. Samuel Hawken sold his business to John Gemmer in 1862, but made the last true Hawken rifles in retirement in the late 1870s. He died in 1884.

The appearance of the first Colt revolver rifles in the 1830s persuaded many inventors that the future lay in multi-chamber guns. However, Colt's patent protected cylinders rotated by the

161, above. *The Indian Trapper*, painted by Frederic Remington in 1889. Note the flintlock Plains Rifle, its butt tacked in typical fashion and the wrist bound with wire. Courtesy of the Amon Carter Museum, Fort Worth, Texas.

hammer and forced his rivals into increasingly complex solutions.

Few were made in quantity. Most survivors were made to the patent granted on 11 June 1829 (US 203) to James Miller of Brighton, New York. Miller died in 1843; his business was then split between his brother John and William Billinghurst, who each made guns to the master patent. A few Billinghurst guns even had a smooth-bore barrel doubling as the cylinder axis pin, later to achieve greater notoriety in the Le Mat revolver.

Many minor gunmakers in upstate New York made Miller-pattern guns, including Holmes of Oswego; Perry of Fredonia; Patrick Smith of Buffalo; William Smith of New York; Charles

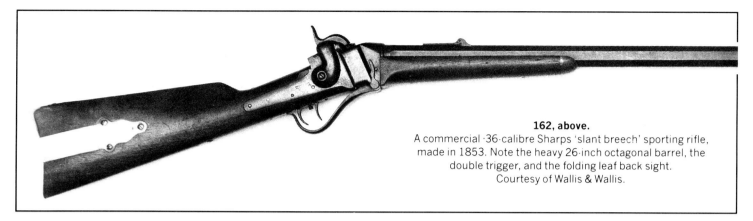

162, above.
A commercial ·36-calibre Sharps 'slant breech' sporting rifle,
made in 1853. Note the heavy 26-inch octagonal barrel, the
double trigger, and the folding leaf back sight.
Courtesy of Wallis & Wallis.

Bunge of Geneva; Calvin Miller of Canadia; and Benjamin Bigelow of Rochester. Bigelow moved to Marysville, California, with the Gold Rush.

Miller-type guns had sturdy bullet deflectors and manually rotated cylinders indexed by a catch at the cylinder-mouth. Many of the original J. & J. Miller guns were pill-locks, though caps were favoured by the copyists.

Jonathan Browning—father of John M. Browning—made small numbers of distinctive manually operated bar-hammer revolver rifles in Kanesville, Iowa, in the middle of the nineteenth century; the rifle patented by Alexander Hall of New York in June 1856 (15,110) had an internal striker, cocked by a lever in the front of the trigger guard behind the fifteen-chamber cylinder. Output of Halls did not exceed fifty.

North & Savage of Middetown, Connecticut, made substantial numbers of revolver rifles—apparently more than five hundred—to a patent granted in June 1852 to Henry North and Chauncey Skinner (US 8,982). They were operated by pulling the front of the trigger guard down, removing the supporting wedge and rotating the cylinder. The hammer was cocked manually. The Springfield Arms Company and James Warner, better known for cap-lock revolvers, made rifles to the same basic designs; quantities were sizable, the former making 250 and the latter about four hundred in a variety of patterns.

The turret repeater was briefly touted as an alternative to the revolver-rifle. Enjoying a brief vogue in the USA contemporaneous with its heyday in Europe, it had a disc-like cylinder with chambers bored radially.

North American guns included the 'Monitor', patented by John Webster Cochran on 28 April 1837 (US 188) and made by Cyrus Allen of Springfield, Massachusetts. The under-hammer Monitor, which had a horizontal cylinder disc, was more popular as a pistol than a ·44-calibre seven or eight-shot rifle. A similar gun patented by Edward Graham of Hillsborough, New Hampshire, in September 1856 (15,734), sought safety by placing the ball in a chamber at an angle to the propellant. The hammer of the Graham rifle was cocked as the cylinder rotating lever was operated.

Guns made by George Foster of Taunton, Massachusetts, for Patrick 'Parry' Porter of Memphis, Tennessee (to US Patent 8,210 of 18 July 1851), had vertical disc cylinders. The earliest "Porter's Cap Box Revolving Rifles" were ·36 or ·50-calibre eight- or nine-shot firearms with special tape-primer locks and offset sights. These were made alongside similar guns using "Colt's Metal-Lined Cap", while those made after 1856 by C.D. Schuberth—Foster's successor—also relied on percussion caps.

Though numbers on Porter rifles run as high as 427, it is unlikely that production exceeded fifty. The inventor is said to have been fatally wounded when, during a demonstration to Samuel Colt (or, alternatively, the Board of Ordnance), one of his rifles revealed the most dangerous feature of a turret-pattern gun by chain-firing. As some radial chambers pointed backward, safety could never be guaranteed.

Typical of the lunatic fringe of multi-chamber cap-locks was the rifle patented by Lucius Gibbs of Oberlin, Ohio, in October 1847 (US 5,316). This extraordinary weapon had nine seven-chamber cylinders. Rotated by a manual lever, each loaded cylinder could be moved forward under gravity when the 'firing cylinder' had been exhausted. The inventor claimed that all 63 shots could be fired in three minutes, though there is no evidence that this was ever achieved.

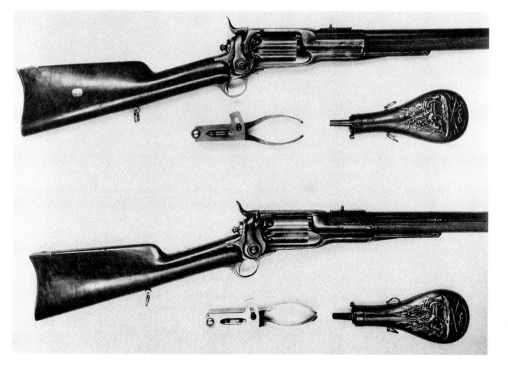

163, left. These two side-hammer Colt Revolver Rifles were presented to grand-dukes Mikhail and Konstantin of Russia in c.1857. Courtesy of the Hermitage Museum, Leningrad, USSR.

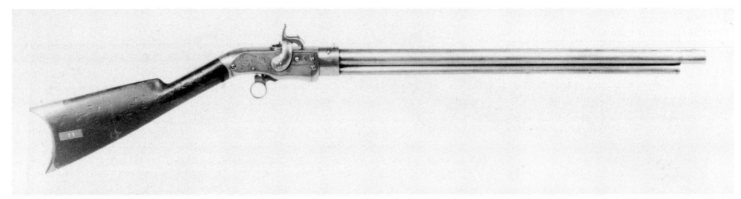

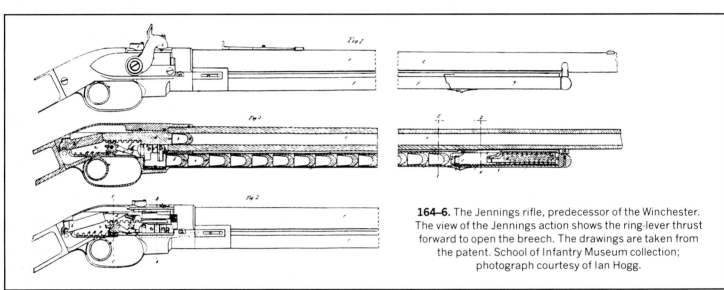

164–6. The Jennings rifle, predecessor of the Winchester. The view of the Jennings action shows the ring-lever thrust forward to open the breech. The drawings are taken from the patent. School of Infantry Museum collection; photograph courtesy of Ian Hogg.

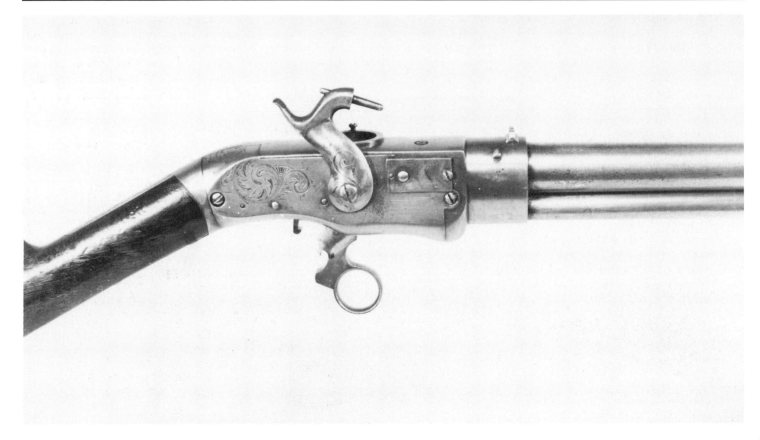

THE VOLITION BALL, 1848-60

An unpractical repeating rifle was patented by Walter Hunt of New York in August 1849. Though only a single example of the twelve shot piston-breech repeater was apparently made, it fired a 'Volition Ball' containing its own propellant and igniter.

Gunsmith Lewis Jennings was entrusted with the difficult task of perfecting the Hunt Rifle, receiving a US patent on Christmas Day 1849. His patent model was a ·54-calibre pill-lock with a 34-inch barrel and an overall length of 53in. A twenty-shot tube magazine lay under the barrel.

Patent rights had been assigned to George Arrowsmith of New York City, who appears to have been a minor entrepreneur. However, once the Jennings rifle had been perfected, Arrowsmith sold the entire project to a syndicate financed by the railroad magnate Courtlandt Palmer. Optimistically, Palmer ordered five thousand Jennings-type rifles from Robbins & Lawrence, but the project failed after no more than a few hundred had been made.

Robbins & Lawrence made two versions of the pill-lock Jennings, each about 44in overall with 26-inch ·54 barrels rifled with seven grooves. The earlier pattern had its ring trigger/operating lever inside a conventional guard and the magazine tube ended level with the muzzle; the later gun dispensed with the guard entirely, its magazine ending behind the muzzle.

Many improvements in the Jennings rifle were the work of Richard Lawrence, junior partner in Robbins & Lawrence and a skilled gunmaker. However, Lawrence subsequently claimed so great a part in the transition from the Jennings to the Volcanic that it is difficult to assess his true contribution. A greater part was probably played by one of Robbins & Lawrence's machinists, Benjamin Henry.

Robbins & Lawrence withdrew when the Jennings rifle failed to excite interest, and Palmer cancelled the contract before it had been completed. In due course, he licensed the Hunt and Jennings patents to Horace Smith and Daniel Wesson.

Younger brother of Edwin Wesson, maker of the Wesson & Leavitt revolver, Daniel had inherited rights to his brother's patents in 1850. A syndicate of heirs and interested parties then formed the Massachusetts Arms Company to make mechanically-actuated revolvers, but had been sued by Colt for patent infringement. After a celebrated duel between two of the most famous attorneys of their day, Colt won. The punitive damages were far too great for the Massachusetts Arms Company to bear, and so the business went into voluntary liquidation in 1853. As no love was lost with Colt, Daniel Wesson was keen to enter partnership with Horace Smith. Smith had formerly worked with Allen, Brown & Luther in Worcester, Massachusetts, and was an experienced gun maker. In June 1854, Smith & Wesson opened a small workshop in Norwich, Connecticut, to exploit—among other things—the Hunt and Jennings patents.

Horace Smith and Edwin Wesson patented an improved magazine pistol in 1854, and series production began immediately.

The Smith & Wessons were lever action repeaters with tube magazines beneath their barrels. They loaded through a port cut in the underside of the magazine tube near the muzzle. Blunt tipped Hunt-type rocket ball were used, bores being ·31, ·36 (often advertised as '·38') and ·44. The pistols were made in several sizes with magazine capacities of 8–10 projectiles, though an occasional carbine was made for special purposes.

In spite of impressive testimonials, the guns were comparatively expensive and inaccurate. There was very little room in the small projectiles for large charges of propellant; in addition, mercuric fulminate was exceptionally corrosive. Unless cleaned carefully and regularly, the bores deteriorated rapidly.

Business declined steadily until it had no future. Smith & Wesson, meanwhile, still apparently financed largely by Palmer, had acquired a patent granted to Rollin White.

Though White's revolver was also unpractical, he had claimed novelty in a bored through cylinder loaded from the breech. Seeing the potential that lay in this one small claim, Smith & Wesson sold the rocket-ball patents to a syndicate of local businessmen in the summer of 1855. In August, the tools, fixtures, gauges and existing components were removed to a factory in Orange Street, New Haven. Only about 1,200 guns had been made during Smith & Wesson's brief superintendency.

New Haven's clock makers, grocers, bakers, carriage makers and entrepreneurs, envious of the flourishing arms trade in neighbouring Massachusetts, formed themselves into the Volcanic Repeating Fire Arms Company. Daniel Wesson was retained as works superintendent until the spring of 1856; Horace Smith left in disillusion, and Benjamin Henry returned to Robbins & Lawrence.

The first president of the Volcanic company, mining financier Nelson Gaston, died suddenly in December 1856. He was replaced by shirt maker Oliver Winchester, who initially held a $2,000 dollar stake in Volcanic. In addition to their personal stakes, however, Gaston and Winchester had each advanced Volcanic large sums of money secured on the Hunt, Jennings and Smith & Wesson patents. When Gaston died, Winchester purchased his Volcanic stakes from his heirs.

By midsummer 1857, Volcanic was insolvent. Sales had never been brisk and the unstable fulminate powder, which sometimes blew the magazine tube off the breech, was a great handicap. Charges of black powder were tried, but cured the fault only at the expense of loss of power. As the rocket ball was inherently weak—muzzle velocity of the ·36 ball was a mere 500 ft/sec—reduction was unacceptable. The answer clearly lay elsewhere.

True Volcanics, made before the sale of the company to Winchester, were invariably ·40 calibre. There were pistols with ring-tipped operating levers, and a selection of carbines whose appearance presaged the Henry rifle.

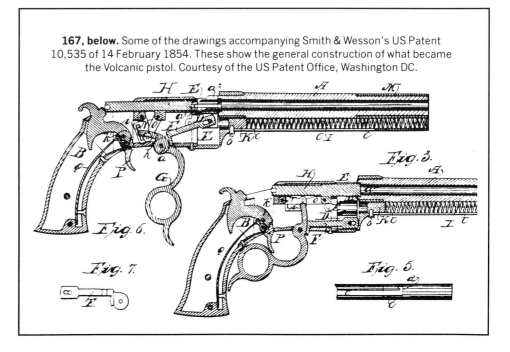

167, below. Some of the drawings accompanying Smith & Wesson's US Patent 10,535 of 14 February 1854. These show the general construction of what became the Volcanic pistol. Courtesy of the US Patent Office, Washington DC.

The longarms were made with barrels of sixteen, 21½ and 25in, their magazines holding twenty, 25 and thirty shots respectively.

The promise that lay in lever action and a tube magazine was hidden by the drawbacks of the Volcanic system. As Hunt, Palmer, and Smith & Wesson had failed, so the Volcanic company finally closed its doors. It had been sold to Winchester—its greatest creditor—for $25,000.

The New Haven Arms Company was formed on 1 May 1857 to purchase the Volcanic patents. Winchester received $40,000 for tools and inventory, plus the patent rights: at least one man had made a substantial profit from the rocket-ball guns!

Winchester acquired the services of Benjamin Henry as works superintendent, the factory was retained, and the guns continued to be sold as the 'Volcanic Repeating Fire Arms'. An 1859-vintage broadsheet advertised three carbines in 'No.2' bore (·40), with barrels of sixteen, twenty and 24in; two ·40 'Navy' pistols with barrels of six or eight inches; a No.1 (·31) target gun with a six-inch barrel; and a ·31 pocket pistol with a four-inch barrel. Magazine capacity varied from six balls in the pocket pistol to thirty in the biggest carbine.

The broadsheets—particularly those issued by Winchester—contain the most magnificent claims, backed up by 'testimonials' gleaned from sources as diverse as clipper-ship captains and Winchester's St Louis agent. The Volcanic system did possess advantages over cap-lock revolvers, particularly in damp conditions, so the opinions of men who claimed to have fired 'over 200 shots from it without even wiping the barrel' or to have had the pistol 'at sea for more than eighteen months, on a voyage around the world, and find…the Balls as good now as when I left New York' are worthy of attention. Less satisfactory are those relating epic deeds.

The New Haven Arms Company also failed to prosper. By 1861, and the dawning of the American Civil War, it was facing insolvency. In the interim, however, Benjamin Henry had developed a new lever action rifle. Its ·44 rim-fire cartridge could propel a 216-grain bullet at 1,200 ft/sec—a vast improvement on the puny Volition Ball. The Henry rifle was the New Haven Arms Company's salvation.

THE FIRST METALLIC-CARTRIDGE BREECH-LOADERS

As European authorities dallied with capping breech-loaders and needle-guns, attempts were being made to perfect self-contained cartridges in metal cases. One of the first steps towards the modern military weapon was taken by Samuel Morse, whose breech-loading carbine

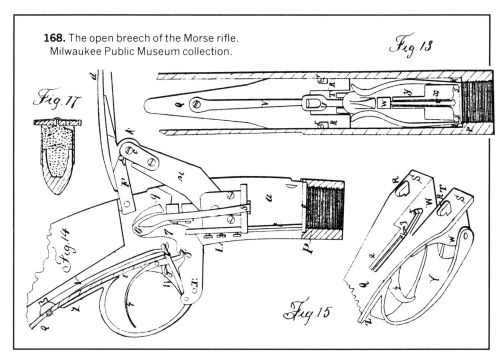

168. The open breech of the Morse rifle. Milwaukee Public Museum collection.

was tested by the US Army in 1857. Morse's cartridge developed no real power, but it had an internal primer and was genuinely self contained.

One school believed that cartridges should carry their own primer (as in the Morse rifle and the Dreyse needle-gun), while another championed external cap locks. Initially, neither could prove its case.

While the Morse gun underwent its trials, the US armed forces experimented in 1858–9 with the Burnside and Maynard Carbines. The former was patented in March 1856 by Ambrose Burnside, later an army commander of renown during the Civil War. Its breech block was dropped by a lever doubling as the trigger guard, the unique tapered copper cartridge case being inserted backward into the block through the top of the frame. As the action closed, the protruding bullet seated in the chamber-mouth. Ignition was provided by a conventional cap lock.

Burnside carbines were originally made by the Bristol Firearms Company of Bristol, Rhode Island. They had a separate breech-lock lever beneath the hammer and lacked a fore-end. Two hundred Bristol-type Burnsides were purchased by the US Army in April 1856, followed by 709 in September 1858.

One gun tested at Washington Navy Yard in 1859 fired 500 shots without malfunctioning, though thirty of the 470 aimed shots missed the eight-feet square target at a range of 500 yards. Penetration at 30 yards was 6·15 inches of pine.

However, the success of the Burnside carbine dissipated after it had received the grudging compliment of being the 'best…imperfect system' submitted to army trials in 1857–8. In

the absence of substantial government orders, its promoter was bankrupted.

Ironically, the new controllers of the patents, reorganised as the Burnside Rifle Company, made thousands of carbines for the Federal Government during the Civil War. The breech locking lever on the later guns was incorporated in the trigger guard.

Designed by a Washington dentist and patented in 1856–9, the Maynard Carbine was an unconventional dropping-barrel gun locked by a trigger-guard lever. Like the earliest Burnside, it lacked a fore-end. Maynards were made by the Massachusetts Arms Company of Worcester. They fired a copper-case cartridge, ignited by the flash from a cap struck by a centrally-hung hammer.

A test undertaken in 1859 showed the Maynard gun to be more accurate than Burnside's, probably owing to its better bullet seating system, and all 250 shots at 500 yards hit the regulation target. At 1,300 yards, fourteen shots out of 43 hit a target ten feet high by thirty feet broad, penetrating an inch of pine. In all, 562 shots had been fired without cleaning. There had been no misfires and the maximum rate of fire proved to be twelve rounds per minute.

In 1860, Major Colston reported to the Commissioners of Virginia Armory that the paper-cartridge Smith loaded easily when clean, but became so foul after sixty shots that it could not be loaded at all; the essentially similar Merrill had proved solid and gas-tight even after a hundred shots; the Burnside shot admirably, with no evidence of fouling; and the Maynard (which Colston regarded as very powerful) shot the best of the special metal-case cartridges.

His conclusion, however, typified conservative ordnance attitudes: he would not recommend Burnside or Maynard carbines, as they could only be reloaded if special ammunition was available.

The Civil War effectively ended the brief heyday of the rifle-musket by confirming the efficacy of the breech-loading rifle and metal case cartridge, even if these vital advances were not heeded immediately. The advantages were partly hidden by the profusion of guns, differing cartridges, suspect ignition and poor-quality propellant.

The earliest metal-case cartridges were heavy enough to worry senior officers concerned with the supply and replenishment of ammunition: the Spencer rifle, accompanied by a Blakeslee cartridge box, could fire twenty shots a minute. When its cartridges had been expended, however, even the Spencer was impotent.

Most senior commanders in the Civil War had seen active service many years previously. Mindful that a cap-and-ball muzzle-loader was not as restricted as a metal-cartridge gun, as long as caps were available, they hindered the progress of the breech-loader for many years. Eventually, the situation became so serious that President Abraham Lincoln ordered the removal of the incumbent Chief of Ordnance—Brigadier General James 'Old Fogey' Ripley—in 1863.

However, when the war ended in 1865 and progressive part-time commanders had returned to civilian life, repeaters were still regarded scornfully by regulars brought up with single-shot muskets. Though many excellent breech loading weapons had been purchased

officially, the US Board of Ordnance and Fortification subsequently chose the slow-firing Springfield-Allin or 'Trapdoor' conversion for its rifle-muskets, condemning troops to poor extraction for more than twenty years.

JENKS RIFLES AND CARBINES, 1838–65

The Jenks was one of the oldest designs to be used in the Civil War. Patented on 25 May 1838, it had an unconventional cap lock with a lateral 'mule ear' hammer. The breech was sealed by a plunger or piston sliding into the back of the chamber from the rear. This was locked by a toggle joint and required no extra locking latches. The breech was opened simply by raising a lever running back from the breech above the stock-wrist. The system was very safe, as it deflected gas leaks down and away from the firer's face.

Though the army rejected the Jenks after the disastrous field trials, the navy was well satisfied with its performance; 6,200 Jenks guns were ordered from Nathan Ames (1,000 rifles and 4,200 carbines) and E. Remington & Son (1,000 carbines) in 1841–5, Remington's guns being the first martial arms to incorporate the Maynard Tape Primer and a cast-steel barrel. They also had double-ear actuating levers and straight-shank hammers.

By 1860, surviving guns had all been withdrawn to store. Though a few original Jenks carbines were reissued to serve during the war, most survivors were transformed by James

Merrill (q.v.) into conventional side-hammer cap locks.

SHARPS RIFLES AND CARBINES, 1848–65

The Sharps was the most popular single shot breech-loader purchased by the Federal government during the American Civil War. Patented by Christian Sharps in 1848 (5,763), it was tested by the US Army as early as 1850. Its breech block was lowered by an operating lever doubling as the trigger guard, on perfected guns, while the combustible paper (later linen) cartridge was ignited by an external cap lock.

Early in 1857, two hundred Sharps carbines were purchased by the Massachusetts–Kansas Aid Committee (one of many anti-slavery organisations) for abolitionists in Kansas. The carbines were shipped in the summer of 1857, but were impounded in Tabor, Iowa. They were subsequently retrieved by John Brown, who had obtained authority to sell a hundred to the Kansas abolitionists and retain the remainder to arm his own anti-slavery forces. After Brown's unsuccessful attack on Harper's Ferry Armory in 1859, 104 carbines and 160 boxes of Sharps Patent Pellet Primers were retrieved. Stored in Harper's Ferry, unclaimed by the Massachusetts Aid Committee, they were subsequently seized by the Confederacy, refurbished in Richmond and issued to rebel cavalry.

As a Sharps Carbine was carried by John Brown, so the genre soon acquired the nickname 'John Brown Sharps' or, alternatively,

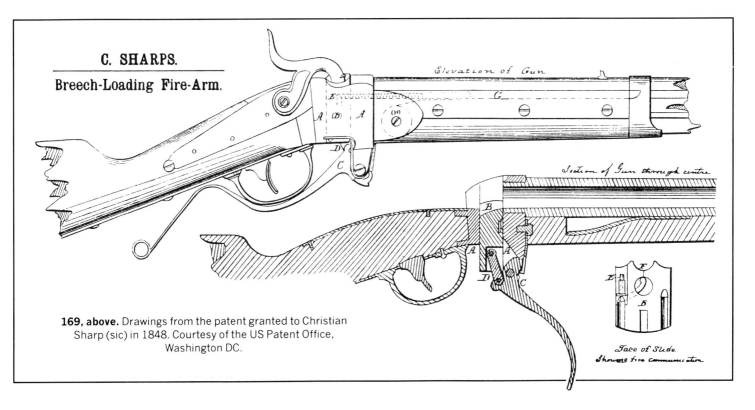

C. SHARPS.
Breech-Loading Fire-Arm.

Elevation of Gun

Section of Gun through centre

Face of Slide.
Showing fire communication

169, above. Drawings from the patent granted to Christian Sharp (sic) in 1848. Courtesy of the US Patent Office, Washington DC.

"Beecher's Bibles" after the notorious Brooklyn preacher Henry Ward Beecher.

A few old-model or 'Slant Breech' Sharps saw action during the Civil War. The Model 1853, used by John Brown, was generally made as a ·52-calibre carbine, 37·8in overall, with a 21·6in barrel and brass furniture. The lock plate contained Sharps' patented pellet magazine, with a slender brass tube of waterproofed priming discs.

The Model 1853 was supplanted by the Model 1855, four hundred carbines being ordered by the US Army in April 1855 and two hundred rifles by the navy in March–September 1856. The ·52-calibre half-stocked rifles were 44·3in long, had 28·3-inch barrels and weighed 9lb without their sabre bayonets. The back sights were graduated to 800yd. Furniture and the single barrel band were brass.

The carbines were essentially similar to the 1853 pattern, with the distinctive slant breech, but Maynard Tape Primers replaced Sharp's own pellet feeder. Sharps' Rifle Manufacturing Company marks appeared on the carbine barrels, with EDWARD MAYNARD/PATENTEE 1855 on the tape primer gate. Official property marks and inspector's initials (e.g., 'U.S.' over 'J.H.–P.') may be encountered on the rear of the barrel.

The Sharps action was sturdy and durable, though not initially gas-tight. This was partly due to great difficulty in sealing breech loaders firing combustible ammunition and partly to the use of the sharpened upper edge of the breech block to shear the base off the chambered cartridge. This inevitably scattered a few grains of powder on the upper surface of the breech; as these often ignited when the gun

fired, adding to the flash of the primer, the guns were unpleasant to use.

Attempts were soon made to improve the seal by letting an expandable gas-check ring into the breech-block face. The first successful system was patented by Hezekiah Conant of Hartford, Connecticut, on 1 April 1856 (14,554). The Sharps Rifle Company is said to have paid Conant $80,000 for rights to his invention, but it was only partly effectual. The situation improved when Richard Lawrence, part-owner of the Sharps Rifle Company, patented an improved seal on 20 December 1859 (26,501). However, the problem was eliminated only cap locks were converted to fire metal-case cartridges after the Civil War.

The improved New Models of 1859 and 1863 had vertical breeches. They fired combustible linen cartridges, with nitrated bases to facilitate ignition, and had conventional external side hammers. In spite of the gas leaks, which varied from gun to gun and could often be minimal, Sharps firearms were very popular; they were sturdy and rarely gave trouble.

The navy ordered nine hundred M1859 ·56-calibre rifles on 9 September 1859. The guns had thirty-inch barrels held in the full-length stock by two bands, and accepted an Ames-made sword bayonet. 1,500 ·52 rifles were then ordered from an agent, John Mitchell of Washington DC, in June 1861.

The first army orders were placed in June 1861, when 'Sharps Long Range Rifles with bayonets' were ordered from C.C. Bean of New York. By 30 June 1865, more than nine thousand rifles had been delivered into Federal stores. Army rifles were similar to the navy's, but—excepting 600 with 36-inch barrels—had

33-inch barrels held by three bands. Most accepted socket bayonets.

The Model 1859 carbine, with a 22-inch ·52-calibre barrel, was 39in overall. It bore Sharps' name on the barrel and acknowledged Lawrence's pellet-feeder patent on the lock plate. A cut-off allowed standard percussion caps to be used if required. Most guns made prior to 1862 had brass furniture, but this was replaced by iron early in the Civil War.

The New Model Carbine of 1863 was all but identical to the 1859 pattern, though it was clearly marked MODEL 1863 on the barrel. The patch box was abandoned some time in the Spring of 1864 to simplify production.

According to ordnance records for the period 1 January 1861 to 30 June 1866, the Federal government purchased 80,512 carbines and 9,141 rifles at a unit cost of $27·49 and $36·17 respectively; 16·31 million combustible paper or linen cartridges cost $2·13 per hundred.

The Sharps rifle attained undying fame in the hands of the two regiments of United States Sharpshooters formed under the supervision of Colonel Hiram Berdan in September–October 1861. Though Chief of Ordnance Ripley wanted the élite units to carry regulation rifle-muskets, Berdan eventually got his way: 1,000 Sharps rifles were ordered for the sharpshooters on 27 January 1862 and another thousand on 6 February. Unlike the standard rifles, they all had double set-triggers. Deliveries to the sharpshooters had been completed by the end of May.

Many other units used the Sharps during the war, including some mounted infantrymen to whom the full-length rifle was something of an encumbrance. Apart from this complaint,

170. Colonel Hiram Berdan, commander of the 1st US Sharpshooters and later renowned as a firearms inventor. Courtesy of the US National Archives, Washington DC.

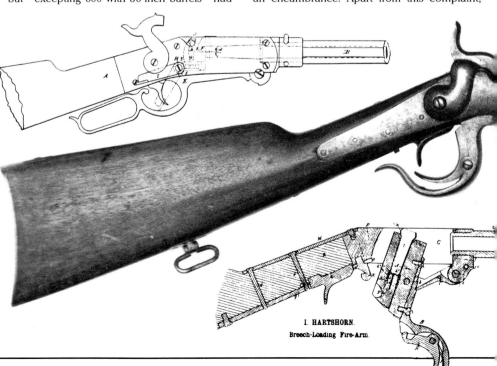

I. HARTSHORN.
Breech-Loading Fire-Arm.

however, and an occasional gas-leak problem, very little was said against the guns.

BURNSIDE CARBINES, 1855-65

Patented by Ambrose Burnside on 23 March 1856 (14,491), but apparently developed two years previously, this distinctive breech-loading carbine fired a unique conical cartridge inserted in the front of the breech block before the action was closed. A small hole in the base of the cartridge case allowed a side-hammer cap lock to be used.

In 1855, before the patent had been granted, Burnside had organised the Bristol Fire Arms Company in Bristol, Rhode Island, in the hope of attracting army attention. The gun underwent several searching trials, culminating in one at West Point, in August 1857, where the Burnside was adjudged the best of several systems under review. Unfortunately, the army order of September 1858 was small—709 guns at $35 apiece.

The absence of large-scale orders coincided with a severe economic depression, which hit the New England firearms industry particularly badly in the autumn of 1857. In desperation, Burnside sold his patents to his creditors and the Bristol Fire Arms Company went into liquidation.

The new proprietors, headed by Charles Jackson, still had faith in their gun and formed the Burnside Rifle Company in 1859. Tooling began in a new factory in Providence, Rhode Island. Once again, the Civil War proved a boon: in July 1861, the Chief of Ordnance, Brigadier General James Ripley, passed Jackson a request

for eight hundred Burnside carbines from Governor William Sprague of Rhode Island. Sprague wished to equip his state cavalrymen with modern weapons.

The order was accepted with alacrity, Jackson promising delivery for the end of 1861. Second pattern carbines were finally delivered in March 1862, lacking the original Maynard Tape Primer and side-mounted locking lever. A new latch had been mounted inside the front of the trigger guard bow.

The original wrapped-foil cartridge, which had a straight-taper case, had been substituted by a 'bell mouth' pattern designed by George Foster, foreman machinist in the Providence factory. Foster cartridges were made in a single piece, a circumferential groove inside the case mouth containing sufficient wax to lubricate the bullet and improve the gas seal. First and second model Burnside carbines had 21-inch ·54-calibre rifled barrels, and measured about 39½in overall.

The third pattern had a short wooden fore-end and a modified hammer profile. The fourth model of 1864, however, displayed a double-pivot breech block and a detachable hinge-pin patented by Isaac Hartshorn, Burnside's sales agent.

The Burnside system, largely because it relied on an external cap lock, was popular with the military authorities. Total Federal purchases amounted to 55,567 between 1 January 1861 and 30 June 1866, ranking the carbines third only to the Spencer and Sharps in distribution. Each gun cost the US Treasury $25·42 each, while the accompanying 21·82 million metal case cartridges were bought at a rate of $2·51 per hundred.

JOSLYN RIFLES AND CARBINES, 1855-65

Benjamin Joslyn contributed two differing carbines to the roster of Civil War breech loaders. The earliest guns, known as the Model of 1855, had conventional side-hammer cap locks. The breech lever ran back along the wrist of the stock, being lifted upward by means of a large finger ring to permit a combustible paper cartridge to enter the chamber. Steel rings in the face of the breech mechanism expanded momentarily on discharge to form a gas seal.

Successful trials with a Joslyn carbine, in September 1857, led to the purchase of fifty in November. Though the army soon lost interest, the navy was keener. Five hundred ·58 rifles were ordered on 9 September 1858 from Joslyn's agent, William Freeman of New York. Owing to problems with the sub-contractor, Asa Waters & Company of Milbury, Massachusetts, delivery was delayed until the Spring of 1861. It has been estimated that only about 150–200 of the 500-gun order were ever forthcoming.

The ·58 Navy Rifles were 45·8in overall, had thirty-inch three-groove barrels and weighed about 8lb. They had half-stocks held by a single band and would accept a sabre bayonet. The ·54-calibre carbines had 22½-inch barrels and measured 38¼in overall. Waters' marks lay on the lock plate. Furniture was brass. The limited efficiency of 1855-pattern Joslyns did not endear them to the ordnance authorities.

A carbine chambering metal-case cartridges appeared in 1861, series production beginning a year later. The new gun had a laterally-

171

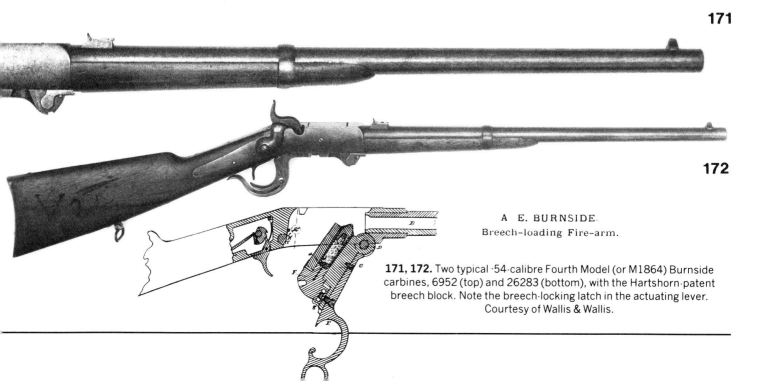

172

A E. BURNSIDE.
Breech-loading Fire-arm.

171, 172. Two typical ·54-calibre Fourth Model (or M1864) Burnside carbines, 6952 (top) and 26283 (bottom), with the Hartshorn-patent breech block. Note the breech-locking latch in the actuating lever. Courtesy of Wallis & Wallis.

hinged block known as a 'cap', as it partially enveloped the standing breech and opened to the left when the locking catch was released. A patent of addition, granted in 1862, added cam surfaces to improve cartridge seating and assure adequate primary extraction.

The Federal ordnance purchased 860 Joslyns from Bruff, Bros. & Seaver of New York City in the period November 1861–July 1862, assigning all but two hundred to units raised in Ohio. Ultimately, Joslyn acquired a much larger contract at the end of 1862 and began volume deliveries in mid-August 1863.

Only about half the guns had been delivered when hostilities ceased. The contract was promptly cancelled on the grounds that the guns failed to meet specifications. Some modern writers have seen government duplicity in this, but it is probable that Joslyn carbines were poorly made (cf., problems with Joslyn revolvers). Benjamin Joslyn was appealing for a review as late as April 1866, while selling the unacceptable guns commercially.

Total Federal purchases amounted to 11,261 carbines from 1 January 1861 until 30 June 1866, each costing the US Treasury $25·09.

Ironically, the first breech-loading rifle to be mass-produced in Springfield Armory was a Joslyn conversion of the regulation M1863 rifle musket, production of which began in 1865. Enough had been delivered by April to equip two infantry regiments, but the guns were too late to see active service.

The 1862-pattern Joslyn carbine, made in Stonington, Connecticut, chambered ·56–52 Spencer rimfire ammunition. It had a 22-inch barrel and was nearly 39in overall. Furniture was brass. There were long upper tangs, a hook on the breech cap, and a single block hinge. The extractor plate was retained by screws.

A few transitional guns made in 1864 combined the basic 1862-type action with the improved breech-cap release catch.

The 1864-model gun chambered ·56–56 Spencer or special ·54 Joslyn cartridges. A chequered finger piece was let into the

underside of the breech hook to improve the lock, a cylindrical firing-pin shroud appeared, a gas vent was added to the breech cap, and a short upper tang was fitted. Guns numbered above about 11,000 had double hinge breeches. They were generally marked '1864' on the lock plate, and the breech-cap markings lay on the back surface instead of on top. Furniture was iron. A 'U.S.' mark graced the butts of government purchases.

GIBBS CARBINES, 1856–65

Patented by Lucius Gibbs in January 1856, this was one of the lesser known Civil War

173-175; below. The Maynard carbine and its patent. Author's collection; drawings courtesy of the US Patent Office, Washington DC.

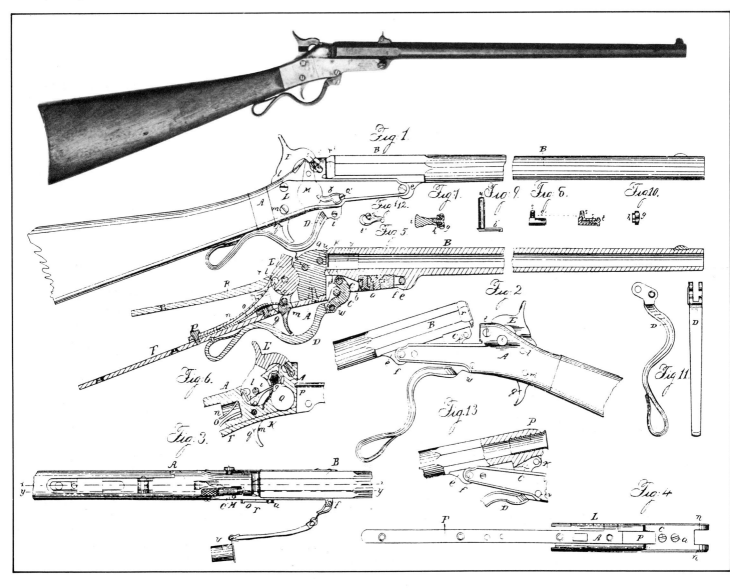

weapons. On 18 December 1861, the Ordnance Department contracted with William Brooks of New York City for ten thousand Gibbs carbines at $28 apiece. Brooks, an iron founder specialising in chimney flues, did not have the facilities to make weapons; consequently, he sub-contracted most of the work to William Marston's Phoenix Armory, which stood on the corner of Second Avenue and 22nd Street.

Deliveries commenced in the late Spring of 1863. On 13 June 1863, however, the Phoenix Armory was destroyed during the New York Draft Riots. With it went the production machinery for the Gibbs carbine and the contract was terminated after only 1,052 guns had been sent into store at a cost to the government of $26·61 apiece.

The ·52-calibre Gibbs operated similarly to the Gallager (q.v.); a lever, formed as the trigger guard, tipped the barrel forward and upward at the breech to receive a new cartridge. Unlike the Gallager carbine, however, Gibbs' pattern fired a combustible paper cartridge. The face of the breech contained an annular collar, expanded momentarily to act as a gas seal, while a conical spigot pierced the cartridge base to facilitate ignition. A conventional side-hammer cap lock was used, the flash passing down the nipple channel and out along the hollow spigot axis.

The carbines had 22-inch barrels, were 39in overall, and had conventional wooden fore ends. A distinctive closed ring appeared on the breech-lever tip.

MAYNARD CARBINES, 1857–65

This interesting little carbine, which saw great success as a sporter in post-war days, was designed by Edward Maynard, a Washington dentist. Ironically, though Maynard made huge contributions to his chosen profession, he is now best remembered for his guns.

Maynard's experiments with metal-case cartridges began with US Patent 15,141 of June 1856, in which the base of a metal tube was closed by a waxed paper disc. He eventually developed a closed iron (later brass) tube brazed onto a sturdy perforated base, which combined excellent sealing properties with a rim offering good purchase for an extractor.

The earliest Maynard carbine did not succeed, but its replacement received excellent testimonials. One gun was tried at Washington Navy Yard in October 1859 in the presence of Commander John Dahlgren, Edward Maynard and William McFarland, Maynard's agent. At a range of 200 yards, the small-calibre carbine achieved 237 hits from 237 shots on a target 3ft broad by 6ft high; at 1,300 yards, it buried a bullet to its length in oak planks.

More than six hundred shots were fired during the experiments, producing minimal fouling, while two cartridge cases—selected at random—had been loaded and re-loaded alternately until each had survived more than a hundred shots without noticeably deteriorating.

Maynard carbines were immediately adopted by the US Treasury for service on the armed revenue cutters.

Though the odd straight-comb wristless butt looked ungainly, Maynards were light and handy, weighing a mere 6lb. Made by the Massachusetts Arms Company of Chicopee Falls, they were 36½–37in overall, had a twenty inch barrel, and were loaded by pushing down on a breech lever formed as the trigger guard. This tipped the barrel so that a new cartridge could be inserted directly into the chamber.

The earliest guns (·35 or ·50) were made with tape primers and a folding back sight on the tang behind the central hammer. No sling bar was fitted, though a ring sometimes lay on the lower tang behind the breech lever.

Later government guns, made in ·50 calibre, lacked the tape primer and patch box, and had a conventional back sight on the barrel above the frame hinge. Federal purchases between 1 January 1861 and 30 June 1866 amounted to 20,002 carbines at $24·47 apiece and 2·16 million cartridges at $3·35 per hundred.

176, below. The 51st New York and 51st Pennsylvania infantry regiments surge over "Burnside's Bridge" during the Battle of Antietam, 17 September 1862. It was named after Ambrose Burnside, one-time firearm inventor, then commanding Federal IX Corps. Courtesy of Philip J. Haythornthwaite.

SMITH CARBINES, 1857–65

Patented by Gilbert Smith, a 'physician' of Buttermilk Falls in New York State, this break action carbine originally fired cartridges with a gutta-percha case. The breech was locked by a sturdy spring-steel bar projecting back from the top of the barrel over a stud on the standing breech. A small locking catch ahead of the trigger lever was pressed upward to release the bar, allowing the barrel to open.

The Smith carbine was tested at Washington Arsenal in the Spring of 1860, very successfully. Praised for simplicity and an unusually gas tight breech, three hundred were purchased for field trials shortly before the Civil War began. They were manufactured by Poultney & Trimble of Baltimore, Maryland, to whom the original patents had been assigned. When hostilities began, Poultney & Trimble obtained a large order from the Federal government and sub-contracted work to the Massachusetts Arms Company.

Work proceeded satisfactorily enough until midsummer 1863. In August, the Massachusetts Arms Company passed part of work on the Smith carbine to Philos Tyler's American Machine Works to free facilities for the Maynard gun. Poultney & Trimble suspected that their project was being given a low priority, and so shifted all work to the American Machine Works in September. The American Arms Company was formed in Chicopee Falls to oversee work.

Though the Smith carbines had originally fired rubber-case ammunition, Poultney was assigned a patent granted to Thomas Rodman and Silas Crispin in December 1863 for an improved 'wrapped-metal cartridge with a strengthening disc or cup'. "Poultney's Patent Metallic Cartridge" transformed the carbine into an even more effectual design, though power was limited by the design of the breech and efficiency by the retention of a side-hammer cap lock.

The ·50-calibre Smith had a 21·6in barrel, measured 39·5in overall, and was occasionally found with swivels on the butt and barrel band.

Federal purchases between 1 January 1861 and 30 June 1866 totalled 30,062 carbines at $24·80 apiece, plus 13·86 million assorted cartridges at an average of $2·72 per hundred. The Smith was the fourth most popular government carbine, after the Spencer, Sharps and Burnside patterns.

MERRILL RIFLES AND CARBINES, 1858–65

The first Merrill to be issued officially, in the US Navy, was an Ames-made Jenks (q.v.) adapted to fire combustible paper cartridges. Submitted by James Merrill of Baltimore in Ohio, the prototype conversion was tested at Washington Navy Yard in February 1858. It was too complex and unreliable, but an improved version with a conventional side hammer cap lock was substituted in June 1858. This proved effectual enough for Merrill to convert three hundred Jenks carbines and make five thousand cartridges for extended trials. These duly satisfied the navy, the conversion being approved on 26 January 1861.

As only a very few Jenks carbines were ever altered to the Merrill system, they are now very rarely encountered. It is not known whether any saw service during the Civil War. The guns had a modified actuating lever, locking on the back sight base, and a conventional side-hammer cap lock instead of the original 'Mule Ear' type.

Merrill had been promoting another carbine, designed in partnership with Latrobe & Thomas in 1856. This embodied a tap or 'faucet' breech closed by rotating a lateral bar behind the chamber. The gun was much too complicated; like its original promoters, it soon failed. However, Merrill persevered with Merrill, Thomas & Company until a satisfactory modification of the Jenks system was made.

The improved carbine accepted regulation combustible paper cartridges or powder and ball, relying on a conventional side-hammer cap lock for ignition. This Merrill claimed as a great advantage, singling out the Burnside, Maynard and Smith carbines (which all fired special cartridges) for especial invective.

The major internal difference between the Jenks and Merrill actions was the annular copper disc on the latter's piston head. This was momentarily crushed by the pressure of firing, expanding outward to provide an effectual gas-seal. A small lug on the actuating lever automatically cleared the spent cap from the nipple and, by blocking the passage of the hammer to the cap, ensured that the gun could not fire before the action was properly locked.

The first sale to the Federal government occurred in June 1861, when twenty carbines, three rifles, a 'Minie Musket' and nine converted Harper's Ferry Rifles (M1841) were acquired for trials. The first major purchase occurred when 5,000 carbines were ordered on Christmas Eve, 1861. In March 1862, 566 Merrill rifles were ordered for the 21st Indiana Volunteer Infantry Regiment, the carbine order

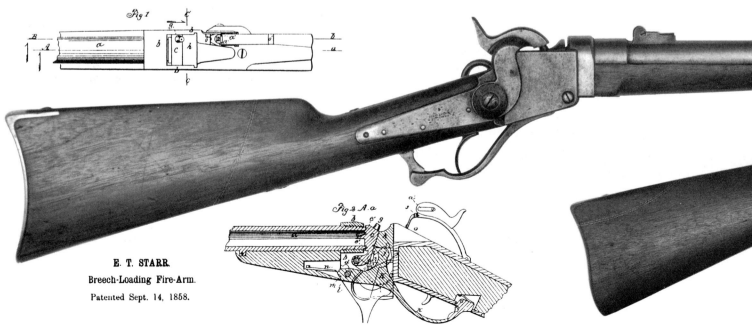

E. T. STARR.
Breech-Loading Fire-Arm.
Patented Sept. 14, 1858.

being reduced accordingly. Merrill rifles were popular, users including the 7th and 10th Michigan Volunteer Infantry, 1st Massachusetts Sharpshooters and the 6th Kansas Volunteer Cavalry. They had a reputation for long-range accuracy and were prized by marksmen. Government purchases amounted to 769 between May 1861 and the end of 1863, but others were acquired privately.

The ·54-calibre Merrill rifles were 48½in long, had 33-inch barrels held by two brass bands, weighed a little over 9lb and accepted sabre bayonets. The first guns had flat knurled breech latches, but these were superseded by a rounded pattern embodying a sprung plunger.

The earliest carbines had 22¼-inch barrels and measured 37½–38in overall. The actuating lever had a flat knurled locking catch, the fore end was tapered, and the furniture was brass.

Later guns had the modified locking catch on the breech lever, the fore-end tip was much less delicate, and the patch box was eliminated. An eagle and the date of assembly were stamped on the lock plates of guns purchased by the Federal authorities; 14,495 carbines had been received by 30 June 1866, costing the US Treasury $25·86 apiece. The combustible cartridges cost $1·92 per hundred.

Testimonials in Merrill broadsheets claimed that carbines equipped the 3rd Wisconsin and 11th Pennsylvania cavalry regiments, 1st New York Mounted Rifles and the 5th Pennsylvania Cavalry.

STARR CARBINES, 1858–65

Patented in September 1858 by Ebenezer T. Starr of Yonkers, New York State (21,523), this single-shot breech-loader was tested favourably at Washington Arsenal early in 1858, eliciting comment that it would be far more effectual than the Sharps carbine if the gas seal could be improved. Accuracy had been well above average, and there had been no misfires. The trial board noted that the Starr—unlike the contemporary Sharps—did not shear the base off the combustible cartridge when the breech closed, and that the breech block had a deep annular recess to fit over the barrel.

The Starr resembled the better known Sharps carbine externally, but was more angular and had a longer receiver. Its two-piece radial breech block was locked by a wedge as the operating lever was closed. A conventional side-hammer cap lock provided satisfactory ignition. The standard ·54-calibre model had a 21in barrel, measured 37·6in overall and had brass mounts.

On 21 February 1865, three thousand guns were ordered for the ·56–52 Spencer rimfire cartridge. These Starrs had a new breech block, fitted with an ejector, and a modified hammer with a short straight shank. They were so successful that an additional two thousand had been ordered within a month. Apart from some conversions and the earliest batches, rimfire guns had iron furniture instead of brass.

Federal purchases amounted to 25,603 prior to 30 June 1866, each gun costing $22·92; in addition, 6·86 million cartridges had been acquired at a rate of $2·05 per hundred.

LINDNER CARBINES, 1859–65

Patented by Edward Lindner on 29 March 1859, this gun existed in three versions. The most basic was a conversion of imported Austrian muskets, cut down to carbine length. Later guns were made by the Amoskeag Manufacturing Company of Manchester, New Hampshire, though they rarely bore anything other than an acknowledgement of Lindner's patent on the breech block.

The carbine had a short grasping handle that rotated the breech cover to the left, allowing the pivoted breech block to be lifted to receive a combustible cartridge. Ignition was provided by a conventional side-hammer cap lock.

The Federal ordnance authorities ordered four hundred Lindner carbines on 6 November 1861, at $20 apiece, in addition to 40,000 cartridges. As these were to be delivered to Washington Arsenal within eight days, it is assumed that guns were in stock. They were duly delivered to the 1st Michigan Cavalry and used during the Second Battle of Manassas.

Lindner carbines had twenty-inch ·58-calibre barrels, and measured about 38½in overall. Federal purchases amounted to 892 at $22·30 apiece, the special combustible cartridges costing about $2·26 per hundred.

GROSS AND GWYN & CAMPBELL CARBINES, 1859–65

Patented by Henry Gross of Tiffin, Ohio, in August 1859 (25,259), this quirky firearm has acquired several different names—'Gross', after its original inventor; 'Cosmopolitan', after its manufacturer; 'Gwyn & Campbell', after the owners of Cosmopolitan; and 'Union' after a mark appearing on many guns.

The onset of the Civil War caused the Federal authorities to seek *any* suitable firearms to

177. The ·54 cap lock Starr carbine resembled the Sharps externally, but was more angular and embodied a radial breech block. This gun has a 21-inch barrel and measures a little under 38in overall. Courtesy of Wallis & Wallis.

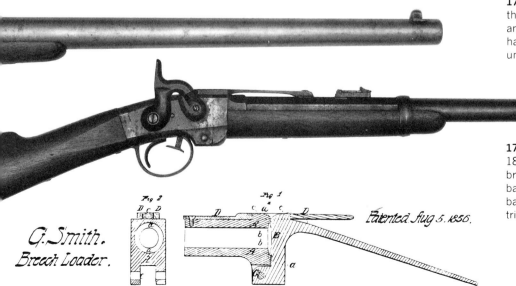

178. This ·52 Smith carbine, no. 6162 of 1863, was an interesting design with a simple breech latched by the spring bar on top of the barrel ahead of the hammer. The actuating bar protrudes into the guard ahead of the trigger lever. Courtesy of Wallis & Wallis.

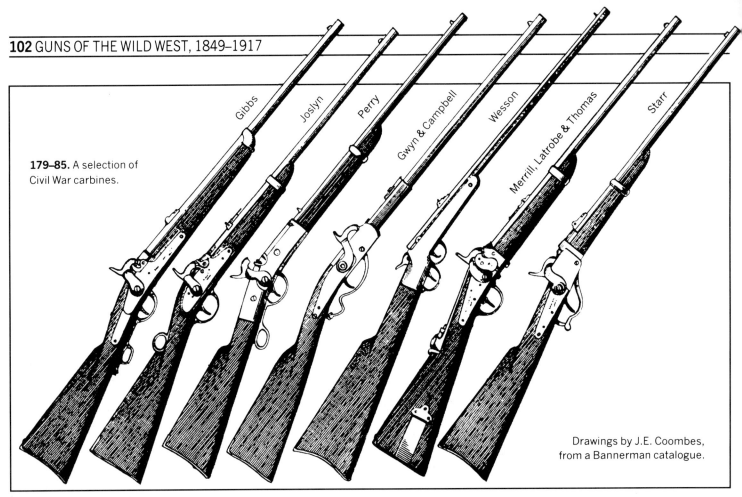

179–85. A selection of Civil War carbines.

Gibbs — Joslyn — Perry — Gwyn & Campbell — Wesson — Merrill, Latrobe & Thomas — Starr

Drawings by J.E. Coombes, from a Bannerman catalogue.

arm units being raised in the northern states. A contract was passed to the Cosmopolitan Arms Company of Hamilton, Ohio, for 1,140 Gross-patent carbines to arm volunteers being mustered in neighbouring Illinois. Production began immediately.

The carbines were made without fore-ends. Pulling the breech lever down pivoted the breech-block face upward as the rear of the breech swung down. A separate breech cover, with an integral loading groove, dropped to allow a combustible cartridge to be pushed into the chamber. The gun was then fired by a conventional cap lock.

The true Gross/Cosmopolitan guns had a serpentine breech lever, doubling as a trigger guard, with a tip recurving to lock into the back of the catch on the frame. They also had a rounded hammer shank. The ·52-calibre guns had nineteen-inch barrels and were about 39in overall.

Once the order had been fulfilled, Gwyn & Campbell simplified the action (Patent 36,709 of 21 October 1862) so that a grooved breech block simply dropped at the front to expose the chamber. The Gwyn & Campbell gun resembled the Gross pattern, but its breech lever locked into the front of the catch on the underside of the butt, and its hammer had flattened sides. The back sight was also simpler.

The Federal government purchased 9,342 Gross and Gwyn & Campbell carbines prior to 30 June 1866, each costing the treasury $21·39.

In addition, about 6·30 million cartridges were acquired at $2·09 per hundred.

WESSON CARBINES, 1859–65

Only 151 Wesson carbines were purchased by the Federal government, being ordered from Benjamin Kittredge & Company of Cincinnati, Ohio, on 7 July 1863 at $23·12 apiece. An additional gun was purchased from Schuyler, Hartley & Graham of New York on 1 August.

Kittredge was an enthusiastic champion of the breech-loading system patented by Franklin Wesson of Springfield, Massachusetts, in 1859 and 1862. He is known to have supplied 1,366 guns to Kentucky and 760 to Illinois, plus hundreds more to individual regiments.

The distinctive frame had two separate trigger apertures. The front trigger released the barrel, which tipped forward and down to elevate the breech. Like many of its contemporaries, the Wesson lacked an extractor; stubborn cases often had to be punched out with a ramrod. 39½in overall, with a 24-inch barrel, carbines usually bore Wesson and Kittredge markings.

SHARPS & HANKINS RIFLES AND CARBINES, 1859–65

The relationship between Christian Sharps and Robbins & Lawrence, makers of guns under

contract to the Sharps Rifle Manufacturing Company, was never strong. Eventually, the two men developed such antipathy that the inventor sold his shares in the company that bore his name.

In the late 1850s, however, Sharps designed an improved carbine loaded by sliding the barrel forward when the trigger-guard lever was pressed. In 1859, armed with a new patent, Sharps went into partnership with William Hankins. Trials of Sharps & Hankins guns were so encouraging that production began in 1861.

The Civil War boosted many gunmaking operations, Sharps & Hankins being no exception. Five hundred 'Old Model' rifles were ordered for the US Navy in April–September 1862, all but a hundred being supplied with a sword bayonet; they were ·52-calibre rimfires chambering the so-called ·52-56 Sharps & Hankins cartridge, were 47·6in overall, had 32·7-inch barrels and weighed 8½lb. They were fully stocked and had three iron bands. The back sight was a Sharps tangent pattern graduated to 800yd.

The army was more interested in the Sharps & Hankins carbine. Some had been bought privately to arm the 9th and 11th New York Volunteer Cavalry during 1862, performing so successfully that the attention of the Federal government was gained. Official orders were forthcoming in 1863, the army eventually receiving 1,468 and the navy taking 6,336. Early or 'Old Model' guns, made in 1861–2, had a fixed firing pin in the hammer face; post-1863 'New Model' examples had a floating pin in the standing breech. A safety slider on the rear of the frame could be used to block the fall of the hammer when appropriate. The guns originally fired ·52-calibre combustible ammunition, and then metal-case cartridges known as '·56 Sharps & Hankins'; a little over a million Sharps & Hankins cartridges were purchased on behalf of the Federal government in 1863–6 at a cost of $2·71 per hundred.

The guns had 23½in barrels and measured 38½in overall. They had brass butt plates and a most distinctive back sight. Navy issue carbines generally displayed inspector's marks (e.g., 'P' over 'H.K.H.') and had a leather protector over the barrel. The leather tube, intended to minimise corrosion, was held to the muzzle by an iron ring doubling as the sight base.

GALLAGER CARBINES, 1860–5

Patented by Mahlon Gallager of Savannah, Georgia, in July 1860, and manufactured in Philadelphia by Richardson & Overman, this gun had a barrel that moved forward and tipped to give access to the chamber. The breech lever doubled as a trigger guard.

The action would have presented fewer problems had not Gallager positioned half the chamber in the standing breech and the remainder in the barrel. The weapon was normally issued with Poultney's or Jackson's patent cartridges, the former made of brass and paper and the latter from iron foil covered in a paper wrapping. Even though one-piece drawn brass cases were eventually produced, the Gallager was notoriously ineffectual. When the breech was opened after firing, the barrel moved straight forward to clear the case—or so the inventor hoped—before tipping upward at the breech. However, owing to the absence of an extractor, spent cases usually stuck fast. Whether they were in the breech or the barrel was a lottery. Though a special combination tool was issued with each gun, it was unequal to the task of prising the cases free. Troops hated the Gallager, which was regarded as far inferior to the other metallic cartridge breech loaders. Unfortunately, the Federal government acquired 22,738 of them at $22·37 apiece, plus 8·29 million cartridges for $2·55 a hundred.

The standard Gallager carbine, which lacked a fore-end and relied on a conventional side hammer cap lock for ignition, had a ·50-calibre 22¼-inch barrel. Overall length was 39¼in. Five thousand modified guns chambering ·56-50 Spencer rimfire cartridges were ordered in March 1865, but were too late to see action.

THE HENRY RIFLE, 1860–5

The first examples of Henry's Patent Repeating Rifle, protected in 1860 (30,446), were made in 1861. They had a 24-inch barrel with a bore diameter of ·420, six grooves ·005 deep, and progressive-twist rifling quickening from a turn in sixteen feet at the breech to one in 33in at the muzzle. The cartridge relied on two grains of fulminate in its rim to ignite 25 grains of black powder. The guns had brass frames, hardwood butts and weighed 10lb unladen. They lacked fore-ends and had comparatively fragile tube magazines beneath the barrel. Series-made Henry Rifles were available from the summer of 1862, whereupon many were sold to state and volunteer units in the face of official Ordnance disapproval.

Brigadier General James 'Old Fogey' Ripley, the incumbent Chief of Ordnance, had a particularly harsh view of the new repeater. As early as the autumn of 1861, Ripley had opined of a prototype Henry that he did 'not discover any important advantage…over several other [single-shot] breech loaders, as the rapidity of fire with these latter is sufficiently good for useful purposes without the objection to increased weight from the charges in the arm itself, while the multiplication of arms and ammunition…is decidedly objectionable, and should, in my opinion, be stopped by the refusal to introduce any more'.

After the Spencer rifle had been approved in 1863, official attitudes softened to the extent that 1,731 Henry Rifles and the staggering total of 4·5 million ·44 rimfire cartridges had been acquired by the end of 1865. It has been estimated than about ten thousand Henry rifles saw action during the Civil War, perhaps eight thousand being purchased for state and volunteer units in addition to the Federal acquisitions. Total production by the end of 1865 amounted to about 11,000.

The Henry was an effectual weapon, greatly appreciated for its high rate of fire—particularly in the days before the 1864-patent Blakeslee Quick Loader elevated the Spencer Rifle to similar heights. Winchester made skilful capital from praise lavished on the Henry, especially if it was to the detriment of rivals such as Spencer.

The Henry was an effectual weapon judged by the standards of the Civil War; indeed, it is hard to argue that it was bettered by any of its rivals, possibly excepting Spencers fitted with the Stabler Cut-off. Though the Spencer

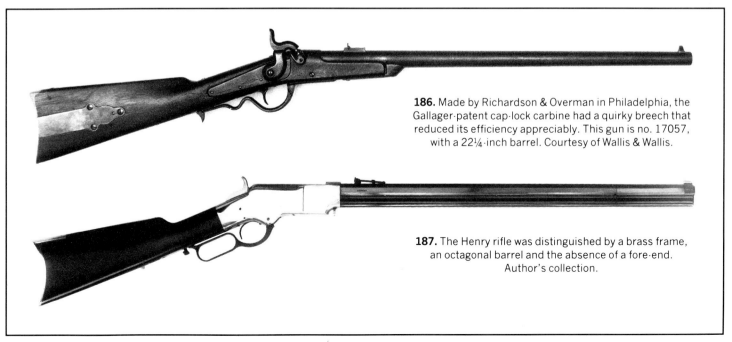

186. Made by Richardson & Overman in Philadelphia, the Gallager-patent cap-lock carbine had a quirky breech that reduced its efficiency appreciably. This gun is no. 17057, with a 22¼-inch barrel. Courtesy of Wallis & Wallis.

187. The Henry rifle was distinguished by a brass frame, an octagonal barrel and the absence of a fore-end. Author's collection.

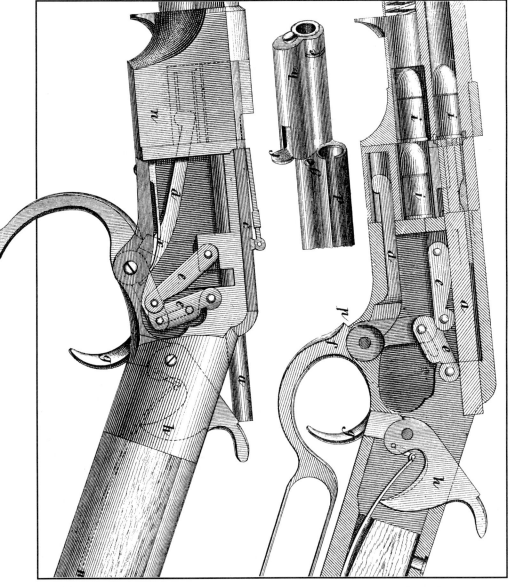

suffered occasional extractor breakages, and was slower to fire owing to its separate external hammer, it was more strongly built; Henry Rifles often suffered damage to their comparatively fragile magazine tubes, in some extreme cases rendering them useless, while the bifurcated firing pin was also prone to fracture.

The Henry was complicated and delicate for a service weapon, and, like all comparable large calibre rimfires, surprisingly low powered. Its principal asset was the speed with which it could be fired. Trials undertaken in Switzerland with an 1866-model Winchester, firing the same ammunition as the Henry (but admittedly easier to load), indicated that even an untrained rifleman could achieve twenty unaimed shots each minute. When the gun was being fired deliberately, accuracy was such that mean radii of four and 24 inches were returned at distances of 300 and 1,200 paces respectively.

The Civil War proved a godsend to the New Haven Arms Company, as the sales of more than ten thousand Henry Rifles—retailing at about $40 apiece—finally placed operations on a stable footing. When hostilities ceased, however, trade slumped; the government sold off so many war surplus guns at knock-down

---

188, left. Longitudinal sections of the Henry rifle, from engravings made in the late 1860s. Author's collection.

189, below left. The 'Color Bearers and Guard' of the 7th Illinois volunteer infantry regiment, pictured by Matthew Brady about 1863. Note the Henry rifles. From an original in the collection of the Illinois State Library.

190, below. A broadside extolling the virtues of the Henry, dating from 1861–2. By courtesy of Ian Hogg.

prices that the market was almost swept away overnight. Only about five hundred new Henrys were sold in the first post-war year.

Yet there were new fields to conquer, as the end of the Civil War gave an extra impetus to attempts to open up the West. American Indians had evolved an effectual technique for attacking small groups of pioneers, but it was based on the premise that the defenders were armed with muzzle-loaders. The Indians would simply send out a small raiding party as bait, presenting the intended victims with a choice; withhold fire and risk death at the hands of the raiding party, or fire and be caught by the main charge while reloading. The advent of repeaters such as the Henry and the Spencer changed the situation, and many a charge was cut down before gaining its objective. From reports of each incident, Winchester and his salesmen made great capital; stories that were already exaggerated needed little attention, others could always be inflated to press the claims.

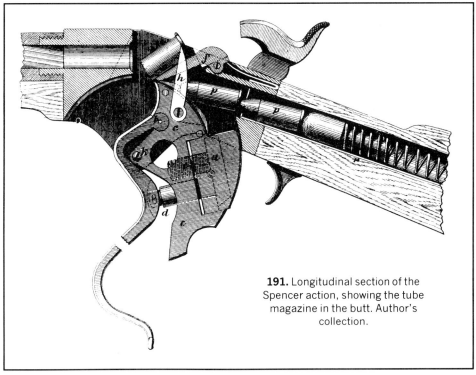

191. Longitudinal section of the Spencer action, showing the tube magazine in the butt. Author's collection.

SPENCER RIFLES AND CARBINES, 1860–5

This repeater, patented in March 1860 (27,393), had a profound effect on local tactics during the Civil War. Designed by Christopher Spencer while working for Cheney Brothers Silk Mills Company of Manchester, Connecticut, even the prototype was potentially very effectual.

The persistent claim that success hinged on a successful demonstration to President Abraham Lincoln in August 1863 has little basis in fact. The Cheney brothers were personally acquainted with Gideon Welles, Secretary of the Navy, and simply submitted the gun to him. Welles was favourably enough impressed to pass the matter to Captain John Dahlgren, then commanding Washington Navy Yard; and even the earliest trials, undertaken on 8 June 1861, were most encouraging—though an inherent weakness was found in the extractor. An improved extractor was eventually patented in July 1862 (36,062).

On 22 June 1861, the US Navy ordered seven hundred rifles and 70,000 rimfire cartridges for large-scale trials. The .52-calibre navy rifles were 47in overall, had thirty-inch barrels retained in the full-length stocks by three iron bands, were sighted to 800yd, and weighed about 10lb unladen. They accepted brass-hilted sword bayonets made by Collins & Company.

Eventually, 703 guns were received by navy ordnance departments on 3 February 1863. Some of the trials were attended by Captain Alexander Dyer of the US Army, later to be Chief of Ordnance. Dyer was impressed by the way in which the rifle coped with rapidity, endurance,

sand and rusting experiments. His favourable report raised the hopes of Spencer and his backers that a large order would be forthcoming. Major General George McClellan directed a Board of Officers to test the rifle at Washington Arsenal in November 1861—again with favourable results—but Brigadier General James 'Old Fogey' Ripley, the Chief of Ordnance, would not be moved.

Exasperated, Charles Cheney turned once more to Gideon Welles. Welles then recruited James Blaine, Speaker of the House of Representatives, and a meeting was convened between the interested parties. Welles, though Secretary of the Navy, took the unprecedented step of authorising purchase of ten thousand Spencer rifles for the *army*. The decision was immediately countersigned by Thomas Scott, Assistant Secretary of War, to prevent a change of heart. On 26 December 1861, Ripley accepted an offer of 10,000 rifles at $40 apiece.

On the strength of this assumption, the newly formed Spencer Rifle Manufacturing Company leased half the under-employed Chickering piano factory in Boston, Massachusetts, to cope with demand. However, unforeseen problems delayed work appreciably. No guns had been forthcoming by 29 January 1862, when notice was received that the Secretary of War had ordered a review of all existing contracts. It was even suggested that the Spencer orders be curtailed in favour of rifle-muskets.

Eventually, the original order for ten thousand guns was reduced to 7,500, a replacement contract being signed on 19 June 1862. The first Spencers were delivered into Federal store on

31 December, the last ones arriving in June 1863. Progress remained slow until August 1863, when Spencer met with Lincoln to demonstrate his carbine. The president was greatly impressed; in no time at all, General Ripley had been replaced by a much more progressive Chief of Ordnance, George Ramsey, and the Spencer's future was finally assured.

The major advantages the Spencer possessed over the rival Henry were its robust construction and larger bullet—·56-calibre and 362 grains, compared with ·44 and 216 grains. Powder charges proved to be 34 grains (Spencer) and 25 grains (Henry) when tested by the Federal Navy in 1862.

Muzzle velocity has been estimated at 900 ft/sec for the Spencer and 1,125 for the Henry cartridges, giving the former a forty per cent advantage in muzzle energy.

The first government-order guns began to reach the troops in the winter of 1862, though many had previously been sold to state and volunteer units. Spencer himself, exasperated by official inertia, had undertaken many promotional tours. The earliest authenticated use of a Spencer was by Sergeant Francis Lombard of the 1st Massachusetts Volunteer Cavalry in a brief skirmish with Confederate horsemen near Cumberland, Maryland, on 16 October 1862. Lombard was acquainted with Spencer and had been given one of the inventor's hand-made pre-production rifles.

Government guns had been issued in time for the campaigns of June/July 1863, though sufficient privately-purchased rifles were in the hands of Colonel John Wilder's men to maul a

192, 193, right and below right. Men of the Clinch Rifles—the 5th Georgia Infantry Regiment—relax in camp (192). Note the short-barrel cap lock rifles and brass-hilt sword bayonets piled on the right. It is probable that these are copies of the Model 1841 rifle. Picture 193 shows men of the 4th Michigan Infantry Regiment, with 1842-model muskets and ·36 Colt Navy revolvers. From *Photographic History of the Civil War* (1911), courtesy of Philip J. Haythornthwaite.

194, below. The cartridge box patented by Erastus Blakeslee in December 1864 proved a great asset to the Spencer rifle. Courtesy of the US Patent Office, Washington DC.

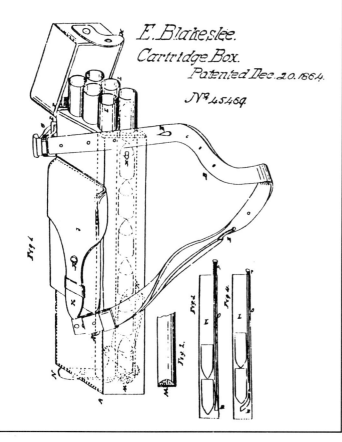

far larger band of Confederates during the Battle of Hoover's Gap. Wilder's Brigade carried 1,369 Spencers, 323 British Enfields, nine Colt revolver rifles, and forty assorted Springfield rifle-muskets.

The superiority was reinforced at Yellow Tavern, Franklin and Five Forks, and as many as 3,500 Spencers helped stem the Confederate advance at the first Battle of Gettysburg on 1 July 1863; by 30 June 1866, 12,471 rifles and 94,196 carbines had been delivered into Federal stores, though it has been estimated that only fifty thousand handy 39-inch 8½lb carbines had been issued.

Each army rifle—identical with the navy pattern, but taking a socket bayonet—cost the Federal treasury $37·48, compared with $25·41 for a carbine. Each hundred of the 58·24 million cartridges purchased between 1 January 1861 and 30 June 1866 cost $2·44.

Spencer ammunition chambered in several other carbines owing to a standardisation begun at the end of 1863.

The Spencer was a seven-shot repeater with a dropping or radial block action operated by a trigger-guard lever. When the lever was opened, the block dropped, the extractor pulled the spent case out of the chamber and the ejector threw it out of the gun; as the lever closed, the tip of the breech block picked up the rim of the first cartridge in the tube magazine—running up through the butt—and fed it into the chamber.

Though the side hammer still had to be cocked manually, the Spencer could be fired very rapidly. Its utility was greatly increased by the introduction of Blakeslee's Cartridge Box, patented by Colonel Erastus Blakeslee of the 1st Connecticut Cavalry in November 1864. This held between six and thirteen seven-round

loading tubes in a wooden block. Reloading was then simply a matter of opening the butt-trap, withdrawing the magazine spring and cartridge elevator, and dropping the cartridges straight out of the tinned sheet-metal Blakeslee loader into the butt. Replacing the magazine spring returned the carbine to working order: the whole cycle took a matter of seconds.

Spencers made after 1864 were fitted with a cut-off patented by Edward Stabler of Sandy Springs, Maryland, which held the magazine in reserve by limiting rotation of the breech block.

Guns were made by the Spencer Repeating Arms Company and also by the Burnside Rifle Company, to whom Spencer sub-contracted 35,000 in June 1864 (30,496 of which were delivered by the end of 1865). A typical ·56–52 carbine, measuring 39in overall with a 22-inch barrel, was marked 'M-1865' if fitted with a Stabler cut-off. The left side of the butt displayed government inspector's marks in a cartouche. Spencers made by Burnside generally had twenty-inch barrels chambered for ·56–50 rimfire cartridges.

The Spencer's fire-rate, without the benefit of the Blakeslee loader, was fourteen rounds per minute compared with 10–12 for the single shot Sharps Carbine, eight for the Colt Revolver Rifle (which was uniquely time-consuming to load), and only three for the rifle-musket. Loading the Spencer took about fifteen seconds—cut to five with the loader, with a corresponding increase in fire to 25 unaimed rounds per minute. The only problems with the Spencer were that the cartridges could be loaded backwards, a potentially dangerous source of premature explosions, and that rapid fire could expend ammunition quicker than quartermasters could replenish it.

Interestingly, there is not one authenticated incident of Confederates overcoming Spencer armed Federals, even when the Northern troops were outnumbered ten-to-one.

RIFLE-MUSKETS IN THE CIVIL WAR, 1861–5

Widespread dissatisfaction with the Maynard Tape Primers, which were susceptible to damp, led to the adoption of the Model 1861 rifle musket. This was practically identical with its 1855-pattern predecessor, apart from a conventional lock firing percussion caps. It had three spring-retained bands and iron furniture.

A total of 265,129 M1861 rifle-muskets were made at Springfield Armory from the beginning of 1861 to the end of 1863, apparently including a few two-band derivatives with 33-inch barrels. These were made for artillerymen during

the Civil War and often incorporated brass components in their furniture.

Adoption of the new weapon coincided with the beginning of the Civil War. To accelerate production, the original patch box was discarded and contracts placed with leading gunmaking firms. Colt's Patent Fire Arms Manufacturing Company of Hartford, Connecticut; the Amoskeag Manufacturing Company of Amoskeag, New Hampshire; and Lamson, Goodnow & Yale Company of Windsor, Vermont, all made the so-called 'Special Model 1861'. This differed from the regulation pattern in its use of screw-retained bands, the omission of the vent screw from the nipple cone, and the shape of its hammer. These special parts could not be exchanged with those of the standard M1861.

The ·58 Rifle-Musket Model 1863, approved on 9 February 1863, was little more than an M1861 incorporating many minor changes made in the Special Model—including screwed bands and omission of the vent screw. Springfield made 273,265 guns in 1863–4.

Additional changes were authorised on 17 December 1863, when solid bands were re-introduced, the back sight changed, and the ramrod head became slotted. Blueing barrel bands and trigger guards was abandoned to simplify production. By the end of 1865, 255,040 M1863 rifle-muskets had been made in Springfield Armory.

In addition to Colt, Amoskeag, and Lamson, Goodnow & Yale, Special Model 1861 and Model 1863 rifle-muskets were made in quantity by Addison Burt of New York City; the Eagle Manufacturing Company of Mansfield, Connecticut; C.B. Hoard's Armory of Watertown, New York; J.T. Hodge of New York City; Alfred Jenks & Son of Philadelphia and

Bridesburg, Pennsylvania; William Mason of Taunton, Massachusetts; James Mowry of Norwich, Connecticut; William Muir of Windsor Locks, Connecticut; James Mulholland of Reading, Pennsylvania; the Norwich Arms Company of Norwich, Connecticut; Parker, Snow & Company of Meriden, Connecticut; the Providence Tool Company of Providence, Rhode Island; E. Remington & Sons of Ilion, New York; Edward Robinson of New York City; Sarson & Roberts of New York City; the Savage Revolving Fire Arms Company of Middletown, Connecticut; Casper Schubarth of Providence, Rhode Island; the W.W. Welch Company of Norfolk, Connecticut; and E. Whitney of Whitneyville, Connecticut.

Most of these contractors can be identified by name. However, the lock plates of Burt's guns simply displayed TRENTON; Jenks used BRIDESBURG; the Norwich Arms Company used NORWICH, which may be confused with the place-name (cf., Mowry); and Welch adopted NORFOLK. A few guns made in New York in 1863 display 'U.A. CO.' for the Union Arms Company, which accepted a 25,000-gun contract in November 1861 but probably delivered less than a thousand. Colt made 113,980 guns to Federal and state orders, Jenks made 98,000, the Providence Tool Company contributed at least 70,000 and there were 50,000 from Lamson, Goodnow & Yale.

A variant of the Model 1863 rifle with an 1841-pattern barrel and lock, the 1855-pattern stock and 1863-type bands, was made by E. Remington & Sons of Ilion, New York. It had a distinctive brass patch box.

The Lindsay Double Musket, patented on 17 December 1863, was based on contemporary single-shot rifle-muskets. However, it had two hammers fired sequentially by a single trigger to

195, below. A selection of Confederate troops, from a fold-out plate in *Harper's Magazine*, 1863. Author's collection.

provide two shots from a single ·58 barrel. Federal authorities ordered a thousand Lindsay rifle-muskets, which proved of value when Indians unwisely pressed home an attack after assuming the soldiers had fired their volley. Experience showed that careful loading was obligatory, or both charges fired at once; Lindsay muskets were strong enough to take the strain, but recoil was fearful.

The rapid expansion of the Federal army could not be satisfied by the meagre supplies of weapons in store, nor by the comparatively limited facilities at Springfield Armory.

Orders for regulation-pattern muskets were placed with leading US gunmaking companies, while Federal and Confederate purchasing agents tramped the length and breadth of Europe in search of weapons. Even the Federal authorities were forced to scour the warehouses of minor manufacturers, wholesalers and distributors.

Many guns purchased in Europe were totally useless; unscrupulous sales agencies, from governments downward, seized the chance to sell the obsolete weapons that cluttered their armouries at a handsome profit.

Ordnance records showed the purchase of 1,472,614 Springfield rifle-muskets, 428,292 Enfields and 795,544 assorted 'Rifles & Muskets' from 1 January 1861 to 30 June 1866. There were also 471 million ·577 and ·58 cartridges, plus about 230 million for the non-regulation muskets, and 1,221 million caps.

The acquisitions ranged from 12,471 Spencer rifles down through 1,673 'Suhl Rifles'—old ex-Prussian Jägerbüchsen—to 5,995 'Garibaldi Rifles' and more than 29,000 'Foreign smooth bore muskets', a category into which anything unclassifiable was lumped. Quality was often poor, only a sixth of one consignment of 3,000 Austrian muskets being passed as serviceable by ordnance inspectors.

The Austrian weapons included a few ·54-calibre Lorenz rifle-muskets, which were effectual enough, but were mostly converted flintlocks. The so-called 'Vincennes Rifle', acquired in France, was a large-calibre musket with a cumbersome sabre bayonet. Recipients were unimpressed. One member of the 148th Pennsylvania Infantry Regiment complained in the winter of 1862 that the 'caliber of the piece may be reckoned as ·69, although the bore is so irregular that, whilst in some instances, ·69 caliber ammunition fits the bore tightly, in others it falls from the muzzle to the breach [sic]… The locks are soft iron and many of them are already unserviceable from wear [and the] rifling adds nothing to the accuracy or effectiveness of the weapons'.

Best of all the imports, the ·577 British P/53 rifle-muskets and P/58-type short rifles were popular in the Confederacy as well as with the Federals. The sabre bayonet of the short rifle proved a boon to recruitment, but increased clumsiness in combat and was often relegated to the status of a sidearm.

Owing to the great ease with which British cartridges could be obtained, the P/53 was the preferred alternative to regulation M1855 rifle muskets—particularly as Springfields would fire .577 (British) and .58 (American) ammunition interchangeably.

About half the infantry regiments raised in New York State in 1861–2 received P/53 Enfields, owing to a shortage of regulation weapons. However, despite 'natty appearance', the British rifle-musket was not always praised. Federal General William Smith opined in 1861 that guns 'were [often] exceedingly rough, and tear men's hands to pieces when they are going through the [drill] manual'. In addition, Smith said, few parts could be interchanged: 'no bayonet, as a general thing, will go on any rifle, except the one it is intended for… But in the case of the Springfield rifles, any one bayonet will fit them all'.

The Enfields acquired by the Federals were generally purchased in Birmingham; the stock was often poor sapwood, furniture was often sub-standard, and finish was generally poor.

The Confederacy fared better, its Enfields being almost exclusively made by the London Armoury Company. Though lacking the finish of the British regulation arms, these guns were superior products; their parts were generally interchangeable.

The regulation, or Springfield, rifle muskets provided the basis for many breech-loading conversions—but few were issued during the Civil War. Most were developed for the US breech-loading rifle trials of 1865–73 and had no commercial success. They included the Miller, patented in May 1865, which cost the Federal treasury $18,000 to prevent a royalty infringement suit; and the Milbank, with a side-hinged breech block, whose brief moment of glory came with a sale to the Fenians in 1867.

BALLARD RIFLES AND CARBINES, 1861–5

This distinctive single shot dropping-block action was designed by Charles Ballard of

196, 197. Two typical British ·577-calibre P/53 ('Enfield') rifle-muskets, with spring-retained bands, typical of those imported into North America during the Civil War. The upper gun was made by Robbins & Lawrence of Windsor, Vermont, under contract to the British Government. Courtesy of Wallis & Wallis.

198, left. Men of the 7th New York infantry regiment pose outside their tent. Though they are Federal troops, they wear grey rather than blue. Note the 1861-model rifle-muskets, which can be identified by the absence of the Maynard Tape Primers.
Courtesy of Dr Francis A. Lord.

The 35 rifles bought by the Federal government were purchased in Florida for $36 apiece; they were apparently issued to sharpshooters of the 34th US Coloured Infantry Regiment.

Perfected Ballard rifles, made by Ball & Williams of Worcester, Massachusetts, in ·44, ·46 or ·56 rimfire, were 45½in long, had thirty-inch barrels and weighed about 8¼lb. Most had three iron barrel bands. The carbines, chambering ·44 or ·54 cartridges, had twenty inch barrels and measured 37¼in overall. They had wood fore-ends, swivels appearing under the barrel band and butt.

GREENE RIFLES, 1861–5

This bolt-action carbine, patented in 1857, had interested the army sufficiently for a hundred to be ordered for trials. James Durrell Greene subsequently patented an improvement (US 34,422 of 18 February 1862), similar to the conversions supplied to Russia. When the Civil War began, Greene, then Colonel of the 4th Massachusetts Volunteer Militia, was promoted into the Federal Army. Attempts were made to sell the rifle to the Ordnance Department, after a few hundred had gone to the Massachusetts volunteers, but fell foul of Chief of Ordnance Ripley. Tests undertaken in

Worcester, Massachusetts, and patented in November 1861 (33,631). Made by Ball & Williams and promoted enthusiastically by Merwin & Bray of New York, the Ballard was sturdy, effectual and sufficiently popular to last into the post-war era.

The breech block contained the hammer and the trigger mechanism, automatically dropping the hammer to half-cock as the action opened.

Though originally designed to take rimfire ammunition, Ballards supplied to the Federal authorities incorporated an auxiliary cap-lock ignition system patented by Joseph Merwin and Edward Bray of New York City in January 1864 (41,166). Seemingly a backward step, this was useful in circumstances where the Ballard cartridges were in short supply. A nipple and vent lay in the block below the hammer nose, the cap being fired by the hammer neck.

Combustible cartridges or loose powder and ball could be used in emergencies, but the breech was far from gas tight. It was better to bore a hole in the base of a spent rimfire case,

then load it with powder and ball. This allowed the brass case to expand to seal the breech, working not unlike the Burnside (q.v.).

Comparatively few Ballards were acquired by the Federal authorities, in view of the efficacy of their design and the widespread enthusiasm of the users. Purchases in 1861–6 amounted to merely 35 rifles at $36·06 apiece and 1,509 carbines at $23·29, though a contract had been signed in October 1862 to supply a thousand rifles and a similar quantity of the carbines. However, the output of Dwight Chapin & Company of Bridgeport, Connecticut, to whom work had been sub-contracted, was so poor that the Ordnance Department rejected all samples.

Six hundred rifles and the thousand carbines were promptly sold to the State of Kentucky, where they were so well received that more orders followed; according to inventories taken in September 1864, the state cavalry and mounted infantry had 3,494 carbines, while the infantry had about 4,600 rifles.

May–June 1862 at Watertown Arsenal were unfavourable. Greene persisted, possibly with high-ranking assistance, until 900 guns and accessories were ordered in January 1863 for $33,266.

They were delivered on 12 March—a speedy response by Civil War gunmaking standards—but were still in store in March 1864.

The fully stocked under-hammer Greene rifles were 52½in long, had 36-inch barrels retained by three iron bands, and weighed 10lb. Among their most interesting features was a Lancaster oval bore measuring ·530 on its minor axis and ·546 on its major axis. The Greene fired a self-contained combustible cartridge with a projectile inserted in its base.

It was sturdy, but had too many odd features to be successful. The breech was opened by pressing a release catch and retracting the bolt. A single bullet was then seated by pushing the bolt handle forward as far as it would go. The bolt was then re-opened, the combustible cartridge dropped into the breech, and the action closed. Rotating the bolt revolved two lugs into seats behind the chamber.

The loaded Greene had one projectile ahead of the charge and a second bullet acting as a gas-seal. After firing, the 'gas-seal' bullet was pushed forward to allow another cartridge to be inserted. The rifle could be used as a muzzle loader if the chamber became too foul.

Greenes are said to have been used during the battle of Antietam in September 1862, enough unused cartridges with reversed bullets being found 'on the battlefield' to create the myth of the Confederate Poison Bullet—owing to the base cavity filled with lubricating grease! The first Federal purchase was made a few months after Antietam; a few rifles may have served volunteers engaged in the action, but evidence has never been forthcoming.

REMINGTON CARBINES, 1863–5

The enviable reputation of the single-shot breech-loading Remingtons was established by the Rolling Block after the Civil War had ended; guns purchased by the Federal authorities during hostilities incorporated the older 'split breech' action, designed by Leonard Geiger and perfected by Joseph Rider.

Patented jointly in the names of Rider and Remington in 1865, the essence of the action

lay in a high-wall receiver and a radial breech block containing the hammer. The nose of the hammer struck the rimfire cartridges through a slot in the top surface of the block.

The Remington-Geiger action was neither as strong nor as effectual as the Rolling Block, though safe enough with low-pressure loads. Fifteen thousand carbines chambering ·56–50 Spencer rimfire cartridges were ordered on 24 October 1864 for $23 apiece. The Remingtons were 34¼in long and had twenty-inch barrels.

They were followed by five thousand smaller guns chambering a weaker ·46 rimfire cartridge, which put less strain on the comparatively weak action. These were ordered in January 1865, for $17 apiece, but few had been delivered before hostilities ended. Their frames were notably smaller than the ·56–50 version, and swivels often lay under the butt and the barrel band.

Soon after the war had ended, Remington retrieved most of the ·56–50 carbines for $15 apiece. They were sold to France—at a good profit—during the Franco-Prussian War.

BALL AND PALMER CARBINES, 1863–5

The repeating carbine developed by Albert Ball—a mechanical genius who held nearly two hundred patents—was perfected in the winter of 1863–4 while its inventor was works

superintendent of E.G. Lamson & Company of Windsor, Vermont. By 6 June 1864, the project was sufficiently advanced for a thousand-gun contract to be accepted from the Federal government. Each gun cost $25·24.

The essence of the Ball action lay in its cartridge elevator, which doubled as a breech block. The carrier took a round from the magazine—a tube beneath the barrel—and transported it to the chamber, then extracted and ejected it. The chamber was formed partly by the rear of the frame and partly by the cartridge elevator, which was to be a weakness in the design; when the action wore, the chambering was less precise than in a new gun.

The action was originally designed for a special ·50 cartridge, delaying progress. No sooner had work begun, however, than Federal authorities ordered Lamson to use ·56–50 Spencer cartridges to simplify ammunition supply. Consequently, perfected Ball carbines would hold nine Spencer or twelve Ball cartridges.

Barrels measured 20·8in, guns being about 37·6in overall. They were delivered in a single batch on 14 May 1865, too late to see service.

Lamson also made carbines patented by William Palmer of New York City in December 1863 (41,017), the first bolt-action pattern firing metal-case ammunition to be adopted by the US armed forces. The Palmer had a collar-type

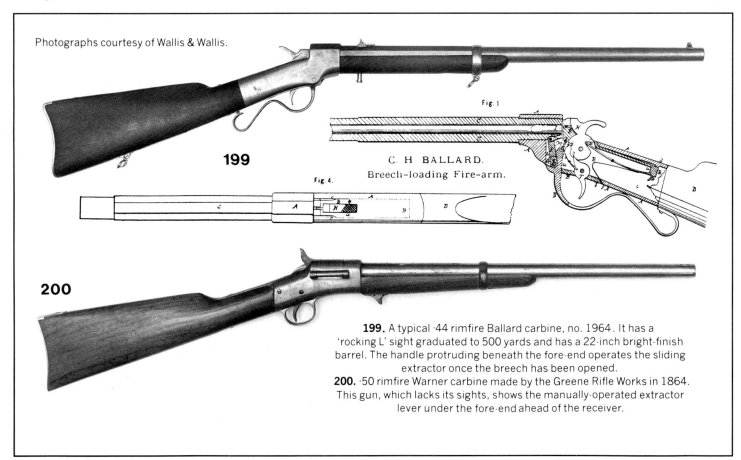

Photographs courtesy of Wallis & Wallis.

199

C. H BALLARD.
Breech-loading Fire-arm.

200

199. A typical ·44 rimfire Ballard carbine, no. 1964. It has a 'rocking L' sight graduated to 500 yards and has a 22-inch bright-finish barrel. The handle protruding beneath the fore-end operates the sliding extractor once the breech has been opened.
200. ·50 rimfire Warner carbine made by the Greene Rifle Works in 1864. This gun, which lacks its sights, shows the manually-operated extractor lever under the fore-end ahead of the receiver.

extractor and a spring-loaded ejector, which elevated it far above many other carbines used during the Civil War. Ignition was supplied by a conventional external side-hammer.

A thousand guns was ordered on 20 June 1864 at $20·90 apiece, but none was delivered before mid-June 1865—too late to see action. They chambered ·56–50 Spencer rimfire ammunition, had 20-inch barrels and were 37¼in overall.

201, right. A longitudinal section of the 1874-pattern Sharps rifle action, from a contemporary manual. Author's collection.

WARNER CARBINES, 1864–5

Made to patents granted to inventor James Warner—41,732 of February 1864 and 45,660 of December 1864—this carbine had a breech block swinging laterally to the right. An extractor lever under the fore-end, ahead of the receiver, could then unseat the spent case.

4,001 Warner carbines were purchased on behalf of the Federal government at $19·82 apiece, 1,501 chambering a special ·50 rimfire cartridge (ordered January–November 1864) and 2,500 taking the Spencer ·56–50 round. The second version was ordered on 26 December 1864, the last gun being delivered into ordnance stores in mid-March 1865.

The Warner was a most attractive brass-frame gun, but had a weak butt and suffered perpetual extraction problems. The special ·50 cartridges often jammed so tightly that they could not be dislodged by the extractor, which lacked adequate leverage. Cases still had to be pulled or shaken from the gun if the extractor worked effectually.

The earlier ·50-calibre Warner had a twenty inch barrel and measured 37·2in overall. A thumb-piece adjacent to the hammer had to be pressed before the breech block could be moved laterally by a lug projecting on its left side. The sling ring was held to an eye-bolt that ran through the frame.

The later guns, chambering ·50 Warner or ·56–50 Spencer ammunition, were made by the Greene Rifle Works in Worcester, Massachusetts. They had a sliding breech-block catch on the left side of the frame—simpler and easier to make than the earlier type—and a sling bar appeared on the left side of the frame.

SHARPS RIFLES, 1865–81

Many pre-1865 gun designs survived to give good service for many years, though many promoters soon failed; some were burdened by irredeemable government debts, while others disappeared as the arms industry declined.

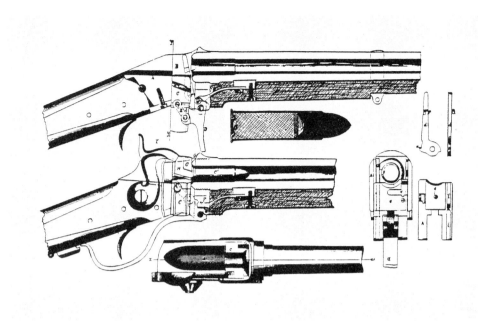

Even in 1870, tremendous numbers of war surplus weaponry were inhibiting commercial sales of new guns.

Sharps' Improved Breech-Loading Metallic Cartridge Rifle, often known as the Model 1869, was based on the 1863-type carbines. The earliest guns chambered ·52–70 rim- or centre fire cartridges, as did many conversions from cap-lock Sharps rifles and carbines; 26-inch octagonal barels were the most common.

The ·52–70 round was short-lived. When the US Army adopted a ·50–70 cartridge, Sharps realised that it was preferable to ream-out and then re-tube old barrels to fire military-pattern ammunition. The ·50–70 Government cartridge was then superseded by ·45–70 in 1873.

Model 1869 Sharps sporters were chambered for a variety of ·44 and ·45-calibre cartridges; however, there were many options, and a wide variety of calibre/barrel length combinations. The earliest proprietary centre-fire cartridges seem to have been ·40 Berdan Short, ·44 Berdan Short and ·44 Berdan Long, dating from about 1870; they were subsequently known as ·40–50, ·44–60 and ·44–77 Sharps.

The Model 1871 rifle was based on the 1869 pattern, improved internally to handle the most powerful sporting cartridges in safety. These guns were made by Sharps Rifle Manufacturing Company of Hartford, Connecticut, until the company failed in 1874. Reorganised as the Sharps Rifle Company, the business moved to Bridgeport in 1876 and went into liquidation in September 1881.

A change in terminology came with the change in ownership, the new 'Model 1874' rifle being the same as the previous Model 1871.

The 1874-pattern Sharps rifle came in many different chamberings. The company's 1879 catalogue notes that these ranged from a

straight-case ·40–1⅞–45 up to an awesome ·50–2½–100 round loaded with a 473-grain paper patched lead bullet.

Rifles were invariably made with characteristic pewter fore-end tips. The earliest catalogues produced by the Sharps Rifle Company offered the Model 1874 with octagonal, half-octagonal or round barrels varying from 26 to 30in. Optional accessories included double set triggers, or a peep-and-globe sighting system. There was also an extra-heavyweight barrel—often as much as 34in long—which could raise the gun weight from its customary 8–11lb to as much as fifteen.

The popularity of the new rifle led to several differing variants: the Creedmoor in 1874; a plain-stocked Hunter's Rifle in 1875; and the Mid-Range target rifle in 1876.

A plain round-barrel Business Rifle made its debut in the summer of 1875, to be followed immediately by a similar Remington; Sharps and Remington, makers of the rifles most greatly favoured by the buffalo hunters, paid great attention to each other's products.

Rifles leaving the Bridgeport factory after April 1876 bore an additional OLD RELIABLE mark on their barrels. Few changes were made by the factory in this era, though gunsmiths such as Frank Freund of Cheyenne patented occasional improvements.

The breech block in the Freund gun of August 1876, instead of moving vertically, rode in a mortise that allowed a certain amount of backward movement as it dropped. When the breech lever was closed, the block moved around its mortise to apply camming action on the cartridge-case base.

The 1877 or English Model Sharps had a slender butt, a minimal fore-end and a lightweight action, often with a much more delicate hammer than normally encountered in the West. The goal was a rifle within the ten-pound limit imposed in many types of competition shooting, but offering the heaviest practicable barrel. Unfortunately, the English Model was very unpopular; many actions are said to have been completed as standard sporting rifles and shipped to gunsmiths such as John Lower of Denver in the early 1880s.

Though the promoters of the Sharps preferred the advantages of long small-calibre bullets to short fat ones, which were inferior ballistically, complaints were soon voiced that even the ·44–77 round did not always drop buffalo with one shot. This resulted in the introduction of the awesome ·50–90 Big Fifty in the summer of 1872, and the virtual end of complaints. Two versions of the ·44–90, one for hunting and the 'Creedmoor' for target shooting, were announced in 1873.

The range of Sharps cartridges was extensive. In addition, the company chambered rifles for cartridges originally introduced for Remingtons or Winchesters—for example, the 'Sharps' ·44–2⁷⁄₁₆ was a Remington pattern, while the ·50–3¼ Big Fifty originated as Winchester's ·50–140 Express. As the years passed, the necked-case ·44 cartridges were replaced by straight ·45 patterns, which were cheaper to make, more easily reloaded, and countered complaints from the plainsmen that necked cartridges were more difficult to extract.

In the late 1870s, the troubled Sharps Rifle Company pinned its hopes on the Model 1878 or Sharps-Borchardt rifle. Designed by German-born Hugo Borchardt and patented in December 1876, the dropping-block action was far in advance of its period. Instead of the familiar external hammer, Borchardt used a spring-loaded internal striker. As the block dropped, it automatically forced the striker back to full cock and applied the safety mechanism. When the action had been reloaded and closed, the firer could override the safety by pressing a secondary trigger.

Sharps, optimistically, saw the Borchardt as a military weapon. Sporting guns gradually appeared—including a mid-range target rifle and a Creedmoor pattern—but the unfamiliar appearance of the Sharps-Borchardt inhibited sales in the West. With the failure of the Sharps Rifle Company in 1881, the effectual Borchardt rifle also disappeared.

MAYNARD RIFLES, 1865–90

The Maynard was a survivor of the Civil War, based on a patent granted to Edward Maynard on 6 December 1859 (30,537). It fired a unique metal-case cartridge with a notably thick rim, ignition being supplied by an external side hammer cap lock. Maynard Tape Primers were standard on pre-1865 weapons. Made by the Massachusetts Arms Company, the guns had a barrel that opened by depressing the breech lever doubling as the trigger guard. Extraction and ejection were accomplished manually, helped by the massive cartridge-case rim.

The original carbine was unprepossessing, with a slab-sided butt and virtually no comb; it lacked a fore-end, but was undeniably light and handy. After the Civil War, substantial numbers of Maynard carbines and Model 1865 sporting rifles (with a mechanical extractor) found their way westward.

External ignition began to prove a handicap in the early 1870s, Maynard patenting a conversion to self-contained cartridges in 1873. However, despite the introduction of a number of proprietary loadings, ranging from ·35–30 to ·50–100, sales were far from brisk—purchasers could only use the idiosyncratic Maynard thick rim cartridges, which were neither widely distributed nor particularly popular.

The 1873-pattern Maynard sporter was offered with half-octagonal or round barrels ranging from twenty to 32in. Pride of the range was the No.14 Long Range Creedmoor, introduced in 1876 to accompany a ·44–100–520 cartridge which taxed the Maynard action to its limit. The gun had a special 32-inch cylindrical barrel, a chequered pistol-grip half-stock, and vernier peep-and-globe sights. It cost $70, substantially less than the Creedmoor rifles offered by Marlin (Ballard), Sharps and Remington.

One of the best features of the Maynard rifle was the ease with which its barrel could be changed; this alone commended it to many Westerners, as a 28-bore shotgun barrel could

202, below. *When Horse Flesh Comes High,* painted by Charles M. Russell in 1909. In addition to the Winchester M1873 rifle being fired by the cowboy in the foreground, what appears to be a Sharps rifle is being carried by the man mounting (left). Courtesy of the Amon Carter Museum, Fort Worth, Texas.

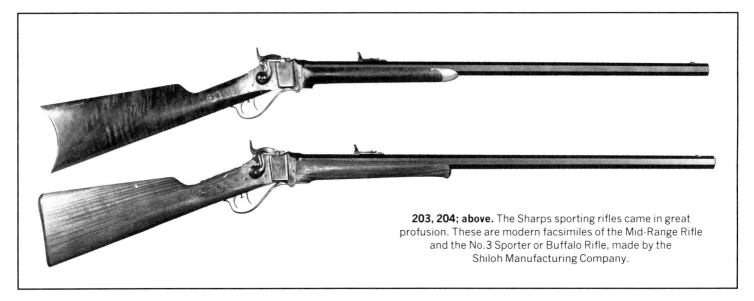

203, 204; above. The Sharps sporting rifles came in great profusion. These are modern facsimiles of the Mid-Range Rifle and the No.3 Sporter or Buffalo Rifle, made by the Shiloh Manufacturing Company.

be fitted at will. In an emergency, a ·55-calibre ball could be fired from the Maynard shotgun cartridge.

The perfected Maynard rifle, announced in 1882, fired conventional centre-fire cartridges. Though it was made of the best materials, the Maynard action was not strong enough to handle smokeless-propellant loadings. Business declined until the assets and liabilities were sold in 1890 to J. Stevens Arms & Tool Company. Edward Maynard, greatly honoured in his lifetime for his services to dentistry in addition to his work with firearms, died a year later.

BALLARD RIFLES, 1865-91

Though never attracting much Federal interest, unlike Spencer or Sharps, Ballard rifles had sold well to state militiamen in Kentucky during the Civil War. Patented by Charles Ballard in November 1861 (33,631), the rifle was effectual by 1865 standards; it survived well enough into the post-war era not only to serve some of the Westerners but also gain an enviable reputation for accuracy on the target range.

The original Ballards had been made by Ball & Williams of Worcester, Massachusetts, but work had passed soon after the Civil War to the transient Merrimack Arms & Manufacturing Company, then to the equally short-lived Brown Manufacturing Company of Newburyport, Massachusetts. Creditors brought a forcible end to Brown's operations in 1873, whereupon rights to the Ballard were acquired by Schoverling & Daly of New York.

Not until 1875 did the partnership find a suitable manufacturer for the rifle, licensing it to John Marlin of New Haven, Connecticut. The Marlin Fire Arms Company was incorporated in 1881, when Charles Daly (of Schoverling, Daly & Gales) became the first president. Ballards

were made in the Marlin factory until 1891, by which time they had been eclipsed by the company's lever-action guns.

The first Marlin-made Ballard rifles were advertised in the Spring of 1876 with "Marlin's Patent Automatic Extractor and Reversible Firing Pin". Dating from 1875, the firing pin could handle rim- and centre-fire cartridges interchangeably.

Guns were sold in a variety of well-known chamberings, including government ·45-70 and ·50-70, but were then offered in proprietary loadings—e.g., ·38-50, ·40-63, ·40-90, ·44-75 and ·45-100 Ballard. Their dropping-block action, opened by a lever doubling as the trigger guard, was sturdy enough to handle impressive powder charges and heavy bullets.

According to *Forest and Stream*, Marlin-made Ballards were initially offered in nine styles ranging from the standard No.1, ·44 rim- or centre-fire, with a round 26-30in barrel and a blued frame ($27-29), to the No.7 'Creedmoor A.1'. The No.7, sighted to 1,200 yards, was offered with ·44 cartridges containing up to 100 grains of powder. It had a 'selected, hand-made pistol grip stock, finest vernier and wind gauge sights, with spirit level' and cost $100.

By 1883, the No.1 Hunter's Rifle had been dropped to leave the No.2 as the basic sporting rifle. This had an octagonal barrel, a reversible firing pin and an open buck-horn back sight; it could be obtained in ·32, ·38 and ·44 'Colt and Winchester Center-Fire'. The ·32 version was sold with a 28-inch barrel, the others with thirty inch patterns. Weights varied between 8¼ and 9lb. The No.3 was a ·22 rimfire gallery rifle, with an octagonal barrel measuring 24-28in and a weight of 7½-9¼lb.

The No.4 Perfection was intended for hunting, being fitted with open 'Rocky Mountain sights'. Available only in ·38-50 or ·40-63, with thirty inch barrels as standard, it weighed about 10lb.

The so-called Everlasting Shells, specifically intended for reloaders, were recommended for this rifle.

The No.4½ A.1 Mid Range, a minor variant of the No.4, appeared c.1878. It had a fine English walnut half stock, Marlin's improved vernier back sight (graduated to 800 yards), and a wind-gauge front sight with bead and aperture discs. The frame was engraved, the butt plate was rubber, and every part was 'finished in the best manner'. The No.4½ was available only in ·40-63, with a thirty-inch barrel.

Ballard No.5 Pacific and No.5½ Montana rifles were essentially similar, introduced in 1876 and c.1879 respectively with the heavy barrels favoured out West. They also had cleaning rods beneath the muzzles, unlike the other guns in the series.

The Pacific rifle had a heavy octagonal barrel and double set-triggers, plus Rocky Mountain sights. Chambered for ·44-40 and ·45-70 rounds in addition to three Everlasting patterns—·40-63, ·40-90 and ·45-100—it had barrels of 30-32in and weighed 10-12lb. The Montana pattern was similar, but even heavier: chambered only for the Sharps ·45-2⅞ cartridge, it had a thirty-inch barrel and weighed about 14lb. No.5 and No.5½ rifles were generally found with ring-tip breech levers instead of the normal spur patterns.

The No.6 Schuetzen Ballard, known as the 'Off-Hand' when introduced early in 1876, was intended for a particular European style of target shooting that was popular in the eastern USA. It was made with an octagonal or half octagonal thirty or 32-inch barrel and weighed 13-15lb. Chambering only ·38-50 Everlasting cartridges, it had a double set-trigger system, Marlin's short mid-range vernier peep and wind-gauge sights. A specially finished Swiss style stock with a cheek piece and a nickel plated hooked butt plate was standard.

The modified ·38–50 No.6½ Off-Hand rifle of about 1880 was also intended for target shooting. Its features included a modified Swiss-pattern walnut stock with a butt plate designed by Milton Farrow, the 'Champion Off Hand Shot of the World'. The 28- or thirty-inch Rigby barrel and Marlin mid-range vernier sights gave the gun a weight of about 11½lb. In common with the No.6, the '6½' action was engraved, and every part was 'highly finished'.

The No.7 Long Range rifle, formerly known as the Creedmoor No.8 (with a pistol grip stock) or No.9 (with a straight-wrist stock), had a 34-inch half-octagon barrel and an improved Marlin vernier back sight graduated to 1,300yd. The wind-gauge front sight was supplied with bead and aperture discs, plus a spirit level.

The rifles all chambered ·44–100 Everlasting cartridges and had hand-made pistol-grip butts. Scroll engraving appeared on the action, with chequering on the pistol grip and the schnabel tipped fore-end. The No.7 A.1 Long Range rifle (formerly No.7 A.1 Creedmoor) was essentially similar to the No.7, but had a Rigby barrel and an 'extra handsome English walnut stock' accompanied by a rubber butt plate. The No.7 A.1 chambered the 'new thin and everlasting shells, ·45 cal, 100 grains'.

The No.8 Union Hill rifle, dating from c.1883–4, was the last of the company's target rifles. In common with many of them, it was often fitted with a Winchester-type finger lever.

PEABODY RIFLES, 1865–83

The original Peabody rifle was, perhaps, the outstanding single-shot breech-loading rifle of the Civil War period. It was patented by Henry Peabody of Boston, Massachusetts, in July 1862 (35,947) and was made exclusively by the Providence Tool Company of Providence, Rhode Island.

Peabody's patent claimed novelty only in the slot in the underside of the breech block and pins on the breech lever that opened the action; a roller on the breech-lever spring to retain the breech block in the loading position; and the combination of the breech lever, the breech block and the sturdy receiver.

The patent was reissued in 1866, noting that the pin-and-slot depressor featured in the original specification was but one of the possibilities. Peabody added a lever-and-slot depressor, plus a pivoting extractor struck by the breech block as it opened. Later patents included one in April 1868 (76,805) to protect the combination rim- and centre-fire striker.

The Peabody had a most distinctive two-piece stock and an all-metal receiver. A back-action lock with an external side hammer was let into the butt. The guns were tested regularly by the US Army, receiving great praise in 1865. The Peabody was a much more effectual weapon than the Allin Springfield, though the latter could be created from existing rifle muskets with comparatively little investment. The Peabody, with its deep receiver and two-piece stock, would have required complete re-tooling.

Not only did the Peabody take much of the strain of firing on the rear inner surface of the sturdy receiver, but the position of the breech block pivot pin prevented the action opening prematurely. The extractor was also much more substantial than the Allin-Springfield pattern.

The end of the Civil War destroyed the market into which the Providence Tool Company had hoped to sell their new gun. Enthusiasm was greater abroad, however, with substantial sales in Romania, Spain and Switzerland.

The original Peabody Sporting Gun, allegedly introduced in September 1865, displayed a half octagonal barrel and a side-barred patch box let into the butt. Small metal plates were let into the fore-end, the breech lever/trigger guard had a scrolled rearward extension, and a folding back sight was to be found on the tang.

A plainer gun had appeared by 1866, with a conventional operating lever and the back sight on the barrel ahead of the receiver. It was offered in a wide variety of rimfire chamberings, including ·45–50–330, ·45–60–420, ·45–70–480 and ·50–45–320, the ·50 round being the only

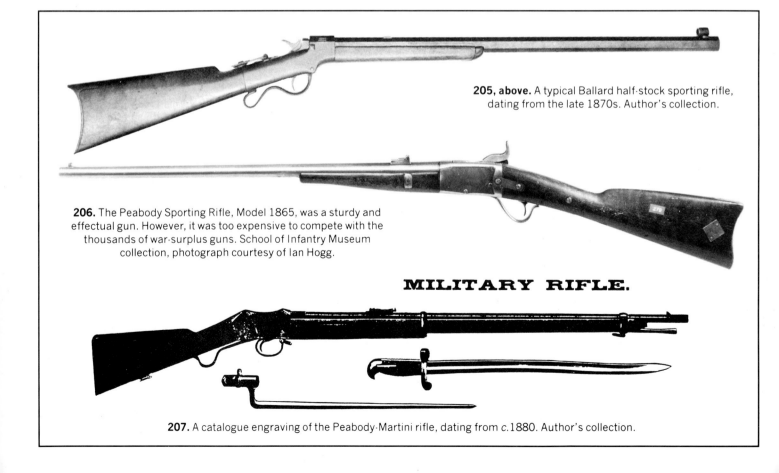

205, above. A typical Ballard half-stock sporting rifle, dating from the late 1870s. Author's collection.

206. The Peabody Sporting Rifle, Model 1865, was a sturdy and effectual gun. However, it was too expensive to compete with the thousands of war-surplus guns. School of Infantry Museum collection, photograph courtesy of Ian Hogg.

MILITARY RIFLE.

207. A catalogue engraving of the Peabody-Martini rifle, dating from c.1880. Author's collection.

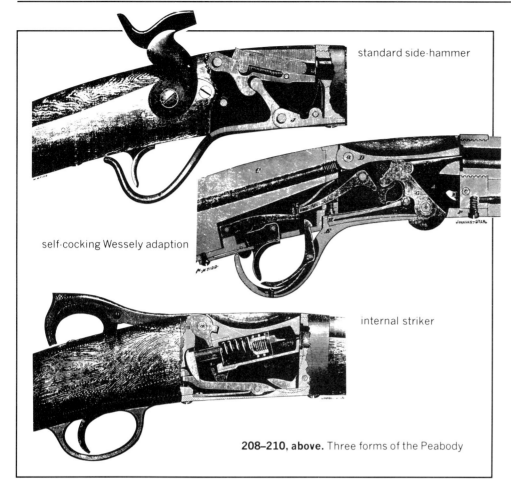

standard side-hammer

self-cocking Wessely adaption

internal striker

208–210, above. Three forms of the Peabody

WHITNEY RIFLES, 1865–82

The Whitney Arms Company or Whitneyville Armory, owned by Eli Whitney the Younger, was another long-established business.

Casting around for a merchantable cartridge rifle at the end of the war, Whitney seized upon an underlever rifle patented by Sebre Howard in October 1862 (36,779) with improvements made by Charles Howard in September and October 1865 (50,125 and 50,358). The sliding breech bolt was locked by a toggle system, an internal striker being cocked as the action was opened.

The Howard rifle was largely tubular, its receiver being a virtual extension of the barrel; the original pattern also had an interesting sliding tube bayonet. Made by Whitney for Howard Brothers & Company of New Haven, Connecticut, guns were entered in the US Army breech-loading rifle trials of 1865 as well as those convened by the Adjutant General of the State of New York in April 1867. Neither board liked the absence of an external hammer, and the ·46 rimfire New York gun was inaccurate.

Sometimes marketed as the Thunderbolt, the Whitney-Howard sporting rifle could chamber virtually any ·44-calibre rimfire cartridge up to and including ·44 Extra Long. A 54-bore shotgun version was also made. A few rifles found their way west in the late 1860s, but were never popular.

Whitney's next move must have caused the Remington family apoplexy: Whitney Rolling Block rifles resembled the Remington pattern so closely that only the knowledgeable could tell them apart at a glance.

Internally, however, the Whitney was based on a patent granted to Theodore Laidley and C.A. Emery on 15 May 1866 (54,743)—though the barrel markings on later Whitney-made guns acknowledged additional patents of 17 October 1865, 26 December 1865 and 16 July 1872. Some also incorporated improvements patented by Eli Whitney in March and June 1871 (112,997 and 115,997).

The Laidley-Emery system was accepted better militarily than the Remington, owing to its safety features, but was not as simple. The prototype rifle, which Laidley called 'My Chick', was successful enough to be selected by the Secretary of War to take part in service trials alongside the Allin Springfield transformation, the Peabody, the so-called 'Split Breech' Remington and the Sharps. However, only the Peabody survived the rigorous programme of over-load charges, the Laidley failing after the second firing.

The Whitney rolling-block rifle contained an auxiliary cam, sharing the hammer-pin, which

---

option available a year previously. There was also a twenty-inch barrelled ·45 or ·50-calibre carbine, and a similar military-style rifle with barrels of 26 or 28in. All were available with a 'Sliding Rear Sight' or an 'Elevating Peep Sight'.

By the summer of 1867, the Peabody had been converted to centre-fire. According to a catalogue produced in 1871, sporting guns were available only in ·45, with barrels of 20–28in and the option of sliding or elevating aperture back sights. Military-style muskets, stocked almost to the muzzle, were available in ·43, ·45 and ·50; military carbines were made in ·45 and ·50.

A few deluxe guns were distinguished by their superior finish, nickel-plating, German silver escutcheons for the barrel-retaining key, half- or fully octagonal barrels, and chequering on the wrist and fore-end.

In a broadsheet submitted to a US Army Board of Officers convened at St Louis in 1870, the Providence Tool Company claimed to be making several versions of the Peabody. There was a standard ·45 side-hammer gun, called the 'Roumanian Model'; a similar ·43 'Spanish Model', with a spiral firing-pin retractor spring; the Peabody Self-Cocking Gun, with a top-lever depressor and a coil-pattern firing-pin spring; the ·42 (Russian) Peabody-Wessely, a modified self-cocking design with an internal hammer; and a method for converting rifle-muskets. The

Peabody was expensive, however; at $40 or more for a plain sporter, it cost more than contemporary Remington and Sharps rifles, which sold for about $32 apiece.

Production of the side-hammer rifles ceased in 1873, when work began on the perfected Peabody-Martini. This had a new internal striker, powered by a coil spring and cocked automatically as the breech was opened.

The new gun was highly successful. Turkey ordered 650,000 rifles in 1873, while others went to Romania and some to state militiamen. Peabody-Martini rifles were made in ·43, ·45–70 and '·45 Necked'.

Peabody-Martini Mid-Range Creedmoor target rifles were offered with a long half-octagonal barrel, a fore-end and a pistol-grip butt of superior quality, a wind-gauge globe front sight, and a folding vernier peep sight on the tang or butt-heel. According to advertisements in *Forest and Stream*, this gun was 'victorious at the Centennial Short-Range Match, at Creedmoor, Sept. 12, 1876, distance 200 yards, off-hand… Only two Peabody-Martini rifles entered, winning first prize, $100 cash and gold medal; and fourth prize, $25 cash and gold medal.'

Unfortunately, the Providence Tool Company was never able to establish the Peabody sporting rifles on the market and left the gun business in the 1880s.

Gun photographs courtesy of
Wallis & Wallis.

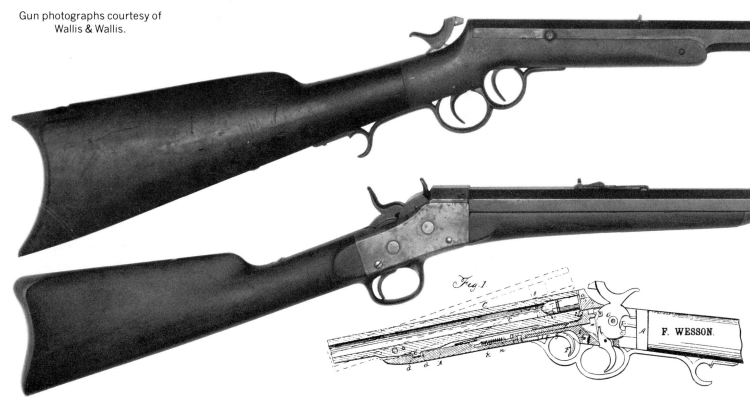

locked into place the instant the breech was closed—even though the breech piece may have been moved no more than a short distance. Unlike the Remingtons, the Whitney rifle loaded at half-cock and its hammer did nothing other than strike the firing pin.

Once production had started in 1872, the action went through several alterations to make it simpler, sturdier and easier to use. The Whitney Rolling Block was offered as a military carbine or rifle, and also as a sporter with round, half-octagon or fully-octagonal 24–30in barrels. There was also a Creedmoor-type target gun, with specially selected woodwork and vernier peep-and-globe sights.

The original Laidley-Emery Rolling Block was difficult to make, production ceasing in the early 1880s in favour of a blatant copy of the Remington. The New System Whitney, which lasted until its manufacturer was purchased by Winchester in 1888, had a special pivoting-lever extractor that was more effectual than most Remington patterns. The basic pattern was improved in 1886 with a main-spring roller and a mechanical firing-pin retractor, but few of the perfected guns were made before Whitney's enforced demise.

One poor feature of the Remington-type Whitneys was the absence of a locking bar, which in most Remingtons prevented the hammer falling from full cock unless the breech piece was shut. If the Whitney trigger was pressed while the breech piece was being shut, the hammer would fall onto the firing pin. The original Laidley-Emery Whitneys were made in

calibres as large as ·58. The largest cartridge chambered in New System guns, distinguished by a rounded receiver, appears to have been ·44–40. Catalogues produced in 1884 listed them in ·22, ·32, ·38 and ·44, with 24–28in octagonal barrels and weights from five to 7lb.

Patented by Eli Whitney III in May 1874, the Phoenix rifle had a side-hinged breech block that lifted up and to the right for loading—awkward for most firers, who would rather have loaded with their trigger hand. The rifle had a massive wrought iron receiver with a central hammer, the receiver being cut transversely to accommodate the breech block. The block, hinged on the right, had an extended thumb piece on the left and contained the firing pin and its coil spring. The rifle had a mechanical extractor, but still

suffered the problems inherent in designs of its type. Consequently, several differing extractor systems were fitted during a production life of little more than a decade. The original breech locking catch shown on the patent drawings was let into the standing breech on the left side of the hammer. Intended to hold the breech closed when the hammer was pulled back to half cock, the catch was soon moved to the front right side of the receiver ahead of the breech block.

Catalogues produced by Whitney in the early 1880s offered the Phoenix as a 9lb military rifle, with three barrel bands, a tangent-leaf sight, and a socket or sabre bayonet; as a 7lb cavalry carbine, with a single band, a ring and a sling bar on the right side of the receiver; and as a sporting rifle. The sporter was made in a variety

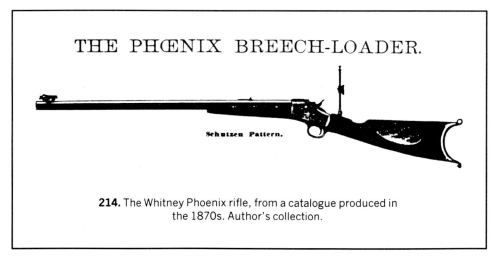

THE PHŒNIX BREECH-LOADER.

Schutzen Pattern.

214. The Whitney Phoenix rifle, from a catalogue produced in the 1870s. Author's collection.

211, above. A ·41 rimfire Franklin Wesson sporting carbine, dating from c.1870. This gun has a 22-inch octagonal barrel and is about 36in long. The front 'trigger' releases the barrel, which tips down to give access to the chamber.

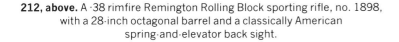

212, above. A ·38 rimfire Remington Rolling Block sporting rifle, no. 1898, with a 28-inch octagonal barrel and a classically American spring-and-elevator back sight.

213, right. A typical North American buffalo, slaughtered in millions by hunters armed with Sharps and Remington rifles. Author's collection.

of styles and calibres, ranging from a plain hunter's gun, with a 26-inch round barrel and open sights, up to a Schuetzen Rifle with vernier peep-and-globe sights, selected woodwork, and a hooked Swiss-style butt plate. Barrels measured between 26 and 32in, weights ranging correspondingly from seven to 10lb.

Military-style Phoenix rifles were offered in ·43, ·45 and ·50; sporters came in ·32, ·38 and ·44 rimfire, plus ·38, ·40, ·44, ·45 and ·50 centre-fire. Individual chamberings included ·40–50 and ·40–70, together with ·44–60, ·44–77, ·44–90, ·44–100 and ·44–105. However, the Phoenix action was prone to jamming when fired with heavy loads, and was never successful.

WESSON RIFLES, 1865–79

Franklin Wesson, proprietor of F. Wesson Firearms Company of Springfield and then Worcester, Massachusetts, made distinctive 'two trigger' carbines during the Civil War.

Wesson supplemented his post-war twin trigger sporters with a Pocket Rifle patented on 31 May 1870 (103,694), and then with two Creedmoor target rifles with vernier peep and globe sights. These appear to have been patented in collusion with C.N. Cutter in July 1877 (193,060), but the business failed a mere two years later.

The Pocket Rifle, offered with a detachable shoulder stock, was a long-barelled pistol loaded by unlatching the barrel and rotating the barrel to the right about its longitudinal pivot. The system was quite adequate for a glorified pistol, but not for a heavy-barrel rifle; consequently, Wesson's Creedmoor rifles embodied a dropping-block action with a Sharps-type side hammer. There was the 'No.1 Long Range Rifle', and the 'No.2 Long & Mid Range & Hunting Rifle' with a brass frame.

REMINGTON ROLLING BLOCKS, 1867–97

Remington dallied briefly with sporting rifles made to the patents granted in the early 1860s to Leonard Geiger and Joseph Rider, the so-called 'Split Breech' military carbines being offered to the post-war commercial market for sporting purposes. These guns are described in greater detail in the section devoted to the guns of the Civil War.

The company also made small numbers of sporting guns to the patents of Fordyce Beals. Confined to 1866–8. these had a 24-inch half octagonal barrel and weighed about 6lb; they were loaded by depressing the breech lever, which doubled as the trigger guard, to slide the barrel forward and away from the standing breech. Unfortunately, the lock was primitive enough to restrict power to ·36 and ·38 rimfire. It was soon replaced by the stronger and more effectual Rolling Block.

The perfected Remington, derived from the Geiger split-breech, was the work of Joseph Rider. Subject of several patents granted during the late 1860s, the breech included a sturdy hammer and an interlocking radial breech piece. The action was opened by thumbing back the hammer to full-cock, then rotating the breech piece backward by pulling on the finger spur. This gave immediate access to the chamber, partially extracting the spent case as it did so. A new round was introduced into the chamber, the breech piece was closed, and the trigger could then be pulled to drop the hammer. The hammer struck the firing pin and fired the gun.

The legendary sturdiness of the Rolling Block derived from the position of the hammer and breech-piece pivots, as the breech could not be opened at all once the hammer shoulder had run forward under the back of the breech piece. Remington rifles regularly withstood trials of utmost savagery; a standard ·50 gun survived a charge of 750 grains of black powder behind forty balls. The director of Liége proof house, Alphonse Polain, reported laconically that 'nothing extraordinary happened' when the gun had been fired.

Remington's sales literature made a great play of such durability. It was sufficient to camouflage comparatively poor extraction, which depended on the breech piece being flipped open as smartly as possible, and hid that the Remington could not be fired as quickly as some rivals.

The Remington enjoyed a brief vogue in the US services, rather longer in the navy than in the army. In the 1872–3 trials, poor extraction with government-issue copper case cartridges persuaded the Board of Ordnance to favour the

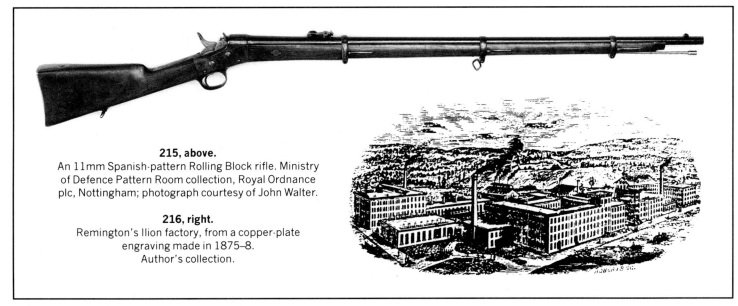

215, above.
An 11mm Spanish-pattern Rolling Block rifle. Ministry of Defence Pattern Room collection, Royal Ordnance plc, Nottingham; photograph courtesy of John Walter.

216, right.
Remington's Ilion factory, from a copper-plate engraving made in 1875–8.
Author's collection.

Trapdoor Springfield. By the time drawn brass cases had been substituted, the US government was committed to the ·45–70 M1873 rifle.

One of the greatest hindrances in army trials arose from loading the rifles with the hammer at full-cock, so alarming boards of officers that a 'Locking Rifle' had been developed. Externally identical with the standard guns, its hammer automatically dropped to half-cock when the breech piece was closed and had to be retracted manually before firing. Locking Rifles were also rejected in 1872–3, though 21,000 were sold to the New York state militia.

Though the US military did not view Remingtons with great enthusiasm, foreign governments were often more accommodating. One of the earliest orders came from Denmark, apparently for 42,000 rifles and carbines, and the Remington gained a silver medal from the Paris Exposition of 1867.

By 1873, Remington was claiming to have sold 16,500 rifles, carbines and pistols to the US Army, 23,000 to the US Navy, fifteen thousand Model 1871 Locking Rifles to New York State, and five thousand rifle-musket conversions to South Carolina. Among the export orders were 75,000 rifles and carbines supplied to Spain for use in Cuba, beginning in 1867, and thirty thousand guns for Sweden from 1868 onward.

Remington's 1876 catalogue offered several military-style rifles—'about 1,000,000 arms of this system now in the hands of troops'—in the hope that they would appeal to impecunious Westerners. They included the ·50-calibre US Model (1871); two adapted Springfield ·58 rifle-muskets, long and short, which mated the original barrel, stock and furniture with a new Rolling Block action; the ·43 or 11mm-calibre Spanish Model with its socket bayonet; the ·43 Civil Guard Model, chambered for the 'Spanish or Russian Cartridge' and offered with

a sabre bayonet; the ·43 French Model and sabre bayonet, chambered for the 'Egyptian Cartridge'; and a ·43 or ·50-calibre carbine.

Together with the Sharps, the Remington Rolling Block swept the plains of the West of the once numerous buffalo. One hunter later ventured his opinion than eight out of every ten buffalo had fallen to guns of these particular makes.

The first commercial Rolling Block was the 1867-vintage Sporting Rifle No.1, offered until 1890 in an assortment of octagonal barrel lengths (24–34in) with weights, according to an 1876 Remington catalogue, ranging from 8½ to 15lb. Chamberings included ·22 Long, ·32 Long, ·38 Long, ·44 Long and ·46 Long rimfires, plus ·40–50, ·44–77, ·44 Creedmoor (·44–90), ·45–45 and ·50–70 centre-fire.

A vast range of optional extras included—among others—peep and globe sights; set triggers; pistol-grip butts; and varnished, or oiled and polished stocks.

Guns made before 1886 were marked E. REMINGTON & SONS, ILION, N.Y. while later ones bore 'Remington Arms Co.' in recognition of the failure of the original business. Patent acknowledgements eventually included 3 May 1864; 7 May, 11 June, 12 November, 24 and 31 December 1872; and 9 September 1873.

The No.1½ Rolling Block, introduced in 1888 and discontinued in 1897, was a lightweight No.1, generally encountered with an octagonal barrel but weighing a mere 7½lb. It was made in a variety of rim- and centre-fire chamberings from ·22 to ·38.

Announced in the late winter of 1872, the New Model Light Rifle, known initially as the 'Gem' and then as the 'No.2', was an ultra-lightweight version. Made for ·22 rimfire, ·25–20, ·32 rimfire, ·32, ·32–20, ·38, ·38–40, ·44 and ·44–40, it lasted until about 1910. The No.2

had a short octagonal barrel, a straight-wrist butt, and a notably concave butt plate. It had a semi-buckhorn back sight and weighed, according to a January 1876 catalogue, between 5½ and 8lb.

The Deer Rifle of 1872–90 was a special model chambering ·46 Long rimfire. It had a 24-inch octagonal barrel, weighed 6½lb and was otherwise similar to the standard No.1. Made from 1874 until about 1890, the Buffalo Rifle had a thirty-inch octagonal or round barrel chambered for cartridges ranging from ·40–50 Sharps to monsters such as ·44–90–400 and the old regulation ·50–70.

The plain finish Hunter, Business and Black Hills rifles (1875–82), minor variants of the No.1, were characterised by their 28-inch round barrels, weighed 7½lb and chambered ·45–70 government cartridges.

By the mid-1870s, with the buffalo all but gone, Remington's reputation with the hunting fraternity gradually moved to the target range. The Mid-Range rifle (1875–90), built on the No.1 action, had half-octagon barrels of 28 or 30in. Weighing about 7½lb without its sights and offered in chamberings ranging from ·40–50 Sharps to ·50–70, the Mid-Range Remington invariably had a pistol-grip butt. A folding vernier aperture back sight, hinged to a block on the upper tang behind the breech, was accompanied by a globe front sight.

The Short Range rifle of 1876–90 was similar to the Mid-Range pattern, excepting that it had a 26-inch half-octagon barrel and chambered rim- and centre-fire cartridges from ·38 Extra Long to ·46.

The most impressive of the Rolling Block target rifles was the Creedmoor, developed by Lewis Hepburn and named after a rifle range—the first in North America—built in 1873 at Creed's Farm, Long Island, on land that had

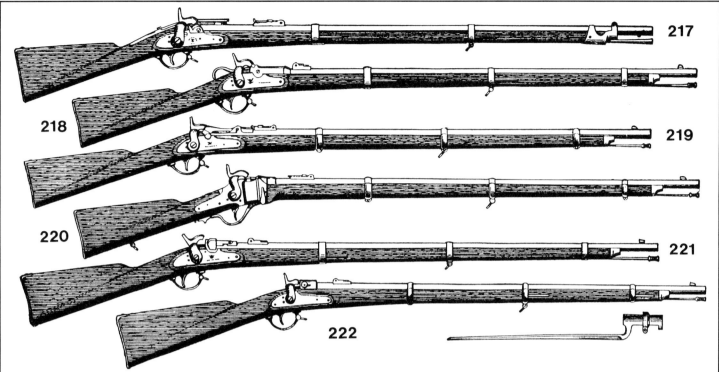

217–22, above. A selection of the breech-loading rifles of the Civil War period: (217) the Merrill alteration of a M1842 musket, dating from the early days of the Civil War; (218) a Peabody alteration of a standard M1861 Springfield rifle-musket, patented in December 1867; (219) the regulation M1866 Allin conversion of an M1863 rifle-musket; a ·50–70 Sharps rifle (220), converted at Springfield in 1870 from old Civil War 'M1863' actions; the Miller conversion system (221), patented in 1865, which saw some success with the militia; and the Joslyn (222), made at Springfield Armory in 1868.

been acquired by the New York State legislature, the embryo National Rifle Association, and the cities of Brooklyn and New York.

The first International Rifle Match was held on Creedmoor Range in 1874, when a team of six Americans successfully defeated the all conquering Irish.

Readied early in March 1874, the Creedmoor Remington was built around specially honed No.1 actions. The first examples were fired against the Irish by Hepburn himself, Colonel John 'Old Reliable' Bodine, and the Lieutenant Henry Fulton.

There was a mild dispute among the proponents of breech-loading, as Fulton, whose score of 171 × 180 was the highest in the 1874 match, loaded his Remington in a unique manner: a blank cartridge was loaded into the breech, but the ball was sized by ramming it down the bore.

Chambered only for ·44–90, ·44–100 and ·44–105, the Creedmoor Remington had a 32-inch octagonal barrel. In 1876, the 'Best Breech-Loading Rifle in the World...shot by Fulton, Bodine, Hepburn, Dakin, Coleman, Canfield, in the great International Contests' was being offered with 'Vernier Peep and Wind Gauge Globe Sight, Pistol Grip' for $100—three times the cost of the basic No.1 sporting rifle. Optional extras included a 'Trunk Shape

Creedmoor Rifle Case' for $20, plus a spirit level and additional sight discs for the globe sight ($5 and $1.50 respectively).

The first guns had a special brass-faced horse-shoe butt plate, but those made after the mid-1880s usually had rubber shotgun-type butt plates.

Creedmoor rifles had selected walnut butts with chequered pistol grips, the matching fore ends terminating in small pewter or German silver finials. The last guns sold about 1890.

The Remington Arms Company inherited large numbers of obsolescent Rolling Block actions, many of which were then completed as Light or Baby Carbines (1888–1908). Chambered only for ·44–40, these little guns had a twenty-inch round barrel and weighed a mere 5½lb. The finish was blue or nickel; the sights, butt and fore-end were traditional military style; and a sling ring was often anchored to a D-bar on the right side of the receiver.

The Remington No.5 rifle of 1898 was overshadowed by its rivals. Introduced as a high-power sporter, chambering 7mm Mauser (7 × 57), ·30 M1903, ·30–30, ·303 British, ·32–40 HP, ·32 Winchester Special or ·38–55 HP, it had a round 'Smokeless Steel' barrel measuring 24–28in, a straight-wrist butt, a rounded fore-end with a schnabel-style tip, and

a semi-buckhorn back sight. Weight was 7–7½lb. Never popular, the No.5 lasted a mere seven years.

THE SPRINGFIELD-ALLIN SYSTEM, 1865–73

The end of the Civil War found the Federal ordnance authorities in disarray. A tremendous variety of weapons had been impressed into official service, while many others existed at state level. A belated effort had been made to standardise the ·56–50 Spencer cartridge for breech-loading weapons acquired after 1864, but had only been partially successful.

In addition, few of the metallic-cartridge guns purchased in 1861–5 were numerous enough to equip even the vastly reduced post-war establishment; only the Spencer carbine would have been suitable, plus the Sharps carbine among the combustible-ammunition cap locks.

In November 1867, the Ordnance Department asked the Sharps Rifle Company to transform the surviving carbines for regulation ·50–70 cartridges. The first thousand was delivered in February 1868; by the end of 1869, about 30,000 had been modified.

Contemporary cavalrymen carried a wide range of weapons. Most of the regulars had

Sharps or Spencers, but state units had greater variety: ·56–52 Joslyns survived in Nevada and Ohio into 1867. As late as 1869, the Ordnance Department approved the issue of a thousand cap-lock Smith carbines to militia in Dakota.

The Spencer was well proven in battle. However, though temporarily retained for cavalrymen—to whom its fire power was particularly useful—it was not acceptable for line infantry. Despite the lessons of the Civil War, breech-loaders were still seen as too complicated and too wasteful of ammunition to be trusted to the common soldier.

As early as 1864, the Chief of Ordnance, Brigadier General Alexander Dyer, had reported that the use of breech-loading arms in Federal service had: "With few exceptions, been confined to mounted troops. So far as our limited experience goes, it indicates the advisability of extending this armament to our infantry also… It is therefore intended to make this change of manufacture at our national armories as soon as the best model for a breech-loader can be established… The alteration of our…muzzle-loading arms is also a very desirable measure, both on account of economy and improvement…"

Advertisements were sent to interested parties at the end of 1864, requesting methods of converting thousands of rifle-muskets on issue or in store. Concurrently, General Dyer asked Erskine Allin, Master Armorer at Springfield, to develop a 'Government Gun' without regard to patent infringements. This was to prove costly.

Trials were undertaken early in 1865 with a variety of single-shot rifles. In April, the board recommended the Spencer repeater and the single-shot Peabody. As the Civil War was ending, the Board of Ordnance merely noted the conclusions and took no further action.

Allin produced his prototype in the summer of 1865, allowing the Chief of Ordnance to order rifles for field trials. The Rifle Musket Model 1865 was a simple adaption of the standard ·58-calibre 1863-pattern cap lock, with a breech block inserted in a cut-away breech. Hinged laterally at the front of the action, the block could be swung up to expose the chamber and operate the ratchet-pattern extractor. Copper-case ·58 rimfire cartridges were used to save rebarrelling.

The first Allin transformation was unduly complicated, only five thousand 'M1865' rifles being made. The extractor was particularly capricious, while the cartridge was ballistically ineffectual. Consequently, a new Board of Officers met in Washington as the first guns were being issued for trials with the 12th Infantry. Testing of more than forty guns continued until June 1866.

The M1865 Springfield-Allin rifle, the initial government entrant in the trials, was replaced by a modified gun with a simplified extractor and the barrel lined-down from ·58 to ·50. This, which became the M1866, was much better than its predecessor.

By the end of the first series of trials, the submissions had all been rejected excepting the Allin, Berdan, Remington, Roberts and Yates rifle-musket conversions, plus the Allin, Laidley, Peabody, Remington and Sharps breech-loaders.

The Berdan was adjudged the best of the conversions, the Peabody was the best new rifle, and—with reluctance, owing to extraction problems—the Spencer repeating carbine was considered best for cavalry. The view was also expressed that ·45 was better than ·50. However, backed by Chief of Ordnance Dyer and General Ulysses Grant, the ·50 Allin was adopted ahead of the Berdan conversion. The enormous quantities of convertible cap locks told against the Peabody, which was by far the best rifle.

The Rifle Model 1866 was a simplified 1865 pattern, chambering a ·50–70 centre-fire cartridge. A U-spring extractor replaced the old ratchet mechanism and, as suggested by Brevet Colonel Laidley, the original ·58 barrels were reamed out to ·64 to take a ·50-calibre liner.

Springfield was ordered to convert 25,000 guns on 26 July 1866, 12,500 with varnished stocks and the remainder plain. Ironically, the sample gun sent from Springfield to the Ordnance Office could be fired without the breech locked…prompting a terse response from General Dyer.

The 1866-pattern Allin conversions, despite their shortcomings, were effectual enough in service. A Board of Officers convened in 1868 to examine future requirements reported that a 'careful examination of more than two hundred monthly reports of Company commanders shows that it is considered a very powerful, accurate, and serviceable Infantry arm'. Few serious flaws had been reported, while the lined barrels had proved highly successful.

Original copper-case inside-head cartridges could not be reloaded. They were also particularly prone to rupture, as the head was no thicker than the case walls. It was very noticeable in the trials leading to the ·45–70 rifle that some of its rivals performed much better with drawn-brass cases than the regulation

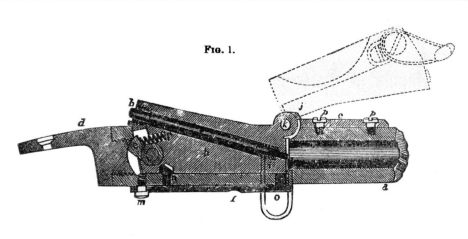

Fig. 1.

223, left. The US Army manuals are greatly sought as sources of original information about (in this case) the Model 1866 Springfield rifle-musket.
224, above. The Allin 'Trapdoor' breech system was embodied in the M1865 and M1866 Springfields. From an engraving in *Description and Rules for the Management of the Springfield Breech-Loading Rifle Musket Model 1866*. Author's collection.

copper varieties. Changes made in the Rifle Model 1868 included the approval of a new 36-inch barrel, though the earlier rifling—three ·0075 grooves making a turn in 42in—was retained. The smaller ramrod was held by a stop inserted in the stock, bearing on a shoulder on the rod about four inches from the tip. There were two bands instead of three, and a special long-range back sight.

The most obvious improvement was a separate receiver into which the barrel screwed, appreciably stronger than the previous method of cutting into the original barrel.

The M1870 was identical with the M1868, except that the receiver was shortened and the breech block was relieved behind the hinge to open farther. The original design sometimes closed unexpectedly when a cartridge was being inserted. A minor adjustment was made to the ramrod, which had a double shoulder, and the sights were refined in detail.

Owing to efforts to reduce ·50 bore in line with contemporary advances in Europe, the M1870 was made only in small quantities and is sometimes considered to be experimental rather than a regulation design.

Several reduced-scale guns were made for cadets. The existence of an 1866-model ·50 Cadet Rifle has been doubted, but 320 were made at Springfield in 1867. They incorporated more than a dozen new non-interchangeable parts. The ·50-calibre Cadet Rifle Model 1869, made only in small quantities, was a diminutive M1868 rifle. It had two bands and a barrel measuring 29½in, shorter than the preceding Model 1866. It was made in several versions, the final one with a flat-face hammer.

The Model 1870 Carbine incorporated the same action as the Model 1870 rifle, but was greatly shortened.

U.S. MILITARY REMINGTONS, 1870–1

While the army was busily experimenting with the Allin conversion, the US Navy, which shared the same chaotic post-war smallarms issue, faced similar problems.

Prior to 1861, the navy had purchased substantial quantities of breech-loading rifles and metal-case ammunition—owing largely to the problems of keeping paper cartridges dry at sea. It was also easier to load from the breech aboard ship, where space was at a premium.

Sharps & Hankins rifles and carbines, plus some Spencer navy rifles, had been acquired during the Civil War. Convinced of the merits of breech-loading, but lacking the enormous numbers of old muzzle-loaders owned by the army, the Navy Bureau of Ordnance began its own trials in March 1869. As the navy had already bought Remington Rolling Block

225–7, below. An external view of the breech and longitudinal sections of the action of the M1870 US Navy Remington, from the original handbook.

BREECH SYSTEM.—Exterior View with Breech Closed.

Sectional View with Breech Closed.

Sectional View with Breech Open.

carbines in 1867, it was no surprise that the report of the 1869 trials board also favoured the Remington breech. The regulation ·50-calibre Springfield barrel was approved, with a brass hilted sabre bayonet and Martin cartridge 'as made by or for the Sharps Rifle Company'.

Additional trials were held in 1869. Among the competitors were ·43 and ·50 Remingtons, and an early prototype Ward-Burton. However, the Navy Bureau of Ordnance preferred to retain the large-calibre Remington and await army experiments with small calibres.

The navy Remington embodied the perfected Rolling Block described in greater detail in the sporting-rifle section. It was manufactured by Springfield Armory and chambered regulation ·50–70 centre-fire cartridges. Its barrel was 32·6in long, rifled with three ·0075 grooves making a turn in 42in, and the distinctive brass-hilt sword bayonet had a fish-scale hilt displaying a Bureau of Ordnance escutcheon. Bayonets were made by the Ames Sword

Company of Chicopee Falls, Massachusetts.

The initial order for ten thousand rifles was placed with the armory on 3 February 1870, but the back sights were positioned wrongly. The rejects were subsequently sold to Poultney & Trimble of Baltimore and re-sold to France during the Franco-Prussian War—at such an advantageous price that, on 27 January 1871, the Chief of the Bureau of Navy Ordnance, Commodore Ludlow Case, requested twelve thousand more rifles. General Dyer, the Army Chief of Ordnance, simply passed the request to Springfield.

Inspired by progress in the navy, the US Army convened a Board of Officers at St Louis in March 1870. Though many differing guns were submitted, only six were tested: in order of preference, the Remington, the Springfield, the Sharps, the Morgenstern, the Martini-Henry and the Ward-Burton. The final report observed that only they [Remington, Sharps and Springfield] 'possess such superior excellence as warrants their adoption by the Government for infantry and cavalry without further trial in the hands of troops. Of these…, considering all the elements of excellence and cost of manufacture, the board are…of the opinion that the Remington is the best system'.

As 504 Remington Rolling Blocks had been made at Springfield in 1868, their characteristics were well enough known for Chief of Ordnance Alexander Dyer to draw the board's attention to inherent defects. The reservations were not severe enough to prevent guns undertaking field trials: by March 1871, Springfield had made 1,001 infantry-pattern Remingtons, 1,020 1870-pattern Springfields, and 501 Sharps assembled from Civil War-era actions. An additional five hundred Sharps was forthcoming by midsummer. They had 32½-inch barrels and a full-length fore-end retained by two bands.

Concurrently, the cavalry tried 313 Remington, 308 Sharps and 341 Model 1870 Springfield carbines. The St Louis board had been sceptical about the Remington carbine, recommending that no issues should be made until a half-cock loading feature had been added, but this does not seem to have been heeded in the desire to complete experiments.

The National Armory also converted 1,108 Spencer carbines to infantry rifles in the autumn of 1871. These had 32½-inch barrels, but chambered rimfire Spencer ·56–50 cartridges instead of the more powerful government ·50–70. The latter was too long to feed

satisfactorily through the old Spencer actions.

Few commanders of companies issued with experimental rifles had a good word for the Sharps, which was regarded as too heavy, too complicated and less accurate than its competitors. Remingtons were greeted with greater enthusiasm, though doubts were expressed over ejection problems and dust jamming the mechanism. Very few respondents liked the idea of loading a gun at full cock.

The Remington Model 1871 rifle was similar to the navy pattern rolling-block rifles being made at Springfield, apart from an additional Locking Bolt. To load an army gun, the firer thumbed the hammer to full cock, retracted the breech-piece spur to expose the chamber, and inserted a cartridge. When the breech-piece was closed, the hammer automatically fell to half cock and the gun could not be fired until it had been pulled back to full cock. Standard Rolling Block actions remained at full cock after the breech piece had been closed.

Army rifles had longer barrels than their navy counterparts, and accepted a socket bayonet rather than a sword pattern.

THE WARD-BURTON, 1871

The ·50-calibre Ward-Burton Model 1871 had been recommended by the St Louis board, though with no especial enthusiasm. Derived from patents granted to Bethel Burton in December 1859 and August 1868, it was

stocked in the manner of the contemporary Allin-Springfield but locked by interrupted threads at the rear of the bolt.

The extractor and the ejector were both mounted on the detachable bolt head; a bolt lock catch appeared on the right rear side of the receiver; and a spring-loaded firing pin was contained in the bolt.

According to a letter written to the Secretary of War by General Alexander Dyer on 31 May 1871, a thousand rifles and three hundred carbines had been ordered from the National Armory. By March 1872, when the first guns were issued for troop trials, 1,015 rifles and 317 carbines had been made.

The Ward-Burton was an interesting design that deserved a better fate. One of its better features, rare in a gun of its class, was the retraction of the firing pin into the bolt as the breech opened. It was difficult to tell when the action was cocked, though the striker tail could have been allowed to protrude through the bolt handle base.

A few units greeted the Ward-Burton with enthusiasm, as it undoubtedly extracted and ejected spent cases far better than its rivals, but views soon changed for the worse.

STEVENS RIFLES, 1871–1917

If the products of Franklin Wesson were seen infrequently on the Frontier, those of Joshua Stevens became increasingly common in the

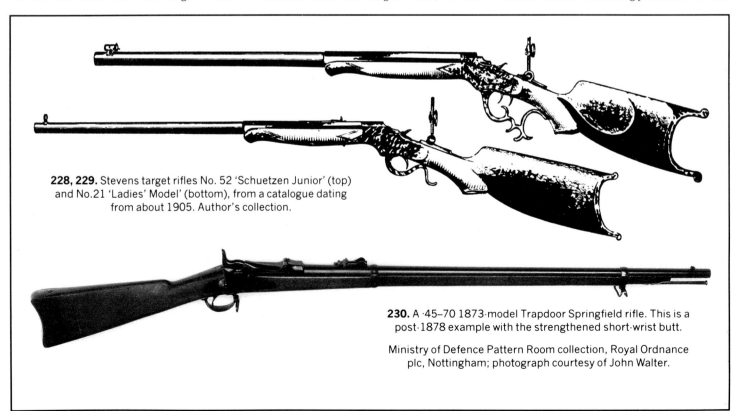

228, 229. Stevens target rifles No. 52 'Schuetzen Junior' (top) and No.21 'Ladies' Model' (bottom), from a catalogue dating from about 1905. Author's collection.

230. A ·45–70 1873-model Trapdoor Springfield rifle. This is a post-1878 example with the strengthened short-wrist butt.

Ministry of Defence Pattern Room collection, Royal Ordnance plc, Nottingham; photograph courtesy of John Walter.

1880s. Stevens' earliest products were simple tipping-barrel pistols, patented in September 1864 (44,123). His first rifles, enlargements of the pistols, did little but amuse the population of the eastern United States.

1871 brought the first effectual Stevens tipping barrel breech-loader, offered in ·22, ·32 or ·38, with barrels of 26–30in. From this inauspicious beginning, J. Stevens Arms & Tool Company made a tremendous variety of sporting guns prior to the First World War. In 1920, however, part of the Stevens equity was acquired by the Savage Arms Company; after swallowing Page-Lewis, Davis-Warner and the Crescent Fire Arms Company, Stevens itself disappeared into Savage in 1936.

Virtually all Stevens tipping-barrel rifles shared the simple transverse barrel-lock system and a sliding extractor powered by a jointed lever attached to a pin in the frame.

Company catalogues display a bewildering variety, ranging from the No.1 to the No.16 Crack Shot. The No.1 had an octagonal barrel, plain sights and lacked a fore-end; the No.16 had a Lyman tang sight, plus a select walnut butt and fore-end. Chamberings included many commercial rim- and centre-fire cartridges— including ·22, ·32, ·38 and ·44—plus proprietary loadings ranging from ·32–35 to ·44–65.

The interchangeable-barrel models often had special readily detachable extractors, while shotguns built on the basic action were offered in 10, 12, 14, 16 and 20-bore.

Most tipping-barrel Stevens rifles had been discontinued by 1900; they were comparatively weak and could not withstand high pressure cartridges. The guns had been supplemented by the so-called Side-Plate rifle, patented by Joshua Stevens on 8 September 1884 and 11 August 1885. This was the first Stevens rifle to feature the swinging block associated with the company's later 'Favorite' series.

An arm on the breech block extended forward beneath the breech, where it was attached by a threaded bolt yet could pivot loosely. It was connected with the breech lever, which doubled as the trigger guard, through an intermediate link that toggled to ensure the breech remained closed during firing. The extractor was a rocking blade activated by the breech block.

Side Plate actions—in two sizes—seem to have been confined to 1885–93, little more than two thousand being made; they were compromised by the removal of the entire right side of the frame to gain access to the action.

Modifications were made in the late 1880s, when the small action was adapted to become the 1889-pattern Favorite, and again in 1894. The larger version became the No. 44.

Introduced about 1890–1, the No. 44 'Ideal' rifle was the mainstay of the Stevens line for many years. Guns sold in vast numbers, as they

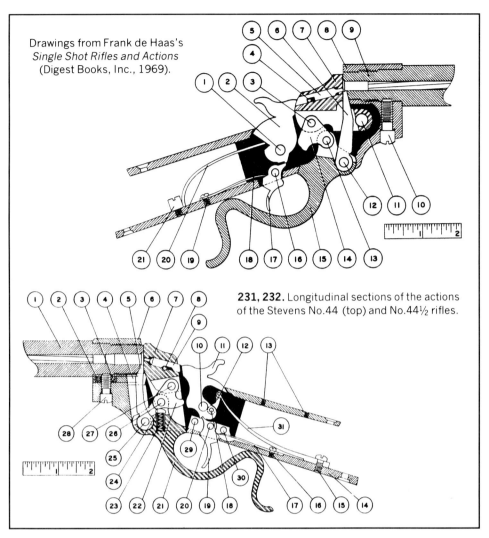

Drawings from Frank de Haas's *Single Shot Rifles and Actions* (Digest Books, Inc., 1969).

231, 232. Longitudinal sections of the actions of the Stevens No.44 (top) and No.44½ rifles.

were cheap and shot extremely accurately. Stevens rifles always had remarkably good barrels, whatever shortcomings lay in their actions. The last No. 44-type rifles—the Model 417 Walnut Hill—did not leave Stevens-Savage warehouses until after the end of the Second World War.

The extractor was moved more centrally from the left side of the action about 1901, and pivot screws were replaced with heavier bolts. An adjustable tension screw in the breech block, intended to keep the breech lever closed, was abandoned when the extractor was moved. However, No. 44 rifles made after introduction of the improved No. 44½ (q.v.) had the latter's spring-and-plunger lever retainer.

The No. 44 was introduced to fire cartridges as powerful as ·32–40 and ·38–55, but these strained the mechanism and were rapidly discontinued. After 1897, therefore, the No. 44 chambered nothing more potent than ·32–20.

No. 44 rifles were made in a bewildering variety of styles, the most common displaying a 26-inch half-octagonal barrel, a straight-wrist butt and a short wooden fore-end with a schnabel tip. However, guns will be found with

spur, ring and ball-tip breech levers, pistol grip butts, hooked Schuetzen-style butt plates, nickel plating, engraving, and specially finished woodwork.

The No. 44½ rifle of 1904–5 was the finest of all the Stevens target rifles, but lasted little more than a decade. Though sharing the general lines of the No. 44 swinging-block rifle, the No. 44½ embodied a true dropping-block action controlled by a breech lever doubling as the trigger guard. As its receiver was made from forged steel rather than a malleable casting, the No. 44½ could chamber cartridges developing twice the breech pressure of those used in No. 44 rifles.

Not only was the No. 44½ action strong, but the block dropped at a slight angle to the true vertical and was canted backward by the finger lever. A spring plunger beneath the barrel held the block in its rearmost position against the back of the receiver. As the breech was closed, the block was cammed forward and could often force poorly seated cartridges into the chamber.

Weaknesses in the No. 44½ action included a primitive extractor, and the omission of a

233, 234; left and below. A lurid version of the Battle of the Little Big Horn, 1876. Apart from the topographical inaccuracies and the condensation of the Last Stand into a tiny area, it is remarkable for a series of errors: very few of Custer's men wore regulation clothing, the Colonel himself favouring a fringed buckskin jacket; his weapons were a pair of Webley 'Royal Irish Constabulary' revolvers; and *no* sabres were carried by the 7th Cavalry on the fateful day. In addition, the longarms appear to be percussion carbines, instead of M1873 Trapdoor Springfield carbines. Author's collection.

firing pin retractor from pre-1908 guns. The inclusion of a hammer-fly in the mechanism, to protect the tip of the trigger if the hammer slipped during cocking, allowed the gun to fire accidentally in adverse circumstances.

However, No. 44½ Stevens rifles were very popular, sturdy and extremely accurate. They were made for a variety of rim- and centre fire cartridges, and in all manner of styles. Particularly effectual were the top-class target rifles, which were offered with heavy barrels, vernier peep and globe sights, double set triggers, butts and fore-ends of the best walnut, and hooked butt plates.

The No. 44½ action was discontinued in 1916. Ironically, the less effectual No. 44 soldiered on for another thirty years.

TRAPDOOR SPRINGFIELDS, 1873–82

Experiments to reduce the calibre of the standard ·50 service cartridge and find an ideal breech-loader continued throughout 1871. However, though participants included Remington, Sharps and Ward-Burton rifles, the Springfield-Allin design was retained.

Trials by a Board of Officers convened in the autumn of 1872 under the presidency of General Alfred Terry—the so-called 'Terry Board'—centred around a newly developed ·45 centre-fire cartridge (·45–70–405).

By January 1873, the board had reduced the rifles from more than a hundred to 21. The British Martini-Henry and the Austro-Hungarian Werndl provided a clue to requirements, while the Elliot no. 80, Freeman no. 76, Peabody no. 63, Remington no. 86, Springfield no. 69 and

Ward-Burton no. 97 were retained. Entered by E. Remington & Sons, the Remington rifle no. 86 with 'Ryder [sic] Power Extractor' was a variant of the standard Remington Rolling Block navy rifle. Springfield rifle no. 69 was similar to the standard Allin-type M1870 (entered as no. 48), except that it had a lightened lock plate. A screw replaced the original main-spring bolster, the hammer was re-shaped and the stock was simplified to save weight. No. 69 eventually proved inferior to the ·45 Springfield entrant, gun no. 99.

The Ward-Burton Magazine Musket, no. 97, was the only bolt-action rifle to qualify. Derived from the ·50-calibre rifle and carbine models of 1870, which had achieved a brief period of semi-experimental army issue, it amalgamated the basic bolt system of the single-shot guns with a tube magazine beneath the barrel. A sliding cut-off prevented magazine feed when appropriate, and the back of the magazine follower was coated with gutta-percha to protect cartridges from recoil.

To prevent accidental ignition, Ward-Burton primers were seated in a deep pocket in the cartridge-case head. The Board of Officers recommended the purchase of Ward-Burton magazine rifles for trials with the cavalry, but this progressive opinion was rejected by Brigadier General Dyer. Thus the cavalry, which had begun the decade at least partly armed with Spencer magazine carbines, was condemned to the single-shot 'Trapdoor' Springfield.

None of the trial guns proved effectual enough to challenge the Allin-breech ·45 Springfield no. 99, which was immediately adopted. Legislation approved on 6 June 1872

by 'the Senate and House of Representatives of the United States of America in Congress assembled' included provisions that were biased in favour of the existing breech system, which had been developed by government employees and would attract no additional royalties; additionally, it was to prevent the trial of many non-Trapdoor guns during the 1870s.

The Model 1873 rifle, approved on 5 May 1873, was a minor adaption of the experimental Springfield no. 99. It perpetuated the Allin system, none of its rivals showing sufficient superiority to be adopted. The breech was familiar throughout the army, while production machinery in Springfield Armory could be adapted to make the new gun without fuss.

Retaining the Allin breech, which had cost the US Treasury more than $124,000 to mollify inventors whose systems it infringed, would also prevent another wholesale payment of royalties.

The M1873 was adapted from the ·50-calibre M1870. The lock plate was lightened, its edges being squared rather than bevelled; the barrel, steel instead of iron, was reduced in diameter; the hammer body was rounded; many screw heads were rounded; a screw replaced the trigger-guard swivel rivet; the ramrod was modified; and the top edges of the stock were rounded from the lock plate forward to the lower band.

On 28 May 1873, Major Stephen Benet, acting on behalf of the Chief of Ordnance, informed Major James Benton, commanding Springfield Armory, that 'The Board...having recommended adoption of the Springfield Breech Loading Gun, caliber ·45, which has been approved by the Secretary of War as the arm for military service, you will proceed to the manufacture of muskets and carbines on this system'. Like all brand-new guns, the M1873 underwent many changes in the earliest years of its life. Originally issued with a trowel bayonet—a composite of designs submitted by Rice and Chillingworth, then refined in the armory—the gun acquired an additional piling swivel in the Spring of 1874.

Among the most important changes were a new Model 1877 back sight in January 1877, with different graduations and an improved sighting notch. The sights were changed again in May 1878, without changing the designation, when a base with curved wing plates replaced the previous stepped design. The height of the arch in the breech block was reduced from March 1878 to give greater rigidity, creating 'Low Arch' guns; internally, the firing-pin spring and the corresponding shoulder on the firing pin were discarded.

Changes made in October 1878 included an increase in the breech-block width and a suitably broadened receiver. In addition,

the gas escape holes through the receiver sides were deepened and extended rearward.

A few 1873-pattern rifles had Metcalfe's Loader, a detachable wooden block on the right side of the stock containing eight cartridges head upward. It has been claimed that only two official Metcalfe-loader prototypes were made in 1874, and that 1,008 allegedly made at the National Armory, Springfield, in 1876 were destined for state militia rather than government troops.

The Model 1873 Cadet Rifle was essentially similar to the infantry pattern, but lacked sling swivels and had a different stacking swivel on the upper band. The Model 1873 Carbine, easily identifiable by its half-stock and short barrel, lacked a butt-trap for the cleaning rods. A stacking swivel was attached to the solitary barrel band.

The first issues were made late in 1874, guns going to the premier infantry regiments. It was some time before distribution was complete, the last to receive guns being the cavalrymen in

Texas and—ironically—Indian country, most of whose carbines were issued in 1876. Men of the Seventh Cavalry, commanded by Lieutenant Colonel George Custer, rode out to the Battle of the Little Big Horn in June 1876 with brand-new Model 1873 carbines.

The subsequent events are too well known to need repeating; Custer and many of his men went to their deaths amid speculation that the new carbines jammed much too frequently.

It was said that copper cases had fused to chamber walls, leaving the extractor to tear through the case rim, but truth was impossible to determine. Indians took all but a few guns from the battlefield and none of the cavalrymen survived to relate what really happened during the Last Stand on 25 June 1876.

The Officer's Rifle, or Model of 1875, had a 26-inch barrel adapted from the contemporary cadet rifle. It was sold to officers who wanted personal weapons of regulation pattern. The half stock had chequering on the the wrist and fore-end, the latter ending in a German silver tip. Foliate engraving appeared on the lock, hammer, receiver, barrel band and butt plate.

Officer's Rifles had a globe-pattern front sight that folded down to allow its pin to serve with the open buck-horn back sight. An additional Sharps aperture back sight folded onto the wrist; it could be adjusted for azimuth in addition to elevation. The trigger had a normal service-pattern pull, but could be set by pushing it forward. The wooden ramrod had nickel-plated brass ferrules, and all rifles made after April 1877 were accompanied by a detachable pistol-grip block. They also had an improved Springfield tang sight, with an attachment block that allowed the leaf to fold closer to the wrist.

About 290 of the first pattern Officer's Rifle were made in 1876–7, then only 187 of the second type (1877–9, 1885). Some of the last to be made—perhaps after regular production had finished—had proper pistol-grip stocks with an elongated schnabel tipped fore-end. They often carried improved sights and lack the ramrod, instead carrying the three-piece rod in a carbine-type 'trapped' butt.

Nine Springfield Marksman's Rifles, made in 1880, had special adjustable vernier back sights and tunnel-pattern front sights with integral spirit levels. The 26-inch cylindrical six-groove barrels, chambered for ·45–80 cartridges, also bore the standard 1879-type buck-horn back sight. The pistol-grip half stock was selected black walnut, distinguished by a German silver nose cap.

The three-piece cleaning rod and dismantling tool were carried in the butt trap. Engraving and the set trigger paralleled those of the Officer's Model described above, though the decoration was somewhat more ornate.

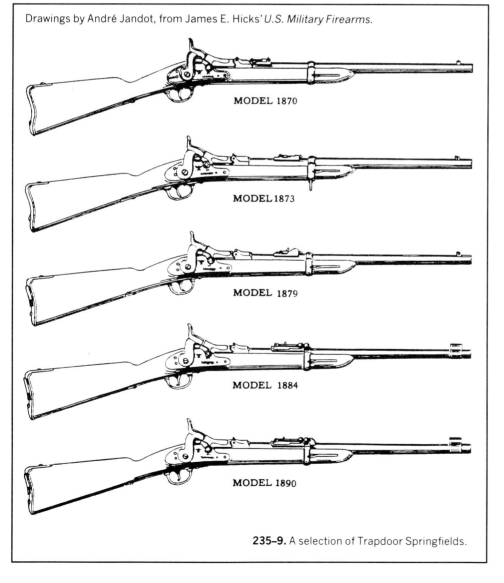

Drawings by André Jandot, from James E. Hicks' *U.S. Military Firearms.*

MODEL 1870

MODEL 1873

MODEL 1879

MODEL 1884

MODEL 1890

235–9. A selection of Trapdoor Springfields.

A mere 151 Long-Range Rifle, destined for competition shooting, were made at Springfield Armory in 1879–80; 24 more followed in 1881. Chambered for ·45–80 cartridges, they had full-length barrels and two spring-retained barrel bands.

Pattern No.1 had a Hotchkiss-pattern butt plate, a full-length stock, a chequered fore-end and wrist (with a detachable pistol grip), a sophisticated Sharps vernier back sight on the tang above the stock wrist, and a laterally adjustable tunnel-pattern front sight with an integral spirit level.

Pattern No.2, sharing the stock design of its predecessor, had an aperture tang sight designed by Freeman Bull of the National Armory and an adjustable globe-pattern front sight. Pattern No.3 had a Hotchkiss butt plate, a full-length stock, a Bull-pattern back sight on the barrel and a regulation front sight.

Progressive improvements made in the basic M1873 led to the Model of 1879, sometimes known as the 'M1873 Improved' or 'M1873 with 1879 Improvements'. Dating from January 1879, a standing plate with two projections improved the sight picture. Known as a 'buck-horn', this went through minor adaptions in October 1879, when the azimuth graduations were placed ·04° apart instead of ·02° and the buck-horn plate was changed; in November 1879, when the upper surface of the leaf-hinge was flattened; and in July 1880, when the notches in the buck horn were revised.

A hole was bored up into the ramrod channel from the front end of the guard plate to reduce the accumulation of dirt (April 1879); a lip was added to the face of the hammer in January 1880; a heavier butt plate appeared in August 1881; part of the under-side of the thumb piece was removed to prevent it striking the lock plate (January 1883); a straight trigger was fitted from March 1883; and a detachable front sight protector was introduced in October 1883.

The Model 1879 Cadet Rifle was a minor variant of the rifle, lacking swivels.

Model 1879 Carbines were essentially similar to their predecessors; however, from December 1879, a rifle-type lower band replaced the special stacking-swivel band. Unlike the rifle, the carbine had a butt trap for the cleaning rod.

The ·45 Rifle Model 1880 was the first to be fitted with a triangular-section rod bayonet, sliding in a channel under the barrel where the ramrod would normally be carried. Though often defended in ordnance correspondence as a means of reducing the soldier's burden—by a whole ten ounces—and saving the US Treasury about 91 cents per man, it was actually a way of avoiding manufacture of socket bayonets. Those in service in 1880 had all been made before 1865, then bushed and re-bushed.

No socket bayonets had been made in North America for some years, whereas rod bayonets could be made by modifying machinery on which ramrods were produced. Colonel James Benton, commanding Springfield Armory, sent a prototype rifle to the Chief of Ordnance, Brigadier Stephen Benet, on 29 May 1880. It elicited sufficient enthusiasm for manufacture of a thousand guns to be approved on 3 June. A total of 1,014 was made in 1881.

Though otherwise essentially similar to the Model 1879, 1880-type rifles could be distinguished by the special nose cap. Their full-length barrels were held by two bands.

REMINGTON-HEPBURNS, 1880–1907

As the years passed, the Rolling Block lost ground to newer guns. There was a concerted challenge from Stevens at the lower end of the market, and the hammerless Sharps-Borchardt threatened at the highest level.

Remington countered with the No.3 or Remington-Hepburn rifle, with a dropping block operated by a lever on the right side of the receiver. It also had a rebounding hammer.

Much more refined than its predecessor, the Remington-Hepburn rifle was patented on 7 October 1879 and introduced commercially in 1880. The standard rifle, touted until 1907, chambered a variety of cartridges ranging from ·22 to ·45, with others available to order. It had a half- or fully octagonal barrel measuring 26–30in, weight being between eight and 10lb. The rifles had pistol-grip butts with chequering, and short fore-ends with pewter or German silver schnabel tips. Blade front and buck-horn back sights were standard.

Actions made after 1893 were strengthened to handle smokeless-powder cartridges. The modified No.3, or 'New No.3', embodying the Hepburn-Walker action described below and chambering cartridges as large as ·45–105 Sharps, had an octagonal barrel of 26–30in and weighed about 8lb. Double set triggers were available to order.

The No.3 was accompanied by the No.3 Improved Creedmoor target rifle (1880–1907), offered in chamberings ranging from ·38–40 to ·45. The rifles had 34-inch round or octagonal barrels, weighed about 9–9½lb and generally embodied set triggers. They had vernier and wind-gauge sights, often incorporating a spirit level. Chequered pistol-grip butts and schnabel tip fore-ends were standard, but rifles could be supplied with cheek-piece stocks and nickel plated Schützen-style butt plates.

A 'Long Range Military Creedmoor' was made for matches in which military-style stocks were obligatory. Chambered only for the Remington ·44–75–520 cartridge, it had a 34-inch round barrel and a full-length chequered fore-end retained by two bands. A steel ramrod was fitted beneath the barrel.

Other Hepburn-system guns included the Match Rifle No.3 (1883–1907), with 28-30in half-octagonal barrels in chamberings ranging from ·25–20 to ·40–65 Centre Fire; the guns weighed 8½–9lb and had vernier wind-gauge sights. They had plain butt plates, chequered walnut pistol-grip butts and chequered fore ends with pewter or German silver schnabel tips. However, cheek pieces and Schützen-style butt plates could be ordered.

The No.3 Hunter's Rifle, dating from 1883, embodied a Hepburn-Walker action with the breech lever doubling as a trigger guard. The guns had plain open sights, 26–30in half octagonal barrels, and chequered pistol-grip butts with curved butt plates. They weighed about 8lb and were available until 1907.

New Model Remington No. 3 Rifle.

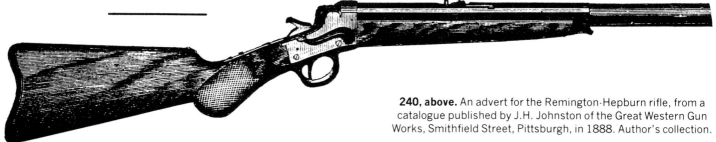

240, above. An advert for the Remington-Hepburn rifle, from a catalogue published by J.H. Johnston of the Great Western Gun Works, Smithfield Street, Pittsburgh, in 1888. Author's collection.

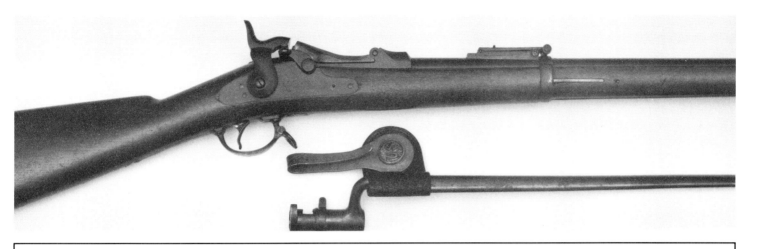

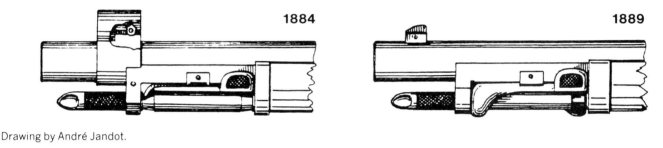

241, above. A ·45–70 1884-model Trapdoor Springfield, no. 463086, dating from 1889. This gun has a Buffington long-range back sight. Courtesy of Wallis & Wallis. **242, below.** A comparison between the 1884- and 1889-type rod bayonet attachments.

1884

1889

Drawing by André Jandot.

The Schuetzen Match Rifle, made in 1904–7 on Hepburn-Walker actions, had an impressively scrolled trigger-guard lever. The rifles had a special vernier wind-gauge aperture sight on the tang, a hooded front sight, and a shallow cheek piece on the straight-wrist butt. Hooked Swiss pattern butt plates were supplied as standard fittings, in addition to folding palm rests beneath the fore-end. The half-octagon barrel measured thirty or 32in, though a 28-inch version could be obtained to order. Guns weighed 11½–13lb and chambered ·32–40, ·38–40, ·38–50 or ·40–65 centre-fire cartridges.

TRAPDOOR SPRINGFIELDS, 1882–9

No sooner had the 1880-pattern rifles been delivered than experiments with universal-issue guns began in the hope of removing the need for infantry rifles and cavalry carbines, as well as their differing cartridges. In February 1882, the Board on Magazine Guns recommended a 'modified Springfield, calibre, ·45' with a barrel of 28in, a lock with a shorter hammer fall, and a full-length stock. With one dissenter, the report also recommended the trial of a thirty-inch barrel on a Sharps action.

Many Sharps rifles were stored at Springfield, making conversion an easy task. The Sharps action was more compact than the Springfield and could accommodate a longer barrel within a specific overall length. Nothing further was done, partly because the guns on hand were ·52-calibre but largely on account of the restricting Federal law enacted in June 1872.

The Model 1882 Short Rifle, sometimes confusingly identified as a carbine, was made with a 27·75-inch barrel. The earliest guns had swivels curved to fit the contours of the stock, to assist insertion into saddle-scabbards, but they were soon abandoned. The barrels tapered to the same muzzle diameter as the standard M1873 rifle and accepted the standard socket bayonet.

A modified short rifle had a triangular-section rod bayonet and a trap in the butt to house the shell ejector and dismantling tool.

Production was minuscule—only a little over fifty of the short rifles being made—and trials with the cavalry at Fort Leavenworth were not successful enough to persuade sceptics of the value of a universal rifle.

A few experimental 1882-model carbines were made with 23·75in barrels, the first pattern being stocked almost to the muzzle. The muzzle band was held with a screw rather than the conventional spring, while a distinctive web separated the muzzle from the ramrod. The shell ejector and the dismantling tool were carried in the butt-trap, while a saddle ring was anchored in a plate on the left side of the breech opposite the hammer. Next came a greatly modified gun with a heavy large diameter barrel, retained by a single band immediately behind the rounded stock tip. A curved swivel lay beneath the band with a more conventional fitting on the under-edge of the butt. The barrels measured 23·75in, the saddle ring slid along a bar anchored in the left side of the stock alongside the breech, Buffington wind-gauge sights were standard, and the three-piece cleaning rod was carried in a trap.

Inconclusive magazine-rifle trials allowed the introduction of new Trapdoor Springfields in 1884. The Model 1884 rifle introduced the Buffington-pattern wind-gauge back sight to service, the first regulation design that ordinary soldiers could adjust in azimuth. The lower band was grooved to accommodate the elongated sight leaf.

Changes were made internally in January 1885, with alterations to the sear and tumbler, and new front sights for rifles (·653 high) and carbines (·738, changed to ·728 late in 1890) were adopted to correct a universal tendency to shoot high at short ranges. The front sight cover became a permanent fixture from March 1886. In August of that year, alterations were made to the Buffington sight to improve its efficacy. The heads of the finger-screws on the wind gauge were enlarged to provide a better grip, and also support the folded leaf laterally by overlapping the base. The security of the binding screw was improved, and the movable base and slide were case-hardened. Minor alterations were made in December 1886, when the firing pin was changed from steel to aluminium bronze, and the rear edge of the rifle front sight block was rounded from August 1887 onward. A new front-sight protector was introduced in February 1888, and a protector band for the back sight was fitted to the carbine from October 1890.

A variant M1884 had a cylindrical rod bayonet, 1,000 guns being authorised by the Secretary of War on 17 December 1884; 1,003 were made in 1885 and issued in the Spring of 1886 to test 'the bayonet fastening and…its effect upon the accurate shooting of the arm'. It was also suggested that an 'improved rear sight with a detachable front sight cover, similar to the front sight protector on the rod bayonet rifle, be approved…for issue to the troops'.

Rod-bayonet guns were issued to selected portions of three artillery and ten infantry regiments, but they were not successful enough to displace the standard Model 1884.

The Model 1889 was the last single-shot rifle to be approved as a regulation US infantry weapon. Ordnance records reveal it to have been expedient, to be made only until a magazine rifle had been perfected.

The quest for a suitable bayonet shuttled between Springfield Armory, the Tactical Board, the Chief of Ordnance—Brigadier General Benet—and the Acting Secretary of War, Major General Schofield, until a cylindrical rod pattern was approved on 5 August 1889. The perfected rifle and its accoutrements were adopted eleven days later.

Many commentators have criticised adoption of a Trapdoor Springfield while the army was so actively seeking a small-bore magazine rifle. Colonel Buffington, commanding the National Armory at Springfield, replied to questions raised by the Chief of Ordnance and the Acting Secretary of War that: '[August 1889]…The statement that the Army is to be rearmed soon with a ·30 caliber magazine rifle is unfortunate. The elements for a ·30 caliber rifle have been practically worked out, but the main element, viz; the powder, is wanting, and all efforts thus far abroad and at home, to produce it have been unavailing. American powder makers, although furnished with the best known foreign brown or black powder and an analysis of the same, have not been able to reproduce it satisfactorily, and the Ordnance Department has not yet been able to penetrate the veil of secrecy that surrounds the manufacture abroad of smokeless powders… It would not do, even were a suitable black powder available, to proceed with the production of a ·30 caliber rifle, because it would be inferior to foreign arms using smokeless powder… A smokeless powder is, therefore, a necessity, and until it can be procured the ·30 caliber arm must remain as a model…without plant to make it.'

WINCHESTER GUNS, 1885–1917

Winchester made a single-shot falling block rifle, designed by John Browning and patented in October 1879 (220,271). Rights were purchased in 1883, the first New Haven-made guns appearing in 1885; by the time production ceased soon after the First World War, 139,725 had been made. Chamberings varied from ·22 rimfire to ·50 centre-fire, small-calibre guns being known colloquially as 'Low Wall' and the larger ones as 'High Wall' owing to the height of the receiver alongside the breech block.

The variants of the Model 1885, universally strong and effectual, ranged from the tiny 4¼lb ·44-40 carbine to a mighty 12–14lb ·32-40 or ·38-55 Schuetzen Rifle. Widely favoured for target shooting, Model 1885 rifles could also be obtained in sporting guise. A 20-bore shotgun was made for some years, and a 'take-down' rifle appeared in 1910.

The Winder Musket was a full-stock ·22 rimfire M1885 variant in Low or High Wall style. Approved for National Rifle Association small-bore matches, many were made prior to 1920.

243, below. An advert for the Winchester M1885 rifle, probably dating from the 1890s. Author's collection.

SINGLE SHOT RIFLE.

THE BEST.

ASK YOUR DEALER TO SHOW THEM.

Send for 76 Page Illustrated Catalogue of Arms and Ammunition.

Winchester Repeating Arms Co.,

Stores, { 312 BROADWAY. NEW YORK
{ 418 and 420 MARKET STREET, SAN FRANCISCO, CAL.

NEW HAVEN, CONN.

244, above. The Browning gun-shop in Ogden, Utah, pictured in the early 1880s. From left to right: Samuel, George, John M., Matthew and Edmund Browning. Far right: Frank Rushton. Note that all six appear to be holding Browning-type single-shot rifles, several hundred of which were made before they attracted the interest of Winchester. Courtesy of the J.M. Browning Museum, Ogden, Utah.

245, below. A longitudinal section of the original Evans lever-action rifle, showing its extraordinary Archimedean screw-type magazine system. Courtesy of Ian Hogg.

THE WINCHESTER MODEL 1866

The New Haven Arms Company, deep in trouble financially, was acquired by the newly formed Winchester Repeating Arms Company in 1865. This was entirely due to Oliver Winchester, who had already received a charter from the state of Connecticut permitting him to establish the 'Henry Repeating Rifle Company'. Winchester did well out of the reorganisation. Selling his shares in the shirt

making Winchester & Davies partnership to become a full-time arms baron, he received 1,500 $100 shares in the Winchester Repeating Arms Company in return for rights to patents previously controlled by the New Haven firm.

The Winchester Model 1866 was simply an improved Henry, with a hinged loading gate designed by Nelson King on the right side of the frame. This allowed the firer to insert cartridges virtually without taking his eyes off the target. The loading gate permitted a fixed magazine and a conventional wooden fore-end to be used.

The powder loading was increased from 25 to 28 grains, a reduction in projectile weight (to 200 grains) increasing velocity. Though the Winchester remained susceptible to mud or dust entering through the top of the action, it was a better weapon than the Henry.

The Model 1866 was made as a rifle, with a 24-inch round or octagonal barrel weighing 9–9½lb; as an 8¼lb musket, with a 27-inch round barrel; or as a 7½lb carbine, with a twenty-inch round barrel. Rifle and muskets each held a maximum of seventeen rounds, though usually loaded with fewer to prevent strain on the magazine spring; carbines nominally held thirteen rounds.

Very few guns were made in 1866, as the factory moved from New Haven to Bridgeport, Connecticut. Listings appeared in catalogues long after the advent of the Model 1873. As late as 1891, 1,000 Model 1866 rifles were assembled, chambered for ·44 S&W centre-fire cartridges and sold to Brazil.

FOGERTY AND ROBINSON RIFLES, 1867–74

Based on patents granted to Valentine Fogerty of Boston, Massachusetts on 23 October 1866 (59,126) and 6 October 1868 (82,819), these rifles were made by the Fogerty Arms Company—reorganized as the American Repeating Rifle Company in the autumn of 1867. Produced as a musket, carbine or sporting rifle, the lever-action Fogerty repeater had a tube magazine in the butt. It bore a superficial external resemblance to the Spencer, but had a rounded tubular receiver and a different action; instead of the Spencer radial block, Fogerty's design relied on cartridges feeding from the side of the carrier-block when the breech lever was operated.

Chambering ·50 rimfire cartridges, the musket was stocked to the muzzle and had three barrel bands; the ·45 rimfire carbine had a half-stock and a single band, while the fore-end of the ·40 rimfire sporting rifle was held to the barrel by a screw under the fore-end. The sporter had a

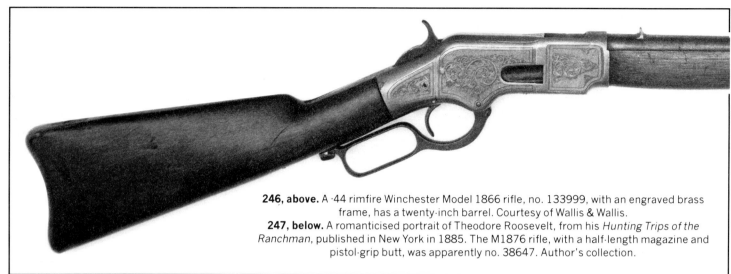

246, above. A ·44 rimfire Winchester Model 1866 rifle, no. 133999, with an engraved brass frame, has a twenty-inch barrel. Courtesy of Wallis & Wallis.
247, below. A romanticised portrait of Theodore Roosevelt, from his *Hunting Trips of the Ranchman*, published in New York in 1885. The M1876 rifle, with a half-length magazine and pistol-grip butt, was apparently no. 38647. Author's collection.

pewter or German silver fore-end tip, and could be supplied with a folding vernier back sight on the tang.

Robinson rifle were made by A.S. Babbitt and then by the Adirondack Fire Arms Company of Plattsburgh, New York. Patented by Orvil Robinson of Upper Jay, New York, on 24 May 1870 (103,504), the gun had a longitudinally sliding breech bolt locked by a pivoting block set into its under-surface. It was operated by pulling back on two knurled finger pieces on the rear of the bolt, a method lacking in mechanical advantage. Robinson patented a toggle-lock rifle on 23 April 1872 (125,988), opened by pulling up on a retractor above the loading gate. New Model Robinsons could be loaded from either side of the receiver.

Production of Fogerty rifles was never large, fewer than five thousand being made in 1867–9. On 6 August 1869, the Winchester board authorised a successful bid for the American Repeating Arms Company, and the Fogerty rifle disappeared into history.

Neither were Robinsons made in quantity; Winchester bought patent rights in 1874, when Adirondack was in dire straits financially, and promptly scrapped the guns.

LEVER-ACTION EVANS GUNS, 1871–80

This curious magazine rifle was patented by Warren Evans on 8 December 1868 (84,685) and 18 September 1871 (119,020). Made by the Evans Rifle Manufacturing Company of Mechanic Falls, Maine, it was touted by Merwin & Hulbert as a potential military rifle—only to be offered as a sporter when the US ordnance predictably ignored it.

The action embodied a Spencer-like radial block, but fed from a capacious Archimedean screw magazine doubling as the spine of

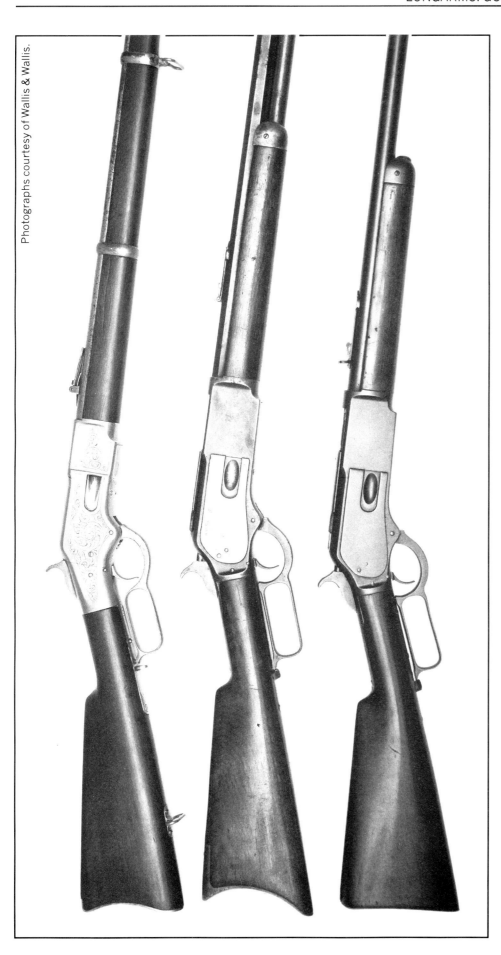

Photographs courtesy of Wallis & Wallis.

248, far left. A ·44 rimfire Model 1866 Winchester, no. 134949, stocked as a two-band musket despite the engraving on the nickel-plated action. This particular gun has a 27-inch barrel and measures 46½in overall.

249, centre left. A ·45–75 Winchester M1876 rifle, no. 40412, with a 28-inch octagonal barrel. Note the design of the receiver, with the half-length raised panel ending level with the loading port, which was shared with the earlier Model 73.

250, left. A ·50–95 Winchester Model 76, no. 56645. Note the short fore-end, which contains the half-length magazine, and the straight butt plate.

the butt. The fluted cartridge carrier made a quarter-turn each time the lever was operated, presenting a new round to the breech.

The greatest advantage of the Evans rifle was its huge magazine, which could hold 34 proprietary ·44 centre-fire cartridges at the expense of great weight and complexity. One gun appeared in the 1872–3 US Army trials, but comprehensively failed the dust test.

The earliest Evans rifles were made as full stock military rifles, with thirty-inch barrels and socket bayonets; as carbines, with 22-inch barrels and half-stocks; and as sporting guns, with 26–30in octagonal barrels and a selection of sights. The sporter weighed 10lb laden.

A New Model Evans (1877) was offered in the same three basic varieties, but with a semi-external hammer and a prominent breech-lever locking catch. It chambered the so-called ·44 Evans Long centre-fire cartridge, reducing magazine capacity to 26.

Sporters were made with round, half-octagon or fully octagonal 26–30in barrels and weighed 9½–10lb. Though guns were sold to Russia during the Russo–Turkish War, apparently for the imperial navy, the Evans company failed in 1880 after about two thousand had been made.

LEVER-ACTION WINCHESTERS, 1873–86

Though the Model 1866 rifle was successful, its utility was limited by a weak cartridge. Its replacement was the Model 1873, offered as a rifle, a carbine, or a military-style musket with a bayonet, chambering ·44–40 (introduced in 1873), ·38–40 (1879) and ·32–20 (1882). A ·22 rimfire version, made for twenty years from 1884, lacked the loading port on the right side of the receiver.

Winchester, a progressive manufacturer with a flair for publicity, was always willing to tailor guns to specific requirements. Consequently, some were made with half-round and half octagonal barrels, half-length magazine tubes, set triggers, rubber shotgun-pattern butt plates, or special decoration.

The Model 1873 was discontinued in the early 1920s after 720,610 had been made. Among its champions had been W.F. 'Doc' Carver, a marksman of international repute. On 13 July 1878, at the Brooklyn Driving Park, Carver broke 5,500 glass balls tossed into the air over a period of eight hours; instead of a shotgun, Carver used a lever-action ·22 rimfire Winchester Model 1873!

The Model 1873 was more successful than its 1866-vintage predecessor, but still lacked power. Buffalo hunters remained faithful to their dropping-block Sharps and rolling-block Remingtons. The lack of a magazine was no great hardship; in the early days of the West, buffalo were so numerous that it scarcely mattered whether a shot was missed.

The single-shot rifles offered large calibres, heavy bullets and capacious cartridge cases. The bullet from the standard ·44–90 Sharps cartridge attained a muzzle velocity of 1,250 ft/sec^{-1} compared with 1,310 ft/sec^{-1} for the ·44–40 Winchester pattern. Though these were similar, muzzle energies—a better indication of hitting power—revealed the tremendous differential: 1,631 ft-lb compared with only 762 ft-lb, due to the weight of the bullet. An experimental ·45–70–405 Winchester, patented

by Luke Wheelock in 1872, was submitted unsuccessfully to the US Army repeating rifle trials in 1872–3.

Prototype Model 1876 rifles were greeted with great acclaim at the Centennial Exposition in Philadelphia, as they offered a much stronger action than any preceding Winchester lever action rifle and could be chambered for cartridges capable of downing the biggest North American game.

The Model 1876 was eventually adapted to handle ·40–60, ·45–60, ·45–75 and ·50–95, gaining favour not so much with plainsmen—who had pursued the buffalo to the edge of extinction—but with ranchers and dilletante Easterners who came westward to seek their fortunes. It also sold well in India and across Africa, establishing impressive credentials in markets that had previously taken nothing but single-shot guns and double rifles made in Britain.

The Model 1876 was also appreciated by Theodore Roosevelt, who recorded the efficacy of his ·45–75 rifle in books and articles; and a particularly impressive gun, engraved by John Ulrich, was presented to in 1881 to the Civil War hero General Philip H. Sheridan. About 750 full-stock Model 1876 carbines were purchased by the Royal North-West Mounted Police of Canada in the 1880s, and, when production ceased in favour of the Model 1886, 63,871 M1876 Winchesters had been made.

LEVER-ACTION WHITNEYS, 1877–88

The first Whitney repeating rifle featured a lever action designed by Andrew Burgess, patented on 7 January 1873 (134,589) and 19 October 1875 (no.168,966).

The Whitney-Burgess, sometimes known as the 'Burgess-Morse' owing to a complicated lawsuit then in progress between George Morse and the US Government, embodied a strong but essentially similar action. The operating lever, which formed the trigger guard, was extended up into the breech. Its short rear face rested against the rear of the receiver while a right-angle arm ran forward along the top inner surface of the receiver. A short breech block was pivoted to the tip of extension arm.

When the breech lever was depressed, it pulled the locking arm down and away from the rear face of the receiver; at the same time, the right-angle extension pulled the breech block back from the chamber. The spent case was ejected, an elevator raised a new cartridge to be caught by the lower edge of the returning block, and the gun was ready to fire.

Burgess had exhibited three guns made in his workshop in Oswego, New York, at the Centennial Exposition in 1876. One of the lever-action rifles caught the eye of Eli Whitney, and a production licence was negotiated in

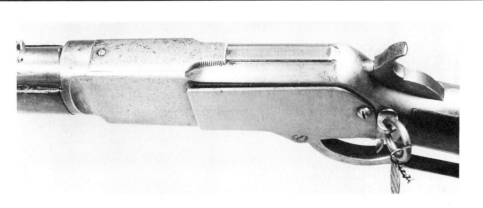

251, 252; below. A Model 1876 Winchester musket and carbine. School of Infantry Museum collection.

253, left. The action of the Model 1876 Winchester, showing the reciprocating breech cover.

Photographs courtesy of Ian Hogg.

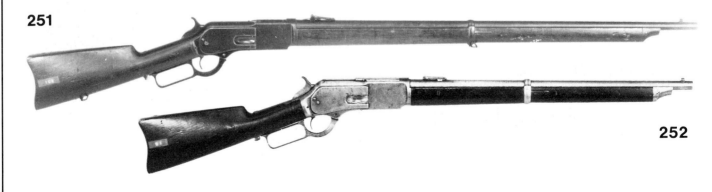

251

252

1877. Two muskets were entered in the US Army breech-loading rifle trials of 1878, but one failed during the rust test.

The perfected gun embodied a cartridge elevator patented in May 1879 by Samuel Kennedy (215,227). As it bore Kennedy's name in the manufacturer's marks, it became misleadingly known as the Whitney-Kennedy instead of the "Burgess Long Range Repeating Rifle with Kennedy's Improvement".

The rifle chambered all the popular revolver cartridges, including ·44–40, and short-case rifle rounds such as ·40–60, ·45–60 and ·45–70. It was made with a round, half-octagon or fully octagonal 24–28in barrel; carbines were also made in small numbers. Double set triggers, long barrels, selected woodwork, engraving and special sights were optional extras.

The 1880-pattern Whitney-Kennedy was soon supplemented by an M1886 rifle, protected by additional patents issued in December 1880 (235,204) and December 1883 (209,393). This new small-receiver rifle was made until Winchester purchased Whitney in 1888. It was offered only as a ·32–30 sporter with a 24-inch round, half-octagon or fully-octagonal barrel; or as a ·38–40 military-style musket.

THE FIRST MILITARY MAGAZINE RIFLES

Though the standard ·45–70 Springfield rifle was reasonably successful as an infantry weapon, the carbine was not favoured by the cavalry—particularly men whose memories stretched back to Spencer repeaters. With an occasional exception, men armed with repeaters had fought off Indian bands many times their size; after the Springfields had been issued, however, the margins of superiority were eroded. The most infamous incident, Custer's defeat at the Little Big Horn, was only one of a series of similar catastrophes.

During the Civil War, the US Army had gained unrivalled experience with magazine weapons. Unfortunately, Union commanders soon forgot how their Spencer-armed men had repulsed Confederates outnumbering them many times over, instead advocating issue of simple single shot guns 'the men could understand'.

The trials of 1872-3 had included magazine guns submitted by (or on behalf of) W.T. Scott, Ward & Burton and Winchester, plus a Swiss Vetterli rifle. In 1878, the Ordnance Department convened a Board of Officers to undertake trials with magazine rifles submitted by or for Andrew Burgess; General William Franklin; Ward & Burton; the Sharps Rifle Company; C.B. Hunt; Lewis, Rice & Lewis; Major Buffington; Bethel Burton; Benjamin Hotchkiss; William Miller; E. Remington & Son; Tiesing; George Clemmons; James Lee; and Chaffee & Reece.

The Ward-Burton, Miller and Clemmons rifles were submitted by Springfield Armory, the Tiesing and Burgess designs came from the Whitney Arms Company, while Winchester backed the Hotchkiss.

In its report of 23 September 1878, the board recommended the Hotchkiss Magazine Gun no. 19. Designed by a French-domiciled American, the rifle had been exhibited at the Centennial Exposition in Philadelphia in 1876. Protected by a patent granted on 17 August 1869 (93,822), it offered good long range performance and durability. Winchester promptly bought US manufacturing rights.

THE REMINGTON-KEENE, 1877–88

This rifle was never used by the US Army, though small numbers—believed to have been 250—were acquired by the Indian Bureau, for reservation police.

Made by E. Remington & Sons under several patents granted to James Keene of Newark, New Jersey, from February 1874 to July 1877, the 8½lb bolt-action repeater had a conventional nine-round tube magazine under the barrel. Indian Bureau guns chambered regulation ·45–70–405, though others accepted ·40 and ·43 Spanish ammunition.

Introduced as a sporter in 1877 and offered until 1888, by which time about five thousand had been made, the Remington-Keene had several unusual features. Unlike

254. A typical ·45–70 Remington-Keene rifle, marked by the US Indian Bureau. Author's collection.

255, 256. The magazine rifle developed by William Gardner, inventor of the manually-operated machine-gun that bore his name, was typical of the idiosyncratic guns developed in the 1870s. Fed from a tube in the fore-end, the action was operated by sliding the barrel/fore-end group forward and then back to lock. The gun was unsuccessful. School of Infantry Museum collection, photographs courtesy of Ian Hogg.

most other tube-magazine guns, it could be loaded from above or below the receiver at will. The cartridges were only transferred from the magazine to the carrier when the breech was opened; in addition, they were held securely on the carrier. Unlike some other lever actions, the Remington-Keene worked perfectly inverted.

The gun was left at half cock after the action had been cycled, requiring the firer to retract the cocking piece before pulling the trigger. This was considered an advantage in certain military circles, though it could be disabled by removing the 'hammer fly' let into the tumbler.

The standard Remington-Keenes were 43½in long and had 25-inch barrels. They proved so inferior to the Lee that Remington ceased promoting them in the mid 1880s.

HOTCHKISS RIFLES, 1878–82

M1878 rifles and carbines were assembled at Springfield Armory from actions supplied by Winchester and standard government-pattern one-piece stocks. The tube magazine in the butt ran up into the receiver ahead of the trigger. Five cartridges could be loaded through a butt-trap, a sixth being inserted in the chamber. Cartridge stops connected to the trigger ensured that, when the trigger was pressed, one round moved forward until its nose contacted the underside of the bolt. Opening the bolt allowed the rim of the cartridge to spring upward far enough to be caught by the lower edge of the bolt as it returned. Closing the bolt pushed the cartridge

258, right. A longitudinal section of the 1879-type Lee bolt action.

259, right. The M1899 small-bore Remington-Lee magazine rifle, from a catalogue produced by M. Hartley & Company of New York in the autumn of 1903. Despite the textual allusion to the M1895 Lee navy rifle, this particular 1899 pattern incorporated a turning bolt.

Author's collection.

forward into the chamber. A cut-off mechanism permitted single shots to be fired while the magazine was held in reserve.

Regulation Hotchkiss rifles had one-piece walnut stocks, their barrels being held by two sprung bands. An 1879-pattern buck-horn back sight lay on the barrel ahead of the bolt mechanism. They had split-bridge receivers and were locked by the bolt-handle rib abutting the front edge of the receiver bridge.

Hotchkiss rifles were not successful enough to shake the army out of its basic conservatism,

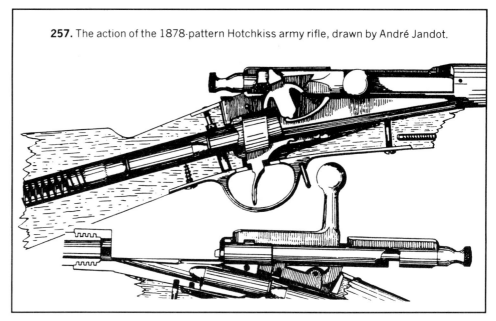

257. The action of the 1878-pattern Hotchkiss army rifle, drawn by André Jandot.

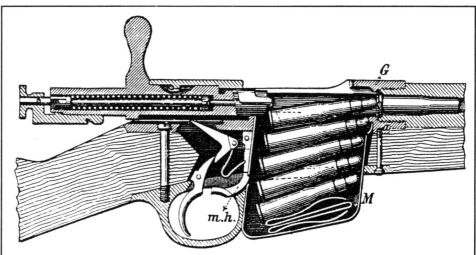

NEW REMINGTON-LEE MAGAZINE MILITARY RIFLE

MODEL 1899.

29-inch special steel barrel.   Five shots.   Total length, 49½ inches.   Weight, 8½ lbs.

This arm is of the well-known bolt type, adopted by military organizations throughout the world on account of its simplicity, durability and ease of manipulation.   The celebrated Lee rifle, formerly in use by the Navy Department, has been altered and adapted to the modern smokeless, high power ammunition, giving great penetration, velocity and flat trajectory with extreme accuracy.

In addition to the bolt locking mechanism on the large calibre Lee, this arm has double-locking shoulders on the bolt head, and is arranged to load with a filler or clip, whereby five cartridges can be placed in the magazine in the same space of time as is ordinarily consumed by the insertion of one cartridge in magazine arms of other types.

List price..$35 00

Knife bayonet and scabbard...   4 00

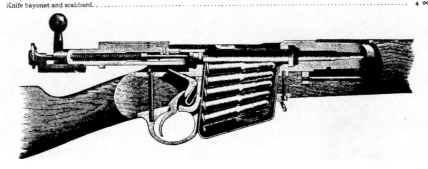

even though some officers opined favourably. Late in 1880 the Chief of Ordnance, Brigadier General Stephen Benet, reported perceptively to the Secretary of War that: 'The Hotchkiss has met…reverses, due to hasty manufacture and imperfect design in some of its minor parts, which can hardly be charged to the invention. It is believed that these defects, in which the mechanical principles…were not involved, have been corrected in the new model, and more favorable results may now be anticipated. The manufacturer's experience with this gun proves that difficulties are ever to be met and overcome in perfecting a new invention that has to stand the severe test of field service.

"The principle of the Hotchkiss is a good one, but there seems to be some prejudice existing in our service against the bolt system and its awkward handle that time and custom may overcome."

About 2,500 Model 1879 Hotchkiss rifles were acquired by the US Navy in 1879–80. These had a modified safety catch and cut-off lever— let into the stock of the army guns—which projected above the stock-side.

A few First (1879-80) and Second Pattern (1880-3) Hotchkiss sporting rifles were also made, but neither was particularly successful in a market dominated by lever-action guns; only 22,521 Hotchkiss-type rifles were made in 1879–83.

LEE RIFLES, 1879–89

The failure of his block-action rifle in the US Army trials, even though 145 had been made at Springfield in 1875, convinced James Lee that the future lay in bolt-action guns.

Lee's patent of November 1879 (221,328) protected a simple turning-bolt action, locked by a shoulder on the bolt handle abutting the receiver and a small opposed lug engaging a seat in the receiver wall. There was a rotating extractor, the box magazine was detachable, and a cut-off allowed the gun to be used as a single-loader.

The Lee Arms Company was formed in 1879 in Bridgeport, Connecticut, sharing premises with the near-moribund Sharps Rifle Company. The earliest prototypes, which used several Sharps-Borchardt components, had their bolt handles behind the receiver bridge.

Lee rifles included in the September 1882 trials chambered regulation ·45–70 cartridges. Gun no. 10, submitted by the Remington Arms Company, was a standard M1879; no. 36, also entered by Remington, had an 'improved bolt' (usually identified as the model of 1882). The Spencer-Lee rifles, numbered 24, 31 and 35, amalgamated Lee-type box magazines with a slide-action loading mechanism.

The US Army had shown so little enthusiasm for the magazine rifle that it was left to the navy to pursue it. Substantial numbers of M1879 Hotchkiss rifles, acquired in 1879–80, were followed by 250 M1880 Remington-Keenes and a similar number of Remington-made M1879 Lee rifles in 1881–2. These not only armed newly commissioned warships, but also allowed long-term testing to be undertaken.

Made in Ilion by Remington, but marked as products of the Lee Arms Company, almost all guns purchased by the navy bore distinctive inspectors' marks—e.g., 'WWK' or 'WMF'—together with an anchor/US marking. They had a one-piece walnut stock with two spring-retained bands, with swivels ahead of the magazine and on the nose-band. The only safety feature was the half-cock notch on the cocking piece.

The rifles were 48½in overall, had 29½-inch five-groove barrels, and weighed about 8½lb. The tangent-leaf back sight was graduated to 500 yards on the base and 1,200 on the leaf. Though the US Navy guns all chambered ·45–70 government cartridges, ·43 Spanish and ·44–77 Necked were available to order.

Navy consensus favoured the Lee. Seven hundred additional guns were purchased in 1884, but whether these were remaining stocks of 1879-pattern guns or 1882 Army-pattern rifles has yet to be determined.

In March 1884, Lee and his employee Louis Diss received US Patent 295,563 for an improved magazine that retained cartridges when detached from the gun. The patent was assigned to Remington and incorporated in the improved 1885-pattern rifle, which also had a separate bolt-head, a non-rotating extractor and a greatly enlarged cocking-piece head.

Rifles still chambered standard ·45–70–405 cartridges, measured 52in overall, had five groove 33½-inch barrels, and weighed about 8½lb. They were stocked and sighted similarly to the M1882, lacking an upper hand guard, and were made exclusively by Remington. Post-1888 guns were marked 'Remington Arms Company', as a result of the collapse of E. Remington & Sons two years earlier. Navy issue displayed 'U.S.' beneath an anchor, together with an inventory number and inspectors' initials; 1,500 were ordered in 1888 to arm newly commissioned warships, pending the introduction of a small-calibre rifle. The last deliveries were made by the autumn of 1889.

Remington-Lee rifles were highly successful in south and central America. By 1900, however, the military Lee in its standard Remington form was losing ground to rival designs. The British had adopted the Lee-Metford and Lee-Enfield, but were making the rifles themselves; the US armed forces were developing the Springfield to replace the Krag-Jørgensen; and most other nations were building production facilities of their own.

As the export markets shrank, so (in 1899) Remington offered sporting guns in an attempt to use up Lee actions. Offered until about 1906, Remington-Lee sporters had five-round detachable box magazines and round barrels measuring 24, 26 or 28in. They had pistol grip walnut half-stocks and weighed 8½–9lb. Though they chambered 6mm (Lee), ·30–30, ·30–40 Government (Krag), 7mm, 7·65mm, ·303 British, ·32 Winchester, ·32–40, ·35 Remington, ·38–72, ·43 Spanish, ·44–77 and ·45–70, and sold quite well in Central and South America, enthusiasm in the USA was feeble: only the Michigan State Militia

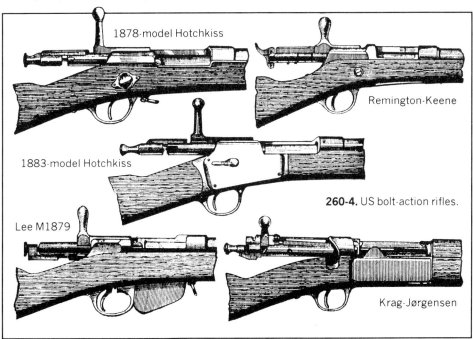

260-4. US bolt-action rifles.

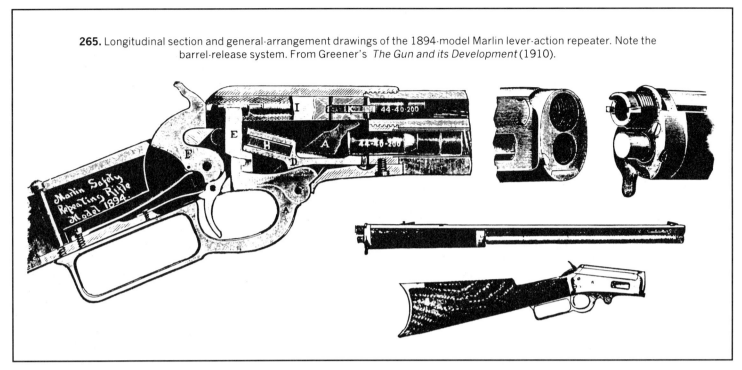

265. Longitudinal section and general-arrangement drawings of the 1894-model Marlin lever-action repeater. Note the barrel-release system. From Greener's *The Gun and its Development* (1910).

purchased Remington-Lee rifles during the crisis created by the Philippine Insurrection.

The bolt system was never popular on the North American commercial market, where its strength and (at least in box-magazine form) an ability to fire ballistically effectual cartridges were reckoned inferior to magazine capacity and speed of action. The Remington-Lee did not break the mould.

LEVER-ACTION MARLINS, 1881–1917

Marlin was one of the few makers of lever-action rifles to remain independent; most

others failed to prosper in the 1880s or were purchased by Winchester.

The Model 1881 was based on patents granted to Andrew Burgess between January 1873 and June 1879, plus an improved cartridge elevator designed by Burgess in collusion with John Marlin (patent 250,825 of 13 December 1881). It also acknowledged elements of Henry Wheeler's February 1865 patent, reissued in November 1880; another granted to Emil Toepperwein in September 1875; and two of Marlin's, issued in December 1879 and November 1880. The Burgess patents were essentially those used by Whitney and Colt. The Wheeler patent was assigned to

Marlin, while Toepperwein's was purchased simply to avoid an embarrassing infringement.

The M1881 rifle was a very simple design, in stark contrast to contemporary Winchesters. The breech-lever extension served as a prop for the longitudinally sliding breech block. When the gun fired, the strain was taken by the breech-lever pivot pin—in theory less than perfect, but in practice quite able to handle substantial pressure. Indeed, a ·45–70 M1881 performed surprisingly well in the US Army repeating rifle trials of 1881–2.

Sample rifles were distributed to Schoverling, Daly & Gales of New York in early in 1881. They had 24–30in octagonal barrels chambering

266, below. The perfected, or 1883-model Winchester-Hotchkiss rifle enjoyed limited military success in central and south America. Note the two-piece stock, which distinguishes this model from its predecessors.

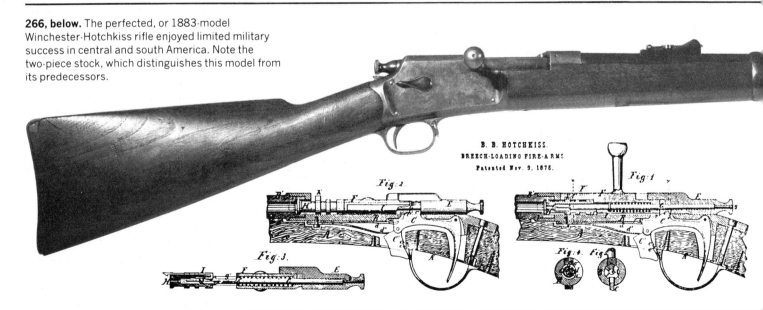

·40–60 or ·45–70 (and ·45–85 from 1885). Under-barrel tube magazines contained 8–10 rounds.

Heavy barrels, double set triggers (from 1883), select woodwork, engraving, and a variety of sights were available to order. There were also a few special 'Light' rifles, weighing about 12oz less than normal; made only in ·40–60 and ·45–70, most of these guns apparently went to Britain. In addition, fifteen smooth-bore shotguns were made in 1884–8.

A small-frame adaption of the M1881 was introduced in 1884 to handle ·32–40 Ballard, followed in 1886 by another variant chambering ·38–55 Ballard.

Production ceased in October 1891 after 21,716 M1881 rifles had been made in series with other Marlins; consequently, numbers ran as high as 51233.

The 1881-pattern Marlin was supplemented by the Model 1888, chambering the most popular handgun cartridges up to ·44–40. This rifle embodied improvements in the Burgess-Marlin action made by Lewis Hepburn, designer of the Remington-Hepburn sporting rifle. It locked by sliding a bolt vertically into the breech block, not unlike the mechanism employed in the contemporary Browning-designed Winchesters. Hepburn received patents on 7 December 1886 (354,059) and 11 October 1887 (371,455), but the 1888-type rifle remained in production for little more than a year before being replaced by the side-ejecting Model 1889 rifle and carbine. These lasted until about 1900.

1893 brought a major redesign of the M1881, necessitated by the introduction of the sturdy 1886 and 1892-pattern Winchesters. The Model 1893 (1893–1936) was simply the 1892-pattern Marlin action enlarged to handle ·32–40 and ·38–55. It was an instantaneous commercial

success, offered in a variety of barrel lengths from 20in for the carbine to a special 32in option for the rifles. Standard guns had 26-inch round or octagonal barrels, open sights, and a straight-wrist butt. Magazines held ten rounds and the rifles weighed 7–8lb.

Variants of the Model 1893 included a 6·75lb Model 1893 Carbine in ·30–30 and ·32–40 only, with a twenty-inch round barrel and a seven round magazine. The Model 1893 Musket, offered with a socket bayonet until about 1915, had a thirty-inch barrel and a full-length fore-end. A cleaning rod lay beneath the barrel.

The Model 1894 was simply the 1893-type gun reduced to accept handgun cartridges. Initially offered in ·25–20, ·32–20, ·38–40 and ·44–40, it had a ten-round tube magazine, a 24-inch round or fully octagonal barrel and weighed about 7lb. It was originally offered with a straight-wrist stock and open sights.

The success of the Model 94 Winchester persuaded Marlin to adapt his 1893-pattern rifle for the new ·30–30 Winchester cartridge, add ·25–36 Marlin to rival Winchester's ·25–35, and then create the Model 1895 rifle to handle cartridges as large and powerful as ·45–90.

When the original Model 1895 was finally discontinued in 1915, it had been chambered for ·33 WCF, ·38–56, ·40–65, ·40–70, ·40–82 and ·45–70. The standard rifles, which weighed 8lb, were offered with 24-inch round or octagonal barrels, straight-wrist butts and open sights.

THE MAGAZINE RIFLE TRIALS OF 1882–5

The US Army appointed a Board of Officers to report on potentially serviceable magazine rifles in 1881. By September 1882, 53 rifles had

been submitted on behalf of twenty inventors and a final eliminator began. Triallists included the Remington-Keene, a rifle designed by Philip Boch of New York City, and a Hotchkiss supplied by Winchester. A Chaffee-Reece was submitted by General James Reece; the Lee was promoted by its inventor; and the Trabue by William Trabue of Louisville, Kentucky. Guns were sent from Fort Union, New Mexico, by Lieutenant Andrew Russell, and from the Marlin Firearms Co. of New Haven.

Charles Dean sent his gun from Fort Walla Walla in Washington State; the Spencer-Lee was submitted by Joseph Frazier of New York City; the Burton came from Walter Burton of Brooklyn; the Springfield-Jones was the work of Sheridan Jones of Menno, Dakota; and, finally, there was a gun from William Elliott.

The most important of the submissions were the Remington-Keene, the Lee, Chaffee-Reece and the Hotchkiss. The board reported on 29 September 1882 that the Lee was preferred ahead of the Chaffee-Reece and the Hotchkiss. The principal advantages lay in the Lee's detachable box magazine—an advantage that was far from universally recognized—and an additional locking lug opposing the bolt handle. The Chaffee-Reece and Hotchkiss actions were locked simply by abutting the base of the bolt-handle rib in the receiver.

Neither Lee nor Chaffee & Reece had backers who could gamble the investment necessary to comply with the government requirements. Hotchkiss already had the support of the Winchester Repeating Arms Company.

E. Remington & Sons were persuaded to produce the Lee, victor of the trials and worthy of support; Chaffee & Reece approached Colt, but the price of $150 per gun was unacceptably high. However, General Reece persuaded the Ordnance Department to use the National Armory. As the unit cost dropped to about a third of Colt's demand, largely by modifying machinery on which Ward-Burton rifles had been made a decade previously, manufacture of Chaffee-Reece trials guns began immediately.

By the middle of 1884, Springfield had completed 753 Chaffee-Reece rifles, though late delivery of 750 Lee and 750 Hotchkiss rifles delayed field trials until the end of the year.

713 examples of each rifle were issued to a wide variety of US Army units in 1884–5. They were distributed to infantry and cavalry alike, with special attention to units engaged along the frontiers.

The trials dragged on until, in December 1885, Benet reported to the Secretary of War that the Lee had proved the most effectual of the magazine guns—but that respondents still favoured the single-shot Trapdoor Springfield! He added that 'I have been and am an

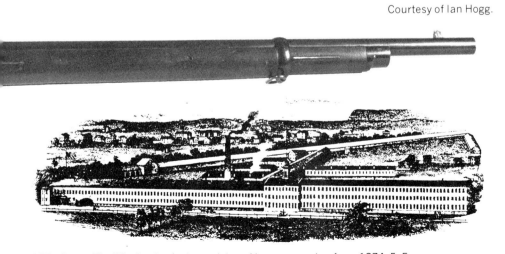

Courtesy of Ian Hogg.

267, above. The Winchester factory, pictured in an engraving from 1874–5. From a company letterhead. Author's collection.

advocate for a magazine gun, but it would seem the part of wisdom to postpone, for the present, any further efforts toward the adoption of a…magazine arm for the service. The Springfield rifle gives such general satisfaction to the Army that we can safely wait…for further developments of magazine systems'.

LEVER-ACTION COLTS, 1883–4

The Colt-Burgess was an improved Whitney Burgess, embodying five patents issued to Andrew Burgess in 1873–82 and a sixth granted to Burgess & Marlin in December 1881.

Colt introduced the first of its ·44–40–200 centre-fire sporting rifles and a short-barrel carbine in November 1883. The rifles offered 25-inch round, half-octagon or fully octagonal barrels; had tube magazines containing fifteen rounds; and weighed 8·5–8·8lb. The carbine had a twenty-inch round barrel, weighed 7·3lb and had a twelve-round magazine. Prices ranged from $24 for the carbine to $27 for the octagon-barrel rifles, an additional dollar being charged for each extra barrel-inch. Decoration and specially selected woodwork were available to order, but rarely used on the Colt-Burgess guns; production life was very short.

The entry of Colt into the lever-action rifle business threatened the sales of 1873 and 1876-pattern Winchesters, which lacked the strength of the Colt-Burgess. Winchester simply let it be known that its effectual experimental revolvers would be put into production to compete against the Colt Single Action Army revolver. As Winchester had also purchased rights to yet another of Burgess's designs—an improved 1873-pattern rifle, patented in December 1883—Colt stopped making lever action guns in 1884, after only 3,810 rifles and 2,593 carbines had been made.

HOTCHKISS RIFLES, 1883–5

The improved 1883-pattern Hotchkiss rifle was similar to the guns made at Springfield in 1879, but had a distinctive two-piece stock. Unlike its predecessors, which were loaded by removing the magazine spring and follower through the

268, above right. The Colt-Burgess lever-action rifle, from a broadsheet published by Colt in 1883. Author's collection.

269, right. The open action of the Winchester-Hotchkiss. Note the cartridge projecting into the feed-way from the tube magazine in the butt. The lever on the side of the receiver is the cut-off. Photograph courtesy of Ian Hogg.

1883   1884

COLT'S New Magazine Rifle,

.44 Cal. CENTRAL FIRE.

CARBINE.

Length of Barrel, 20 inches.
Number of Shots, 12.
Weight, - - 7¼ lbs.
Price, - - - $24.00.

SPORTING RIFLE, ROUND BARREL.

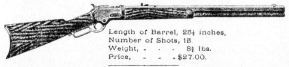

Length of Barrel, 25¼ inches.
Number of Shots, 15.
Weight, - - - 8½ lbs.
Price, - - - $25.00.

SPORTING RIFLE, OCTAGON BARREL.

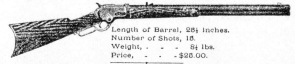

Length of Barrel, 25¼ inches.
Number of Shots, 15.
Weight, - - - 8½ lbs.
Price, - - - $27.00.

SPORTING RIFLE, HALF OCTAGON BARREL.

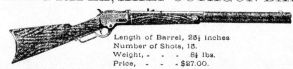

Length of Barrel, 25¼ inches.
Number of Shots, 15.
Weight, - - - 8½ lbs.
Price, - - - $27.00.

If longer barrels and magazines are required, $1.00 for each additional inch will be charged.

This Company has for some time been engaged in developing and perfecting a Magazine Sporting Rifle. It is now completed and samples will be issued to the trade on application. **This Rifle possesses advantages over all other Magazine Guns now in market. The materials** used in the construction of the arm are the **best of their kind,** and the **workmanship is equal** to that of the other arms manufactured by us. The cartridge used in this rifle is the same as that used in our **"Frontier" .44 Cal. Army Pistol;** it contains 40 grains of powder and the bullet weighs 200 grains, and it can be obtained from all Arms dealers in the United States and Mexico. The list above gives the details of the various rifles produced, and the prices.

TERMS CASH.

ALL COMMUNICATIONS MUST BE ADDRESSED TO

COLT'S PATENT FIRE-ARMS MANUF'G COMPANY,
HARTFORD, CONNECTICUT.

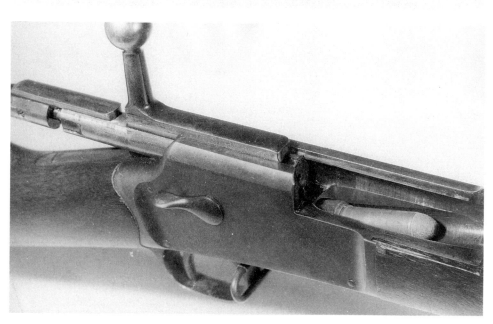

butt trap, the M1883 was loaded through the top of the open action. Cartridges could be inserted rim-first into the feedway and pressed back and down into the magazine tube, enabling the 1883-pattern magazine to hold six rounds instead of five. The bolt lock and the magazine cut-off lay on the side of the receiver.

The success of the rifle in the 1882 trials, when the Hotchkiss placed third behind the Lee and the Chaffee-Reece, persuaded the Ordnance Department to order 750 1883-type guns at $15 apiece from the Winchester Repeating Arms Company. Unfortunately, the field trials failed to generate enthusiasm for bolt-action magazine rifles; in addition, the Winchester, though overhauling the complex Chaffee-Reece into second place, was still inferior to the Lee.

Winchester's January 1884 catalogue, which contained the first large-scale promotion of the Hotchkiss Model 1883, stated that the gun resulted from 'the experience of six years of manufacturing and the valuable suggestions of many experienced officers who have used it in the field. It is a most simple and solid repeating gun, capable of doing good service under the most disadvantageous circumstances'.

The Hotchkiss Sporting Rifle was offered with 26-inch round, half-octagon or fully octagonal barrels, and weighed about 8½lb. Guns generally had pistol-grip butts, set-triggers being supplied to special order.

Unfortunately, the sporting market was still far more accustomed to lever-action rifles. With the advent of the Browning-designed Winchester Model 1886, which could handle high-powered cartridges with equal facility, the Hotchkiss sporter was relegated to comparative obscurity.

The M1883, made as a rifle, carbine or musket, was exclusively chambered for the regulation ·45–70–405 cartridge. A ·40–65 version was announced in Winchester catalogues in the summer of 1884, but there is no evidence that it was made.

The six-shot 9lb M1883 musket—made with a 32-inch barrel until 1884 and a 28-inch pattern thereafter—proved popular in militia circles; by far the majority of the 62,034 examples made before assembly ceased in 1899 had been muskets. In 1913, however, Winchester scrapped all the remaining Hotchkiss parts.

THE CHAFFEE-REECE, 1884

This gun was designed by Reuben Chaffee and General James Reece of Springfield, Illinois, the principal patent (US no.216,657) being granted in February 1879; 753 were made at Springfield Armory in 1884.

The rifle bore resembled the 1879-model Hotchkiss externally, as the stock was almost identical. Internally, however, a bolt-actuated oscillating double-rack system replaced a conventional magazine spring. As the bolt moved back, the mobile rack was pushed down the magazine until retainers slipped under and behind the rims of the cartridges. A fixed rack simply held the rounds in place. As the bolt was closed, the mobile rack pulled the cartridges forward. The bolt face caught the rim of the first cartridge, raised by an elevator, and fed it into the chamber.

The Chaffee-Reece action was interesting, as it separated the rounds. In the rival Hotchkiss, the nose of a cartridge touched the primer of the preceding round. However, the advantages of the oscillating rack system were hidden among a welter of breakages. Tube magazines predictably proved to be inferior to the Lee pattern box in the service trials. The troops were not particularly fond of the Chaffee-Reece, partly owing to excessive breakages, partly to tortuous dismantling and reassembly, and partly because closing the bolt lifted all the remaining cartridges in the magazine. The rifle had one brief ·30-calibre resurrection during the trials of 1892–3, but was otherwise ignored by posterity.

LEVER-ACTION BULLARDS, 1884-9

This handsome and extremely sturdy lever action rifle was patented by James Bullard on 16 August 1881 (245,700) and 23 October 1883 (287,229), and made by the Bullard Repeating Arms Company of Springfield, Massachusetts, in 1884–9.

Levers and rack-and-pinion gear moved the breech bolt, which was locked at the rear by a variant of the Remington Rolling Block. The Bullard rifle soon gained a reputation for an extremely smooth operating stroke, one gun allegedly firing twelve shots in five seconds in a trial where its nearest rival—presumably a Winchester—managed only eleven shots in seven seconds.

Bullard repeaters were made in a variety of sizes. According to adverts in *Forest and Stream*, dating from 1884–5, these included 26- or 28-inch round, half-octagon or fully octagonal barrels, weights ranging from eight to 9·75lb. Magazine capacity was generally eleven cartridges, though an extra one could be carried in the breech.

The standard rifles were made with straight wrist stocks, pistol grips being just one of the many optional extras. There were half length magazines, specially-selected butts or fore-ends, chequered to order, and receivers were often colour case-hardened. Beach and Lyman sights were available, though even the standard Bullard rifles were expensive; the ·32

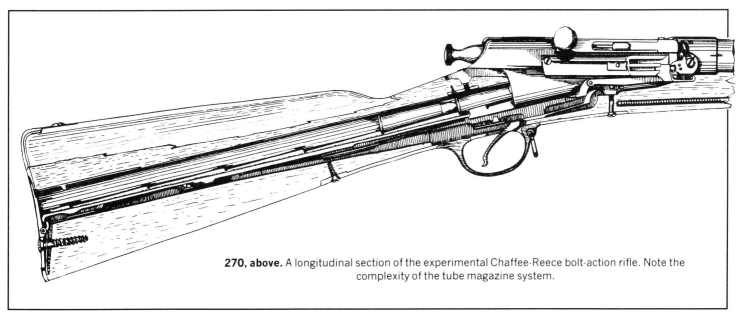

270, above. A longitudinal section of the experimental Chaffee-Reece bolt-action rifle. Note the complexity of the tube magazine system.

version, with a standard 26-inch round barrel, cost $33 in 1885.

Bullards were offered only in proprietary chamberings such as ·32–40, ·38–45, ·40–75, ·40–90, ·45–60, ·45–75, ·45–85 and ·50–115, though a few were also made for the ·45–70 US Government cartridge.

An advert in the July 1884 *Forest and Stream* challenged rivals to '…produce a Repeater that can compare with ours in ease of operation, safety, workmanship, style, finish, rapidity of fire, trajectory, penetration and accuracy'. Unfortunately, though the guns were sturdy enough to handle ·50–115 Express—one example being owned by Theodore Roosevelt—they were unable to withstand competition from Winchester and Marlin, and the Bullard Repeating Rifle Company had failed by 1890.

SLIDE-ACTION COLTS, 1884–1900

The Colt-Burgess was succeeded by the New Model Lightning slide-action repeater, locked by a Burgess-type pivoting wedge beneath the breech bolt. The subject of patents granted to William Elliott on 29 May 1883 (278,324) and

18 September 1883 (285,020), the Lightning handled well once initial ejection problems had been overcome. It could be fired merely by operating the slide with the trigger held back.

The medium-frame Lightning appeared at the end of 1884. Sold until 1900, it chambered ·32–20, ·38–40 or ·44–40 cartridges. The rifle magazine held fifteen rounds to the carbine's twelve. A ·25–20–86 version is said to have been offered commercially, but none has been authenticated.

Medium-frame Lightnings were offered in rifle form, with a 26-inch round or octagonal barrel, and a fifteen-round magazine; as a twelve-shot carbine with a twenty-inch round barrel; and as a scarce Baby Carbine (chambered for ·44–40 and experimentally for ·32–20) with a special twenty-inch barrel, a twelve-round magazine and a weight of just 5¼lb. A selection of sights, finishes and woodwork was available.

The first of the small-frame ·22 rimfire and large-frame Express rifles appeared in 1887, their barrels bearing additional patent acknowledgements—26 May 1885, 15 June 1886 and 22 February 1887. Apart from differences in size, their most obvious feature was the breech cover: pre-1887 medium-frame guns had an exposed breech bolt. Handling

cartridges such as ·38–56–256, ·40–60–260, ·45–60–300, ·45–85–285 and ·50–95–300, the Lightning Express Rifle (1887–94) presented better established lever-action guns with an effectual rival. Ten-shot Expresses were made with 28-inch round or octagonal barrels and weighed 9½–10lb. There was a 9lb carbine with a 22-inch barrel, and an uncommon 'Baby Express Carbine' weighing 8lb.

A set trigger patented by Frederick Knous in December 1885 was occasionally fitted, plus an unsuccessful auxiliary bolt-locking arm patented by Carl Ehbets in April 1885.

The Lightning was discontinued after 89,777 standard medium frame and 6,496 large-frame Express rifles had been made. A few had been sold to the San Francisco Police Department, but orders of this type had been rare.

LEVER-ACTION WINCHESTERS, 1886–1917

The improved Model 1876 remained structurally similar to the Model 1873, relying on the toggle joint lock derived from the Henry. By the 1880s, however, single-shot guns were handling bullets as heavy as 550 grains in 3-inch cases.

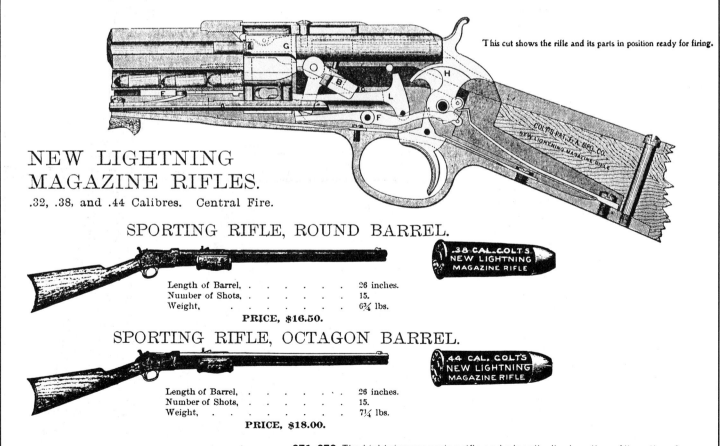

This cut shows the rifle and its parts in position ready for firing.

NEW LIGHTNING MAGAZINE RIFLES.

.32, .38, and .44 Calibres.   Central Fire.

SPORTING RIFLE, ROUND BARREL.

Length of Barrel,	26 inches.
Number of Shots,	15.
Weight,	6¾ lbs.

PRICE, $16.50.

SPORTING RIFLE, OCTAGON BARREL.

Length of Barrel,	26 inches.
Number of Shots,	15.
Weight,	7¼ lbs.

PRICE, $18.00.

271, 272. The Lightning magazine rifle and a longitudinal section of its action, from Colt's advertising literature, *c.*1894. Author's collection.

These cartridges would not feed through the Winchester actions; in addition, though necking reduced case length, the 1876-pattern action could not handle high pressures.

Winchester's management chanced upon gunsmiths John and Matthew Browning in the small town of Ogden, Utah. Interest centred on a promising single-shot dropping block gun, which became the Model 1885, and also on an improved lever action locked by sturdy vertically sliding bars.

The Model 1886 rifle was such an instant success that it immediately inhibited sales of the Model 1876. By the time the M1886 had been superseded by the Model 71 in 1936, 159,994 had been made. The chamberings included ·38–56, ·45–70, ·45–90, ·50–100–450 and ·50–110 Express. Barrel lengths, finishes, triggers and decoration were tailored to the whims of the customer. Owing to the power of the cartridges, most 1886-type Winchesters were made with barrels of normal length, carbines being rare.

A full-stock carbine was described in the company's 1887 catalogue, but may not have been made. The standard short-barrel carbine, with a half-length fore-end, was pictured from 1889 onward. A 'take-down gun' was offered in 1894—but merely 350 were made.

Theodore Roosevelt, a long-time champion of Winchester rifles, replaced his Model 1876 with ·45–90 M1886 no. 9205. Many other hunters concurred, taking the guns all over North America and across the Atlantic to Africa and beyond. The last grizzly bear in California was downed with a M1886 near San Juan Capistrano, and many a trophy-head gained by courtesy of Winchester graced study walls.

For most normal purposes, however, the Model 1886 was too expensive. In the early 1890s, therefore, the company's engineers produced the Model 1892, a diminution of its predecessor available in rifle and carbine form with an occasional military-style musket. A few take-down variants were made prior to the First World War, but were never popular. Barrel lengths ranged from fourteen to 36 inches—the

273, right. The 1886-pattern Winchester, designed by John Browning, was the first of the company's lever-action rifles capable of handling the most powerful sporting rifle cartridges. This gun, no. 124931, chambers ·50–110 Express and has a half-length magazine contained in the fore-end.

274, 275; centre and far right. Examples of the 1892-model Winchester: ·38–40 no. 51262 with a 24-inch round barrel (274) and ·32–20 no. 702027, with a 24-inch half octagonal/half round barrel (275).

Courtesy of Wallis & Wallis.

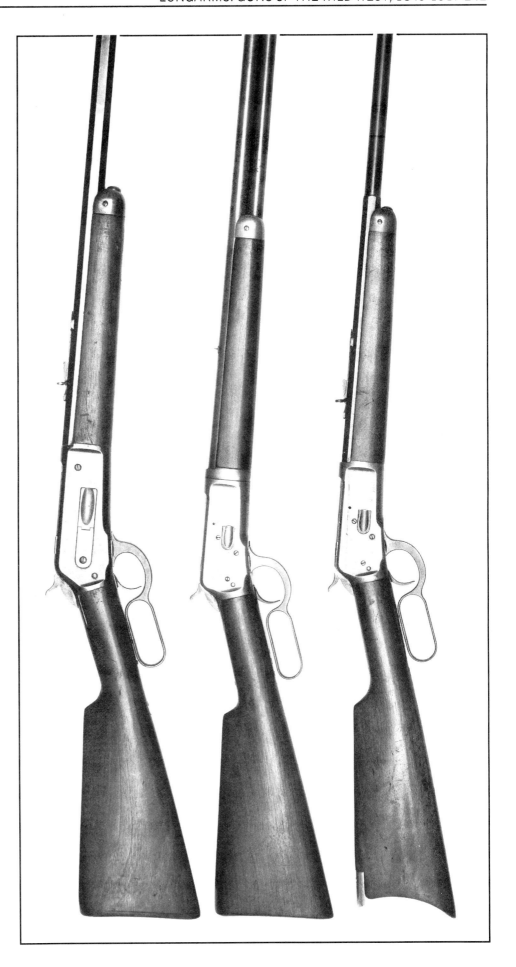

WINCHESTER - Model 1886

.50-100-450.

—A New Cartridge.—

.50 Caliber,
100 Grains Powder.

50-100-450
WINCHESTER
MODEL 1895

450 Grain

Solid Bullet.

LIST PRICE, $48 PER 1000.

To meet the demands of our friends for a .50 caliber carrying a heavy bullet, we are now prepared to furnish the above. The bullet has a penetration of about 16 pine boards 7⅜ inch thick, and a trajectory of about 13 inches at 100 yards. This cartridge cannot be fired with good results out of the .50-110-300 rifle, but requires a barrel especially rifled for it.

Winchester Repeating Arms Company,

NEW HAVEN, CONN.

Send for our 112 page catalogue—free.

latter on special order only—while half- and threequarter-length magazines, selected wood, set triggers and pistol-grip butts were available.

The M1892 was offered in ·32–20, ·38–40 and ·44–40, plus ·25–20 from 1895. Beginning at number one, 1,004,067 guns had been made by 1941. The basic design never altered, though details had been refined in 1924—creating the Model 53—and then again ten years later to give the Model 65.

The 1892-pattern rifle was followed by the Model 1894, a Browning design specifically intended for cartridges loaded with smokeless powder. It was needed to compete against the 1893-pattern Marlin, chambering the same ·32–40 and ·38–55 cartridges.

If the M1892 was successful, then the Model 1894 gladdened the Winchester treasurer's heart; it remains in full production, having been through several modifications (including the Models 55 and 64) before reverting to its orignal designation. The millionth rifle went to President Calvin Coolidge in 1927; no. 1500000 to Harry Truman in 1947; and the two millionth to Dwight Eisenhower in 1953.

The Model 1894 has been made as a rifle, carbine and musket, and also as a take-down rifle. There have been many barrel lengths, finishes and accessories. Chamberings have included ·32–40 and ·38–55 (1894), followed by the high-velocity ·25–35 and legendary ·30–30 in 1895, and then by the short-lived ·32 Winchester Special in 1902.

The Model 1895, another Browning design, incorporated a box magazine to handle high

276, above. An advertisement promoting the Model 1886 rifle. The announcement of the ·50–100–450 cartridge dates it to 1895–6.

277, 278; below. The 1892 and 1894 Winchester actions. The earlier design pivots the locking bar directly on the finger lever, and the lock seats in shoulders cut in the breech bolt. The later bar, attached to an auxiliary lever, rises behind the bolt.

power small-calibre smokeless cartridges with sharply pointed noses—a dangerous liability in tube magazines. That it also had appreciable military potential was more than evident in its chamberings: ·30–40 Krag, ·30 M1903 and ·30 M1906, plus ·303 (British). These co-existed with sporting rounds such as ·35 Winchester, ·38–72, ·40–72 and ·405 Winchester. Production had reached 425,881 by the time the M1895 was finally discontinued in 1938.

About five thousand low-number guns were made with a flat-side receiver, lacking the perfected rebated surface.

Not surprisingly, in view of his previous affections, the Model 1895 was popular with Theodore Roosevelt; 'Teddy' owned one rifle chambering ·30–40 Krag cartridges and two ·405 examples. Others were used by the world-renowned big game hunter Stewart Edward White.

The 1895-pattern Winchester, approved by the National Rifle Association of America for use in shooting competitions, was equally popular with militia and volunteer units participating in the Spanish-American War. The Winchesters were infinitely superior to the converted single shot Trapdoor Springfields being carried by many other units.

The most impressive military sale, however, came from the imperial Russian government; 300,000 Model 1895 Winchesters chambering the clumsy Tsarist 7·62mm rifle cartridge were ordered in 1915. Hasty modifications were made, production began as soon as possible and 293,816 guns had been delivered prior to the 1917 revolution. They were

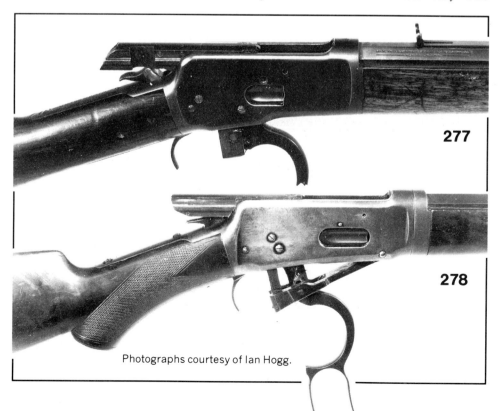

277

278

Photographs courtesy of Ian Hogg.

279, 280; right. Markings on the tang and barrel of an early octagonal-barrelled Winchester Model 1894 rifle. Courtesy of Ian Hogg.

281, below. The Winchester Model 1894 is probably the most successful of all lever action rifles, eclipsing the Model 73. This gun, ·30–30 (·30 WCF) no. 884958, has a twenty-inch round barrel. Courtesy of Wallis & Wallis.

281

exclusively full-length rifles, accompanied by sword bayonets. These Winchesters are rarely encountered in the West, most being lost in Russia. However, the contents of more than fifty original cases were offered commercially in the early 1920s.

THE MAGAZINE RIFLE TRIALS OF 1890–2

By 1890, even the US Army agreed that the Trapdoor Springfield was obsolescent. On 16 December 1890, therefore, a Board of Officers met in New York City to decide the rules for a repeating-rifle competition. The closing date was originally set at 1 June 1892 and circulars were sent to interested parties. During the summer of 1892, Frankford Arsenal made a hundred thousand ·30 rimmed cartridges firing a 220-grain bullet at about 2,000 ft/sec⁻¹.

Trials of 53 guns were subsequently held at New York Arsenal, a report being made on 19 August 1892. The submissions had included a variety of well-known designs in addition to the work of many lesser lights. There were six Krag-Jørgensens; five ·30 Mausers, based on the Belgian Mle 89; two 8mm Austrian-style Mannlichers and a 6·5mm Romanian gun; a German 7·9mm Gewehr 88; a Portuguese 8mm Kropatschek; an 8mm Japanese Murata; a 7·5mm Swiss Schmidt-Rubin; a 7·62mm Russian Mosin-Nagant; three French-pattern Berthiers submitted by the Hotchkiss Ordnance Company, Washington; an M1888 Schulhof; and a Swiss Rubin rifle.

Lee-system rifles, which had enjoyed success in the US Navy, included an 1885-model ·30-calibre ten-shot gun submitted on behalf of the Lee Arms Company of South Windham, Connecticut; two similar rifles from the Remington Arms Company of Bridgeport, Connecticut, ·303 No. 25 and ·30 No. 26; and a ·303-calibre British Lee-Metford rifle No. 1 masquerading as the 'Lee-Speed', entered—like all foreign service weapons—by the Chief of Ordnance.

Three single-shot ·30 Trapdoor Springfields were submitted by the Chief of Ordnance as control weapons. Even at an early stage, the trials board decided to seek a rifle firing rimmed ammunition; it was seen as a single loader with a magazine held in reserve.

The Krag No. 1 was the 8mm Danish m/89; No. 2 was a similar gun in ·30-calibre with a Mauser-type safety, a pivoting ejector and a different cocking piece; No. 3 was identical to No. 2, but had greater head-space; No. 4 was No. 2 with a dust cover over the bolt and a downward-opening loading gate; No. 5 was the same as No. 4, without the dust cover; and No. 6 was a variant of No. 5 chambering a rimless ·30 cartridge.

The trials resolved in favour of Lee No. 3, Belgian type Mauser No. 5 and Krag-Jørgensen No. 5; the Krag was victorious because fresh cartridges could be inserted in the magazine even when the bolt was shut and cocked on a loaded chamber. The standard US Krag magazine was adapted from an experimental Norwegian trials rifle, with a gate swinging down to serve as a loading platform rather than pivoting forward.

The Krag was a turning-bolt repeater with a single lug locking vertically in the receiver behind the chamber, a weak system that prevented the army developing high-velocity cartridges prior to 1900. Ironically, Krag & Jørgensen developed a twin-lug gun in the early 1890s—US Patent 492,212 of 21 February 1893—and one experimental gun survives in the Smithsonian collection.

The Krag rifle was officially adopted on 15 September 1892 but production of the new 'US Magazine Rifle, Caliber ·30, Model of 1892', scheduled to begin in 1893, was soon deferred. Though the original trials had been undertaken with scrupulous honesty, American inventors were outraged by the adoption of a foreign rifle. They successfully petitioned Congress to withhold approval for the Krags until more tests could be undertaken—even though Springfield continued to tool for the new rifle.

Convened in March 1893, the new Board of Officers tested fourteen guns—a Spencer-Lee, a Lee, a Savage, four Dursts, two Blakes, three Russell-Livermores, a Hampden and a White—and reported on 16 May 1893 that none of the triallists had even approached the efficiency of the Krag.

THE KRAG-JØRGENSENS, 1892–1901

The first two M1892 rifles were assembled in Springfield Armory on 1 January 1894, but first issues were delayed until 6 October.

Problems were reported as soon as the guns entered service. As the sights had been calibrated in the depths of the New England winter, guns shot high and to the left in warmer conditions until corrections were made. The original flat butt-plate was replaced by a rounded pattern from 23 December 1895, as the toes of many stocks broke when they were struck on the ground during 'Order Arms'. By the end of 1896, nearly forty changes had been made to the M1892, though few guns received all the minor modifications.

The standard US Krag-Jørgensen had an elegant straight-gripped walnut stock, with a grasping groove in the fore-end and a hand guard from the breech to the barrel band. An open stacking swivel was attached to the the nose cap, the upper surface of which was solid prior to 16 August 1894. A lug beneath the nose cap accepted the M1892 knife bayonet, copied from the Swiss M1889, and a full-length cleaning rod protruded below the muzzle. 24,562 Model 1892 Krags were made at Springfield Armory, though most were subsequently converted to M1896 standards.

Though placed in production in December 1895, the Krag Cadet Rifle was officially known as 'M1896'; only 404 were made. It was essentially similar to the standard M1896, but had a barrel-band spring and lacked sling swivels. However, 398 survivors were returned for the installation of swivels in November 1900

and 1901-pattern back sights were fitted in 1902.

The Magazine Rifle, Caliber ·30, M1896 was standardised on 19 February 1896—though the decision was arbitrary and there was little difference between the last of the much modified 1892s and the first 1896 apart from the radically different back sight and the three-piece cleaning rod carried in a butt-trap. 61,897 true M1896 rifles were made.

Many 1892-pattern Krags were converted to 1896 standards by filling the ramrod channel in the fore-end, modifying the butt to accept the three-piece rod, substituting the Model 1896 back sight (often later replaced by the M1901), and adding a bolt hold-open notch in the receiver for the extractor pin. Work started in March 1897 and, by 1902, 18,559 of the 24,562 original M1892 rifles had been transformed. These do not bear MODEL 1896 marks on the side plate and still simply read '1892'.

The first experimental Krag carbines, made in 1893, were simply rifles with 22-inch barrels and reduced nose caps without the bayonet lug. A cleaning rod was carried in the stock and a saddle ring appeared on the left side of the stock-wrist.

Though the Chief of Ordnance directed carbine production to start in May 1895, development had only commenced a mere three months previously. A pattern gun was approved on 17 May 1895, production carbines being designated 'M1896'. The first guns had

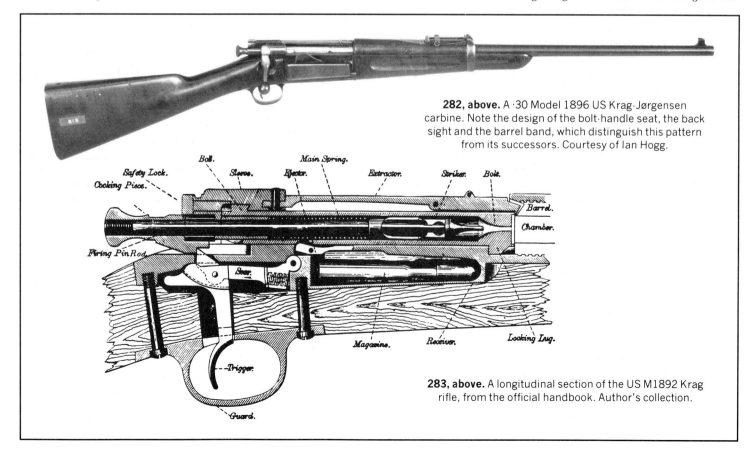

282, above. A ·30 Model 1896 US Krag-Jørgensen carbine. Note the design of the bolt-handle seat, the back sight and the barrel band, which distinguish this pattern from its successors. Courtesy of Ian Hogg.

283, above. A longitudinal section of the US M1892 Krag rifle, from the official handbook. Author's collection.

284, 285; left. Typical of the grandiose headquarters of the pre-1917 US militia were those of the 74th Regiment in Buffalo, New York (284), and the 5th Regiment in Baltimore, Maryland (285). From picture postcards of the 1910–25 period. Author's collection.

Production amounted to 22,493 M1896, 5,002 M1898 and 36,051 M1899 Krag carbines.

The original M1892 back sight was a tangent leaf pattern, graduated from 300 to 1900 yards, with a stepped base. No azimuth adjustment was provided on the leaf. The M1896 sight had a 'stepless' or continuously curved base; azimuth adjustments were absent, though a binding screw was added to the slider. The rifle sight was graduated to 1,800 yards; the carbine pattern, distinguished by a large 'C', ran up to 2,000.

Next came the short-lived M1898 or Dickson Sight, a tangent pattern for 200–2,000 yards, with an azimuth adjustment on the three-notch back sight block in addition to a binding screw on the slider. An essentially similar carbine sight was marked 'C', but neither was long lived owing to the failure of the high velocity cartridge for which they were graduated.

The M1901 Buffington Sight had a stepless base, azimuth adjustments being made by pivoting the entire sight base across the barrel surface before locking it with a clamp screw. The Buffington sight was replaced by the M1902 Dickson-type tangent pattern, similar to the M1898 but with only one sight notch and a spring plunger in the slider to engage the serrated left edge of the leaf.

The so-called Sergeant's Peep, a pivoting aperture plate designed by Franklin Bull of Springfield Armory, was added to the M1902 sight in January 1904 and intermediate 25-yard graduations appeared in April.

Identifying Krags is complicated by the periodic changes of sights. On 30 June 1903, the inventory stood at 2,244 M1898 rifles with 1892-pattern sights; 55,973 with 1896 sights; 39,956 with 1898 sights; 66,713 with 1901 sights; 7,410 with 1902 sights; and 9,600 rifles with no sights at all!

The army was never entirely satisfied with the Krag-Jørgensen, particularly as the single lug action was too weak to cope with higher velocities and rising chamber pressures.

Experiments were underway to find a better gun by 1900; and, after only a decade's service, the Krag was replaced by the Mauser-action M1903 Springfield. Ironically, the smoothness of the Krag action was such that it was readily accepted by sportsmen, many thousands being converted to NRA Carbines in the 1920s.

Many obsolescent carbines were transformed into so-called Philippine Constabulary Rifles,

thin-wrist stocks, a saddle ring and bar assembly on the left side of the stock above the trigger guard, and a two-piece cleaning rod in the butt.

An oiler was carried in the butt after February 1897, but most guns subsequently received the 1899 carbine stock. Cut-offs were reversed in 1900, but the carbines were relegated to militia cavalry after the summer of 1901. Nine thousand were refurbished and sold to the Guardia Rurales in Cuba in 1912.

Approved on 14 March 1898, the 'Magazine Rifle, Caliber ·30, M1898' was the first major revision. The bolt mechanism, receiver and the magazine loading gate were modified to simplify machining, while the bolt-handle seat was milled flush with the receiver to ease inletting problems.

The first true M1898 rifles were delivered from Springfield on 9 July 1898, but none saw service during the Spanish-American War. Total

production amounted to 324,283. Many guns made between 28 April 1899 and 11 October 1900 had a headless cocking piece introduced in an unsuccessful cost-cutting exercise.

The M1898 Carbine was essentially similar to its predecessor but incorporated the improved 1898-pattern rifle action. Only 5,002 guns were made in 1898, owing to the trouble with the high velocity cartridges for which the 1898 tangent-pattern back sight had been graduated. Many guns were subsequently fitted with 1899-type stocks and a selection of sights.

The 1899-pattern Carbine had a plain stock, a fore-end lengthened by about three inches, and (originally) an 1896-pattern sight. However, most guns subsequently received the M1901 sight and then, after complaints, the M1902 hand guard was added to protect the sight leaf when the carbine was thrust in its saddle scabbard.

officially known as the 'Carbine M1899, altered for Knife Bayonet and Rifle Sling'. This was authorised in 1906, when Springfield modified 350 service carbines for Girard College in Philadelphia. Larger numbers were supplied to the forces in the Philippines, where the small rifle was ideally suited to the stature of the native troops. Conversion work was undertaken by Manila ordnance depot, where 5,100 were modified in 1907, and then by Springfield Armory (3,724 guns, 1908–15) and Rock Island Arsenal (613 guns, 1911–14). Though virtually all the carbines were originally of 1899 pattern, a few M1898 and a very few M1896 examples were among them.

Constabulary Rifles accepted the standard 1892-pattern knife bayonet, though most of the Combination Intrenching Knife-Bayonets and Wise bolo bayonets made in 1900–3 had also been sent to the Philippines.

THE LEE NAVY RIFLE, 1895

Though ·45–70 Remington-Lee rifles had been ordered in 1888, the US Navy Bureau of Ordnance was well aware of the small-calibre experiments being undertaken in Europe. Specifications for a new small-bore rifle were issued in 1892.

Meanwhile, Lee had been granted a series of patents for bolt-action rifles and improved box magazines; a turn-bolt Russell-Livermore with a box magazine; and a prototype straight pull Lee.

A Luger, a Durst and another Briggs-Kneeland were subsequently admitted, all apparently embodying turning bolts. Mindful of problems that had arisen with the Krag, the navy had decided to favour the Lee; competition was as much to humour American inventors as ensure that no better gun appeared unexpectedly.

Lee's Straight-Pull Rifle was recommended in May 1895 and ten thousand were ordered from Winchester; 19,563 were made in 1896–8, but not all reached the navy.

The ·236 (6mm) M1895 was the first ultra small calibre clip-loader to be adopted for US service. A clip containing five semi-rim cartridges was inserted in the magazine with the bolt open, automatically releasing tension on the case rims so that the clip fell out of the action after the first or second round.

The ·236 cartridge was powerful for its day, its jacketed bullet piercing 23in of pine at fifty yards compared with eighteen for the Austrian 8mm cartridge and only ten for the ·45–70. The back sight leaf, lacking azimuth adjustment, was graduated from 800 to 2,000 yards, battle sights being provided for 300 and 600 yards.

An extraordinary wedge-type locking block lay beneath the bolt. Pulling back on the bolt handle disengaged the wedge so that the entire mechanism could be retracted. However,

though potentially fast when well lubricated, the inclined operating stroke was awkward when the rifle was shouldered. The Lee was very unpopular in service; in addition, the curious floating extractor/ejector, the firing-pin lock and bolt-lock actuator gave constant trouble. Tension in the ammunition clips also proved difficult to regulate.

The rifle was handy—47·6in overall, 8½lb with sling and bayonet—and had a conventional one-piece pistol-grip walnut stock. It had a single barrel band and a most distinctive nosecap.

The Model 1899 Lee rifle, modified by Edward Parkhurst, had dual-opposed lugs on the front of the bolt. Protected by US Patent 604,904 of 31 May 1898, the modified bolt also originally incorporated a Mauser-type extractor collar. The lugs locked into the receiver immediately behind the chamber, where, backed up by the bolt-handle seat, they provided much greater strength than in the original Lee design. A new combination bolt-stop/ejector was designed by William Larraway (US Patent 579,096 of March 1897), and improvements to the safety were patented by Edward Parkhurst in February 1898 (599,287).

The standard M1899 measured 49½in overall, had a five-groove 29-inch barrel and weighed about 8lb 6oz; however, a 39½-inch carbine was also made in small numbers. The M1899 rifle was stocked as the M1885 Remington-Lee,

286, above; 287, below. The ·236-calibre M1895 Lee Navy Rifle, made by Winchester, was unsuccessful; it had been replaced by the Krag by 1905. Courtesy of Ian Hogg.

magazines. The most important group was 506,319–506,323 (three of which protected straight-pull bolts), plus the similar 506,339 granted to Francis Richards and assigned to Lee. These were followed by 513,647 of January 1894, granted to Lee to protect a straight pull bolt-action rifle with a clip-loaded magazine and a special cartridge-lifter arm; 547,582 of 8 October 1895, for a perfected five-round clip system; and 547,583 for an improved straight pull system.

Twelve rifles were tested at the US Navy's Torpedo Station in Newport, Rhode Island, on 2 October 1894. There was a Miles turn-bolt rifle with a side magazine; a Briggs-Kneeland; five turn-bolt Remington-Lee guns; a slide-action Van Patten, with a tube magazine beneath the barrel; two turn-bolt French Daudetau rifles with

288, left. A page from the 1906–7 catalogue produced by Von Lengerke & Antoine of Chicago, showing the 1899-model Savages. These were handled alongside imports such as Mauser sporting rifles, small numbers of which reached the West before the First World War. Author's collection.

followers. However, though highly satisfactory, they were not good enough to beat the bolt action Krag-Jørgensen.

Savage, meanwhile, had been granted Patent 491,138 on 7 February 1893 to protect a refinement of the rotary magazine in which each cartridge was carried in a separate cradle. Eager to exploit his design, Savage and his backers incorporated the Savage Repeating Arms Company of Utica, New York, in April 1894. The Savage Arms Company, formed at the end of 1897, remained independent until its assets were acquired by the Driggs-Seabury Ordnance Company in 1915.

The Model 1895, the first perfected Savage rifle, was made by Marlin in several styles. Chambered for a unique smokeless ·303 Savage cartridge, the rifle soon presented a serious rival to Winchester and Marlin. The military version chambered ·30–40 Krag cartridges, had a six-shot magazine and weighed 8lb 11oz. The carbine was similar, excepting for its 22-inch barrel, half-stock and saddle ring. A sporting rifle chambering ·303 Savage High Velocity was made with round, half-octagon or fully octagonal barrels.

Five thousand M1895 sporters had been sold by 1900, but Savage then made improvements in the basic design. The resulting Model 1899 was made in a new factory in Utica in the same three variants as its predecessor.

The capacity of the magazine was reduced to five, with a sixth round carried in the breech. A cocking indicator (in the top surface of the bolt) and a firing-pin retractor were added at the same time.

Savages were operated by depressing the finger lever, a long curved extension of which then withdrew support from under the rear of the breech block. The block dropped clear of the locking shoulder in the top of the receiver behind the magazine, and was withdrawn clear of the magazine. The return stroke closed the breech, loading a fresh cartridge, and finally tilted the breech block up into the receiver.

The system was simple and very sturdy; though the breech block was placed under stress during firing, it could handle the most powerful high-velocity cartridges available prior to 1917. In addition, unlike rival lever-action rifles with tube magazines, it could handle pointed-nose bullets in perfect safety.

The Model 1899 military rifle and carbine (1899–1908) were available in ·303 Savage

but had a short upper hand guard extending forward to the rear band. Like all Lee designs, the 1899-pattern mechanism cocked on closing, but the extractor was let into the left side of the detachable bolt head. The rifle took a standard Remington knife bayonet; the carbine, however, had a plain rounded half-stock.

The 1895-model Lee navy rifle was also made in sporting guise, apparently to rid Winchester of as many sets of components as possible after the failure of the gun militarily. Unfortunately, the tiny ·236-calibre (6mm) bullet, despite developing an extremely high velocity for its day, had very poor knock-down capabilities on game. Consequently, only about 18,000 muskets and 1,500 sporting rifles were made before the Lee straight-pull system was finally discontinued in 1904.

LEVER-ACTION SAVAGES, 1895–1917

Arthur Savage's first patent, granted in July 1887, protected a modified Peabody-Martini rifle loaded from a tube magazine in the butt. Prototypes were made in ·45–70 and ·44–40, but hinged-block actions were unsuited to magazine feed; Savage, defeated, turned instead to a tilting-block action feeding from a magazine ahead of the trigger.

Work on the perfected lever-action rifle began in the late 1880s, Savage lodging an application for what became US Patent 502,018 in April 1889. Two 'M1892' rifles had been entered in the US Army rifle trials, featuring thirty-inch barrels, nine-shot rotary magazines with radial arm and, briefly, in ·30–30. The rifle had a full-length fore-end, a tangent-leaf back sight, two barrel bands, a cleaning rod beneath the muzzle, and could accept sword or socket bayonets. It had a 28-inch barrel and weighed 8lb 12oz. The carbine had a twenty-inch barrel, a leaf sight, a sling ring on the right side of the receiver, and a half-length fore-end retained by a single band. It weighed 7lb 4oz.

Unfortunately for Savage, the M1899 military rifle, effectual enough to elicit impressive testimonials from the New York National Guard and the Mexican army, never sold in large numbers.

The pre-1917 M1899 sporter chambered an assortment of cartridges, including ·25–35, ·30–30, ·303 Savage, ·32–40 and ·38–55. Its barrels—round, half-octagon or fully octagonal—ranged from 22 to 26in. The butts originally had straight wrists, though pistol-grip patterns, once optional, gradually became standard. Variety existed among fittings and sights, with engraving and specially selected woodwork obtainable to order.

Savage was particularly keen on his rimmed ·303 cartridge and promoted many proprietary loads. According to the company's 1904 catalogue, these included ·303–5 with a lead bullet; ·303–15 Miniature, with a nickel plated jacketed bullet; ·303–20 Schuetzen, with a paper-patched lead bullet; ·303–28 Smokeless with a 'Regular or Expanding Bullet'; and ·303–40 Black Powder.

A centre-fire ·22 high velocity round was introduced in 1912, to be followed within a year by the famed ·250–3000 Savage—which, with an 87-grain jacketed bullet, could generate a muzzle velocity of 3,000 ft/sec[-1].

The enormously successful Savage was made in differing solid-frame and 'take-down' forms,

the millionth Model 99 being presented to the National Rifle Association on 22 March 1960.

MILITARY EXPERIMENTS, 1897–1909

A few Krag rifles with an experimentally reversed cut-off were made in 1897–8. A similar change was applied to service rifles from February 1900 onward.

A rifle chambering a ·30 rimless cartridge, tested briefly in July 1899, was abandoned in favour of the Parkhurst & Warren Device—a charger ('stripper-clip') patented by Edward Parkhurst combined with an adaptor block designed by Lyman Warren. A hundred M1898 rifles and a similar quantity of M1899 carbines were converted by Springfield Armory in July 1900, but the Parkhurst Clip was abandoned when progress was made with Mauser rifles.

Two hundred Krag-Jørgensen sub-calibre training devices were made in 1899–1909, and a hundred Board of Ordnance & Fortification Rifles—with 26-inch barrels and special sights—were issued in the autumn of 1902. Though the short barrel increased recoil and muzzle blast, as well as reducing accuracy, the rifle was well liked.

Six M1898 Krags were converted for 8 × Cataract Tool & Optical Company telescope sights in February 1901 and issued for trials. Others adapted for the Hyposcope (periscope) were exhibited at the National Matches in 1903. Neither variant was successful.

The ·22 Gallery Practise Rifles were rimfire versions of the standard ·30 M1898 infantry rifle, originally developed for Extra Long and then revised for ·22 Long Rifle cartridges. Assembled from old and rejected parts on hand after Krag production had ceased in November 1904, 341

rifles and 124 barrelled receivers emanated from Springfield Armory in 1906–7.

MAGAZINE RIFLE TRIALS, 1900–1

The Spanish-American War showed that the Spanish Mausers were vastly superior to the Krag-Jørgensen, as were similar designs being adopted throughout Latin America.

On 2 October 1900, a Board of Officers convened at Springfield Armory to test a 'Rifle, caliber ·30, Model 1900' amalgamating the best features of the Krag-Jørgensen with those of the Mauser. The gun had a distinctive clip-loaded Mannlicher-pattern magazine, and a bolt with two lugs on the head plus a third (or safety lug) opposite the bolt handle base. A cut-off pivoted laterally above the magazine housing.

The board reported that the experimental rifle had '...successfully passed the tests to which it has been subjected, the minor difficulties which were experienced being only what might reasonably be expected in the case of a new gun'. The action was approved, though the magazine was to be adapted to fit in the stock.

The Model 1901 rifle embodied most of the changes suggested by the 1900 Board of Officers. Though much the same length as the M1898 Krag, it was appreciably lighter (9·47lb with its bayonet compared with 10·64lb) and chambered a semi-experimental ·30 rimless round firing a 220-grain bullet at 2,300 ft/sec[-1]—compared with only 2,000 ft/sec[-1] for its predecessor.

Manufacture of five thousand M1901 rifles was subsequently approved by the Secretary of War. Springfield Armory's Krag production machinery was to be adapted to make 125 new rifles daily after the initial order had been completed, and a duplicate line was to be installed in Rock Island Armory with a capacity of two hundred rifles per day.

Making M1901 and Krag rifles simultaneously was a waste of resources, so about a hundred partially hand-made Model 1901 guns were assembled at Springfield Armory to resolve details before production of the Krag-Jørgensen was disrupted. The rifling of guns made in 1902 made a turn in eight inches instead of ten.

The Model 1901 had a straight-wrist butt, a tangent-pattern back sight, and a rod bayonet. Its magazine was loaded through the top of the open action, losing the one real advantage of the Krag—which could be replenished even when there was a cartridge in the chamber.

Series production of 1901-pattern rifles had not begun when the Short Magazine Lee-Enfield rifle appeared. The US Ordnance Department had developed an experimental universal-issue M1882 Springfield twenty years previously; now it was time to reconsider.

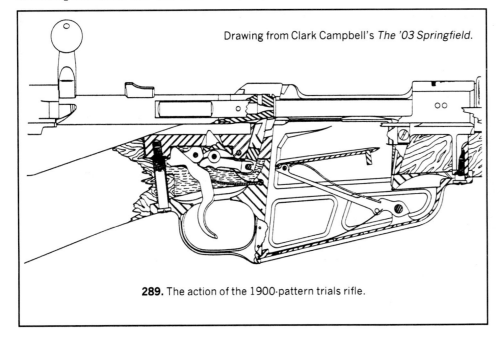

Drawing from Clark Campbell's *The '03 Springfield*.

289. The action of the 1900-pattern trials rifle.

THE SPRINGFIELD RIFLE, 1903–17

A Board of Officers convened at Springfield Armory in 1902, under the presidency of Captain Frederick Foltz of the cavalry. Trials soon showed that the M1901 barrel could be reduced to 24in without affecting its performance. Changes to the back sight, the hand guard and the lower band were recommended. The 1901-type rod bayonet was retained, though its diameter was increased from ·27 to ·30 and the protrusion when fixed reduced from 15¼ to ten inches.

Approved by the Secretary of War on 19 June 1903, the 'United States Magazine Rifle, Caliber ·30, Model of 1903' was ordered into immediate production. It measured 43·41in overall, had a 24-inch barrel protected by a hand guard running back to the receiver ring, and weighed 8·94lb. The rifling twist had reverted to a turn in ten inches, as the 1-in-8 pattern had worn too quickly.

Daily production was to be 225 guns at Springfield Armory (soon raised to four hundred) and 125 at Rock Island Arsenal. By 30 June 1904, Springfield had made thirty thousand M1903 rifles; production began at Rock Island in May 1904.

Sufficient guns had been made by the end of 1904 to equip the standing army, though

issues had scarcely begun when the President, Theodore Roosevelt, wrote to Secretary of War William Taft condemning the rod bayonet as 'about as poor an invention as I ever saw' and casting doubt on the efficacy of the short barrel. Work on the M1903 was suspended on 11 January 1905.

The Chief of Ordnance, Brigadier General William Crozier, attempted to defend bayonet and barrel-length, but was unable to prevent an investigation authorised by Chief of Staff Adna Chaffee. On 1 April 1905, Lieutenant General Chaffee reported that the committee had not found 'the rod bayonet with which our new rifle is furnished as fully answering the purposes of a bayonet'. He also recorded that he was 'of the opinion that we should no longer attempt a combination tool, viz, bayonet and intrenching tool'.

The new sword bayonet was similar to the Krag pattern, though the locking mechanism differed and the blade was extended by several inches to compensate for the corresponding reduction in barrel length.

The report of the investigating committee was accepted by Taft on 3 April 1905. Existing rifles were recalled, to be modified by substituting a new stock and an upper band bearing a bayonet-attachment lug. Rifles were issued with slings—leather M1907 or webbing M1917—and the M1905 sword bayonet was accompanied by M1905 or M1910 scabbards.

A Board of Officers was appointed to consider the design of the M1903 back sight on 20 April 1905, leading to a suspension of the 1902-style tangent-leaf sight. On 24 May 1905, the board recommended an improved version based on that fitted on the experimental rifles of 1901. The hand guard, front sight and sight-cover were modified at the same time.

The leaf of the M1905 sight was hinged at the rear of a mobile base, which was in turn attached to a flap-topped sleeve-mount over the barrel. The leaves were graduated from 100 to 2,400yd.

Advances made in Germany, where the S-Patrone was about to be issued in quantity, led to the 'Cartridge, Ball, Caliber ·30, Model of 1906', approved by the Secretary of War on 15 October 1906. The muzzle velocity of Model 1906 pointed-nose ball ammunition was 2,700 ft/sec[-1] compared with 2,200 ft/sec[-1] for the M1903, necessitating altered sight leaves graduated to 2,850yd.

Re-chambering the existing barrels was easy, though they were shortened by one turn of the breech-screw. Concurrently, the M1905 sight gained a solid tubular mount instead of the original cut-away pattern. Work had been finished by 1909.

The perfected M1903 or 'Springfield' rifle was very successful, and few major problems were discovered even after it had seen extensive use. Minor changes were made prior to the First

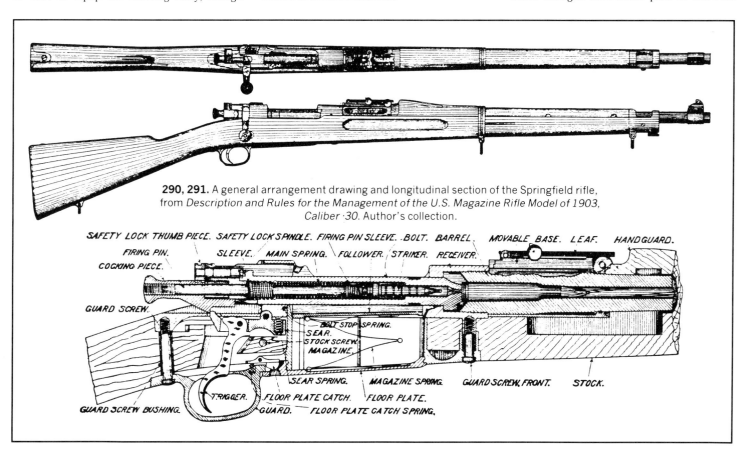

290, 291. A general arrangement drawing and longitudinal section of the Springfield rifle, from *Description and Rules for the Management of the U.S. Magazine Rifle Model of 1903, Caliber ·30.* Author's collection.

292. A standard Remington-made M1903 Springfield rifle. Courtesy of the Remington Arms Company.

293. The back sight components of the M1903 rifle. From the US Army handbook. Author's collection.

294. The M1905 bayonet, from the US Army handbook.

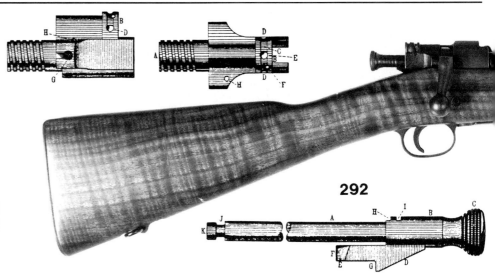

292

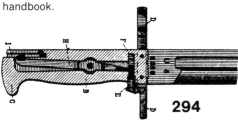

294

World War, including a flute cut in the top surface of the hand guard; an increase in the diameter of the azimuth adjustor on the back sight from ·45 to ·58; and the addition of a recoil bolt through the stock above the front of the trigger guard. A new chequered butt plate was also introduced.

An additional recoil bolt was added beneath the chamber in 1917–18, and the bolt handle was swept perceptibly backward after 1918.

Most guns will be found with standard ordnance marks, though a few display a 'flaming bomb' above 'N.R.A.'. This mark was added, after 30 March 1915, to rifles sold to members of the National Rifle Association by the National Board for the Promotion of Rifle Practise.

Sufficient Springfields had been made by November 1913 to allow the authorities to close the production line in Rock Island Arsenal, though it re-opened in February 1917.

Rifles selected for Expert marksmen were fitted with Telescope Musket Sights of 1908 or 1913. These impressive-looking Warner & Swazey prismatic patterns offered limited performance. Though greeted with enthusiasm by men accustomed to open sights, their limitations soon became apparent. They served throughout the First World War in small

numbers, but attempts were made to replace them after 1918.

WINCHESTER AUTO-LOADERS, 1903–17

The self-loader interested neither military authorities nor the sporting fraternity until the early part of the twentieth century. This was partly due to conservatism, but also to problems with early smokeless propellant. Variable pressures, fouling and erosion were handled comparatively simply in manually operated rifles, but the self-loaders depended on consistent ammunition performance for reliability.

Spurred on by the efforts of John Browning, many North American gunmakers attempted to compete with auto-loading guns introduced in Europe by Fabrique Nationale.

Winchester's first attempt, the Model 1903, was a hammerless ·22 rimfire blowback designed by Thomas Johnson. It loaded through a port cut into the right or outer side of the butt and chambered the unique ·22 Winchester Automatic Smokeless cartridge.

Emboldened by the comparative success of the Model 1903 on the pre-1910 market, but

equally aware of its lack of power, Winchester announced the Model 1905 at the beginning of 1906. Another Johnson design, the M1905 chambered ·32 and ·35 centre-fire cartridges. A detachable box magazine replaced the original tube in the butt, but the rifles were expensive and ineffectual. Blowback operation restricted the maximum permissible chamber pressures and, therefore, the power of the cartridges. Only 29,113 rifles were made before production ceased in 1919.

The Model 1907 was an enlargement of the Model 1905, sharing the same operating system but chambered for the ·351 Winchester Self Loading (WSL) cartridge. Made in Standard, Fancy and Police grades, the M1907 shared the principal vices of the M1905. It was expensive, but not powerful enough to convince the sporting market of its utility.

The Police Model, complete with sling and a knife bayonet, was offered only in 1934–7. Total production of M1907 rifles amounted to 58,490, but sales were painfully slow after 1920 and the last gun did not leave Winchester's warehouse

295, below. The action of the ·30 M1903 rifle. This gun, no. 348540, was made at Springfield Armory in 1908. Courtesy of Ian Hogg.

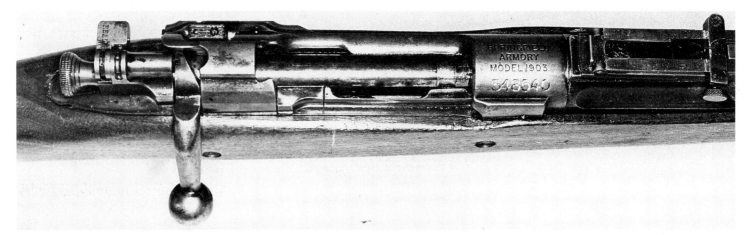

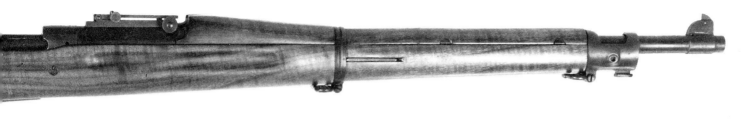

293

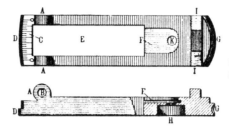

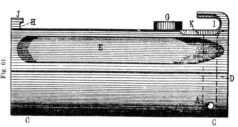

Fig. 61.

296, left. A page from the 1906–7 catalogue of Von Lengerke & Antoine of Chicago, showing Winchester Model 1903 and Model 1905 semi-automatics (bottom right).

---

10   VON LENGERKE & ANTOINE, 277 Wabash Ave., Cor. Van Buren St., Chicago.

WINCHESTER REPEATING RIFLES
MODEL 1890--22 CALIBRE
TAKE DOWN.   ALL RIM FIRE.   NEW MODEL.

Stock and barrel can be separated by turning of screw.

The same rifle will only load one length of shell.　Made for 22 short, 22 long and 22 Winchester rim fire cartridges, both black and smokeless.
Magazine of 22 short will hold fifteen 22 short cartridges; magazine of 22 long will hold twelve 22 long cartridges; magazine will hold ten 22 Winchester cartridges.
Octagon barrel, 24-inch, 5¾ lbs...............................**$10.26** net

FANCY FINISHED WINCHESTER RIFLES
MODEL 1890, "TAKE DOWN"

FANCY

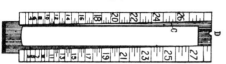

Calibres, 22 short, 22 long or 22 Winchester rim fire.
24-inch Octagon barrel, plain trigger, pistol grip stock of fancy walnut, checked, weight about 6 pounds.　Price.......................**$19.88** net

WINCHESTER REPEATING RIFLE
MODEL 1892--15 SHOTS

Special high velocity smokeless cartridges now furnished for this model.

Cartridges for this model loaded with both **black and smokeless** powder.
Made in 25-20, 32, 38 and 44 calibres, center fire.
This system is the same as the model of 1886. This rifle is light, strong, handsome and simple in construction, will be furnished with 24-inch round or octagon barrels, plain triggers and straight-grip stocks.　The 44 calibre rifle, with 24-inch octagon barrel, will weigh an ounce or two less than 7 lbs. The 38 and 32 calibres will weigh a little more than the 44 calibre rifle.　Cleaning rods will not be put in butt stock, but each gun will be accompanied with slotted hickory rod without charge.
Round barrel, solid frame............................**$11.55** net
Octagon barrel, solid frame..........................12.50 ne

"TAKE DOWN"
Octagon barrel, full magazine.....................16.04 net

WINCHESTER REPEATING RIFLES
MODEL 1894

Strong, Light and Elegant

The Breech-bolt, worked by a finger-lever, is automatically locked by a vertically moving block, which shows on the top of the gun when closed, and covers the whole rear of the breech-bolt.　The firing pin is automatically withdrawn and the trigger locked until the parts are in firing position.
32-40 and 38-55 calibre, round barrel, 26-inch, weight 7½ lbs., solid frame.........................**$11.55** net
.32-40 and .38-55 calibre, octagon barrel, 26-inch, 10 shot, weight 7½ lbs., solid frame.....................12.50 net
.25-35, .30 and .32 Winchester special calibre, round, octa-gon or half octagon barrel, 26-inch, nickel steel, 10 shot, weight 7½ lbs., solid frame.....................14.75 net
The .25-35, .30 and .32 special are not made in extra length barrels.

WINCHESTER MODEL 1894--"TAKE DOWN"
32-40 and 38-55 calibre, octagon barrel, full magazine................. **$16.04** net
25-35, 30 and 32 special, octagon barrel, full magazine, or half oct-agon barrel, half magazine..................................... 17.95 net
Model 1894 Rifles with **interchangeable barrels**, to special order only, as barrels must be fitted at factory.
Model 1894 "Take down" rifles can be furnished with interchangeable barrels, the .25-35 interchanging with the the .32-40 and the .30 Winchester interchanging with the .32 Winchester Special and the .38-55.
Extra barrels, complete with magazine, forearm, etc......... $ 7.70 net

MODELS 1892 AND 1894, "TAKE DOWN"

FANCY
MODEL 1894
Calibres, 25-35, 30-30 and 32 Winchester Special.
26-inch half octagon barrel, half magazine, pistol grip stock and fore-arm of fancy walnut checked, rifle butt, weight about 7½ lbs.......................
Price..**$27.58** net

MODEL 1892, FANCY
25-20 CALIBRE
24-inch half octagon barrel, half magazine, pistol grip stock and fore-arm of fancy walnut checked, rifle butt, weight about 7½ lbs.
Price...**$25.65** net

WINCHESTER AUTOMATIC RIFLE
MODEL 1903

.22 Calibre Automatic

Hammerless, "Take Down," Independent Safety, uses 22 cal. Winchester Automatic Smokeless r. f. cartridge only. Holds 10 shots. Recoil from exploded cartridge ejects the empty shell, cocks the hammer and throws a fresh cartridge into the chamber.

CAUTION
Bear in mind that after the first cartridge is thrown into the chamber, the **gun is always loaded until the last cartridge is fired or the magazine emptied by hand.**

High velocity, great accuracy, great rapidity of discharge.

Blued trimmings, plain walnut stock and fore-arm, not checked, 20-inch round barrel, open front and rear sights, length over all 36 inches, weight 5¾ lbs., stock 13¾ inches long. Price..................**$16.04** net

FANCY AUTOMATIC WINCHESTER 22 CALIBRE RIFLE
Has fancy walnut pistol grip stock and fore-arm, checkered...... **$25.65** net

GRAVITY CHARGER
Holds 10 cartridges, very convenient to load magazine.............. **$0.71** net

WINCHESTER MODEL 1905 SELF-LOADING RIFLES
32 AND 35 CALIBRE   "TAKE DOWN"

As name implies, this rifle is self-loading.　The recoil is used to eject empty shell, cock the hammer and insert a fresh cartridge in chamber. Box maga-zine holding five cartridges.
Round Barrel, 22 inches long, plain trigger, plain walnut stock and fore-arm, not checked, weight about 7½ lbs....................**$17.95** net
Fancy Finished, same as above, but with fancy walnut pistol grip, stock and fore-arm, checked, weight about 8 lbs............. 27.58 net
Extra Magazines, each.. 1.00 net

---

until 1957. The Model 1910, made in Sporting Rifle and Fancy Sporting Rifle grades with extra decoration available to order, was a heavier version of the M1907. It chambered the effectual-sounding ·401 WSL, one of the world's most useless cartridges. Compared with bolt action rifle cartridges of comparable calibre, ·401 was much too expensive and far too weak. Only 20,786 rifles were made prior to 1936.

REMINGTON AUTO-LOADERS, 1906–17

The first centre-fire auto-loader to be made in North America was the Browning-designed recoil-operated Remington Model 8, offered commercially from 1906 until superseded by the improved Model 81 in 1936. Sold only with a 22-inch round barrel and a five-round detachable box magazine, the 7lb 10oz Model 8 was chambered for ·25, ·30, ·32 and ·35 Remington.

Standard guns had two-piece stocks with a straight-wrist butt and a schnabel fore-end tip, though half pistol grips could be obtained on request. Rifles were offered in five grades, each a little more luxurious than its predecessor. They all acknowledged Browning's US patents issued on 9 and 16 October 1900 (659,507 and 659,786) and 3 June 1902 (701,289). Guns made after 1918 added patents granted in May 1907 and February 1911.

SLIDE-ACTION REMINGTONS, 1912–17

Envious of the success of Winchester and Marlin, Remington determined to find a high

power gun of its own. The success of the slide-action rimfire Model 12 inspired an enlargement of the sturdy Pedersen action to handle centre-fire cartridges. The Model 14 was introduced commercially in 1912. Made with a 22-inch round barrel, a straight-wrist butt and a ribbed slide, the standard guns had a six-shot tube magazine and weighed a little under 7lb. Half pistol-grip butts and a selection of finishes were available to order.

Rifles bore Remington Arms–Union Metallic Cartridge Company markings until 1918 and 'Remington Arms Co.' thereafter. They also acknowledged John Pedersen's patents of 12 October 1909 and 5 July 1910. Chambered for 25, 30, 32, 35 Regular and High-Speed ammunition, the Model 12 was the first truly successful slide-action centre-fire sporting rifle. It lasted until 1936 and the introduction of the improved Model 141 Gamemaster.

The Model 14R carbine (1912–34) had an 18½-inch barrel and a straight-wrist stock, while the Model 14½ and Model 14½R were rifle and carbine-length derivatives handling 38 and 44-40 Winchester catridges. Their action was substantially shorter than that of the guns chambering regular rifle rounds, but they were unpopular and had been discontinued by 1925.

THE NEWTON RIFLES, 1916–17

Charles Newton began his experiments with a 22 centre-fire high-velocity cartridge adapted from the 25–35 Winchester case. The 22 Newton soon interested Savage, who wished to chamber it in a Model 99 lever-action rifle, but the 22 Savage High-Power encountered head-space problems. It was followed by the outstandingly successful 250–3000 Savage, another Newton design.

Encouraged by acclaim that greeted the cartridges, Newton introduced his own rifle commercially in April 1916. His gun had a turning bolt locked by seven lugs on the head and two ahead of the bolt handle. Careful design ensured that the lugs aligned when the breech was open, allowing Newton to avoid an elevated bridge.

A clever three-position radial safety lay on the right side of the bolt plug, while a lightweight one-piece striker reduced the lock time. The original rifles accepted chargers—unusual in an American sporting rifle, though common militarily—and their unique magazine floor plate could release the barrelled action from the stock.

A readily adjustable set trigger system was standard on early guns, an auxiliary lever at the back of the guard reducing the pull on the trigger necessary to release the sear from about eight to 2lb. The bolt handle was pitched low enough to clear a telescope sight, then more popular in Europe than in North America. Segmental rifling was preferred, though Newton subsequently accepted that a ratchet pattern prolonged barrel life. Newtons had slender stocks with straight-comb pistol grip butts.

Chequering graced the pistol grip and the fore-end, which had a schnabel tip.

Newton cartridges performed spectacularly for their day, though only 30 and 35 had been introduced commercially before the first rifle's inglorious demise. The 30 cartridge contained a 172-grain bullet generating about 3,000 ft/sec[-1] at the muzzle, figures for the 35 being 250 grains and a claimed (but undoubtedly optimistic) 2,975 ft/sec[-1]. Original rifles were very light, weighing 6½–7lb, and recoil was appreciable; indeed, the uncomfortably narrow comb could gouge the unwary firer's cheek.

Made in Buffalo, New York State, the Newtons were little more than a passing fancy. The commencement of production coincided with the entry of the USA into the First World War. Rifle production stopped and even the distinctive cartridges disappeared; though the components had been made by UMC, they were assembled in Buffalo.

The Newton Arms Company entered voluntary liquidation in April 1918. About four thousand guns had been made in the Buffalo factory, but quality control was so poor that only about half were fit for sale. Several hundred sets of components were subsequently assembled and sold by the liquidators. The remaining parts—many of which were virtually useless—were sold to an unscrupulous machine-tool refurbisher. Guns made from these parts were hawked as the products of the 'Newton Arms Corporation' until the inventor successfully sued, the injunction being granted in July 1920.

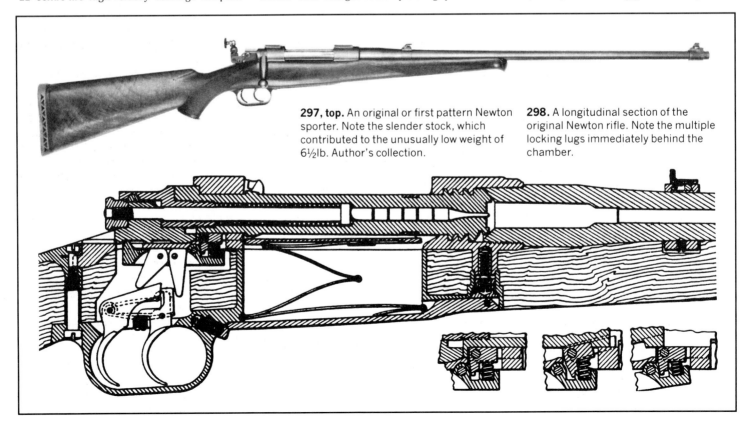

297, top. An original or first pattern Newton sporter. Note the slender stock, which contributed to the unusually low weight of 6½lb. Author's collection.

298. A longitudinal section of the original Newton rifle. Note the multiple locking lugs immediately behind the chamber.

THE SHOTGUNS

299. The 1878-pattern Colt, from a catalogue published by J.H. Johnston of the Great Western Gun Works, Smithfield Street, Pittsburgh, 1888. Author's collection.

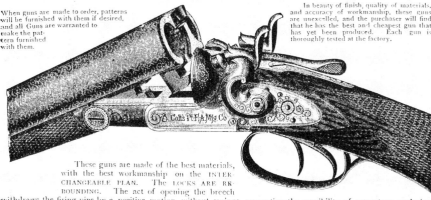

Throughout the entire period of the Wild West, shotguns were important in remote districts where factory-loaded metal case ammunition was difficult to obtain.

They were widely used during the Civil War—particularly by the Confederacy, which had such a poor manufacturing base that even front-line cavalry units had to make do with smooth bores. Many surviving accounts testify to the limitations of these guns in skirmishes with Federal troops.

THE EARLY REPEATERS, 1866–75

The cap-lock Colt was introduced shortly before the Civil War began. It outwardly resembled the contemporary revolver rifle, but was smooth bored.

Slightly more than a thousand Colt 10- and 20-bore revolver shotguns were made. They had round barrels, plain trigger guards, and Root patent creeping rammers—the 10-bore version being recognisable by its mushroom-headed rammer plunger. The plain straight-wrist butts had flat butt plates, while the short fore-end featured a brass tip and a brass escutcheon for the barrel-retaining key. Colt shotguns were not particularly popular, as they were expensive, cumbersome and prone to chain-firing, but they achieved much wider distribution than those made by Otis Whittier or North & Savage.

On 10 April 1866, Sylvester Roper of Roxbury, Massachusetts, patented a shotgun (53,881) with a bolt mechanism and a revolving cylinder magazine. Cocking the hammer withdrew the breech bolt, extracting a spent cartridge from the barrel as it did so. When the hammer had been retracted, a magazine spring revolved a new cartridge into line with the chamber; pulling the trigger released the bolt to fly forward and fire the chambered round in a 'slam bang' motion.

To reduce the shock, the hammer could be lowered onto the chamber and then pulled back to an intermediate position from which the cap on the cartridge-base nipple could be fired without partially extracting the case.

Made originally in 16 and (later) 12-bore by the Roper Repeating Rifle Company of Amherst,

Massachusetts, the shotgun was a minor success. Most examples had a detachable choke patented in July 1868 (79,861).

The Roper Sporting Arms Company, formed in Hartford in March 1869, was effectively a partnership between Christopher Spencer and Charles Billings. Production of ·40 rifles and 12-bore shotguns continued into the early 1870s, but never in sufficient quantity to make any real impact.

SINGLE-BARREL HAMMER GUNS 1867–1917

The Sharps Rifle Company made a few smooth-bore dropping-block guns, while the Massachusetts Arms Company made the 20 or 28-bore M1865 and M1873 tipping-barrel Maynards.

From 1867 until c.1892, Remington advertised the Remington(-Rider) Rolling Block Shotgun No.1, with a plain round barrel chambering 16 or 20-bore cartridges. It weighed 6½–7lb, depending on barrel length. The Shotgun No.2 was simply a smaller or 'juvenile' 30-bore No.1, built on a smaller action.

The Whitney Arms Company offered a few shotguns based on the action of the Howard patent rifle (q.v.), before concentrating on

the swinging-block Phoenix; Joshua Stevens contributed 12, 14 and 16-bore shotgun versions of his 'Pocket Rifle' with barrels of 28–32in; and Hopkins & Allen offered a dropping-block shotgun in 12 or 16-bore into the 1880s.

Springfield Armory completed the first 20-bore Forager shotguns in October 1881 to enable troops on the frontiers to supplement issue rations; the last of 1,376 guns left the factory in the summer of 1885. They had a standard 1873-pattern 'Trapdoor' lock, dated in cursive script, but lacked rifling. Their plain-tipped tapering fore-end was attached to the barrel by a single screw.

Many obsolete ·50–70 Model 1865 and Model 1866 Trapdoor Springfields were converted in the 1880s by replacing the barrel and shortening the fore-end. These ultra-cheap 12 or 16-bore conversions were supplemented by 12-bore 'Zulu' guns—ex-French Tabatière breech-loaders purchased in Europe after the Franco-Prussian War.

Dexter Smith, son of Horace Smith of Smith & Wesson, produced a single-shot 12 or 16-bore shotgun in 1872–5. Patented by Martin Chamberlain of Springfield, Massachusetts, on 14 February 1871 (111,814), then improved by Smith & Chamberlain in March 1871 (112,505) and finally by Chamberlain alone in July 1872

(129,393), Smith's gun was externally very similar to the popular Remington Rolling Block. However, its action was locked by the trigger.

Made in 1882–1900 by the American Arms Company, a partnership of Henry Wheeler and George Fox, the 12, 16 or 20-bore Fox semi-hammerless shotgun was cocked by a thumb lever on the right side of the breech. Production moved from Boston to Milwaukee in 1893, but the American Arms Company was purchased by Marlin in 1901.

Simple single-barrel shotguns with box locks and exposed central hammers included the 'American', made by Hyde & Shattuck of Hatfield, Massachusetts (1876–80) and then by C.S. Shattuck & Company (1880–1908); the 'Champion' of the John P. Lovell Arms Company of Boston, Massachusetts (1885–90); and unnamed guns made in 1887–1902 by first Forehand & Wadsworth and then Forehand & Company of Worcester, Massachusetts.

Others may be encountered with the marks of Iver Johnson of Worcester and then Fitchburg, Massachusetts ('Side Snap'); the Massachusetts Arms Company of Chicopee Falls; or the Davenport Arms Company of Norwich, Connecticut. Some bore 'A.J. Aubrey' marks, explained below.

By 1908, Harrington & Richardson were offering a selection of single-barrel hammer guns. These included the Model 1900 ejecting pattern in 12, 16 and 20-bore, with a patented hinge pin, and the smaller (but otherwise similar) Model 1905 in 24 and 28-bore, ·44 and ·45, 12 and 14mm, and '·410 Eley'.

The H&R M1908, ejecting or non-ejecting, was an improved Model 1900 with a snap fore-end and a hook-type barrel retainer.

DOUBLE-BARREL HAMMER GUNS, 1874–1917

Most of the double-barrel shotguns sold in the USA prior to 1875 were made in Europe, ranging from the output of the very best makers to cheap weapons produced in Birmingham and Liége.

One of the first American hammer doubles was made by Ethan Allen to a patent (49,491) granted on 22 August 1865. Its hinged breech block was locked by a pivoting latch set into the right side. The patent also showed a ratchet extractor, operated by a finger-ring, but a trigger guard system was used on guns made in 1868–71.

Patented by William Miller on 13 November 1866 (59,723), the shotgun made by the Meriden Manufacturing Company and then by Parker Brothers & Company of West Meriden, Connecticut, had a sprung locking bar in the top of the breech. This was pushed out of engagement by a vertically sliding latch ahead of the trigger guard. The guns were well made, cheap and effectual enough to find a ready market. Made in 10 and 12-bore, with barrels of 24–32in, they were available by 1868.

The Wesson Fire Arms Company was formed in May 1867 by Daniel and Franklin Wesson, Horace Smith and J.W. Storrs. The 12-bore Wesson shotguns were opened by pushing forward on a thumb-lever above the breech. They incorporated several features patented by Daniel Wesson, John Blaze and John Stokes between 17 December 1867 (72,434) and 24 November 1868 (84,314), but only about two hundred guns were made before the company assets were sold in 1870—apparently to Dexter Smith (q.v.).

After toying with a sliding-barrel pin fire shotgun, Eli Whitney the Younger, Charles Gerner and Frank Tiesing received US Patent 93,149 on 27 July 1869. The dropping-barrel action was locked by a lever ahead of the trigger guard. Guns made in 1869–70 lacked a guard for the barrel-release catch, but a second bow was subsequently forged in the trigger guard. The Whitney was amongst the cheapest double-barrel guns available in the West. One was used by John H. 'Doc' Holliday, but sales were not brisk enough for production to continue after 1875.

The Model 1874 Remington was patented by Andrew Whitmore on 8 August 1871 (117,843) and 16 April 1872 (122,775). Pushing forward on the thumb piece of the top-lever withdrew a longitudinally sliding bolt from lugs under the breech. Guns were made only in 10, 12 and 16-bore, with barrels of rolled or damascus-twist steel. Faults hastened their demise in 1878.

The breech of the original Fox shotgun, made by the American Arms Company of Boston, Massachusetts, pivoted laterally to the right. The gun was patented by George Fox on 4 January 1870 (98,579), but was not made in quantity until the mid 1870s; only a few had been sold before an improvement was patented by Fox and Henry Wheeler on 6 November 1877 (196,749). The side-swinging action was simple, strong, by no means new—comparable guns had been made in Europe before the Civil War—but enjoyed a lengthy period in vogue.

On 31 August 1875, William Baker of Lisle, New York, received a patent (167,293) to

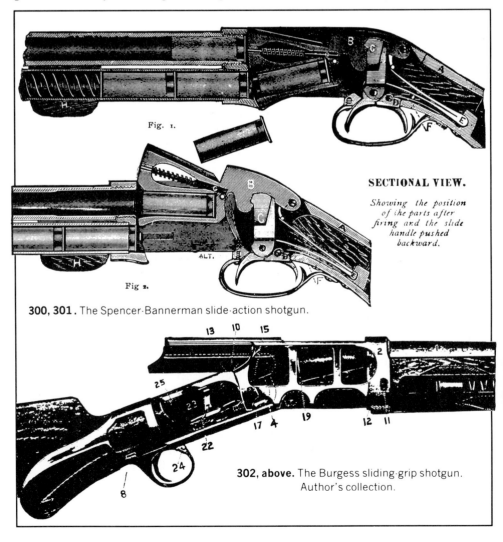

Fig. 1.

SECTIONAL VIEW.

Showing the position of the parts after firing and the slide handle pushed backward.

ALT.

Fig 2.

300, 301. The Spencer-Bannerman slide-action shotgun.

302, above. The Burgess sliding-grip shotgun. Author's collection.

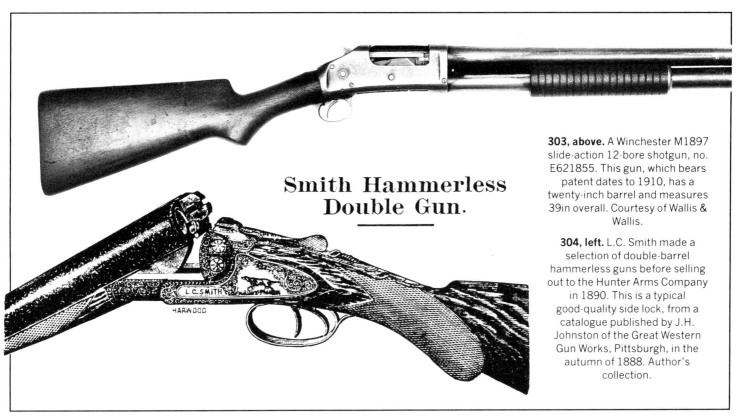

Smith Hammerless Double Gun.

303, above. A Winchester M1897 slide-action 12-bore shotgun, no. E621855. This gun, which bears patent dates to 1910, has a twenty-inch barrel and measures 39in overall. Courtesy of Wallis & Wallis.

304, left. L.C. Smith made a selection of double-barrel hammerless guns before selling out to the Hunter Arms Company in 1890. This is a typical good-quality side lock, from a catalogue published by J.H. Johnston of the Great Western Gun Works, Pittsburgh, in the autumn of 1888. Author's collection.

protect a gun-lock opened by pressing the front trigger forward. The Baker shotgun, therefore, lacked external levers or latches. Side-lock shotguns and a few European-style combination guns—with two smooth-bore barrels above a single rifle—were made by W.H. Baker & Sons Company of Syracuse until 1880. One of the partners, Lyman Smith, then bought the business and renamed it 'L.C. Smith & Company'; contemporaneously, William Baker and Lyman Smith's brother founded the Ithaca Gun Company in Ithaca, New York.

Patented by Joshua Stevens and made in Chicopee Falls from 1877, the Stevens hammer double was offered in ten or twelve-bore with 24–32in barrels. It had a 'locking trigger' in an auxiliary guard to operate a sliding under bolt mechanism. Rifle-shotguns, popular in North America, were added from c.1880 in accord with Stevens' patent of 28 January 1879 (211,642). Like virtually all Stevens products, these guns had shortcomings in construction, but were cheap enough to sell in substantial numbers.

In contrast to Remington, a maker of shotguns in great quantity, Colt's first experience with the genre was short-lived. The 'Colt Breech-Loading Shotgun, Double barrel, Hammer Model 1878' was made only in ten and twelve-bore, with barrels of 28–32in.

The guns had side locks with rebounding hammers, Purdey-type under-lugs and a top lever. Their barrel-blocks—imported from Birmingham—included damascus, laminated,

and fine twist patterns. Butts were English or Circassian walnut, with straight wrists or a half pistol-grip. The Colt shotguns, which weighed 7½–11½lb, were based on patents granted to Andrew Whitmore and William Mason. Series production continued until 1889, by which time 22,683 had been made—though a few more were assembled from parts in the early 1890s. Perhaps forty double rifles were also made on the 1878 action, chambered for ·45–70, ·45–85, ·45–90 and ·45–100 centre-fire cartridges.

Envious of the success of other double-barrel shotguns, the Sharps Rifle Company briefly marketed 'Old Reliable' guns from 1879. They were purchased in England, mainly from P. Webley & Sons. The project was abandoned when Sharps collapsed in 1881.

The first shotguns to bear Winchester's name were also made in England, by C.G. Bonehill and W.C. Scott & Sons, though they bore Winchester marks on the barrel ribs. Advertised as the 'Model 1879', they were classical side by side 10- or 12-bore doubles ranging downward from the de luxe Match Gun to plain class D.

An improved Baker action with a radial top lever was patented on 25 May and 1 June 1880 (228,020 and 228,165). These box-lock guns were made by the Ithaca Gun Company of Ithaca, New York, which had been formed in 1880 by William Baker and L.H. Smith.

In 1883, Alexander Brown of Syracuse (L.C. Smith's factory manager) patented a rotary self-compensating locking bolt—US 274,435 of 20 March 1883—and an improved hammer

mechanism (289,062 of November 1883). Smith then stopped making Baker-patent side-locks in favour of the Brown pattern.

The Lefever hammer and semi-hammerless doubles were remarkable for their special self-compensating actions, which minimised the effects of wear. Patents were granted in June 1878 (205,193) and June 1880 (229,429), but not until US Patent 264,173 was granted to Daniel Lefever and Frederick Smith on 12 September 1882 was volume production considered. The 1882 patent protected the Lefever Ball Joint, a hemispherical-tip bolt acting on the cup-face barrel under-lug. Wear in the action could be cured simply by tightening the bolt.

The perfected or 1882-pattern double-barrel Parker had a top-lever with a doll's head bolt, though the earlier rocking bar mechanism retained its popularity for another decade.

Remington's New Model of 1882 (offered until 1910) had a top lever breech-lock, low 'Circular Hammers' and rebounding locks. It was available in seven grades. Made in 10, 12 and 16-bore, the 28–32in barrels were rolled or damascus-twist steel and had matted ribs. The guns had chequered half-pistol grip butts, and weighed 6½–10½lb. Double triggers were standard. New Model Heavy guns, discontinued in 1895 and offered only in 10-bore, had an extension rib and weighed up to 11lb.

Offered until 1908, the Model 1889 Remington was an improved 1882 pattern distinguished by recurved hammer shanks. Made in 10, 12 and

16-bore, with barrels of 28–32in and weighing 7–10lb, it invariably had a pistol-grip butt and Remington Arms Company barrel marks.

By 1910, hammer doubles suited to smokeless ammunition were still being made by L.C. Smith, Ithaca, Hopkins & Allen, Stevens and others—though Lefever had made none since the introduction of its first hammerless gun in 1885. According to the 1906–7 catalogue issued by Von Lengerke & Antoine of Chicago, prices ranged from $11.85 for the 16-bore Stevens Model 225 to $23 for a 10-bore L.C. Smith New Model Hammer Gun with damascus barrels.

SLIDE-ACTION GUNS, 1882–1917

The earliest effectual slide-action shotgun was patented by Christopher Spencer and Sylvester Roper on 4 April 1882 (255,894), and then by Roper alone on 21 April 1885 (316,401). It used a stubby fore-grip to pivot the breech block. Five cartridges could be inserted in the tube magazine beneath the barrel, a sixth being inserted in the chamber if required.

A Spencer-Roper rifle was offered to the US Army in 1882 without notable success. By 1884, however, it was being touted as a 12-bore shotgun with a thirty or 32-inch barrel. The Spencer Arms Company failed in 1889, its assets passing to Pratt & Whitney and thence to Francis Bannerman & Sons of New York. Production recommenced in Brooklyn, the first or 1890-model Bannerman-Spencers being all but identical with the 1882 pattern apart from their ribbed cylindrical handles. The perfected 1900 model, however, had a better dismantling system.

Bannerman made much of a successful test by the US Army in 1884, but others drew attention to the regularity with which unfired cartridges were ejected.

When the slide-action Winchester shotgun appeared in 1893, Bannerman sued on the grounds that the 1885 Roper patent was being infringed. After protracted wrangling over the existence of earlier patents, the case resolved in Winchester's favour in 1897; Bannerman appealed, but the case was finally dismissed in 1900. Ironically, it was the existence of the *original* Spencer & Roper patent that finally unhinged Bannerman's case.

Competition afforded by Winchester and then Marlin slide-action guns forced Bannerman out of production about 1900. The Brooklyn factory was still being offered for sale in 1907.

The Burgess sliding-grip gun was another thorn in Winchester's flesh. Based on patents granted to Andrew Burgess—210,091 of 19 November 1878, 213,866 of 1 April 1879 and 216,080 of 3 June 1879—it was not marketed commercially until the 1890s.

An action for infringement brought against Sylvester Roper in the mid 1880s established that Burgess had made the first North American guns with a slide action, but the case was lost on a technicality: Burgess had neglected to claim against the Spencer & Roper patent granted in 1882. The Burgess Gun Company was organised in Buffalo, New York, in 1892 and the first 12-bore slide-action guns were assembled in 1893.

The perfected Burgess was loaded by sliding the pistol grip down the underside of the butt, then returning it to chamber a fresh cartridge and close the bolt. When the gun was fired, the bolt opened automatically to eject the empty case. Cycling the pistol grip then reloaded and closed the bolt ready for another shot.

Production of the effectual but expensive weapons, offered in several grades, continued until Burgess sold out to Winchester in 1899. A rifle had been introduced in 1896, and a folding rifle—chambered for ·30–30, ·30–40 or ·44–40—made a fleeting (but noteworthy) appearance in 1897.

Winchester's Browning-designed Model 1893 slide-action gun had an exposed hammer and a five-cartridge tube magazine. Made only in 12-bore, generally with barrels of 30–32in, it could be obtained with differing decorative finishes. Production was confined to 1894–7, a little over 34,000 being made.

Its successor, the legendary Winchester Model 1897, was made only in 12-bore (solid frame) or 12- and 16-bore ('Take Down'). The M1897 was offered as a trench and riot gun, or for specialist tournament work. Serial numbers had advanced from 34151 to 1058850 by 1957.

Marlin's 12-bore 'Take Down' slide-action Model 1898 shotgun was made until 1905. Offered in four grades with 26–32in barrels and a five-cartridge tube magazine, it weighed 7–7½lb. It was joined by the 16-bore Model 16 (1904–10) and then replaced by the short

305, 306; left and right.
The Topperweins, Adolph and Elizabeth, were among the most renowned shots of their day. Shown here in photo-postcards dating from *c.*1920, he holds a Winchester lever-action rifle (probably a Model 94) while she has a Model 12 shotgun. Author's collection.

307, opposite page.
A broadsheet promoting the Remington Model 10 shotgun, 1912. Author's collection.

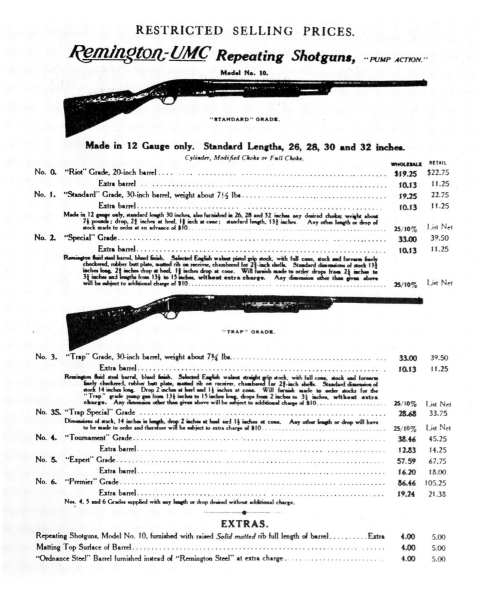

RESTRICTED SELLING PRICES.

Remington-UMC Repeating Shotguns, *"PUMP ACTION."*

Model No. 10.

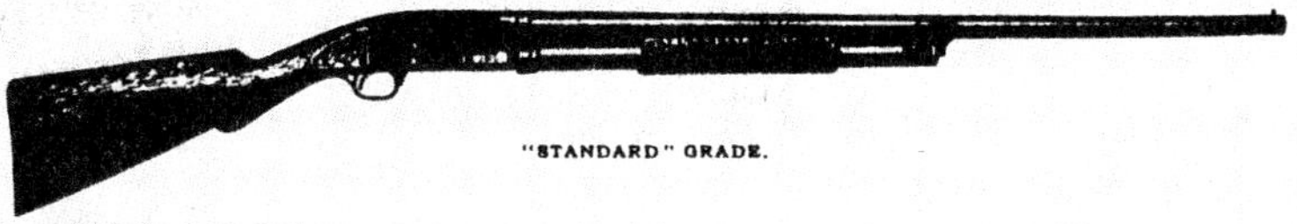

"STANDARD" GRADE.

Made in 12 Gauge only. Standard Lengths, 26, 28, 30 and 32 inches.

Cylinder, Modified Choke or Full Choke.

		WHOLESALE	RETAIL
No. 0.	"Riot" Grade, 20-inch barrel	$19.25	$22.75
	Extra barrel	10.13	11.25
No. 1.	"Standard" Grade, 30-inch barrel, weight about 7½ lbs	19.25	22.75
	Extra barrel	10.13	11.25
	Made in 12 gauge only, standard length 30 inches, also furnished in 26, 28 and 32 inches any desired choke; weight about 7½ pounds; drop, 2⅝ inches at heel, 1⅝ inch at cone; standard length, 13⅞ inches. Any other length or drop of stock made to order at an advance of $10	25/10%	List Net
No. 2.	"Special" Grade	33.00	39.50
	Extra barrel	10.13	11.25
	Remington fluid steel barrel, blued finish. Selected English walnut pistol grip stock, with full cone, stock and forearm finely checkered, rubber butt plate, matted rib on receiver, chambered for 2¾-inch shells. Standard dimensions of stock 13⅞ inches long, 2⅞ inches drop at heel, 1⅝ inches drop at cone. Will furnish made to order drops from 2¼ inches to 3¾ inches and lengths from 13¼ to 15 inches, **without extra charge.** Any dimension other than given above will be subject to additional charge of $10	25/10%	List Net

"TRAP" GRADE.

No. 3.	"Trap" Grade, 30-inch barrel, weight about 7¾ lbs	33.00	39.50
	Extra barrel	10.13	11.25
	Remington fluid steel barrel, blued finish. Selected English walnut straight grip stock, with full cone, stock and forearm finely checkered, rubber butt plate, matted rib on receiver, chambered for 2¾-inch shells. Standard dimension of stock 14 inches long. Drop 2 inches at heel and 1½ inches at cone. Will furnish made to order stocks for the "Trap" grade pump gun from 13½ inches to 15 inches long, drops from 2 inches to 3½ inches, **without extra charge.** Any dimension other than given above will be subject to additional charge of $10	25/10%	List Net
No. 3S.	"Trap Special" Grade	28.68	33.75
	Dimensions of stock, 14 inches in length, drop 2 inches at heel and 1½ inches at cone. Any other length or drop will have to be made to order and therefore will be subject to extra charge of $10	25/10%	List Net
No. 4.	"Tournament" Grade	38.46	45.25
	Extra barrel	12.83	14.25
No. 5.	"Expert" Grade	57.59	67.75
	Extra barrel	16.20	18.00
No. 6.	"Premier" Grade	86.46	105.25
	Extra barrel	19.24	21.38

Nos. 4, 5 and 6 Grades supplied with any length or drop desired without additional charge.

EXTRAS.

Repeating Shotguns, Model No. 10, furnished with raised *Solid matted* rib full length of barrel . . . Extra	4.00	5.00
Matting Top Surface of Barrel	4.00	5.00
"Ordnance Steel" Barrel furnished instead of "Remington Steel" at extra charge	4.00	5.00

lived 'Take Down' Model 19 of 1906–7. The Model 19 was essentially similar to the Model 1898, but had double extractors and a matted sighting groove. Other exposed-hammer Marlins included the 7½lb solid-frame Model 17 of 1906–8—also made as a riot and brush gun, with twenty and 26-inch barrels respectively.

The Marlin Model 21 was a variant of the Model 19 with a straight-wrist stock, while the strengthened Model 24 (1908–15) had a 'recoil safety lock'. The Model 26 was a solid-frame variant of the Model 24, while the Model 30 of 1910 was a 16 or 20-bore version of the original Model 16 with a recoil safety lock.

The first hammerless slide-action Model 28 Marlin made its debut in 1913. A 'Take Down' 12-bore 8lb five-shot repeater, it was offered with 26–32in barrels, pistol-grip butts, and ribbed slide handles. Production of the plainest version continued until 1922, the three better grades being abandoned in 1915

Marlin introduced the Model 31, essentially a reduced-scale Model 28 chambered for 16 or 20-bore cartridges, in 1915–16. Made until 1922 with 25–28in barrels, it weighed merely 6¼–6½lb.

The slide-action Remington Model 10 was protected by patents granted to John Pedersen on 3 February 1903 (719,955) and 18 May 1905 (789,755). A six-shot repeater with an under barrel tube magazine, it was introduced commercially in 1907. Made only in 12-bore, but in six grades of finish, it had barrels of 26–32in and weighed about 7½lb. Pedersen's design was successful enough to remain in production until 1929.

The Model 10-C Target had a ventilated over barrel rib and a straight-wrist butt, while the 10-S Trap Special had a matted barrel top.

DOUBLE-BARREL HAMMERLESS GUNS, 1883–1917

The market for good-quality hammerless shotguns was initially satisfied by European imports. Harrington & Richardson commenced production of Anson & Deeley guns in 1881.

The hammerless Model 1883 Colt derived from patents issued to Whitmore & Mason on 22 August and 19 September 1882. Made in 10- and 12-bore, with damascus-twist 28–32in barrels, the box-lock Colts had top levers. The cheapest gun—plain finish, English walnut stock, damascus barrels—cost $80 in 1893; specially finished examples could be $300. Production ceased in 1896, when only 7,366 had been made.

Daniel Lefever of Syracuse, New York, was offering his Automatic Hammerless gun as early as January 1885. Easily recognizable by the thumb-catch on the tang, the double-trigger gun was introduced in seven grades ranging from 'F'—the plainest at $75—to the special 'AA' at $300. An 'Optimus' pattern ($400) was introduced some time prior to 1893. A few double rifles and combination guns were made in this era. Lefevers all had compensated actions, compensated cocking levers and a host of other advanced features.

An improved top lever shotgun of 1894 remained in production until Daniel Lefever sold his business to the Durston family in 1901. The first ejector guns had been made in 1891, and a single-trigger system had been developed about 1898.

Production of standard guns continued under the new ownership while D.M. Lefever, Sons & Company was formed in Bowling Green, Ohio, to make box-lock guns. Apart from the patented self-compensating ball joint, these bore little similarity to the Lefever Arms Company side locks. They were also much rarer: only 2,500 box-lock Lefevers were made (*c.*1903–6), compared with about 72,000 pre-1919 side locks.

Box-lock Lefevers were offered from '0 Grade Excelsior', $60 in 1905, to the quaintly named 'Uncle Dan Grade' at $400. Bowling Green operations were closed on Daniel Lefever's death, while the Lefever Arms Company continued to make guns until purchased by the Ithaca Gun Company in 1915. New side-lock Lefevers were available from dealers' stocks until 1921.

The first L.C. Smith hammerless shotgun made its début in 1886. In 1888, however, Smith sold the business to John Hunter; it transferred to Fulton, New York, in 1890. 'The L.C. Smith Shot Gun' marking was retained.

Smith shotguns could be obtained with the special Hunter One-Trigger, designed by Allan Lard of St Joseph, Missouri, to whom relevant US patents were granted between August 1899 (630,061) and December 1903 (747,191). The perfected Lard single trigger mechanism—introduced *c.*1906—was guaranteed never to double or jam.

The 1906–7 Von Lengerke & Antoine catalogue listed the standard L.C. Smith hammerless guns alongside the Automatic Ejector Pigeon Gun and the lightweight Field Gun. Prices ranged from $37 for a 12-bore non-ejector 'New Grade 00', with thirty or 32-inch barrels, to $140 for an ejecting 12-bore Pigeon Gun.

Hammerless doubles were also made by the Baker Gun & Forging Company of Batavia, New York (active 1890–1919). They differed from those being made contemporaneously by the Ithaca Gun Company to earlier Baker patents, being similar externally to L.C. Smith examples. An improved hammerless box-lock gun was introduced in 1912, but the gunmaking division of the Baker Gun & Forging Company was sold to H. & D. Folsom Company of New York soon after the end of the First World War. Assembly of Baker-type guns continued into the 1920s. Batavia-brand guns were budget-price Bakers; the 'Batavia Special' cost merely $25 in 1909.

Hammerless top lever box-lock Fox shotguns were made by the Philadelphia Arms Company (c.1903–5) and then by the A.H. Fox Gun Company until business passed to Savage in 1930. They were based on patents granted to Ansley Fox between June 1896 (563,153) and May 1908 (921,220, with George A. Horne).

Parker Brothers & Company also made high quality hammerless box-lock doubles, the first being introduced about 1890. Parker was acquired by Remington in 1934, though guns bearing the Parker name were made until the end of 1941.

Box-lock 'Remington Hammerless Double Barrel Shot Guns' or Model 1894, made until 1910, had a top lever, automatic ejectors and an automatic safety. They were supplied in 10, 12 or 16-bore, with rolled or damascus-twist steel barrels (28–32in), and weighed 7–10lb. The best grades were delicately engraved, with

fine cut-chequering on the half pistol-grips. Fore-ends, which also often featured first class chequering, were of Purdey snap-on pattern.

The M1900 Remington was an improvement on its predecessor. Based on patents granted to Rimmon Fay and George Humphreys, guns had 10, 12, 16 or 20-bore barrels of damascus-twist steel. A Trap Gun derivative of the M1900 was introduced in 1902 with straight-wrist butt and 30–32in 12-bore barrels. It weighed 7½–8lb.

The 'Remington Special Model 1900' was the finest double-barrel shotgun made by the company. Offered with a Greener-type treble bolt action, and 26–32in barrels of ordnance, nickel or Whitworth steel, it had a straight wrist butt and fore-end of Circassian walnut. Gold escutcheon plates were let into the wood. Available only in 12-bore, weighing 6–8lb depending on pattern, the guns cost $750 apiece in 1906—a staggering price for the era.

At the other extreme, the Crescent Arms Company of Norwich, Connecticut, made box lock non-ejectors to retail at $10 or less, camouflaged by brandnames ranging from 'Faultless' to 'Square Deal'. Crescent was purchased in 1893 by H. & D. Folsom Arms Company of New York. Contemporaneously, Sears, Roebuck & Company of Chicago created the Meriden Fire Arms Company in Meriden, Connecticut. Sears guns were named 'A.J. Aubrey' after the first factory superintendent.

Among the most interesting pre-1917 sporting guns were made by the Three Barrel Gun Company of Moundsville, West Virginia. The inventor, Frank Hollenbeck, had worked for the Syracuse Gun Company and the Baker Gun & Forging Company. His sturdy European style combination guns, with two smooth-bore barrels above a single rifle, were made to US Patent 752,492 of 1 March 1904. Excepting 'Grade O' (12-bore, ·32–40 and ·30–30 only),

Three Barrel Guns were made in 12, 16 and 20-bore, plus ·22 centre-fire, ·25–20, ·25–25, ·25–35, ·30–30, ·32–20 and ·32 40. Barrels usually measured 28in and the guns weighed 6·5–7·8lb. They cost $65–$262·50 in 1906.

The original manufacturer appears to have been succeeded by the Royal Gun Company (c.1908–10) and then by F.A. Hollenbeck & Company, but the project had failed by 1913.

SINGLE-BARREL HAMMERLESS GUNS 1887–1917

Among the earliest guns of this type—less popular in North America than exposed hammer patterns—were those made for Amos Dickerman of New Haven, Connecticut, whose patent dated from 6 September 1887 (369,437). The guns were apparently sub-contracted, possibly to Marlin.

The Remington No.3 of 1893–1902 was a simple single-barrel semi-hammerless design, with a radial top-lever breech lock and a cocking lever on the left side of the frame. Made in 10, 12, 16, 20, 24 and 28-bore, with barrels of 30–34in, the ultra-plain No.3 weighed 5·7–6·5lb.

The semi-hammerless Remington No.9 of 1902–10 was an improved No.3 distinguished by its spurred trigger guard. The ejector was automatic, while the rolled-steel barrels measured 30–34in. Made from 10-bore down to 28-bore, it had walnut woodwork and weighed 5·75–6·5lb. The barrels acknowledged patents issued to Rimmon Fay on 30 October 1894, 16 June 1902 and 28 June 1904.

Among the lesser manufacturers were Forehand & Wadsworth and the Forehand Arms Company, whose guns dated from c.1887–1902. Iver Johnson made a 'Top Snap' pattern, while others will be found with the marks of the

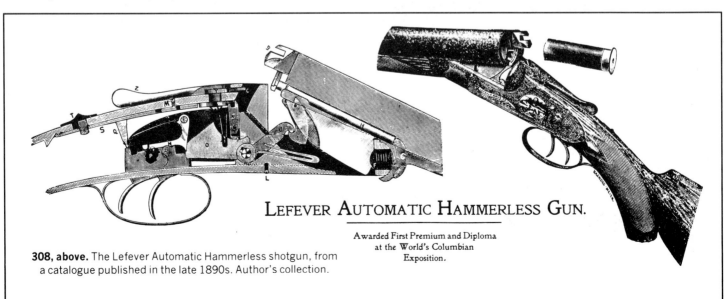

308, above. The Lefever Automatic Hammerless shotgun, from a catalogue published in the late 1890s. Author's collection.

LEFEVER AUTOMATIC HAMMERLESS GUN.

Awarded First Premium and Diploma at the World's Columbian Exposition.

These are made in all grades and weigh as light as 6 lbs. in 12 gauge. These **Featherweights** are without doubt the **ideal field gun of today.** **Entirely Hand=made. Unequalled for quality of material, workmanship, finish, shooting qualities and wear.**

FRANCOTTE "X" EJECTOR
Quintuple Wedge=fast Action

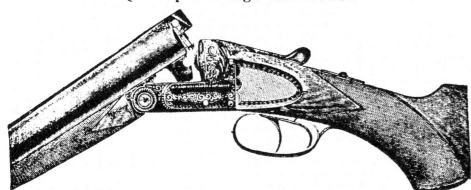

"Siemen-Martin" Steel Barrels. **12 gauge, 6 to 8 lbs., 26 to 30 inch.** **Field Weights**—12 gauge, 26-inch 6 to 6½ lbs. 28-inch, about 6½ lbs. **Trap Weights**—12 gauge, 30-inch. 7½ to 8 lbs.

Latest improved Anson & Deeley lock action, Greener Cross Bolt through "Doll's Head" extension, with Purdey side projections, preventing any possible lateral motion of the barrels.

There is nothing made that can equal this gun in value. The action is the strongest yet produced and especially suitable for the heavy continuous work that guns are put to in our artificial target shooting. This gun has Francotte's Improved Safety Intercepting Sear, and the engraving and finish throughout is of superior quality. Price..**\$140.00** net

FRANCOTTE "A" PIGEON EJECTOR
Quintuple Wedge=fast Action

FRANCOTTE "AA" FEATHERWEIGHT EJECTOR

Francotte Ejector "A"

Superior Quality and Finish.

Crescent Gun Company or the Baker Gun & Forging Company. The high-quality Baker top lever box-lock Trap Guns appeared in 1909.

LEVER-ACTION GUNS, 1887–1917

The Spencer slide-action shotgun enjoyed limited success in the 1880s, but Winchester initially chose the lever-action Model 1887 designed by John Browning. 64,855 were made in 1887–1901.

Chambered for 10- and 12-bore cartridges, M1887 barrels ranged from a twenty-inch riot pattern to 32in. Chokes, finish and decoration were all often left to the whims of clients. The last of Winchester's lever-action shotguns was the Model 1901. A variant of the Model 1887, strengthened for smokeless ammunition, it was made only in 10-bore and its frame was blued instead of case-hardened. The standard guns had full, modified or cylinder-choke 32-inch barrels, though a Riot Gun, with a twenty-inch barrel, was touted briefly in 1898.

309, left. A page of imported Francotte box- and side-lock hammerless shotguns, from the 1906–7 Von Lengerke & Antoine catalogue. Author's collection.

Model 1901 Winchesters, never popular, were discontinued in 1919 after less than fourteen thousand had been made. Their numbers extended the series begun by the earlier Model 1887, running on from 64856.

AUTO-LOADING GUNS, 1905–17

Remington's Model 11 was the first successful auto-loading shotgun made in North America. Based on patents granted to John Browning on 9 October 1900 (659,507), 17 December 1901 (689,283), 30 September 1902 (710,094) and 16 June 1903 (730,870), the Model 11 had an interesting history.

Much of the Browning brothers' work had previously been sold to Winchester on a cash-for-rights basis. Eventually, John Browning demanded royalty agreements; his guns, after all, were making many a manufacturer's fortune. Winchester refused to produce the shotgun, so the Brownings had approached Remington–UMC.

Unfortunately, Marcellus Hartley, President of Remington–UMC, died in his office as the brothers awaited a crucial meeting. The Brownings then took their gun to Fabrique Nationale d'Armes de Guerre in Liége, Belgium, where their pistols were already in production. North American rights on the recoil-operated shotgun were licensed to Remington on their return from Europe.

The patents had been drafted with the help of advisers working for Winchester, anticipating that the shotgun would be made in New Haven. When Remington proceeded with the Model 11, Winchester designers needed five years to produce an effectual competitor.

Made in 12, 16 and 20-bore, the Remington Model 11 had a five-round tube magazine beneath the barrel and ejected laterally. Offered with a half pistol-grip stock in six grades of finish, plus assorted combinations of barrel and choke, it sold in great quantity before being discontinued in 1948.

The Winchester Model [19]11 was the work of Thomas Bennett, who needed several years to develop a shotgun that circumvented Browning patents. Bennett's design was not especially effectual; only 82,774 were made in 1911–25.

The hammerless Winchester M12, designed by Thomas C. Johnson, was outstandingly successful: 1,968,307 guns had been made by 1963. Few variants were available prior to 1917, though a handful of highly decorated guns was engraved by Winchester's leading craftsmen.

This index provides a guide to the gunmakers featured in this book; the summary of contents (page 5) should be used to locate guns. Dates of operation should be considered as approximate.

The suffix 'i' indicates a reference containing an illustration.